D1830247

The
General Principles
Of
Hindu Jurisprudence

Owing to the antiquity and rarity of this book, certain pages are regrettably absent, and readability is compromised due to the blurring of the original text. If you possess any insights regarding the availability of these missing sections, kindly inform us. Your assistance is crucial in ensuring the completion of this significant work for the benefit of future generations.

Tagore Law Lectures -1909:

The General Principles Of Hindu Jurisprudence

Priyanath Sen

GYAN

Published by

Gyan Publishing House
5, Ansari Road
Daryaganj, New Delhi-110002
Phone: 011-47034999, 9811692060
E-mail: books@gyanbooks.com

Distribution Network
gyanbooks.com
India, USA, Canada, UK, Australia

© Publisher
All rights reserved. No part of this work may be reproduced, stored, adapted, or transmitted in any form or by any means, electronic, mechanical, photocopying, micro-filming, recording or otherwise, or translated in any language, without the prior written permission of the copyright owner and the publisher.

ISBN: 978-93-7169-656-2 (HB)
First Published, 1918

2nd Impression 2025

Printed at: Gyan Press, Delhi.

The book is sold subject to the condition that it shall not, by way of trade or otherwise, be lent, resold, hired out, or otherwise circulated without the prior publisher's written consent.

TAGORE LAW LECTURES-1909:
THE GENERAL PRINCIPLES OF HINDU JURISPRUDENCE
Author: PRIYANATH SEN

Tagore Law Lectures, 1909

The General Principles of Hindu Jurisprudence

Tagore Law Lectures, 1909

The General Principles of Hindu Jurisprudence

By

Priyanath Sen, M.A., D.L.,

Tagore Law Professor, Premchand Roychand Scholar, Vakil, Calcutta High Court
and sometime Member of the Faculty of Law and Board of Studies
in Law of the Calcutta University.

Published by

The University of Calcutta

1918

Dr. Priyanath Sen

A Short Life Sketch*

Priyanath Sen was the second son of Babu Dinanath Sen Sarkar, a member of a Vaidya family of great respectability in Eastern Bengal. He was born on Sunday the 2nd February 1873, (the day of the Saraswati Puja), in village Japsa in the District of Faridpur, in the ancestral family dwelling house which has now been washed away by the erratic Padma. From a very early age, he showed signs of uncommon intelligence, and his father, who had been himself a teacher by profession and a Sanskrit scholar of some attainments, did all he could with his limited means to impart a sound education to the boy. Priyanath passed the Middle English Examination from the school of his native village, and by his special proficiency in English won the prize awarded by Raja Surja Kumar Roy of Rajbari. He then joined the Dacca Collegiate School, from which institution he passed the Entrance Examination of the Calcutta University in 1889 and obtained a first grade junior scholarship. He next came to the metropolis and joined the Presidency College. At the F.A. Examination of 1891 he headed the list of successful candidates and carried off the Duff scholarship for science, as also the Gwalior gold medal. He passed the B.A. Examination of 1893 with first class Honours in Sanskrit and second class Honours in Philosophy. His relative position amongst all the candidates of the year was first, and he obtained the Burdwan scholarship

* Reprinted (by kind permission) from the Calcutta Law Journal. 10 C. L. J., Vol. 37-39.

and the Eshan scholarship, each of Rs. 50 per month. He was also awarded the Radhakanta gold medal for proficiency in Sanskrit. At the M.A. Degree Examination in 1894, he was placed first in the first class in Philosophy and obtained the University gold medal and prize. Meanwhile, he had been invited by the University to be a candidate for the Government of India scholarship tenable in England, but he declined the offer on account of the opposition of his mother to whom he was always deeply devoted. In 1896, he passed the B.L. Examination in the first division, and having served his articles of clerkship with Babu Baikunthanath Das, was enrolled as a Vakil of the High Court on the 7th September 1897. About this time Rai Jotindranath Chowdhury of Taki offered through the Bangiya Sahitya Parishad, a prize of Rs. 500 for the best essay in Bengali on Adwaitavada. Priyanath had studied Vedanta Philosophy critically from the original sources, and at the request of his father, competed for the prize which was eagerly sought after by pundits who had specially studied the Vedanta for years. The prize was equally divided between him and a well-known teacher of Vedanta Philosophy, Pundit Durgacharan Vedanta Sankhatirtha. His essay named Adwaitavada Vichara, which was subsequently published in Dacca in August 1897, shows great acuteness of argument and clearness of presentation. In 1899, Priyanath won the Premchand Roychand Studentship, the Blue Ribbon of the University as also the Mouat Medal. In February 1903 Priyanath submitted to the University his thesis on the Philosophy of Vedanta as required by the Regulations for the Studentship. It was examined by Mahamahopadhyay Mahesh Chandra Nayaratna and Babu Kalicharan Banurji who reported " that it bore ample evidence of special investigation and was in particular a thoughtful contribution to Vedantic Apologeties." In 1904 Priyanath passed the examination for Honours in Law, and on the strength of a thesis on the Interpretation of Negative Precepts of Hindu Law, he was admitted in 1905 to the Degree of Doctor of Law. In August 1908, the Senate appointed him Tagore Professor of Law, and the subject he chose for his lectures was the General Principles of Hindu Jurisprudence of which he had made a special study in the original Sanskrit. He then submitted to the University a complete manuscript copy of the lectures, but did not live to deliver them, as he died on Monday, the 18th of October, 1909. Since 1907 he had been a member of the Faculty of Law and of the Board of Studies in Law of the University, and he had on several occasions acted as one of the examiners for the B.L. Examination.

From the establishment of the Calcutta Law Journal he had been one of its editors and took great interest in the success of the undertaking. In the first volume (p. 9*n*), he contributed a paper on the Interpretation of Promise which attracted the notice of Sir Frederick Pollock and was commented upon in the Law Quarterly Review Vol. XXI, p. 219 as an indication "that the subtelty of Hindu Lawyers is amply capable of finding a new field in the Common Law." To the third volume he contributed (p. 1*n*) a paper on Acceptance of an offer by Post. The fourth Volume (pp. 21*n*, 27*n*, 35*n*, 63*n*, 75*n*) contains his thesis on the Interpretation of Negative Precepts in Hindu Law. These papers are all characterised by great learning and acuteness, and are models of contribution on legal subjects.

Dr. Priyanath Sen, at the time of his death, had been a member of the profession for twelve years, and had earned the reputation of being an able and erudite lawyer. After the usual struggle of the junior, he had latterly been gaining a sure footing in the ranks of the leaders, and if he had been spared, a place in the very front rank of the profession or a seat on the Judicial Bench would have been only a question of time. He was scrupulously fair as an advocate, and was held in high regard by all members of the profession who had the pleasure to know him. His early death is an irreparable loss to the country, and we are not likely to get for years to come another man of his type—the modest and accomplished scholar of unblemished character.

Nine long years have elapsed since the talented author of these lectures passed away. During this period there have been many difficulties in the way of their publication. Shortly after the manuscript of the first four lectures had been sent to the University Press, the Press together with the manuscript was destroyed by a fire which broke out in an unexplained manner. Fortunately, the first draft prepared by the author was in existence, and the manuscript was restored with considerable difficulty. Almost equal difficulty was felt in identifying the original texts mentioned in the lectures. The entire work has been seen through the press by Babu Asiranjan Chatterjee, M.A., B.L., and Babu Sailendranath Chatterjee, M.A., B.L., two of the Professors of the University Law College. They have also drawn up the full Index which finds a place at the end of the volume.

A. M.

October 6, 1918.

TABLE OF CONTENTS

LECTURE X.

LECTURE XI.

LECTURE XII.

LECTURE XIII.

LECTURE XIV.

APPENDIX A.

APPENDIX B.

TABLE OF CASES CITED

THE

General Principles of Hindu Jurisprudence.

LECTURE I.

INTRODUCTION.

Province of law.

The province of law is the establishment of rules for the regulation of human conduct amidst the diversity of inclinations and desires, so as to reconcile and harmonise the wishes of the individual with the interest of the community in which ultimately the interest of the individual is also involved; it curtails the fictitious freedom of unregulated desires by subordinating the particular nature of individual men to the discipline of the community acting upon universal rational principles, and thereby gradually tends to bring about the higher freedom which consists in the dependence of the individual on the dictates of reason, which, while governing the community, is also his. It may be that this conception of the aim of law is not consciously recognised at the outset, but there can hardly be any doubt that the various systems of law exhibit, on a careful analysis, so many efforts towards the realisation of the end indicated above at different stages of development. In so far as the conditions of different societies and the stages through which they have passed are not exactly similar, these systems of law which they have severally evolved are more or less dissimilar to one another; yet the unity of human constitution and the universality of human reason concur in producing an essential similarity in all those systems which exhibits itself to a scientific observer amidst the diversity of details. It is the province of general or abstract jurisprudence to analyse and systematise these essential elements underlying the infinite variety of legal rules without special reference to the institutions of any particular country. 'The proper subject of general or universal jurisprudence,' says Austin, 'is a description of such subjects and ends of laws as are common to all systems, and of those resemblances between different systems which are bottomed in the common nature of man.' Jurisprudence, however, becomes particular or concrete, when it takes its data from a particular system of law, and exhibits the essential ideas and principles, which go to constitute jurisprudence proper,—not in an abstract form, but coloured and shaped, as it were, by the concrete details of that particular system. It does not, it is true, enter into a discussion of all the complex rules which enter into the composition of the actual system of law on which it has its basis, but, while exhibiting the essential conceptions of law, it does not altogether isolate them from the concrete shapes which they have assumed in that particular system, owing to the particular line of evolution through which it has passed and the particular stage of development which it has attained. Identical social needs have been met by different communities in different ways; but, in as much as the needs are the same, and the forces which work for their removal are similar in their character, the differences in detail conceal within them a deeper unity. General Jurisprudence or Jurisprudence proper, concerns itself to exhibit these elements of unity irrespective of their historical or geographical adjuncts; concrete

General Jurisprudence and Particular Jurisprudence.

Jurisprudence, having reference to a particular system of law, exhibits what shapes those elements have assumed by reason of the characteristic development of that system under the influence of historical and other particularising accidents.

Hindu Jurisprudence: what it means.

It is not necessary for me, in this connection, to consider the view advocated by certain jurists, that the term 'Particular Jurisprudence' is a misnomer, and that the principles of Jurisprudence, in so far as they are scientific truths at all, are always general and of universal application; the subject of my proposed lectures being 'The General Principles of Hindu Jurisprudence,' all that is at present necessary for me to enquire is what the expression 'Hindu Jurisprudence' must be taken to imply as distinguished from general or abstract Jurisprudence having no special reference to any particular system of positive law. Now, it will follow from what I have already stated about the scope and methods of Particular Jurisprudence, that the aim and object of a dissertation on Hindu Jurisprudence must be the examination and ascertainment of the Hindu conceptions about the general topics of Jurisprudence as unfolded in the works of Hindu lawgivers of recognised authority, with a view to exhibit the characteristic development of the Hindu Law in relation to the essential conceptions and principles common to all systems of law. Hindu Jurisprudence may therefore, be regarded as Hindu Law viewed from the standpoint of Jurisprudence, or as Jurisprudence reflected through the medium of Hindu Law. It will perhaps be better to explain my meaning by an illustration: Ownership, for instance, is one of the fundamental juristic conceptions common to all systems of law, and it is the function of Jurisprudence to explain its character and determine the conditions under which it may be acquired, transferred, or extinguished; abstract jurisprudence discharges this function without special reference to any particular system of law; it analyses the constituent elements of ownership as a juristic conception, and considers and systematises the conditions of its acquisition, transfer, and extinction. Now, Hindu Jurisprudence also would do the very same thing, but *not* without reference to the Hindu system of law; it would take notice of the line of evolution which the Hindu Law has pursued and the extent of development which it has attained; it would analyse and exhibit how Ownership has been understood by the Hindu jurists; it would examine and classify the conditions under which, according to the Hindu Law, it could be acquired, transferred, or extinguished; and, if necessary, it would seek to indicate, as far as possible, what position the Hindu Law is entitled, in this reference, to occupy in the evolution of juristic conceptions. As with ownership, so with other fundamental juristic conceptions; and, furthermore, our study would not confine itself to the substantive branch of Hindu Law alone, but must also pass under review the adjective branch thereof.

Importance of the study of Hindu Jurisprudence.

Having thus briefly indicated the character and scope of the subject of our discourse, it may not be out of place to say a word or two about the importance of the study which we have thus undertaken. "Hindu Law," says Mr. Mayne,[1] "has the oldest pedigree of any known system of jurisprudence, and even now it shows no signs of decrepitude. At this day it governs races of men, extending from Cashmere to Cape Comorin, who agree in nothing else except their submission to it. No time or trouble can be wasted, which is spent in investigating the origin and development of such a system, and the causes of its

[1] Preface to the first Edition of Mayne's Hindu Law.

influence." At the same time, it must be remembered, that though so ancient, it cannot, in all its departments, be pronounced to be very familiar to any of us; owing to altered conditions of the Hindu community, a considerable portion of it does not at all attract the attention of a practising lawyer, and, whatever its intrinsic antiquarian and theoretic interest may be, it will not be an exaggeration to say that it has practically remained a sealed book to most of us. "The law," says Dr. Ghose, "which moved the admiration of Sir William Jones has ceased, in one sense, to be living law, and must be sought at the present day, not in our books of report, but in the texts of our sages, and in the writings of the successive Jurisconsults by whom Hindu law was gradually moulded into system;"[1] and, as he further observes, "Legal antiquities ought to engage our special attention as India offers a rich and varied field for such enquiries. The harvest has long been ripening for the sickle, but as yet, to our reproach, the reapers are few in number, and that wealth of materials which should be our pride is now our disgrace."[2] It, therefore, gives me unfeigned pleasure to find that the Calcutta University has been pleased to prescribe 'The General Principles of Hindu Jurisprudence' as one of the subjects for the Tagore Law Professorship; and who knows that, if properly pursued, it may not furnish at least some materials for the fulfilment of Dr. Ghose's prediction that "Hindu Law will, at no distant date, render the same service to Jurisprudence that Sanskrit has already done to the sister science of Philology."

Difficulties in the study of Hindu Jurisprudence.

We cannot, at the same time, shut our eyes to the immense difficulties which lie in our way in pursuing

---

[1] Dr. Rash Behary Ghose's Law of mortgages, 4th Edn. p. 35.

[2] Do. p. 63.

(i) due to the peculiar character of the Hindu Dharmaśastras.

this study. In the first place, the Hindu Dharma-śástras, which are the principal sources of Hindu Law, do not confine themselves to the enunciation of juristic rules for the guidance of human conduct; ceremonial rules moral and religious injunctions, and strict legal precepts are found mingled up, and no clear line of demarcation is uniformly maintained, so as to keep them separate, and prevent a confusion of ideas in minds not sufficiently familiar with the rules of logic and canons of construction by which they have to be discriminated from one another. This difficulty in the study of Hindu Law and the proper understanding thereof has been very forcibly pointed out by their Lordships of the Judical Committee of the Privy Council, in the case of *Sri Balusu Gurulingaswami* v. *Sri Balusu Ramalakshmamma*,[1] where their Lordships observe as follows :—"Their Lordships had occasion in a late case to dwell upon the mixture of morality, religion, and law in in the Smritis: *Rao Bulwant Sing* v. *Kishori*. They had to decide whether a prohibition on alienation of property away from a man's family, certainly based on religious grounds, had a purely religious or also a legal bearing. They then said :—'All these old text-books and commentaries are apt to mingle religious and moral considerations, not being positive laws, with rules intended for positive laws. In the preface to his valuable work on Hindu Law, Sir William Macnaghten says: 'It by no means follows that because an act has been prohibited it should therefore be considered as illegal. The distinction between the *vinculum juris* and the *vinculum pudoris* is not always discernible.' They now add that the further study of the subject necessary for the decision of these appeals has still more impressed them with the necessity of great

[1] I. L. R. 22 Mad. 398, at p. 415.

caution in interpreting texts of mixed religion, morality, and law, lest foreign lawyers accustomed to treat as law what they find in authoritative books, and to administer a fixed legal system, should too hastily take for strict law precepts which are meant to appeal to the moral sense, and should thus fetter individual judgment in private affairs, should introduce restrictions into Hindu Society, and impart to it an inflexible rigidity, never contemplated by the original lawgivers." It is impossible not to recognise that there is considerable force in the above observations, and that a student of Hindu Jurisprudence must critically examine and discriminate the precepts intended to have a strict legal bearing as distinguished from those having merely a moral or a religious application. At the same time, it must not be forgotten that the complete abstraction of the legal rules from their moral and religious adjuncts may sometimes be calculated to throw into the shade their real character, and invest them with an altogether foreign garb, and that this must especially be the case with regard to some of the most important ceremonies of our domestic life, such as marriage and adoption, which with us have both a religious and a secular aspect. On the whole, therefore, it seems to me that in order to be properly studied and understood, the legal rules must be separated but not completely detached and isolated from their moral and religious adjuncts, especially in those cases where the ceremonies to which the legal rules relate partake of both a religious and a secular character. In the second place, besides the above difficulty arising from the peculiar character of the Hindu Dharma-sástras, there is another due to the peculiar character of the science of jurisprudence itself. Jurisprudence, as we have it, is pre-eminently a Western science; it had its foundation in the Roman Law, which, for the first time among

(ii) due to the peculiar character of the science of jurisprudence.

the Western nations, reduced legal rules to order and coherence, and throughout its development, its divisions and classifications have been modelled on the divisions and classifications of the Roman Law. The result is that in the study of Jurisprudence, whatever may be the system of law which furnishes us with materials for the same, we start with certain preconceived ideas about and a pre-arranged scheme of classification for juristic conceptions borrowed from the Roman Law. This works well enough so long as we confine our attention to the Western systems of law, for they have all, more or less, been based upon and influenced by the Roman Law; but to approach the study of Hindu Law with an expectation to find the exact counterparts of the ideas and classifications referred to above, may not always prove equally convenient or successful. In order to be properly appreciated and understood, Hindu Law must, therefore, be studied from within, with such light as it itself affords and under such guidance as we may receive from a study of analytical and comparative Jurisprudence as regards the points on which we should bestow our special attention; and when in this way we succeed in grasping the fundamental conceptions and principles contained therein, we may proceed to arrange and systematise them with reference to similar topics in other systems of law, and compare and note striking points of similarity or contrast wherever such comparison may be instructive or interesting.

(iii) a third difficulty due to uncertainty of chronology.

While on this point, there is yet another difficulty which occurs to us; Hindu Law has had a development of its own, and whatever the orthodox assumption may be, it can scarcely be conceived that the Hindu Jurisprudence furnishes an exception to the general law of evolution, and that there the same conceptions and the same rules have prevailed from almost the dawn of human civilisation up to relatively modern times; the question, however, is, how far is it possible to trace the course of gradual development in Hindu juristic ideas? Now, I have often thought that there is nothing so uncertain as Hindu chronology, and the researches of modern antiquarians in this direction have given rise to so many hopelessly divergent conclusions and haphazard generalisations, that one may be excused if one feels considerable hesitation in relying upon their conjectures in any case. The only way, therefore, out of the difficulty, is to apply, with adequate caution and circumspection, the critical method of enquiry upon the materials furnished by our lawgivers with a view to discover in them, as far as possible, under the light furnished by comparative jurisprudence, the record of the onward march of juridical ideas along the line of progressive evolution; in pursuing this enquiry we should avoid the error of extremes; on the one hand, we should not rashly rush into conjectures which are not fully warranted by the evidence available to us, and, on the other hand, we should not allow ourselves to be overawed by the phantoms of superstition which may stand in our way, under various subtle disguises, and endeavour to keep us fastened to the prejudices of the past.

Sources of Hindu Law.

Having observed upon the importance of the subject of our discourse and some of the difficulties which one must encounter in its study, I think it will not be now out of place to enquire what are the sources of Hindu Law. The character of our subject requires such a preliminary enquiry, and I must pursue it although the subject has been so often discussed that I may not have much new information to impart. As it has been often noticed that the expression 'sources of law' is not altogether free from ambiguity, I may at once make it clear that I take the expression 'sources of Hindu Law' to denote what Vijñáneswara calls, ज्ञापक हेतु, *i.e.*, the sources from which our knowledge of that law must be derived. The question, therefore, is, what are the sources to which we must refer in order to obtain a knowledge of Hindu Law ?

Fourfold indices of 'dharma' according to the Hindu Sages.

Now, as we all know, there are, according to the Hindu sages, four indices by reference to which 'dharma' or approved conduct may be ascertained. Thus Manu declares,—'The Veda, the Smriti, the usage of good men, and what is agreeable to one's soul, the wise have declared these to be the fourfold indices of 'dharma' or approved conduct.'[1] The word 'dharma' used in this passage no doubt covers a wider field than positive law, but the latter, according to the Hindu conception, has no existence apart from the former, for positive law is but a portion of the sacred law which, by reason of its peculiar character and the exigencies of the community, is enforced by the king. That being so, it is only proper that we should examine how far the four indices enumerated above may be regarded as the sources of positive law as understood and obeyed by the Hindus.

(1) The Vedas.

Doctrine of revelation.

(1) The Vedas—There can be no doubt that every Hindu lawyer must admit that theoretically the Vedas must be regarded as the primary authority on all questions relating to the proper conduct of a man, including questions falling within the sphere of positive law, wherever any guidance may be obtained from them with reference to such questions. The authority of Vedic texts containing precepts for the regulation of human conduct is founded on direct revelation; the wisdom of

[1] वेदः स्मृतिः सदाचारः स्वस्य च प्रियमात्मनः ।
एतच्चतुर्विधं प्राहुः साक्षाद्धर्मस्य लक्षणम् । मनुः । अ २ श्लोक १२

these precepts and their authoritative character are fundamental assumptions of Hindu Law which are not to be questioned or tested by the application of sceptical reasoning. I have elsewhere tried to explain the theoretical basis of this view in these words: "The sphere of revelation has reference to two kinds of topics: (1) that which is (सिद्ध) and (2) that which ought to be done (साध्य). The Vaidika Philosophers of India maintain that with regard to the latter topic the usual secular sources of knowledge (*i.e.* observation and inference) must necessarily be imperfect, for the rightness or wrongness of an action is not one of its sensible characters that can be directly perceived; and moreover, if in ascertaining the ethical character of an action one has to refer to its result, even then the shortcoming of observation and inference is apparent, for although they may enable a person to measure approximately the effect of an action so far as it exhibits itself during the short span of a man's life, there remains an illimitable region beyond which they cannot encompass within their range. This shortcoming, then, has to be mended by reference to the Vedas which contain injunctions and prohibitions indicating what actions should be performed and how they should be performed."[1] But whatever the theory may be, practically we derive very little light from the Vedas in regard to any question of positive law. As Babu Golap Chandra Sarkar points out: "The *Sruti* contains very little of lawyer's law; they consist of hymns, and deal with religious rites, true knowledge, and liberation. There are, no doubt, a few passages containing an incidental allusion to a rule of law or giving an instance from which a rule of law may

Practical value of the Vedas on questions of positive law.

---

[1] 4 C. L. J. 22 n.

be inferred."[1] For all practical purposes, therefore, we must refer to the Smritis or Dharma-śástras for the ascertainment of positive law.

(ii) The Smritis.

(2) The Smritis or Dharma-śástras—Theoretically the authority of the Dharma-śástras is derivative in its character. Not containing a direct record of the revelation, it is advanced that they embody the purport of Vedic texts as recollected by the sages who were their authors, and it is contended that even where the Vedic texts corresponding to the precepts contained in the Smritis are not expressly found, it must be inferred that they did exist but have now been lost owing to the frailty of human memory or some other cause of a similar nature. Hence Jaimini declares, 'the Smritis having been compiled by sages who were also the repositories of the revelation, there arises an inference that they are founded on the Śruti or revelation, and should therefore be regarded as authoritative. But if there be conflict, the precept of the Smriti must be disregarded, since the inference arises only when there is no such conflict.[2] But however that may be, practically, as I have already pointed out, recourse can very seldom be had to Vedic texts on any question of positive law, and the Smritis must be regarded as constituting the principal source of a lawyer's law.

There are numerous Smritis ascribed to the authorship of different sages, and twenty of these have been enumerated in the well-known text of Yájñavalkya which runs as follows:—'Manu, Atri, Vishnu, Hárita,

---

[1] Hindu Law, 3rd Edition, p. 11.

[2] अपि वा कर्तृ सामान्यात् प्रमाणमनुमानं स्यात् । पूर्व्वमीमांसा १ अ ३ पा २ सू ।
विरोधे त्वनपेक्ष्यं स्यादसति ह्यनुमानम् ॥ पूर्व्वमीमांसा १ अ ३ पा ३ सू ।

Yájñavalkya, Angiras, Usanas, Yama, Apastamba, Samvartta, Kátyáyana, Brihaspati, Parásara, Vyása, Samkha, Likhita, Daksha, Gautama, Sátátapa, and Vasishtha are the compilers of Dharma-sástras.'[1] But these are not all, for, as the Mitakshara points out, the enumeration is not exhaustive, so that compilations of Baudhayana, Narada and others are also regarded as authoritative Dharma-sástras. Theoretically all these Dharma-sástras are of equal authority, for all of them are supposed to have been based on the pronouncements of the Vedas; a superior position, however, is, by universal consensus, accorded to the Institutes of Manu; so Brihaspati declares, 'The first rank (among the lawgivers) belongs to Manu, as he embodied the true sense of the Vedas in his work; that Smriti (or text of law) which is opposed to the tenour of the law of Manu is not approved'.[2] It may naturally be expected that there being so many Smritis their pronouncements would not always be found to agree, but apparent conflict would be found to exist among them. The possibility of such conflicts is recognised even by the Smritis themselves, although commentators make every possible effort to reconcile conflicting texts and harmonise them into one consistent whole, it being an established rule of construction that no conflict should be admitted to exist where it is possible to find an interpretation which would explain away the apparent conflict

Conflict among Smritis—how reconciled.

---

[1] मन्वत्रिविष्णुहारीतयाज्ञवल्क्योशनोऽङ्गिराः
यमापस्तम्बसम्वर्त्ताः कात्यायन-बृहस्पती ।
पराशर-व्यासशङ्खलिखिता दक्षगौतमौ
शातातपो वशिष्ठश्च धर्म्मशास्त्र-प्रयोजकाः । याज्ञवल्क्यः, १अः,४।५।

[2] वेदार्थोपनिबन्धृत्वात् प्राधान्यं हि मनोः स्मृतम् ।
मन्वर्थविपरीता या सा स्मृतिर्न प्रशस्यते ॥ बृहस्पतिः ॥

and make the whole thing consistent. It is not necessary, in this place, to advert in any detail to the various ways in which commentators try to reconcile conflicting texts; sometimes, out of two conflicting texts, the one which is more rigid is pronounced to be more commendable, and the laxer one is treated as meant for those who are unfit to abide by the strict rule; sometimes they are reconciled as having different spheres of application, the texts being turned and twisted in interpretation with a view to enable them to stand together without contradiction, and so on; and we shall meet with examples of these ingenious devices in the subsequent parts of our discourse. The modern method of explaining the existence of these conflicting texts by referring them to different periods in the evolution of legal ideas is, for obvious reasons, not generally recognised, although instances of variation in legal rules with the progress of time, or rather, as the Hindu lawyer would prefer to put it, with the progressive degeneration of human capacities, are not altogether unknown, the most glaring assertion of such a variation being contained in the text of Parásara declaring that 'the *Dharmas* of men vary in the several Yugas in keeping with the character of each Yuga'.[1] When, however, the conflict cannot thus be easily explained away, it seems

The place of reason in the domain of sacred law.

that the sages contemplated that preference should be given to the view which is more consonant with reason; so Nárada says, 'In a case of conflict between Dharmasástras, that which is consonant with reason should be adopted as the proper course'.[2] But later commen-

---

[1] अन्ये कृतयुगे धर्मास्त्रेतायां द्वापरे परे ।
अन्ये कलियुगे नृणां युगरूपानुसारतः । पराशरः १ अः २ । २ ।

[2] धर्मशास्त्रविरोधे तु युक्तियुक्तो विधिः स्मृतः । नारदः । १ अ ४० श्लो ।

tators explain this by saying that it is not meant by texts like the above that in a case of conflict between two texts of Dharma-sástras one should judge by the exercise of his independent reason which one should be preferred, but that he should exercise his reason with a view to reconcile the two texts by interpreting them in such a way that they may stand together without contradiction Thus Viramitrodaya, referring to the text of Yajnavalkya, 'In a case of conflict between Smritis, reason prevails according to usage',[1] observes, 'The import of the above text is that the Smriti which accords with reason prevails over another which does not accord with it, and therefore the one which does not accord with reason should be explained as having a different import.'[2] It may be observed that this view of the commentators maintaining that the proper function of reason in the domain of sacred law is to explain away apparent conflicts and reconcile and harmonise the various texts of Dharma-sástras, and not to assume a superior and independent position and adjudge the relative merits of conflicting texts, is but a logical corollary from the assumption that the sages who were the lawgivers were infallible and they truly reproduced the purport of the Vedic texts of which they were the repositories, and it seems to be in keeping with the spirit of Manu's declaration, 'By Sruti (revelation) is meant the Veda, by Smriti (tradition) the Institutes of the sacred law: these two must not be called into question in any matter, since from these two the sacred law shone forth. Every twice-born man, who, relying on the science of dialectics despises those two sources is fit to be cast out

---

1 स्मृत्योर्विरोधे न्यायस्तु बलवान् व्यवहारतः । याज्ञवल्क्यः । २ अ, २१ श्लो ।

2 तत्रायमाशयः न्यायानुपष्टब्धस्मृत्यपेक्षया न्यायोपष्टब्धा स्मृतिर्बलवतीति न्यायानुपष्टब्धस्मृते स्तात्पर्यान्तरकल्पना कार्य्या । वीरमित्रोदयः । अर्थ । ५

by the virtuous as the scorner of the Veda'[1]. The place of reason in the domain of sacred law is, therefore, according to the commentators, a circumscribed and subordinate one, its function being to ascertain the real meaning of the various pronouncements of Dharma-sástras and harmonise them with one another, and never to supersede their place, subvert their authority, or sit as an arbiter between them. It may not be quite safe to speculate upon a subject like this, but it seems to me that in this extreme reverence towards each and every pronouncement of the Dharma-sástras and the curtailment of the scope of reason in relation thereto, the commentators display a return to the earlier rigidity and stricter orthodoxy of Manu's time from which later lawgivers, such as Yájnavalkya, Nárada, and Brihaspati, were prepared to allow a qualified departure.

(iii) established usages.

(3) Sadácháras, or the established usages of good men furnish a supplementary criterion for ascertaining the nature of approved conduct. There is, however, a dispute as to whether such usage can at all prevail as evidence of commendable conduct, when it conflicts with an express text of Smriti.

How far authoritative when in conflict with Smriti.

The leading commentators seem to be of opinion that in a case like this the express text must prevail, and the reason they assign is this :—An established usage not supported by any available text of Smriti still raises the presumption that there must have been some text of Smriti at the basis of the usage which has now been lost or forgotten ; this presumption is, however, rebutted

[1] श्रुतिस्तु वेदो विज्ञेयो धर्म्मशास्त्रन्तु वै स्मृतिः ।
ते सर्व्वार्थेष्वमीमांस्ये ताभ्यां धर्म्मो हि निर्बभौ ॥
योऽवमन्येत ते मूले हेतुशास्त्राश्रयाद्द्विजः ।
स साधुभिर्बहिष्कार्य्यो नास्तिको वेदनिन्दकः ॥ मनुः । २ अ, १०।११ श्लो

when we find an express text of Smriti condemning the conduct. The basis of the presumed propriety being thus gone, it follows that the prevalent usage can no longer be supported as proper. In support of this proposition, I may refer to the discussion contained in one of the Adhikara*n*as of Mádhavácháryya's Jaiminîya-nyáya-málá-vistara, which runs as follows:—"In Southern India, there is a custom among the learned of marrying one's maternal uncle's daughter. This custom being in conflict with an express text of Smriti prohibiting such marriage, the question arises whether it can be accepted as good evidence (of conduct approved by sacred law) or not. It may be contended that it is good evidence like other established usages, but that is not correct because it is opposed to Smriti. The weight attached to the usage of the learned arises from the inference that it is based on Smriti (although an express text may not be traceable), but when there is an express text opposed to the usage, the inference must give way".[1]

It should, however, be observed that this view does not imply that an established usage, where it conflicts with an express text of Smriti, should be condemned by the king. The condemnation proceeds from the broader standpoint of *Dharma* which has a religious reference, but by reason of the existence of the established usage, conduct in consonance with it must be tolerated though not approved by the king. Thus Brihaspati expressly declares:—"Local, tribal, and family customs wherever they prevail from before must be respected; otherwise, the subjects become agitated, popular disaffection springs up,

[1] यो मातुलविवाहादौ शिष्टाचारः स मा नवा ।
इतराचारवन्मानममानं स्मार्त्तबाधनात् ॥
स्मृतिमूलो हि सर्वत्र शिष्टाचारस्ततोऽत्र च ।
अनुमेया स्मृतिः स्मृत्या बाध्या प्रत्यक्षया तु सा ॥ जैमिनीय न्यायमाला
१ अ, ३ पा, ५ अधि ।

and the strength and the treasury (of the Government) suffer in consequence; (then giving certain instances of customs condemned by the Smritis, Brihaspati proceeds to observe), by such a conduct those (who pursue it) do not render themselves liable to expiation or punishment";[1] and commenting upon these passages, the Vîramitrodaya observes as follows:—"The author of Madanaratna says that the prescription of punishment and expiation for the performance of such acts in other Smritis applies to localities other than those specified in these texts. We are, however, of opinion that the visible harm such as popular discontent spoken of in the text indicates that the king should in no way inflict any punishment in such a case; but the absence of expiation has been spoken of with reference to social intercourse, and not with reference to purity in the life to come, for which latter purpose expiation is of course requisite, so that there arises no conflict with other Smritis. When conduct opposed to Sruti and Smriti extends over an entire locality, the sinfulness of the conduct loses its force of obstructing social intercourse (through excommunication), but its force of causing hell (*i.e.* misery after death) remains in tact, because on a consideration of the preamble, the purpose of the texts quoted above being fitly fulfilled on ascribing this much of meaning to them, it is improper to imagine an absolute want of guilt; hence it has been said by A'pastamba: 'Local, tribal, and family customs are authoritative when they are not opposed to sacred law'. In the text, *viz.* 'those who follow customs handed down

---

[1] देश जातिकुलानां च येधर्म्माः प्राक् प्रवर्त्तिताः ।
तथैव ते पालनीयाः प्रजाः प्रक्षुभ्यतेऽन्यथा ॥
जनापरक्तिर्भवति बलं कोषश्च नश्यति

* * * *

अनेन कर्म्मणा नैते प्रायश्चित्त दमार्हकाः । बृहस्पतिः ।

through successive generations and acted upon by predecessors incur no guilt thereby; not so with other people', the expression 'incur no guilt' means 'do not become liable to excommunication and punishment from king'; otherwise, it becomes difficult to avoid conflict between these two texts."[1]

The introduction of political considerations is a very noticeable feature of these texts, and the commentator therefore contends that although these considerations may be sufficient to induce the king not to punish those who follow these established usages condemned by the Dharma-sástras, and although by reason of their wide prevalence no question of social ostracism can possibly arise as a punishment for infraction of sástric injunctions, yet, in so far as they are opposed to express directions of Dharma-sástras, they can at best be tolerated but not approved. The conclusion, therefore, is that such customs or usages wherever they exist must be tolerated and recognised in the administration of justice, but must not be recognised as affording any index of 'Dharma' or commendable conduct and encouraged as such. Their Lordships of the Privy Council have laid down in the case of

[1] यत्तु स्मृत्यन्तरेष्वेतत्कर्म्मकरणे प्रायश्चित्तदण्डस्मरणात्तदेतद्वचनानुपात्तदेशविषयमिति मदनरत्नकारः। वयन्तु प्रजाप्रक्षोभादिदृष्टदोषकथनाद्राजदण्डा तत्र दण्डो न कार्य्य एव। प्रायश्चित्ताभावस्तु व्यवहारविषयः। परलोकशुद्ध्यर्थं प्रायश्चित्तं भवेदेवेति न स्मृत्यन्तरविरोधः। तत्तद्देशव्यापकश्रुतिस्मृतिविरुद्धाचरणे व्यवहारप्रतिबन्धिकाशक्तिस्तज्जन्यपापस्य नास्ति, नरकजनिकास्त्येव। उपक्रमपर्य्यालोचनादेतावदर्थकत्वमेव चैतद्वचनोपपत्तौ सर्व्वथादोषाभावकल्पनस्यानुचितत्वात्। अतएव आपस्तम्बेनोक्तं देशजातिकुलधर्म्माश्चाम्नायैरविरुद्धाः प्रमाणमिति। येषां परम्पराप्राप्ताः पूर्व्वजैरप्यनुष्ठिताः। त एव तैर्न दुष्येयुराचारैर्नेतरे पुनरिति। न दुष्येयुरव्यवहार्य्या राजदण्ड्याश्च न भवेयुरित्यर्थः। अन्यथैतयोरेव वचनयोः परस्परविरोधः दुष्परिहारः स्यादिति ब्रूमः। वीरमित्रोदयः। व्यं। ९

Collector of Madura v. *Mootoo Ramalinga*[2] that 'Under the Hindu system of law, clear proof of usage will outweigh the written text of the law.' There can be little doubt that for all practical purposes this statement is correct enough, although it may require some qualification, as indicated above, from a standpoint outside the scope of positive law. All that their Lordships should, therefore, be taken to lay down is that an act or transaction in consonance with an established usage cannot be treated as illegal or void of legal effect merely because it transgresses a written text of Dharma-sástra, and the position thus understood cannot possibly be doubted or assailed.

It should be mentioned that besides local, tribal, and family customs, the existence of special customs among commercial classes was also recognised, and the king was enjoined to give due weight to them in actions involving their consideration.

On the whole, therefore, it follows that besides the Dharma-sástras, established usages may be regarded as affording a supplementary source of Hindu Law, but it need hardly be observed that being essentially circumscribed and variable in their character, they cannot be of much assistance in a discussion on the general principles of Hindu Jurisprudence which must principally be gathered from the Dharma-sástras themselves.

(iv) Self-satisfaction.

(4) A'tma-tush*t*i, or self-satisfaction—is also mentioned as an index of 'Dharma' or commendable conduct. It is, however, explained that this criterion should only be resorted to when no guidance can be obtained from the Dharma-sástras themselves, and a man has to choose between alternative courses of action according to his own lights. So a passage ascribed to Garga declares that

[2] 12 Moo. I. A. 397, at p. 436.

self-satisfaction is the guiding principle among optional alternatives.[1] It need hardly be stated that this criterion has nothing to do with any question of positive law; it is not an external objective standard at all, but is an internal ethical standard by reference to which one should settle one's line of action among several courses left open by the *Sástras*.

Having thus passed under review the four sources from which, according to Manu, the knowledge of "Dharma" may be obtained, we find that the Smritis and the established usages may, for all practical purposes, be regarded as the two principal sources of positive law. Besides these we should also mention the Purá*n*as which are often cited by commentators and writers of Nibandhas as authorities on questions of Hindu Law.

(5) the Purá*n*as.

(5) The Purá*n*as—There are numerous works known as Purá*n*as among which eighteen are called 'Mahápurá*n*as' or principal Purá*n*as. Curiously enough, all of them are ascribed to the authorship of Vyása, though there can be no doubt that they belong to different periods and bear unmistakable marks of not being the works of the same author. They generally start with a mythical account of the origin of the creation, and then proceed to record the history of various ancient families interspersed with mythological stories and sectarian disputes; jurisprudence is not a subject with which they are directly concerned, but incidentally they sometimes deal with questions of law, and are cited by later commentators and writers on Hindu Law as authorities on such questions, although it is recognised that they can never be allowed to override the Smritis but must yield to the superior authority of the latter, if any conflict be found to exist between them.

1 वैकल्पिके चात्मतुष्टिः प्रमाणम् ।

The above review, however, is not exhaustive, for it only deals with what may be called the original sources of Hindu Law, and it is necessary to enquire how they were supplemented in later times, when people would no longer accord the dignity of a direct lawgiver to any of their contemporaries. This brings us to the commentaries and 'Nibandhas' (compendia) written by learned writers of more recent times.

(vi) Commentaries and Nibandhas.

(6) Commentaries and Nibandhas—As it has been already indicated, in the course of the development of Hindu Law there came a time when the productive period, if I may say so, was succeeded by a critical period. The criticism of commentators and Nibandhakáras, however, could not, for obvious reasons, be of an avowedly aggressive character; the authority of the Dharma-sástras they did not and could not possibly disown, and their task consisted in interpreting them and reconciling their pronouncements whenever any apparent conflict stared them in the face. The task was no doubt a difficult one; the original sources of the law remained constant of which no portion could be discarded as unauthoritative, or improved upon as erroneous or defective; conflicts between their pronouncements had to be explained away and reconciled; and beyond these there were perhaps the demands of a progressive time which had to be met not by the introduction of avowed innovations but by ingenious interpretation working upon old materials. It need hardly be said that these writers could not lay claim to any independent authority; their pronouncements were authoritative only in so far as they were deemed to correctly interpret the original sources, and any body was free to show that they were wrong. But it so happened that when the views of a particular writer, who, by reason of his superior scholarship and sanctity of life, commanded

The growth of different Schools in Hindu Law.

the reverence of the people of a particular locality, got a firm hold upon those people and began to mould their lives and institutions, the chances of those views being easily shaken off diminished from day to day, and at last there came a time when his interpretations might be said to have almost superseded the original authorities on which they were based, although theoretically this could never be and no commentator could, as of right, claim to have said the last word on any disputed question of law. It was in this way that different schools sprang up recognising the superior authority of different commentaries and compendia within the regions governed by them, and at the present moment one need not feel much reluctance to endorse the view of the Privy Council, as stated in the case of *Collector of Madura v. Mootoo Ramalinga Sathupathy*,[1] that the duty of a Judge who is under the obligation to administer Hindu Law "is not so much to enquire whether a disputed doctrine is fairly deducible from the earliest authority, as to ascertain whether it has been received by the particular school which governs the District with which he has to deal," with this qualification, which has been laid down in other cases, that a family, which has migrated from one Province to another, continues to be governed by the law as it obtains in the Province from which it has migrated unless and until it either expressly or impliedly adopts the law of its new domicil.[2] The importance of commentaries and Nibandhas of recognised authority therefore stands on a double basis: in the first place, they collect and harmonise the diverse texts of Dharma-sástras bearing on various topics of law, and in the second place,

Importance of commentaries and Nibandhas.

[1] 12 Moo. I.A. 397 at p. 436.

[2] See Soorendranath v. Mt. Heeramonee 12 Moo. I. A. 91; Parbati Kumari v. Jagadis Chunder I.L. R. 29 Cal. 433.

the interpretations which they put upon them acquire a sort of independent authority in the particular Provinces specially governed by them. In the part which commentators have thus played in the devolopment of Hindu Law, it is difficult to discriminate how far established usages have tinged the interpretations which they have put upon the texts of Dharma-śástras, and how far their interpretations themselves have moulded and modified those usages; all that can be safely surmised is that there must have been interaction between the two, so that interpretations influenced by usages did, in their turn, influence the usages themselves. However that may be, the conclusion at which we arrive from the above discussion is that the main sources to which reference must be made by a student of Hindu Jurisprudence are the Dharma-śástras and their expositions in the recognised commentaries and treatises of later writers.

The sources of authority of the Hindu Law.

Having thus discussed the question as to what are the sources from which we must seek to obtain materials for the treatment of our subject, I now proceed to trace the sources from which the Hindu Law derives its authority or imperative character. I have already indicated that the Hindu Law-givers included legal rules, as well as moral and religious precepts, within the broader con-

Dharma—what it means, and whence it derives its authority.

ception of 'Dharma.' Etymologically, the word 'Dharma' signifies that which supports and sustains; from the standpoint of the individual, it supports and sustains him through the temptations and vicissitudes of life, and from the standpoint of the community at large, it is the source of its solidarity and strength; nay, the Taittiriya sruti declares, 'it is the support of the entire world.'[1] There can be no doubt that this broad conception of 'Dharma' was the result of a reflective generalisation which must

[1] धर्मो विश्वस्य जगतः प्रतिष्ठा।

have been preceded by the enunciation and recognition of concrete rules of action, and in the Vedic age of Hindu Society these rules of action demanded obedience on the score that they were grounded on direct revelation. In this way such a connection was established between the idea of 'Dharma' and revelation, that even in the age of the Dharma-śástras, which succeeded the Vedic age, the sages, who did not claim to be the recipients of direct revelation justified the precepts laid down by them on the ground that they also were ultimately based on or deducible from the precepts of the Vedas, and Jaimini, the author of the Mimánsá aphorisms, declared that 'revelation being the root of Dharma, whatever is not (directly or indirectly) based on revelation need not be attended to.'[1] But as I have indicated, implicit obedience to an external mandate, however hallowed it may be by the reverence due to revelation, cannot proceed very long without being followed by a rational reflection. My natural inclinations impel me to proceed one way; the śástras command me to follow another; why should I follow the latter course in preference to the former? The question must have suggested itself very early in the evolution of Aryan thought and the answer was afforded by the differentiation between the pleasurable and the good. So, in the Kathopanishad we find, 'The good is different, the pleasurable is different; they both induce a man to diverse kinds of activities; among the two, he who takes up the good attains welfare, but he who selects the pleasurable misses it.'[2] It will thus appear that two different but interconnected ideas clustered around the term Dharma, (1) foundation on revelation, and

Connection between Dharma and revelation

The idea of the good.

---

[1] धर्मस्य शब्दमूलत्वादशब्दमनपेक्ष्यं स्यात् ।

[2] अन्यच्छ्रेयोऽन्यदुतैव प्रेयः । ते उभे नानार्थे पुरुषं सिनीतः ॥
तयोः श्रेय आददानस्य साधु भवति । हीयतेऽर्थाद् य उ प्रेयो वृणीते ॥

4

5797

(2) conduciveness to true welfare, and both these ideas are conveyed in the definition of Jaimini, 'Dharma is that object of welfare which is indicated by an injunction.'[1] The final end of 'Dharma' indicated above is distinctly set forth by Vasishtha where he says that 'after studying the Vedas, enquiry should be made about 'Dharma' with a view to the ultimate attainment of permanent welfare (salvation); knowing it and regulating one's conduct accordingly, the virtuous becomes most commendable in this life or after death';[2] and Kanada in his Vaiseshika Aphorisms expressly defines 'Dharma' as the source from which welfare and eventually salvation are realised.'[3]

How 'dharma' contains its sanction within itself in the certainty that its obedience will lead to welfare.

The above discussion will make it clear that according to the Hindu ideas 'dharma' or sacred law contains its authority within itself; the king is not superior to it, but, like other human beings, is subject to it. It is authoritative because its observance is conducive to welfare and ultimately to salvation, and its violation is reprehensible because that is sure to lead to misery. Within the sphere of sacred law, the king has his own function which is partly general and partly special in its character; it is general in so far as it is his duty to obey the law himself like other individuals, and it is special in so far as, unlike other individuals, it is his duty to enforce its obedience in others to a certain extent. The Law is supreme; the will of the king is not its originator, and its sanction is not derived from any extrinsic or accidental agency, for it contains its sanction within itself in the certainty that obedience to law will lead to welfare and its violation to misery. It may, however,

---

[1] चोदनालक्षणोऽर्थो धर्मः।

[2] अथातः पुरुषनिःश्रेयसार्थं धर्मजिज्ञासा। ज्ञात्वा चानुतिष्ठन् धार्मिकः प्रशस्यतमो भवति लोके प्रेत्य वा।

[3] यतोऽभ्युदयनिःश्रेयससिद्धिः सधर्मः।

be asked whence does this certainty arise? Is it to be supposed that the law represents commands issuing from God whose will upholds them by attaching due reward or punishment to actions in conformity with or in violation of those commands? No doubt this may seem to be the most natural standpoint, but, in fact, the Mîmánsakas who may be said to have dealt with the Philosophy of the Law did not introduce divine intervention in order to explain the fruition of human actions; they maintained that every action had an invisible force which subsisted even after the cessation of the action, and brought about the due consequence either in this life, or, at any rate, in the life to come. This invisible force was designated by them as Apûrva, which is thus explained by Mr. Colebrooke than whom no European writer had better understood the true spirit of Hindu Legal Philosophy. "The subject," says Mr. Colebrooke, "which most engages attention throughout the Mîmánsá, recurring at every turn, is the invisible or spiritual operation of an act of merit. The action ceases, yet the consequence does not immediately arise; a *virtue* meantime subsists unseen, but efficacious to connect the consequence with its past and remote cause, and to bring about, at a distant period or in another world, the relative effect. That unseen virtue is termed *Apûrva*, being a relation superinduced, *not before* possessed." By the introduction of this theory of Apûrva or invisible force, the Mîmánsakas sought to escape from the admission of a *Deus ex machina* which they considered to be unnecessary or untenable. This has led some to suppose that the Mîmánsá system of Jaimini was atheistic in its character, but Mádhaváchâryya in his *Samkara Viyaya* maintains that it was not Jaimini's intention to deny the existence of God, but merely to show that the nonscriptural arguments advanced by the Vaiseshikas to establish his existence

Whence does this certainty arise?

The theory of *apûrva*

Was the Mîmánsá system atheistic?

were in themselves insufficient and inconclusive. However that may be, this impersonal conception of the law bases its obligatory character upon the inscrutable authority ascribed to the *sástras*, as explained above, and operates upon human will by maintaining that *sástric* injunctions and prohibitions show us the true way and give us the sure warning that the adjustment of our actions in accordance with them will lead to welfare and their violation to its reverse.[1]

How positive law differentiates itself from ceremonial rules and moral and religious injunctions.

Having thus traced the source of the authority of Hindu law in the sanction which it carries along with it, let us now consider how that portion of it which may be characterised as positive law, and with which we are more directly concerned in the treatment of our subject, differentiates itself from the other portions which deal with ceremonial rules and moral and religious injunctions. The true explanation of this is to be found in the special function of the King in the Hindu polity. While the law directs an individual to do certain things and avoid certain others, it directs the King in addition to his other duties to take steps that the law may be respected and obeyed, and to mete out punishment to those who in violation of the law inflict injury upon others; the positive law may be said to comprise that portion of the law the violation of which calls for the interposition of the King in order to provide an adequate remedy to the injured party, or

---

[1] It may be added in this connection that the Sàmkhya system agreed with, but the Vedánta differed from the Mimánsá theory regarding the admissibility of dependence on divine causation in explaining the fruition of human actions. Mádhaváchárya in his commentaries on the Parásara Smriti tries to reconcile the Vedántic and the Mimánsaka doctrines by maintaining that the apparent conflict between them on this question should be understood as due to the different aims and scopes of those two systems.

(विवक्षाविशेषेण तत्समाधानात्)

chastise the delinquent for his transgression, or, in other words, it is that portion of the law which is enforced by the King. So Yájñavalkya declares,—"if a person, molested by others in a way which contravenes the Smriti or established usage, complains to the King, that gives rise to a topic for a judicial proceeding,"[1] and this implies three characteristic elements, *viz.*, (1) transgression of law as laid down in the Smriti or established by usage, (2) injury to some one other than the transgressor, and (3) intervention of the King in his judicial capacity. If these elements are duly considered, I hope it will be found that the Hindu conception of positive law was not very different from the modern or Austinian conception thereof. In the first place it emphasises that 'law was added because of transgressions'; in the second place it shows that intervention of the King is called for because and in so far as these transgressions cause injury to people other than the transgressors; and in the third place it indicates that whether the transgression be of some rule of action laid down in the Smritis or of some established usage, in either case it is the intervention of the King, who is the protector of the people and dispenser of justice, that converts religious or customary law into positive law. The only points of difference between the Hindu view and modern or Austinian view are, that while according to the latter view, law, in its normal form, consists of commands issuing from the King, and the duty of enforcing the same is a self-imposed duty, according to the former view, the law issues from a source superior to the King, and the duty of enforcing the same is cast upon him from above, so that the infliction of punishment

Three characteristic elements involved in the conception of positive law.

The Hindu conception compared with the Austinian.

---

1 स्मृत्याचारव्यपेतेन मार्गेणाधर्षितः परैः ।
आवेदयति चेद् राज्ञे व्यवहारपदं हि तत् ॥

is itself regarded as a Dharma as indicated in the well-known text of Manu, "penalty keeps the people under control, penalty protects them, penalty remains awake when people are asleep, so the wise have recognised punishment itself as a form of Dharma."[1]

The place of administration of justice in the functions of a Hindu King.

It may be noticed that there is a wide-spread idea, from which even well-known writers and reputed scholars are not entirely free, that the main function of Oriental Empires was the gathering of taxes and the levying of armies, and that they seldom concerned themselves with the enforcing of legal rules; but so far as India was concerned, a study of its ancient institutions, as disclosed in the works of the sages, at once demonstrates that nothing could be farther from the truth, for such a view really reverses the true order of things. According to the Hindu conception, it was the protection of the people, and not the collection of taxes, that was regarded as the principal duty of the King, and the administration of justice was one of the principal means to keep the people in order and to protect them in the proper enjoyment of their rights; of course the King had a right to collect taxes, but the right involved a corresponding obligation to afford protection to those who paid them, and whoever failed to discharge the obligation while enjoying the advantages of the right was condemned in no doubtful terms. Thus Manu declares: "a King who without protecting his subjects collects revenue from them may be said to be the collector of all the impurities to which they are subject;"[2] to the same effect is the following text of Yájñavalkya which lays down that 'whatever sin the

---

[1] दण्डः शास्ति प्रजाः सर्व्वाः दण्ड एवाभिरक्षति ।
दण्डः सुप्तेषु जागर्त्ति दण्डं धर्म्मं विदुर्बुधाः ॥

[2] अरक्षितारं राजानं बलिषड्भागहारिणम् ।
तमाहुः सर्व्वलोकानां समग्रमलहारकम् ॥

people commit being unprotected by the King, half of that goes to the King since he takes revenue from them."[1] It was, thus, one of the principal duties of the King to administer justice among his people, for administration of justice and maintenance of order go hand in hand, and one cannot conceive the one without the other. It was not, however, his function to legislate except in minor matters of local or temporary importance; the general body of the law was contained in the śástras, and their exposition was in the hands of learned Brahamans who, by reason of their piety and intellectual eminence, were specially fitted for the task. This is not the place to pause and consider how far this bifurcation of functions was conducive to the welfare of the community, but it certainly kept up the idea of sacredness which the Hindus attached to their law as emanating from a higher wisdom and not originating from the fiat of the royal will, although enforced by the temporal power which was vested in the King.

Arrangement and division of the subject.

Having thus considered the source from which the Hindu Law derives its authority, I will next endeavour to fix the limits of my subject by laying down an orderly scheme of discussion. The subject is a vast one, and it is apparent that it cannot be conveniently treated without appropriate arrangement and division. Let us, therefore, consider how best we can arrange and divide the subject of our discourse. I have already stated that the sphere of 'Dharma', as dealt with in the Dharma-śástras, includes a good deal more than positive law which furnishes the subject-matter of jurisprudence; it may, therefore, be reasonably inferred that the classification of 'Dharma', taken in its broadest sense, as given by the commentators is not

---

[1] अरक्षमाणाः कुर्व्वन्ति यत्किञ्चित् किल्विषं प्रजाः ।
तस्मात्तु नृपतेरर्द्धं यस्मात् गृह्णात्यसौ करान् ॥

-kely to serve the purpose of an adequate classification for positive law. Take, for instance, the sixfold division of Dharma as stated by Medhátithi in his commentaries on the Institutes of Manu and by Vijñáneswara in his commentaries on the Institutes of Yájñavalkya: The six divisions of 'Dharma' are:—(1) वर्णधर्म or duties peculiar to the several castes, (2) आश्रमधर्म or duties relating to the several stages of life, (3) वर्णाश्रमधर्म or duties appropriate to the several castes in relation to the several stages of life, (4) गुणधर्म or duties of special quality arising from special position, (5) निमित्तधर्म or secondary duties arising, for instance, from the nonperformance of primary duties, and (6) साधारणधर्म or duties of general obligation, and it is apparent that this classification is not at all appropriate to our purpose, being based upon a principle of division which cannot be adapted to jurisprudence. In the Institutes of Yájñavalkya we find व्यवहाराध्याय or chapter on positive law separated from आचाराध्याय or chapter on rituals and प्रायश्चित्ताध्याय or chapter on expiation; this division has the merit of discriminating positive law which has to be administered or enforced by the King in his judicial capacity from other topics discussed in the Dharmaśástras, and is calculated to save a student of Hindu jurisprudence from a good deal of confusion; it must, however, be remembered that the chapter on rituals is not completely foreign to jurisprudence as there are certain rituals, such as marriage and adoption, which create juristic relations and thereby produce, in an indirect way, certain juristic results. The main question, however, is how to divide the subject-matter of positive law so as to base thereon an orderly treatment of the general principles of Hindu jurisprudence. In considering this question, one primary distinction at once suggests itself to us, viz., the distinction between substantive law and adjective law, and it is a distinction which was recognised by our jurists, who dealt with adjective law under the head of व्यवहारमातृका, as distinguished from the different topics of substantive law which were treated after it in the order of discussion. For our purposes, however, I propose to deal with substantive law before I take up the discussion of adjective law, for some knowledge of the former division seems to be a necessary preliminary to the proper understanding of the latter. The next question is, how to divide the sphere of substantive Law itself ; it appears that the principal commentators and writers on Hindu law, who have dealt with positive law as a separate and relatively independent branch of study, have generally followed the division of topics of litigation as given by Manu in the following passage :—" Of these forms of action, the first is the recovery of debts ; the others are, (2) deposit, (3) sale by one who is not the owner, (4) partnership, (5) resumption of gift, (6) nonpayment of wages, (7) transgression of compact, (8) rescission of purchase and sale, (9) dispute between the master and the herdsman, (10) boundary-dispute, (11) personal violence, (12) verbal abuse (including defamation), (13) theft (including other cognate cases involving deceit), (14) violent crimes involving the use of force (such as robbery), (15) seduction of women (including adultery), (16) mutual duties of husband and wife, (17) partition of heritage, and (18) gambling and betting,—these are the eighteen topics on which litigation rests ; "[1] and Brihaspati

[1] तेषामाद्यमृणादानं निक्षेपोऽस्वामिविक्रयः ।
सम्भूय च समुत्थानं दत्तस्यानपकर्म च ॥
वेतनस्यैव चादानं संविदश्च व्यतिक्रमः ।
क्रयविक्रयानुशयो विवादः स्वामिपालयोः ॥
सीमाविवादधर्मश्च पारुष्ये दण्डवाचिके ।
स्तेयञ्च साहसञ्चैव स्त्रीसंग्रहणमेव च ॥
स्त्रीपुंधर्मौ विभागश्च द्यूतमाह्वयमेव च ।
पदान्यष्टादशैतानि व्यवहारस्थिताविह

said that "those who were true examiners would find these eighteen topics enumerated in the Dharma-śástras at the root of every possible litigious dispute,"[1] thereby implying that on careful analysis all seemingly different causes of action might be resolved into these. No doubt it was early recognized that in the diversity of human transactions the eighteen topics mentioned above were capable of being subdivided into numerous branches as Nárada and Kátyáyna expressly declared, but the eighteen-fold division was in the main retained with very little modification, perhaps the only modification which is worth mentioning being the introduction of a chapter dealing with nonservice by one who has accepted service, and of another dealing with miscellaneous obligations towards the king which did not readily come under any of the topics enumerated above, and for the violation of which the king, of his own motion, might call the transgressor to account. On the whole, therefore, it must be admitted that the division of the subject-matter of substantive law into eighteen topics, as indicated above, has the sanction of antiquity and general recognition, but one cannot fail to observe that it does not bear the impress of any scientific principle of classification, but represents an enumeration of certain causes of action apparently taken at random, but, in all probability, chosen and grouped together because they frequently arose at that period of social evolution in which it was first introduced; when, however, it was adopted by Manu and sanctioned by his great authority, it tended to become stereotyped and was accepted by subsequent law-givers without much modification. It, therefore, follows that a logical and systematic discussion

---

[1] पदान्यष्टादशैतानि धर्म्मशास्त्रोदितानिच ।
मूलं सर्व्वविवादानां ये विदुस्ते परीक्षकाः ॥

of juristic principles cannot conveniently follow the division and arrangement of topics indicated above, although the enumeration of causes of action contained therein may serve the purpose of a useful historical landmark showing the nature of the disputes that used to come up before a Court of Justice in those remote days, and may even be so explained as to include within its scope all possible legal disputes that may arise at any time. I am thus called upon to outline for myself a convenient method of arranging the topics of law treated by the lawgivers in order that I may adopt it for the purpose of an orderly discussion of the principles of Hindu jurisprudence, and this I will now proceed to do. I have already noticed the striking distinction between the substantive law and the adjective law, and stated that in the order of treatment the former branch should find a place before the latter. Dealing next with the substantive law, one is at once reminded of the distinction drawn by the Roman jurists between the law of things (jus quod ad res pertinet) and the law of persons (jus quod ad personas pertinet) including within the latter branch what the German writers call 'Familien-recht' or the law of the family meaning thereby that portion of the substantive law which deals with the special rights and obligations arising from special conditions of family relationships, and I propose to adopt it as a very convenient, though not a scientifically accurate, principle of classification. It should, however, be noted that there has existed some doubt as regards the positions of the law of succession and of the law of obligations within this scheme; as regards the law of succession, inasmuch as succession is one of the modes of acquisition of ownership, I consider it proper to include it within the part dealing with the law of things, although being founded on personal relationship it may have some affinity to the law of persons, and as regards the law of obligations I prefer to class it apart. To these must be added the law of crimes, which, being regarded as a part of the public law, is generally considered to be outside the abovementioned divisions; I am, however, disposed to think that as the law of crimes bears a strong affinity to the law of torts which, although generally regarded as a part of the law of obligations, was not, under the Hindu law, sharply discriminated from the same, it may not be inconvenient to separate the law of torts from the law of obligations and discuss it along with the law of crimes, thereby confining the law of obligations to rights and duties arising from contracts as distinguished from delicts or wrongs. In the result, the divisions thus obtained may be arranged as follows :—

A. Substantive law:—(1) The Law of things dealing with (*a*) ownership, (*b*) pledge, (*c*) various kinds of bailment, and (*d*) such other rights over things as are not included in the above.

(2). The law of persons dealing with (*i*) the law of special status or conditions which may be distinguished as (*a*) parental and quasi-parental, (b) marital and quasi-marital, and (*c*) dominical, and (*ii*) the law of defective status of condition arising out of infancy, insanity, etc.

(3) The law of contractual obligations dealing, for instance, with recovery of debts, recovery of wages, partnership, suretyship, and transgression of compact.

(4). The law of torts and the law of crimes.

B. Adjective Law :—Including the law of procedure, the law of evidence, and the law of sanctions and remedies.

Acting upon this arrangement of topics, I may divide and distribute the proposed course of lectures in the following way:—

LECTURE II.—Ownership: its nature and the modes of its acquisition.

LECTURE III.—Transfer of ownership (including the law of gift and the law of sale).

LECTURE IV.—The law of prescription.

LECTURE V.—The law of succession.

LECTURE VI.—The law of pledge.

LECTURE VII—The law of bailments and other incorporeal rights.

LECTURE VIII—The law relating to parental and quasi-parental relationship.

LECTURE IX.—The law relating to marital and quasi-marital relationship.

LECTURE X.—The law of dominical relation, and the law of defective status in general.

LECTURE XI.—The law of contractual obligations.

LECTURE XII.—The law of torts and the law of crimes.

LECTURE XIII.—Adjective law.

LECTURE XIV.—Concluding remarks.

Concluding remarks.

Having thus outlined the scheme of my future lectures, I propose to conclude my introductory observations. I have not attempted in this lecture to anticipate any of the discussions which will be elaborated in their proper places in the following lectures, for, the introduction of inadequate accounts of subjects which will be fully treated afterwards is not only superfluous, but may also be productive of wrong impressions. All that I can at present do is to express a confidence that whoever will patiently follow the account of Hindu Jurisprudence, as contained in the following pages, will be convinced that much of the hostile aspersion that has been cast against Hindu Law by some able but ill-informed critics is the result of ignorance and prejudice acting and reacting upon each other. I do not, of course, mean to assert that Hindu Jurisprudence was in all respects as perfect as one could desire, but I hope to be able to show that, in the main, it will not compare unfavourably with even the most developed system of ancient Jurisprudence, the Roman. The assertion may seem to be somewhat too bold, but I do not see any intrinsic improbability about it and I hope that those, who know anything about the contributions of the Hindu mind in other dspartments of knowledge, will not meet it with irrational scepticism. As regards those who go into raptures at the bare mention of the Twelve Tables, but shake their heads at the mention of the name of Manu, and talk about 'feeble civilization' and 'cruel absurdities' without feeling the absurdity of criticising upon a subject which they had no opportunity to study, I am content to leave them to their convictions, and to the satisfaction which they derive from the same.

LECTURE II

OWNERSHIP : ITS NATURE AND THE MODES OF ITS ACQUISITION.

In the previous lecture I have explained the scope of Hindu Jurisprudence, and set forth a scheme for the discussion of the various topics which require consideration. The first of these topics is ownership, which is acknowledged on all hands to be one of the fundamental juristic conceptions common to all systems of law. I will, therefore, endeavour to place before you in this lecture an exposition of the conception of ownership as understood by the Hindu Jurists, and also explain some of the modes in which it could be acquired according to the Hindu Law-givers.

Ownership what it means.

In analysing the conception of ownership, we at once see that it is based upon the distinction between persons and things, and implies a certain peculiar kind of relation between them ; this relation, whatever its exact character may be, is capable of being viewed from two different stand-points ; on the one hand, we may start with the 'persons' in whom a bundle of rights constituting ownership inheres in relation to particular things ; on the other hand, we may take up the 'things' as they are, and view them as subject to a special kind of control from particular individuals, which makes us regard those 'things' as the property of those individuals. The *idea* which underlies the conception of ownership (स्वामित्व) on the one hand and the conception of property (स्वत्व) on the other,

Difference between ownership and property.

is fundamentally the same, so that they may be regarded as mutually inter-dependent correlatives connoting two different aspects of the same identical relation ; ownership, therefore, may be said to inhere in persons in relation to things in so far as they are objects of ownership, and property may be said to characterise things in so far as they stand related to persons who are their owners.

The distinction and inter-connection pointed out above between the conceptions of ownership (स्वामित्व) and property (स्वत्व) is, I need hardly say, fully recognised and explained by Hindu Jurists with their usual analytical subtlety, and they point out that the correct logical way of comprehending them both is to regard the one as the determinant of the other, so that if you start with ownership as a peculiar condition of the person in whom it inheres, it should certainly be regarded as having a determinate character in so far as it is related to the thing which thereby becomes the property of that person ; for ownership in the abstract has no meaning apart from its object. This inter-relation between the conceptions of ownership and property is characterised by Hindu Jurists as mutual determination. (निरूप्य निरूपक भाव).

I have introduced this discussion at the outset in order to make it clear that an exposition of one of these two conceptions necessarily explains the other, in as much as they are but two aspects of the same idea, just as fatherhood and sonship which designate the same relationship viewed from opposite sides.

Having thus explained the inter-relation between the conceptions of ownership and property, I will next

Siromani's view

proceed to explain what is meant by them. But before I do so, it may not be out of place to observe that although ownership inheres in the person, and property in the thing in relation to the owner, neither of them can, in the opinion of Siromani, be regarded as falling within the classification of categories* (पदार्थ) recognised by the Vaiseshikas ; an exhaustive enumeration and exposition of these categories is beyond the scope of these lectures and I do not propose to undertake this task ; it will be sufficient to point out that what is chiefly meant by this remark is that 'ownership' on the one hand, and 'property' on the other, represent a superinduced relation between the person who owns and the thing that is owned not included within the essential attributes, which characterise the person and the thing respectively ; so that they cannot be regarded as attributes (*gunas*) of either the person or the thing. Hence arises the necessity of admitting an additional category (अतिरिक्त: पदार्थ:) supplementing the sevenfold division of the Vaiseshikas, to indicate that the conception of ownership or property is an outcome of social evolution which clothes the persons with a bundle of rights in relation to things which are objects of ownership. It is, however, unnecessary to enter into the intricacies of these discussions which can be properly understood only by those who are sufficiently acquainted with the Hindu Philosophical systems, and I merely indicate them as testifying to the deep logical insight with which the Hindu Jurists pursued these discussions ; it may be easy to scoff at these niceties, but it is not quite so easy to understand them or to help admiring the subtlety of logical acumen displayed by those who introduced them.

Recognised definition of property.

Leaving behind these logical niceties, I will now proceed to explain what the term property (स्वत्व) signifies,

---

* द्रव्यंगुणा स्तथाकर्म सामान्यं सविशेषकम् ।

समवाय स्तथाभाव: पदार्था: सप्त कीर्त्तिता: ॥

According to Srikrishna Tarkalankar.

or in other words, what is meant when it is said that a particular thing is the property of a particular person. Srikrishna Tarkalankara in his commentary on Dayabhaga says that according to the old established explanation it signifies fitness for free disposal as indicated by the Sastra.* If you analyse this definition, you will at once find that it consists of two distinct elements which may be treated separately, viz. (1) that the idea of property is exclusively indicated by the Sastra (शास्त्रैक समधिगम्यत्व); and (2) that it signifies fitness for free disposal by the person who owns it (यथेष्टविनियोगार्हत्व). I will now proceed to deal with these two elements separately.

Controversy about the view that property is exclusively indicated by Sastras. Jimutavahana and Vijnaneswara.

(1) According to some Hindu Jurists the idea of property is exclusively indicated by Sastras and ownership can only be acquired in the modes recognised by them. This view is advocated by Dhareswara, Jimutavahana and their followers. On the other hand Vijnaneswara and his followers maintain that the idea of property has its basis on popular recognition without any dependence on Sastras, the object of the rules laid down in the Sastras about the modes of acquisition of ownership being to collect and prescribe those means of acquisition recognised by popular usage that are regarded as commendable and as such worthy of being pursued. This latter view is denominated as लौकिक स्वत्ववाद *i.e.*, the doctrine that property has its basis on popular recognition. It is not possible within the short scope of this lecture to enter into a detailed examination of this remarkable controversy, and all that I can attempt to do is to present before you an idea of the controversy with some of the arguments advanced by the disputants in support of their respective opinions. The real point in the controversy resolves itself

---

* यथेष्टविनियोगार्हत्वं न शास्त्रबोधितत्वमिति भावः ।

into this: there are certain modes of acquiring ownership recognised by the people on all hands; they are also the modes laid down in the Sastras as leading to acquisition of ownership; now, the question is which is prior? Do the Sastras merely summarise the modes of acquisition of ownership which they find already recognised in popular usage, or does the popular usage merely follow and give effect to the Sastric rules laying down the conditions for the acquisition of ownership? Dhareswara and Jimutaváhana advocate the latter view, while Vijnaneswara and Mitra Misra maintain the former. I need hardly say that I feel inclined to give preference to the former view as more consonant with reason and common sense; let us, however, examine some of the objections advanced in opposition to this view.

Objection to Vijnaneswara's view.

(a) "Fitness for free disposal" is not a sound test.

(*a*) It has been objected that if 'fitness for free disposal' is what, according to you, characterises the conception of property without any reference to the Sastric rules regulating the acquisition of ownership, then, how is it that you do not ascribe ownership to the thief over the stolen articles which are as much within his control as any other thing acquired by honest means? It will not do to say that the thief cannot freely dispose of the stolen articles for fear of detection and consequent punishment, for even an honest owner cannot dispose of his property in any way he likes, in as much as his power of free disposal is to some extent limited by Sastric injunction, as for instance, he cannot set fire to his own house so as to burn the houses of his neighbours; in either case the exercise of the power of free disposal is in practice limited to some extent, but the power is there, and no one can stop its exercise provided the person is prepared to pay the penalty for the same. The shortest answer, however, to this objection seems to be that it is altogether erroneous to assume that popular usage recognises the thief as the owner of the stolen articles, so that it is unnecessary to seek the assistance of Sastric injunctions to establish that theft causes no transfer of property, although the real owner, so long as he is unable to trace the articles, loses his control over them ; if this loss of control argued loss of ownership, you might as well maintain that a person who left his home and went to a distant land, thereby lost his ownership over everything which he left behind him.

(*b*) Sastric rules become unnecessary.

(*b*) It may, however, be asked that if the different modes of acquisition of ownership are recognised in popular usage without any reference to Sastric rules, then why is it that the Sastras quite unnecessarily lay down those rules prescribing various modes in which ownership can be acquired ? Surely, it is not reasonable to suppose that the Sastras would undertake the quite unprofitable task of repeating without any purpose what is otherwise well-known to the people, so that those who assert that the various modes of acquisition of ownership are developed out of popular usage and recognised by the people without any reference to the Sastras must explain the object which those rules are calculated to serve, and thereby justify their insertion into the Sastras. To this it may be replied that it cannot be said that even a bare collection of rules which we find recognised by popular usage is altogether unprofitable, for a scientific presentation of such rules is not without its value, and it is widely recognised that a good portion of what is called positive law consists of rules collected from popular usage set forth in well-defined and systematic forms. Moreover, it may be pointed out that a specification in the Sastras of some of the recognised modes of acquisition of ownership does not amount to a mere useless repetition of what is already recognised by popular usage, for it serves the useful purpose of enunciating the approved methods of acquisition of ownership, and thereby indirectly reprobates those other methods of acquiring property which are opposed to directions contained in the texts of the Sastras,—in other words, although these texts may not exhaustively enumerate the methods of acquiring property which are to be gathered from popular usage, yet they may have as their object the useful end of regulating human conduct by indicating what courses may be pursued, and thereby indirectly suggesting what courses should not be pursued by people belonging to the several castes in their endeavour to acquire property.

To illustrate this view, Viramitrodaya refers to the rule laid down in the Sastras that a man should take his food with his face turned towards a particular direction; this does not signify that whoever violates this rule does not enjoy his meal or satisfy his hunger, but it merely indicates that an infringement of the rule is not conducive to welfare; similarly, when the Sastras point out certain modes of acquiring property and give specific directions about them, it does not follow that ownership will not arise unless those directions are strictly complied with, but all that may be inferred is that a violation of those directions is not proper, and should be avoided as far as possible. In other words, acquisition of ownership is not an outcome of Sastric injunctions; they are not creative, if I may use the expression, but are partly illustrative and partly regulative in their character.

Having thus answered the objections of the other side, the supporters of the doctrine that the growth of ownership is an outcome of social evolution and not a deduction from Sastric injunctions urge that the very fact that the conception of ownership is not confined to the people who recognise the authoritative character of the Sastras furnishes a strong argument in support of their position; this argument seems, at the first sight to be almost unanswerable, but it may perhaps be replied that although there are people who do not revere the Sastras prevalent among us, yet they have got some authoritative works among them which supply them with their law, so that the controversy discussed above does not become impossible even with them. Understood in this wider sense, the controversy appears to resolve itself into a question regarding the relative priority between the unwritten rules about the acquisition of property evolved by the popular mind and observed in popular usage, and the written rules inculcated and systematised in authoritative works on positive law. When we come to consider the question carefully from this stand-point, it seems difficult to deny that in the order of evolution the unwritten rules evolved by the popular mind occupy a prior position, although they may be subsequently moulded and modified by written works of acknowledged authority, and this seems to be the opinion more widely recognised among the Hindu Jurists. I have already mentioned that Vijnaneswara and his followers, such as Mitra Misra, advocate this view; I may also add that renowned Mimansakas, such as Guru, Kumarila Swami and Parthasarathi Misra are also of the same opinion.

"Fitness for free disposal" special significance of the word "fitness."

(2) Having discussed the first of the alleged characteristic elements in the definition of property mentioned above, I now pass on to consider the second element, *viz.* 'fitness for free disposal.' It is important to notice in this connection the special significance of the word 'fitness' used as a part of the above definition; it is not denied that in actual practice it is found that the disposition of property by the owner is not absolutely capricious, but is

regulated to some extent by the motives furnished by the control exercised by the King and by the Sastric injunctions; still this admission does not militate against the view that the term 'property' connotes fitness for free disposal; for although my dealing with my property may not be absolutely unfettered by the considerations indicated above, yet that does not imply that I have not got the power to deal with my property in any way I like, or, to put it in another way, that my 'property' is not, by its very nature, liable to be disposed of by me according to my will. Hence the Viramitrodaya observes that if an unrighteous man disposes of his property in a way prohibited by the Sastras, he may be committing a sin by reason of his violation of the prohibition, but it cannot be said that his action is not an exercise of his proprietary right; or, to look at the matter from another stand-point, although a man may, and usually does, refrain from dealing with his property in a way prohibited by the Sastras, it cannot be said that his proprietary right did not extend to invest him with the power of acting according to his pleasure in relation to his property, provided he was prepared to undergo the penalty consequent upon the infraction of the Sastric prohibition. Hence it follows that although in practice one's dealings with one's property are regulated by various considerations, yet the word 'property' in its fullest sense connotes fitness for free disposal by the owner, and ownership implies, to borrow an expression of Dr. Holland, a plenary control over its object. To illustrate this view the Viramitrodaya mentions the simile of a seed which contains within it the capacity to germinate and be converted into a sprout; this capacity may, in individual cases, be impeded by extraneous causes, but still it cannot be said that the capacity was not there and the seed was not, by its very nature, fit for developing into the shape of a young plant; similarly an owner may not actually exercise his power of dealing with his property unrestrained by the extrinsic considerations of prudence and propriety, but that does not show that he was not invested with the power of disposing of his property according to his inclination, or that the term 'property' did not connote 'fitness' for free disposal by the owners. A practical application of this characteristic element in the conception of property will be found in the oft-quoted dictum of Jimutavāhana that 'a fact cannot be altered by a hundred texts'; a father, according to Jimutavāhana, is the full owner of his property and his sons do not acquire any co-ownership with him by reason of their birth; now there are certain texts which prohibit the father from alienating certain kinds of his property without the consent of his sons; but this prohibition, argues Jimutavāhana, cannot have the effect of invalidating an alienation by the father in violation thereof, because the alienation becomes operative by reason of the ownership which inheres in the father to the exclusion of his sons, and 'a fact', he says, 'cannot be altered by a hundred texts.'

Austinian conception of property compared.

While explaining the conceptions of 'ownership' and 'property' according to the Hindu Jurists, one cannot help being struck by the similarity of their views on this point with those of some of the eminent western writers on modern Jurisprudence. Thus, in his lectures on Jurisprudence, Austin points out that "in the Institutes of Gaius and Justinian, the right of property or dominion is not defined at all. Things are described; the modes of acquiring property in them are described; servitudes are described; but of the right of property or dominion no direct description is given", and he himself defines the term property or dominion as being "applicable to any right which gives to the entitled party an indefinite power or liberty of using or dealing with the subject." (Lecture XLVIII). Similarly, Dr. Holland defines ownership as 'a plenary control over an object', but he points out at the same time that in accordance with the maxim 'sic utere tuo ut alienum non laedas', it must always be enjoyed in such a way as not to interfere with the rights of others. (Chap. XI). It is hardly necessary to point out how closely these definitions approach the view of the Hindu Jurists which I have tried to lay before you in the foregoing exposition. The resemblance is not confined merely to the definitions, but also extends to the limitation indicated in the latter part of the passage quoted from Dr. Holland's Jurisprudence, for this limitation is ultimately reducible to the control exercised by the king and by the Sastric injunctions, which is fully recognised by the Hindu Jurists, as already pointed out. On the whole, therefore, I may trust that I shall not be accused of an idle pride in the merits of these discussions introduced by the Hindu Jurists, if I affirm that in point of logical subtlety and analytical skill they have scarcely been excelled even by the most modern exponents of Western Jurisprudence.

Qualified property.

It will be seen that in the above exposition of the conceptions of ownership and property I have taken those terms in their strictest sense; it must not, however, be thought that the Hindu Jurists did not acknowledge that the unfettered power of using or dealing with one's own property, which constitutes ownership in the strictest sense, is susceptible, under special circumstances, of being limited or circumscribed to various extents, for, as a matter of fact, the Hindu Law does recognise the existence of qualified ownership or property, and the restriction upon the right of free disposal may even go so far as almost to deprive the owner of his right of alienating the property according to his choice. Thus, a Hindu widow succeeding to the property of her deceased husband cannot ordinarily alienate that property except under certain special contingencies, which, for the sake of conciseness, are described by the expression 'legal necessity'. Now, is not the widow the owner of the property? No doubt, she is, but her ownership does not fully correspond to the idea which I have tried to explain above, but is ordinarily limited to the right of enjoyment of the usufruct without detriment to or destruction of the corpus; hence this kind of qualified property is said to imply fitness for enjoyment (भोगोपयोगि स्वत्व) as distinguished from fitness for free alienation.

Srikrishna's view.

So also Srikrishna Tarkalankara expressly recognises the existence of various concurrent rights to one and the same thing vested in different persons provided there be no incompatibility in the co-existence of such rights. He thus distinguishes between property of the same kind and property of different kinds, and maintains that the existence of the property of one kind in a particular person is incompatible with, and so excludes, the concurrence of the same kind of property in another person (सजातीय स्वत्वं प्रति सजातीय स्वत्वं विरोधि), where as there is no such incompatibility in the co-existence of different kinds of property in relation to the same thing residing in different individuals. This position involves the admission of diverse rights inhering in different persons constituting different fragments of the totality of rights comprised by ownership taken in its strictest sense; when we use the term 'property' in relation to cases of this description, it is no doubt used in a qualified sense; still the question may arise as to who should be regarded as the true owner of the thing, for, in strict legal parlance one of these persons should be treated as being the owner, and the other should be regarded as being invested with rights over the object in the ownership of the former. In most cases, the solution of this question is not found to be beset with much difficulty, for we can generally trace the mode in which these subordinate elements of ownership constituting 'jura in re aliena' have been carved out and transferred to different individuals, while the residuary right of ownership has remained where it was. There may, however, be cases where the question may not be altogether free from doubt or difficulty; as an instance, I may refer to the interesting discussion about the nature of king's right in the soil within his dominion, which is owned and occupied by private individuals. The discussion is contained in the Viswajidadhikarana of the Mimansa, and the more widely recognised opinion seems to be that the private individuals are the true owners of the soil, the title of the king being generally limited to the right of collecting revenue from them. Nilakantha in his Vyavaharamayukha and Srikishna Tarkalankara in his commentary on the Dayabhaga seem to endorse this view and regard the *bhoumikas* (Landlords) as the real owners of the soil held by them, while they ascribe to the king merely the right to collect revenue from the landlords as representing his proper share of the produce of the soil to which he becomes entitled by reason of the protection which he affords to them in the peaceful enjoyment of their property. Jagannath, however, seems to contend that, looking at the origin of the proprietary right, this limited conception of the right of the sovereign is not justifiable; he maintains that if ownership primarily arose from first occupation, it would be more reasonable to suppose that the sovereign being the stronger party, would have the prevalent right, such rights as the subjects possessed, being permissive in their character, and terminable at his option by the withdrawal of the permission

The nature of king's right in the soil.

Mimansa.

Nilakantha. Srikrishna.

Jagannath.

at the end of the year. It is thus curious to observe that the more modern view gives a greater latitude to the rights of the sovereign as opposed to the rights of the people, and it may not be unreasonable to presume that this was to some extent due to the influence of foreign domination which had effected an alteration in the conception of sovereignty among the Hindus. The perplexity felt by Jagannatha was, however, mainly due to his attempt to go to the root of the matter, and determine how originally the rights of the sovereign came to co-exist with the rights of the subjects; and none of the various hypotheses which suggested themselves appeared to him to be altogether free from difficulty. If the ownership of the subject arose from occupancy, he argues, why could not the sovereign prevent it by his superior power, or if it was due to a grant from the sovereign, what was the exact character of the grant? Questions of this kind are essentially speculative and are not at all easy to solve, so that the better course seems to be to confine our enquiry to the actual state of the ideas prevalent in a particular society at a particular stage of its evolution; and looking at the question from this standpoint, it seems that among the Hindus the property of the sovereign to the soil within his dominion in the occupation of private owners had at an early period been confined to the right of realising a certain share of the produce as revenue, as a recompense for the protection afforded by him. The view of Jagannatha that the private owners might be regarded as if they were so many lessees from year to year finds very little support from the Dharmasastras which, although they dilate upon the divine character of the sovereign and the reverence due to his position, do not furnish any basis for maintaining that he was the absolute master of his territory, free to deal with the lands within his dominion in any way he liked to the prejudice of the settled rights of his subjects. It must, however, be understood that I am not here speaking of king's private lands over which he had complete and absolute control; it may also be that with regard to lands within his dominion which had not been appropriated by private owners as their own, his right was supreme and superseded the claim of his subjects; but as regards lands under private ownership his right was limited by the concurrent rights inhering in private owners. How and why the right of the sovereign came to be limited in this way it is very difficult to explain, and I think it ought to be enough for us to take note that it was so. "This earth", says Jagannatha, "is the cow which grants every wish; she affords property of a hundred various kinds (inferior, if the owner need the assent of another proprietor—superior, if his right precede assent); while she deludes a hundred owners, like a deceiving harlot, with the illusion of false enjoyment; for, in truth, there is no other lord of this earth but one, the Supreme Lord."

Sastric means of acquisition of ownership.

Having thus explained the correlated conceptions of ownership and property according to Hindu Jurists, I now proceed to deal with some of the means of acquisition of ownership recognised in the Dharmasastras. I have already stated that the enunciation of these means contained in the Dharmasastras was not meant to be exhaustive; hence we find different law-givers giving different lists which do not exactly agree. Thus Manu declares:[1]

Manu.

'There are seven virtuous means of acquisition of wealth,—inheritance, gain, purchase, conquest, application (of wealth), employment of work and acceptance of gifts from

[1] सप्त वित्तागमा धर्म्या दायो लाभः क्रयो जयः ।
प्रयोगः कर्मयोगश्च सत्प्रतिग्रह एव च ॥ Manu X 115.

* *

Gautama.

proper persons.' Gautama gives almost the same list with a little modification when he says that ownership arises from succession, purchase, partition occupation (of unappropriated property) and finding (of hidden treasures or the like), to which may be added acceptance of gifts in the case of Brahmins, conquest in the case of Kshatriyas, commerce and agriculture in the case of Vaisyas, and wages of labour in the case of Sudras.[1] Narada enters into a little more detail, and says that there are twelve different modes of acquiring wealth of which three are general (*i.e.*, open to all castes), and the rest are peculiar to the several castes. Succession, gifts of affection, and marriage presents received with the wife,—these are common to all the castes. There are three special sources of acquiring wealth in the case of Brahmins which are free from stain, *viz.*, acceptance of free gifts, performance of priestly duties and receipts from disciples; similarly there are three special sources of wealth in the case of Kshatriyas, *viz.*, revenue, gains of war and penalties of law; so the Vaisyas acquire wealth in three distinct ways, *viz.*, through agriculture, herdsmanship and commerce; and the Sudras gain wealth by serving the aforesaid three castes. These specific modes of acquiring wealth are proper for the several castes, and any contravention is reprehensible unless forced by pressing necessity. It is hardly necessary to point out that although the Dharmasastras lay down certain modes of acquiring property as specially appropriate to a particular caste, it is not thereby implied that any contravention of these directions will in any way affect the growth of ownership; for instance, if a Brahmin instead of following the usual avocations of his own caste takes up those of a Vaisya and becomes

Narada.

Enumeration of means not exhaustive.

---

[1] Gautama Chapter X.

a cultivator, it must not be understood that the produce of his agriculture will not be his own, for, to adopt the terse and at the same time significant expression of Jimutavahana, 'a fact cannot be altered by a hundred texts.' The real meaning of these rules is that such conduct as leads to a confusion of functions among the several castes is reprehensible unless justified by pressing necessity and ought to be avoided as much as possible.

Modes of acquisition of ownership.

I will now proceed to deal with some of the specific modes of acquisition of ownership indicated above, and among these the first that requires consideration is the one by which ownership is acquired in respect of a thing which had no previous owner. This is indicated by the word *parigraha* which literally means appropriation and is explained in the Viramitrodaya as signifying the appropriation of previously unappropriated property such as straw, water, logs of wood, etc., from a forest which is open to the public as not being under the ownership of any particular individual.[1] The explanation above quoted does not limit the extent of *parigraha* or first appropriation as a means of acquisition of ownership, but indicates that it can only be effective in respect of things which are not already under the ownership of somebody else and that at the time when the Viramitrodaya was written, the other, and if I may say so, older examples of its operation had become obsolete. It will perhaps be understood that in speaking of these examples, I am referring to the acquisition of ownership in a wild animal by the person whose arrow strikes it down, and in a previously unappropriated field by the person who first reclaims it and makes it fit for cultivation. I have said that these

Parigraha or occupatio.

[1] परिग्रहः पूर्व्वमपरैरस्वीकृतस्यारण्यादिसाधारण प्रदेशसम्बन्धिनस्तृणजलकाष्ठादेः स्वीकारः। Viramitrodaya on Partition.

* *

examples had become obsolete in the days of the Viramitrodaya; but this is saying very little, for, as it seems to me, they had become obsolete even in the days of Manu.

Manu.

Thus in one passage Manu says, "Those who were versed in the ancient lore regarded this earth as the wife of its first king Prithu, and they declared that the field belonged to him who reclaimed it and the (hunted) animal to him whose arrow struck it down.[1]" In this passage Manu distinctly traces the origin of ownership to what is called *occupatio* in Roman Law, and the way in which he puts it indicates that this was a view which was handed down to him from the past, but had very little practical application in his days when settled ownership was the rule and creation of first ownership in things which had no previous owner was only heard of in ancient traditions; it is therefore quite natural that we find very little upon this subject in the works of our law-givers beyond the enunciation of the general rule indicated above. It may, however, be interesting to notice that in the case of a hunted animal, Manu ascribes ownership to the person whose arrow first strikes it down, and the ownership of the land where the game is killed does not seem to affect the question. This seems to resemble the Roman Law which lays down that it is immaterial whether a man takes wild beasts or birds upon his own ground or that of another, and to differ from the English Law which does not seem to ascribe ownership to a trespasser who kills game on another person's land.

I have already pointed out that Manu declared that according to ancient tradition ownership in a field belonged to him who first reclaimed it and brought it under culti-

---

[1] पृथोरपीमां पृथिवीं भार्य्यां पूर्व्वविदो विदुः।
स्थाणुच्छेदस्य केदार माहुः शल्यवतो मृगम्॥ Manu IX 44.

vation. Sir William Markby, however, observes that "we find an example of occupancy without ownership in the (so-called) Institutes of Manu. The ownership of cultivated land (as distinguished from the homestead and the pasture attached thereto) is not mentioned in that work; and as there are no rules as to how such land is to be disposed of when the family breaks up, it seems clear that when that book was written it was not owned but only occupied." I must confess that I find it extremely difficult to follow these observations, and it seems to me quite clear that there is no foundation for them. Manu distinctly speaks of the ownership of cultivated lands, and says that, according to ancient tradition, it arose originally from the reclamation of previously unappropriated waste lands; he further declares that as between the person to whom the field belongs and another who sows his seeds in it, the crops belong, to the former, in the absence of a special contract under which both may become sharers in the produce,[1] —— a proposition which may be compared to the well-known maxim '*quicquid plantatur solo solo cedit*. In fact, Manu speaks more often about the ownership of cultivated fields than about the ownership of homestead and pasture grounds. I may, therefore, take this opportunity to warn you once for all against accepting upon trust the remarks of foreign writers upon Hindu Law, who, however eminent and able they may be in other respects, had very little first-hand knowledge of the subject of their discussion. I need hardly say that I have the highest respect for the spirit of research which these

---

[1] येऽक्षेत्रिणो बीजवन्तः परक्षेत्र प्रवापिणः ।

ते वै सस्यस्य जातस्य न लभन्ते फलं क्वचित् ॥ ९ । ४९

क्रियाभ्युपगमात् त्वेतद् बीजार्थं यत् प्रदीयते ।

तस्येह भागिनौ दृष्टौ बीजी क्षेत्रिक एव च । ९ । ५२

Adhigama: finding of treasure troves.

writers have evinced, but the materials at their command have often been of a very limited character, and very few of us, I am sorry to say, have taken the trouble to pursue their enquiries and correct their mistakes where necessary.

Shares of the king and the finder.

The next topic to which I will now turn is अधिगम or the finding of hidden treasures or the like, of which the owner is unknown.[1] The law regarding treasure-trove is thus stated by Yajnavalkya:—If the king discovers the treasure-trove, then he will take half and distribute the other half among Brahmans; if a learned Brahman finds it, then he may keep the whole himself; in other cases, the king will give one-sixth to the finder, and take the rest himself; but if the finder does not bring the fact to the notice of the king, then he will, on coming to know of it, extract the whole and also punish the finder. To this Mitakshara adds, on the authority of Manu, that even in such a case if the real owner comes forward and establishes his title, the king will restore the treasure to him after retaining one-sixth or one-twelfth for himself, or, according to Nilakantha one-fourth for himself and one-twelfth for the finder. This latter direction clearly indicates that a treasure-trove must not be regarded as a *res nullius*, for although it may have remained unclaimed for a long time, still that cannot have the effect of extinguishing the title of the real owner; at the utmost it can give rise to a presumption of abandonment which, however, is capable of being rebutted by the real owner.

Treasure-trove not *res-nullius*

Comparison with rules of Roman and English Law.

It may be interesting to compare these rules with those of the Roman Law and of the English Law upon the subject. According to the Roman Law, if any treasure was found by the owner of the land where it lay concealed, he could keep the whole of it himself; if another person found it, the finder and the owner of the land divided it

[1] अधिगमोऽज्ञात स्वामिकस्य निध्यादेः प्राप्तिः । वीरमित्रोदयः ।

equally. According to English Law, however, neither the finder nor the owner of the land had any interest in it, but it belonged entirely to the crown, and it was an offence not to give notice of its discovery. I may be wrong, but it strikes me that, taken as a whole, the rules laid down in the Hindu Law reconcile the rights of the king to unclaimed property within his dominion with the natural expectations of the finder, which both the Roman Law and the English Law fail to do.

Difference between treasure-troves and articles lost by one and found by another.

I may mention that there is a clear distinction between treasure-trove and articles lost by the owner and found by a stranger; the distinction consists in this, that in the case of the former all hope of tracing the owner is lost, while in the case of the latter it is not so. Hence, in the case of lost articles found by a stranger, the Hindu Law directs that the king must detain them in safe custody for some time awaiting the appearance of the owner to claim them ; if, however, nobody appears within that time to claim those articles, then the king may appropriate them for his own use after making over one-fourth to the finder. The period of detention is differently given, somewhere as one year and somewhere as three years, and the difference is reconciled by laying down that where the owner appears within one year he will get his articles back without any deduction, but where he comes forward after one year and within three years, the king will retain a small share as a charge for the detention out of which he will make over one-fourth to the finder. Here the Mitakshara adds a note that if the owner comes forward even after three years, and establishes his claim, the king shall restore the articles or their equivalents to him, for title, according to the Mitakshara, cannot be lost by mere lapse of time. It is not necessary to consider the rules laid down upon the subject in the western legal systems,

Refinement introduced in Mitakshara.

Bijita : or conquest of war. Not *res nullius* as in Roman Law.

but it may be said without hesitation that the rules of the Hindu Law indicated above are on the whole as just and equitable as any that are to be found in the western systems of Law.

I will next consider विजित or conquest as a source of acquisition of property. According to the Roman Law the property of the enemy was regarded as *res nullius*, so that the victorious party could deal with it in any way they liked. Pressed to its fullest extent it leads to the conclusion that even the property of private individuals in a conquered country can be freely disposed of by the conquering state, and no private rights can be set up against it. Our Hindu Law, however, did not recognise this fiction which is founded upon the assumption that the institution of private property falls into abeyance upon the outbreak of hostilities and explains a simple fact by what is less simple and less easily understood. According to the Hindu Law, conquest is an independent source of acquisition of ownership, and we need not seek to explain it by introducing the fiction that the ownership of the conqueror arises from a sort of 'occupatio' in relation to the enemy's property which, so far as the conqueror is concerned is to be regarded as no body's property. Then further, the conquest, according to the Hindu Law, did not sweep away all private rights, its only effect being to invest the victorious king with the rights (and, I may add, with the obligations also) of the vanquished king, so that although the former might claim full ownership in the exclusive property of the latter, his right, so far as the property of the subjects were concerned, did not extend to anything more than the right of collecting revenue from them. So, Srikrishna Tarkalankara distinctly says that the property (स्वत्व) of a particular kind only excludes the property of the same kind (inhering in

Extent of right of conquest : private property not interfered with.

others), which implies that a king by his conquest acquires only the right of receiving revenue from the subjects of the conquered territory in relation to property lying within it which has devolved upon them by inheritance or otherwise[1], and Yajnavalkya broadly enjoins that 'a king bringing under his control a foreign territory becomes subject to the very same duties as are cast upon him in protecting his own state.' Referring to the fact that the rules which International Jurisprudence derives from the positions of Roman Law, indicated above, 'have sometimes been stigmatised as needlessly indulgent to the ferocity and cupidity of combatants,' Sir Henry Maine observes that 'those who pass such strictures are unacquainted with the history of wars,' and 'are consequently ignorant how great an exploit it is to command obedience for a rule of any kind;' that may be quite true; but the end of law is, I suppose, to curb and control the natural passions of men, and we may sometimes be too prone to assume that they do not admit of any further regulation than what we already find; at any rate we may be justly proud that the Hindu Law was less indulgent to the ferocity and cupidity of combatants and Sir Henry Maine, when he talked glibly of the 'feeble civilization' of the Hindus might well have taken notice of this.

Prayoga: or application of pre-existing property.

'Accessio' in Roman Law.

प्रयोग or application of already existing property is a source of new acquisition. Thus, if a field produces crops or a domestic animal bears offspring, the produce in each

[1] सजातीय स्वत्वं प्रति सजातीय स्वत्वं विरोधि। सजातीयेति करग्रात् पराजित नृपति-राज्यान्तर्वर्त्ति तत्तत्पुरुषीय क्रमागतस्थावरादी-जयादिनाजेतुर्नृपतेः करग्रहणोपयोगि स्वत्वोत्पादः।

य एव नृपते धर्मः स्वराष्ट्र परिपालने।
तमेव कृत्स्नमाप्नोति परराष्ट्रं वशं नयन्।

Fruits of animals and produce of and accessions to land belong to the owner of the animal and the land.

case belongs to the owner of the field or the animal unless there has been some previous agreement modifying the general rule. This corresponds to what is called *'accessio'* in the Roman Law.

An analogous instance is furnished by what is called alluvion. The rules of the Hindu Law upon the subject seem to have been these :—if a river which flows between two villages and forms the boundary between them encroaches upon one bank and attaches newly formed land to another, then the owner of the bank on which the formation takes place becomes entitled to it as an accretion to his property; this sort of gain is characterised by Brihaspati as a gain due to good fortune; he also lays down an exception to the rule, and says that where by the force of the current of a stream a field with crops standing on it is detached from the main land, there the rights of the original owner remain unaffected by the change; on this the Viramitrodaya observes that the exception only applies to the standing crops and after they are reaped the rule of accretion holds good ; where, however, there is no question of accretion and the river after having inundated the lands on its bank again recedes, there, Narada says, the former ownership continues over its old site, its position being determined, in the absence of old land marks, by inference based upon other evidence. It will be observed that these rules clearly recognise the acquisition of land by right of contiguous accretion, and nothing depends, so far as this right is concerned, on the gradual or sudden nature of the change, which, according to the English Law and the rules introduced in India by Regulation XI of 1825, seems to furnish the guiding principle on this question. An accession to one's land by the recession of the river was treated as if it were a gift made by the river due to the good luck of the riparian

Exception.

Comparison with Roman Law.

owner, and it made no difference whether it came all on a sudden, or gradually by slow and imperceptible advance. The Roman Law also does not seem to have recognised this distinction, and a careful comparison will show that the rules laid down in that system upon this subject have many points of resemblance to those indicated above.

Dealing with the question of accession one is reminded of the question also discussed in the Roman Law of the extent of the right of a person building a house upon the land of another with his own materials. On this, Narada lays down that a person who pays rent to the owner of the land and lives there by building a house upon it, may, when he is required to leave the land, take away the materials with which he built the house; where, however, no rent was paid, and there was no special contract about the removal of the materials, there the builder of the house being evicted from the land cannot take the materials away with him, and must leave them behind for the owner of the land. These rules are, on the whole, fair and reasonable, for the only case where the builder of the house loses the materials is where he did not pay for the occupation of the land and erected the house without the consent of the owner of the land and without entering into any previous understanding with him regarding the future disposal of the house or its materials; in such a case it may well be presumed that the builder knowingly accepted the risk of losing the house and its materials on his eviction from the land; at any rate these provisions are less severe than those of the English Law which by a somewhat stringent application of the maxim 'quicquid plantatur solo solo cedit' allow the land-owner to sweep off everything that is attached to his land.

Karmayoga or employment of work.

Here I propose to conclude the present lecture. Among the other sources of acquisition of ownership, कर्मयोग or employment of work does not require any special treatment, the receipt of remuneration for work done being generally the result of a sort of contractual obligation to which I will devote one of my future lectures. The next three lectures will be devoted to the law bearing upon some of the most important sources of what I may call derivative acquisition of ownership, *viz.*, the law of transfer, the law of prescription, and the law of succession.

LECTURE III

TRANSFER OF OWNERSHIP.

In this lecture I propose to deal with the law of transfer of ownership by a voluntary act on the part of the owner. Prescription, which also effects a transfer of ownership, but is based not upon an act but upon an omission of the owner, will be discussed in the next lecture; and Succession, which does not depend upon any voluntary act or omission on the part of the previous owner, will be treated in the lecture after that.

Difference between gift and sale.

In dealing with voluntary transfer of ownership, we come across two distinct types of it, *viz.*, sale and gift, and they typify all acts of translation of ownership by the act of the owner with or without consideration. Where the owner parts with his ownership for a consideration, *i.e.*, in exchange for some substantial benefit conferred or promised to be conferred, the act amounts to an act of sale; where, however, there is no such consideration, the act of the owner in parting with his property is an act of gift. A little consideration will shew that these two transactions (*i.e.*, gift and sale) have a common basis; in both, the transfer is a voluntary one and proceeds from an act of the previous owner intended to effectuate a translation of ownership from him to some body else, and hence it is but natural that many of the principles which govern them must be common to them both. I shall therefore begin with the simpler of the two transactions, *viz.*, an act of gift, and discuss the principles bearing upon it, and I shall then supplement the discussion by dealing with those peculiar incidents of an act of sale which require separate consideration.

Gift: its definition.

Gift.—Gift may be defined as the renunciation of property in favour of a sentient being having the result of extinguishing the ownership of the donor and creating ownership in the donee. (स्व स्वत्व-ध्वंसपूर्व्वपरस्वत्वापत्तिफलक चेतनोद्देशपूर्व्वक त्यागो दानम्). If we analyse this definition, it will be found that it is required that there must be a doner, a donee, a proper object of gift, and a transaction involving certain formalities. Let us now consider, what, according to the Hindu Law, are the essentials of a valid gift.

Essentials of a valid gift.

Formalities:

Nature of the transaction and its attendant formalities.—I have stated that a gift involves a renunciation of property on the part of the donor in favour of another person. But is mere renunciation on the part of the donor sufficient to invest the person, in whose favour the renunciation is made, with ownership of the property given without a corresponding act on his part accepting the gift, or, to put it shortly, is ownership transferred to the donee without acceptance? The question is not free from difficulty, as it has formed the subject of a well-known controversy between the Dayabhaga and the Mitakshara Schools. Jimutavahana maintains that property is not created by acceptance on the part of the donee, but by gift on the part of the donor, and he argues that if it had been otherwise, then, since the root *da* signifies the extinction of ownership in one and creation of ownership in another, the acceptor would have been called the donor; it is true that the Sanskrit word for acceptance is स्वीकार, which signifies the reduction into one's property of a thing which was not so before, but it implies no more than this that though property had already arisen from the act of gift, still it is now by the act of the donee subsequently recognising it for his own, rendered liable to free disposal. The argument, which I have tried to

Can ownership arise without acceptance of gift?

Jimutavahana's view.

summarise above, is based upon the peculiarities of Sanskrit Grammar, and I cannot hope to be able to make it clear to those of you who are not sufficiently acquainted with the niceties of that language; moreover, it does not seem to me to be at all conclusive, for, as Viramitrodaya has shown, it is not at all impossible to explain the grammatical construction of the word 'दाता' which means a donor, without accepting the proposition that transmutation of ownership takes place even before the acceptance of the gift. The real bone of contention seems to be this: the donor being the owner of the property, it ought to be taken that he has got the right to devest himself of that ownership without the concurrence of any body else; but can he at the same time invest the donee with ownership without his concurrence? Now, in cases where gift and acceptance take place simultaneously, the problem suggested above creates no practical difficulty, for the two acts being concurrent and simultaneous, it makes no practical difference whether you say that it is the acceptance which following upon the gift causes the transmutation of ownership or that it is the gift which transfers the ownership from the donor to the donee; but the acceptance following upon it takes the ownership up, so to say, and makes it subject to determinate enjoyment. Where, however, there is a clear interval between the gift by the donor and the acceptance or non-acceptance of it by the donee, as the case may be, the question assumes practical importance, and requires definite solution. Now, according to Jimutavahana, ownership is transferred to the donee by the very act of the donor, but it is liable to be defeated by the refusal of the donee to accept the gift, or to be perfected by his acceptance thereof, so that in the interval between the gift and its acceptance or non-acceptance, as the case may be, the donee is vested with an inchoate ownership which is either perfected or defeated on the donee either accepting or refusing to accept the gift. Vijnaneswara and his followers, however, are of opinion, that although the donor may, by his act, divest himself of ownership over a particular property, he cannot, at his option, invest another person with ownership without the consent of the latter, so that in the interval between the gift and its acceptance or non-acceptance the object of gift does not become the property of the donee. The principal objection against the former view is that at the time when the gift is made, it cannot be pronounced for certain whether the donee will or will not accept the gift, so that the completion of the transfer of ownership hinges upon an uncertain contingency at that time, and if that be so, why should you say that the gift alone is sufficient to cause a transmutation of the ownership from the donor to the donee? Does not your own position involve that the gift is not the sole cause of the transfer, but स्वीकार प्रागभाव (or antecedent absence of acceptance, which implies subsequent acceptance), to use the language of the Naiyayikas, is also an auxiliary cause? And if you accept this, is it not better to avoid this sort of circuitous exposition and admit that the donee is not invested with ownership until he accepts the gift? The real difficulty of the latter view seems, however, to be this;—the donor can, by the act of gift, divest himself of the ownership over the property given; if by that act the donee is not invested with ownership, in whom does the ownership inhere during the interval between the gift and its acceptance or non-acceptance by the donee? Does it become a *res nullius*, so as to become liable to be appropriated by any person who may choose to take possession of it? To this Viramitrodaya replies, that this difficulty does not really arise, for although the donor may lose his ownership in so far as it involves the right of free disposal, he does not lose his right of custody

Mitakshara view.

Objection against Dayabhaga view.

(परिपालनीयत्व रूपस्वत्व) which prevents any one besides the donee from taking possession of it; otherwise, by assuming that the donee becomes the owner although he may know nothing about the gift, you are forced to admit, in case of his ultimate refusal to accept, that the ownership did arise only to be extinguished upon this refusal, an admission which would involve the fault of complexity of assumptions (गौरव). I need not, however, attempt to decide upon the relative merits of these two views; it is enough for my purpose that I have given you an idea of the difference that exists between the Dayabhaga and the Mitakshara Schools upon this question, and I hope, I have also incidentally shown what amount of logical subtlety these Hindu Jurists brought to bear upon discussions of this kind.

Acceptance, as Mitakshara points out, may be of three kinds, mental, verbal, and corporeal: mental acceptance consists of a determination of the mind regarding the property as one's own; verbal acceptance is that mental state which finds expression in such words as 'this is mine' or the like, intimating the acceptance of the gift; corporeal acceptance in constituted by the assumption of possession or some sort of corporeal control over the object of gift denoting the mental acceptance of the gift. In the case of movable property, the three kinds of acceptance explained above may take place at once, but in the case of immovable property, there can be no corporeal acceptance without some enjoyment of the produce, which cannot often take place all at once; hence the question may arise whether a gift can become complete without corporeal acceptance, or in other words, without assumption of possession, which, in the case of land, involves at least some little enjoyment of its produce. Dealing with this question Mr. Mayne observes that 'few propositions have

Three kinds of acceptance.

Can a gift become complete without corporeal acceptance?

Mayne's observations.

Mitakshara view explained.

been laid down with more confidence than the doctrine that under Hindu Law a gift is invalid without possession.' 'Yet,' he correctly points out, 'Hindu Law, properly so called, appears to lay little stress on any such as specially applicable to gifts'. He then extracts a passage from Mitakshara to shew what its position really is, and I think I may also quote that passage here in order to enable you to see whether the position that gift is invalid without possession is itself valid. After remarking that acceptance may be of three kinds, and explaining them in the way already stated by me, the author of Mitakshara goes on to observe that 'in the case of land, as there can be no corporeal acceptance without enjoyment of the produce, it must be accompained by some little possession; otherwise,' says he, 'the gift, sale or other transfer is not complete. A title, therefore, without corporeal acceptance consisting of the enjoyment of produce, is weaker than a title accompained by it or with such corporeal acceptance. But such is the case only where, of these two, the priority is undistinguishable; but when it is ascertained which is first in point date, and which is posterior, then the simple prior title affords the stronger evidence. Or the interpretation may be as follows :—

'Evidence is said to consist of documents, possession, and witnesses.' This having been premised as the general rule, the texts 'a little is more powerful than possession unaccompained by hereditary succession' and 'where there is not the least possession, there a title is not sufficient,' have been propounded to point out to which the superiority belongs, where the three descriptions of evidence meet.' The above extract makes it quite clear that in the opinion of Vijnaneswar delivery of possession was not absolutely essential to constitute a valid gift, but it is necessary to remember that a gift unaccompanied by possession is of a very risky kind, because, in a case of conflict between two apparent titles, in the absence of any evidence to the contrary, that which is accompained by possession must prevail.

It seems to me that the position indicated above with regard to the relation between transfer of ownership and delivery of possession is eminently logical and reasonable; the transfer of ownership is the result of the manifestation of intention on the part of the transferor to part with the ownership *in presenti* in favour of another who thereupon accepts the situation, agrees to become the owner, and does, by the combined effect of renunciation (त्याग) on the one hand and appropriation (स्वीकार) on the other, become the owner. Assumption of possession and enjoyment of usufruct are not factors essentially requisite to complete the transfer of ownership, but they are acts indicative of an existing ownership which they seem to presuppose. It is true that a transfer of ownership unless coupled with or followed by a transfer of possession is a very risky affair; in the first place, the transfer of ownership in such a case is often very difficult to prove; in the second place this state of things, if it continues for some time, may very naturally give rise to a presumption that the person who has not got possession must have parted with any title that he might have acquired, and in the third place, in a case of conflicting claims, in the absence of any other test, the title which is coupled with possession must prevail; yet it cannot be doubted that delivery of possession need not be a necessary condition to the transfer of ownership which can be accomplished even without it by the co-ordinated desire of the transferor and the transferee; and a system of law which perceived the real relation between the two things, and viewed them in their true light must be admitted to have advanced very far in the development of juristic ideas.

Roman Law compared.

It may be mentioned in this connection that according to the Roman Law property could not be transferred by mere agreement unless it was accompained by delivery of possession; 'Traditionibus et usucapionibus, non mudis pactis dominia tranferentus.' (Codex Just. iv 3,20). According to Mahomedan Law too, there can be no gift without delivery of seisin, and it is difficult, as Sir W. Markby observes, to say when the idea of transferring ownership without transferring possession became familiar in modern law. 'To some minds,' says he, 'it can scarcely be said to be familiar still.' Thus he points out that 'Heineccius solemnly declared it to be a universal maxim of law that there can be no acquisition of ownership without tradition, and, an English lawyer, Mr. Serjeant Manning, has made a similar assertion'; it is therefore highly interesting to notice that more than a thousand years ago our Hindu Jurists correctly grasped the true relation between alienation and transfer of possession which has escaped the analysis of even some of the modern European lawyers; the inability to conceive transfer of ownership without delivery of possession betrays an imperfect power of abstraction from which the subtle minds of the Hindu Jurists were entirely free.

I shall now turn to the other formalities of a transfer prescribed by the Hindu Law. It does not appear that with regard to the transfer of movable property, any particular formality was required beyond what has been already mentioned; but with regard to land the Mitakshara quotes an anonymous text which lays down that 'land passes by six formalities; by consent of co-villagers, of kinsmen, of neighbours and of heirs, and by gift of gold and water'; in explaining this text the Mitakshara says 'that the consent of the co-villagers is required for the publicity of the transaction, since it is provided that 'acceptance of a gift, especially of land, should be public; but the transaction is not invalid without their consent, and the approbation of neighbours (residing near the boundary) serves to obviate any dispute concerning the boundary'; as regards the other formalities, I shall explain their purpose according to the Mitakshara after I have done with these.

Other formalities: Consent of co-villagers and neighbours.

Turning, then, to the consent of the co-villagers and of the neighbours, I may observe that the grounds on which their requirement is explained by the Mitakshara cannot be said to be far-fetched or unreasonable; it is but natural that one should desire that the transfer of the most important property which one could possess should be attended by certainty and notoriety, and for that purpose nothing could be better than to require that at the time of the transfer the consent of the co-villagers and of the neighbouring land-holders should be obtained so as to give publicity to the transaction, as well as to obviate the chance of a future dispute. Mr. Mayne, however, suggests that these requirements might probably be the relics of a still older system in which 'the rights of a family in their property were limited by the rights of others outside the family'. It is not at all easy to speculate upon a subject like this with any amount of confidence, but if we consider the formalities of a 'mancipation under the Roman Law which was the mode of conveyance by which *Res Mancipi* including land and some other commodities very highly valued by the early Romans were transferred before Justinian allowed its place to be taken by tradition or delivery of possession, and compare them with the requirements of Hindu Law as noticed above, we may trace a certain amount of resemblance between the two systems which may not be altogether accidental. Referring to the requirement of five witnesses besides the actual parties in a Roman Mancipation, Sir William Markby observes that the number is, he thinks, 'not to be referred to the imperfection of oral testimony, but to the requirement that the transfer should take place in the presence of and be consented to by the community at large, whom these five persons may be taken to represent'; it cannot be said that a similar interpretation cannot be placed upon the original requirement of the consent of the co-villagers and the neighbouring land-owners as laid down in the text cited above; but, however that may be, it is quite clear that that interpretation had long been forgotten in the days of the Mitakshara, and the explanations which that book furnishes are those which suggest themselves to one who lives is a progressive society which has outlived the stage of communal ownership.

Markby's observations.

Turning next to the requirement of the consent of kinsmen and heirs, it will be observed that kinship and heirship may or may not involve co-ownership; where the heirs and kinsmen are not co-owners, their consent, says the Mitakshara, is required for the facility of the transaction by obviating the possibility of any future dispute about the character of the property and the nature of the right of the transferor; in such a case the transferor has full power of alienation and the transaction is consequently valid even without the consent of those kinsmen; Apararka goes further and says that the object of requiring the consent of such kinsmen is to indicate that where they are not unfit or indifferent, an alienation of immovable property should be made in their favour and not in favour of strangers.[1] Where, however, the heirs and kinsmen whose

[1] दानादि योग्येषु विभक्तेषु दायादेषु सत्सु तेभ्य एव स्थावरमर्पणीयमयोग्येषु निरपेक्षेषु वाऽन्येभ्यः । इति अपरार्कः । दत्ताप्रदानिकप्रकरणम् ।

consent is desiderated are co-owners, the effect of the absence of that consent will depend upon the nature of the co-ownership which, as it is well-known, is differently conceived by the Mitakshara and the Dayabhaga Schools of Hindu Law. As I propose to discuss the subject more fully in a future lecture, I refrain from dwelling upon it at this place beyond pointing out that the conception of joint ownership of the members of an undivided family under the Mitakshara school is fundamentally different from that under the Dayabhaga School, and the result is that while an alienation of the joint property or any portion thereof by a Mitakshara co-parcener without the consent of the other co-parceners is generally regarded as invalid, a similar alienation by a Dayabhaga co-parcener is regarded as valid and operates to the extent of the share which belongs to that individual according to the Dayabhaga conception of joint ownership.

Gift of gold and water: its significance. Mitakshara explanation.

The next formality that requires consideration is the gift of gold and water accompanying an act of alienation of immovable property. One would have wondered what it meant, were it not for the explanation furnished by the Mitakshara which runs as follows: 'Since the sale of immovables is forbidden ("In regard to the immovable estate, sale is not allowed; it may be mortgaged by consent of parties interested"); and since donation is praised ("Both he who accepts land and he who gives it are performers of a holy deed and shall go to a region of bliss"); if a sale must be made, it should be conducted for the transfer of immovable property in the form of a gift, delivering with it gold and water (to ratify the donation)'. It may here be interesting to pause for a moment and consider the special significance of the explanation given above, for it illustrates the tenacity with which old formalities cling to their existence even after the ground of their origin has ceased to exist. Under the early Hindu Law it seems that a sale of immovable property was not allowed to be made, but a gift of it for spiritual benefit of the doner was not similarly restrained, but was on the other hand commended as a meritorious act; hence when under the growing exigencies of the community a sale of land came to be tolerated, it was not yet looked upon as altogether free from stain; and was made to resemble in its form an act of free gift; this purpose was served by the accompaniment of gift of gold and water by the vendor which symbolised, as it were, the ratification of a gift. Gradually, however, it has fallen into disuse, and nobody would have known anything about it but for the passage in the Mitakshara to which I have referred above.

Sale assimilated to gift: its parallel in the Roman Mancipation.

This assimilation of a sale to an act of gift has got its parallel in the Roman Mancipation, but there it was not a sale that was assimilated to a gift, but a gift was made to resemble an act of sale. The formalities of mancipation are thus described by Gaius: "Mancipation is effected in the presence of not less than five witnesses who must be Roman citizens of the age of puberty, and also in the presence of another person of the same condition, who holds a pair of scales, and hence is called *libripens*. The purchaser taking hold of the thing says and affirms 'this thing is mine, *ex jure Quiritium*, and it is purchased by me with this piece of copper and these scales'. He then strikes the scale with the piece of money, and gives it to the seller as a symbol of the price". It will be remembered that under the early Roman Law, till the modification introduced by Justinian *Res Mancipi* including solum Italicum could only be transferred by the formalities of a mancipation; what, then, do these formalities signify? I have already indicated the original purpose which the presence of the five witnesses was perhaps designed to fulfil;

but what was the significance of the presence of that peculiar personage, the Libripens, with his pair of scales, and what did the ceremony of striking the scales with a copper coin symbolise ? It seems pretty clear that the ceremonies described above closely simulated an actual sale with the accompaniment of payment of price ; the Libripens was there with his pair of scales to weigh, as it were, the coins payable as price, and the striking of the scale with a piece of money was emblematic of their payment ; the question is, why, when no sale was actually in contemplation, as in the case of a gift or of that particular form of testamentary devise which was known as the testament *per aes et libram*, did the ceremonies simulate those of an actual sale including the payment of price ? The explanation seems to be this : free alienation of immovable property was not favoured by any system of ancient law, but in course of time the old restraints on alienation were gradually relaxed in order to meet the demands of a progressive community undergoing social and economic modifications ; it however so happened that the course pursued by one community in gradually removing the old impediments to alienation did not always agree with that followed by another, although both were ultimately moving towards one and the same destination. I have already explained that under the Hindu Law the first move was made in favour of an act of gift, which being regarded as a pious act was excepted from the general restraint on alienation of immovable property, and gradually, when a sale for price came to be tolerated, it appeared, as far as possible, under the garb of a gift ; under the Roman Law, however, the course of transition seems to have been different ; there the first exception seems to have been made in favour of a sale for valuable consideration, and when gradually other kinds of alienation began to be introduced, they simulated in outward appearance a sale for price, and that appearance was kept up, even when its original significance had been forgotten, by the presence of the libripens with his pair of scales and the striking of the scales with a piece of copper which served to symbolise the payment of price although no payment was actually intended. The difference above set forth, therefore, indicates different lines of progress towards free alienation; among the Hindus the first step was taken in favour of pious gifts; among the Romans sales for price furnished the first exceptions; and when gradually the old trammels came to be further relaxed, among the Hindus a sale was assimilated to an act of gift, while among the Romans gift was made to resemble an act of sale. It will be unprofitable to speculate why the course of transition towards free alienation took different directions in the two communities, but it may, I think, be truly observed that the line of transition in each case was in perfect harmony with the genius of the race. Be that as it may, I shall not be wrong if I say that whatever the original significance of these formalities might have been, they gradually came to be regarded as non-essential, and their prescription was explained in the way indicated above, as being intended either to give greater publicity to the transaction, or to ensure security from future dispute, or to lay down merely moral injunctions not touching the validity of the transaction; in short they were treated as directory and not as mandatory; and provided the donor was the owner of the thing, had the necessary capacity to make a gift of it, and acted freely, the non-observance of any of these formalities would not in any way invalidate the transfer on the principle succinctly set forth in Jimutavahana's dictum that 'a fact cannot be altered by a hundred texts', a principle which must not be taken to be a

Difference set forth above indicates different lines of progress towards free alienation.

peculiar doctrine of the Bengal School, but is a doctrine equally resognised by all the schools of Hindu Law.

I have so long considered how far the validity of a gift depends upon the nature of the transaction including its attendant ceremonies ; I now propose to pass under review the other factors of a valid gift. A complete gift implies the existence of two parties, *viz.*, a donor and a donee ; the donor gives the property and the donee accepts the gift and it is the conjunction of gift and acceptance that completes the transfer of ownership from one to the other. Hence it has been said that in order that there may be a valid gift the donee must be a sentient being in existence at the time of the gift. This rule has not been laid down in so many words by any Hindu Law-giver, but it is a deduction from the definition of a gift which I have given above, as well as from the fact that no gift can be complete without acceptance. You will remember that I have defined a gift as the renunciation of property in favour of a sentient being having the result of extinguishing the ownership of the donor and creating ownership in the donee ; this necessarily implies that there must be a sentient being whom the donor intends to benefit by his gift and in whom the ownership becomes vested upon the extinction of the ownership of the donor by his own renunciation ; moreover, the completion of the transfer of title depends upon the acceptance of the gift by the donee, and this cannot possibly take place unless he be a sentient being in existence ; therefore the gift must be made in favour of a being who has got the capacity to accept, and in as much as such a capacity can only be attributed to a sentient being in existence, it follows that the donee must be a sentient being in existence at the time of the gift ; the rule was authoritatively laid down by the Judicial Committee of the Privy Council in the celebrated care of

Donee must be a sentient being in existence.

Tagore *vs.* Tagore (9 B. L. R. 399 ; s. c. 18 W. R. 359) and has ever since been scrupulously followed. It should be noted that the rule insists on the existence of the donee as a sentient being capable of accepting the gift at the time of the gift, and not at any future time ; for instance it is not open to me to make a gift of my property in favour of the son who may be born to A in future, so as to enable the son so born to take the property under the gift at the time when he comes into existence ; it will be easy to understand this if we remember that a gift operates *in præsenti* to divest the owner of his ownership and to invest the donee with the same, which cannot take place unless the donee is already in existence ; for, to suppose that the donor has lost his ownership while no one else has been invested with it will be to reduce the object of gift to the condition of a *res nullius* which may be appropriated by any one at his pleasure ; in fact to speak of a gift in favour of a person who at the moment does not exist and therefore in future may or may not exist involves a contradiction in terms, and a gift in favour of a person who may come into existence in future can amount to nothing more than a promise to make a gift when the occasion will arise in future by that person really coming to exist ; a gift, it must be understood, is a complete conveyance and not a mere promise to convey, and that being so, the requirement that the donee must be a sentient being in existence at the date of the gift is but a logical deduction from the very nature of the transaction. There is very little trace of the existence of testamentary power under the Hindu Law, save and except the rule laid down by Katyayana that in certain cases a promise to give made by a father which he has not been able to carry out during his life time must be fulfilled by the son after his death ; but when gifts by will gradually came into use, it was but natural to apply to them the analogies of the law of a gift *inter vivos.* 'The Law of Will,' says the Privy Council, 'has grown up, so to speak, naturally, from a law which furnishes no analogy but that of gifts and it is the duty of a tribunal, dealing with a case new in the instance, to be governed by the established principles and the analogies which have heretofore prevailed in like case'. Hence applying the principle applicable to a gift *inter vivos* to the case of a testament, it has been held that no one can take under a will unless he be in existence at the death of the testator which is the time from which the will comes into operation. There are, however, two apparent exceptions to this rule, *viz.*, the cases of an infant child in its mother's womb and a son adopted after the death of the testator under an authority from him; but these are not real exception, since such persons are by a fiction of law considered to have been in existence at the death of the testator and are thus capable of taking from him. The exceptions, therefore, really prove the rule. It is, however, possible to carry the rule too far, and an extreme application of it is to be found in certain decisions of the Calcutta High Court* which have laid down that a gift to an idol, which

Apparent exceptions referrable to a fiction of law.

An extreme application of the rule.

* Upendra Lal Baral *v.* Hem Chandra Baral, (1897) I. L. R. 25 Cal. 405; Rojomoyee Dasee *v.* Troilokho Mohini Dasee, (1901) I.L.R. 29 Cal. 260; Nagendra Nandini Dassi *v.* Binoy Krishna Deb (1902) I. L. R. 30 Cal. 521; Promothanath Roy *v.* Nagendrabala Chaudhurani (1908) 12 C. W. N. 808.

Note. Since these lectures were written a Full Bench of the Calcutta High Court has overruled those decisions and held that the rule which requires that for the validity of a gift, the relinquishment must be in favour of a sentient being does not apply to bequests to trustees for the establishment of an image and the worship of a Hindu deity after the testator's death. See Bhupatinath Smrititirtha *v.* Ram Lal Maitra, (1909) 10 C. L. J. 355, s. c., 14 C. W. N.

is not in existence at the death of the testator but has been directed to be consecrated after his death is invalid, though the deity to be represented by the idol is always in existence. The ground of these decisions is that there could be no gift to the deity as such, and as regards the idol, it could not be the recepient of a gift before its consecration, so that in the absence of a duly consecrated idol at the time of the testator's death the gift could not take effect and the property would vest in the person who could take it if there were no dedication at all. To this it may be replied that it is difficult to understand why it should be taken that there can be no dedication of property to the deity as such, for, in fact the dedication to an idol is really a dedication to the diety, the idol being no more than the visible image through which the deity is supposed specially to manifest itself by reason of the ceremonies of consecration; hence, when a person dedicates a property to an idol to be consecrated and established at a particular place, the dedication is really in favour of the ever-existent deity subject to the direction that its worship should be carried on at that place and through the image to be consecrated and established there; the establishment and consecration of the image does not bring into existence a new deity who did not formerly exist; but it merely gives, as it were, a local habitation to the deity in order to facilitate the worship of those who require the help of symbols to aid their devotion; it is therefore wrong to apply the analogy of a gift to an unborn person to the dedication of property to the deity coupled with the direction that the worship should be carried on by establishing an image of the deity at a particular place and consecrating the same; if any analogy were required, we might liken a dedication of this kind to the gift of property to an existing individual on condition that the gift should take effect when and so long as that individual resided at a particular place; in such a case it could not be said that the gift would be invalid because at the date of the gift the individual was not residing at that place, and the only result would be to postpone the enjoyment of the property until he began to reside there; similarly a dedication to the deity cannot fail on the ground that before the consecration of the image there was no recipient of the gift to validate the transaction, and all that can be said is that the intention of the testator cannot be effectuated and the object of the endowment cannot be fulfilled until the consecration of the image upon which the dedication takes a definite shape and the property becomes liable to regular disposal for the purposes of the endowment; just as it is the duty of the trustee to carry on the worship, so also it is his duty in a case like this to establish and consecrate the image for the purpose of worship, for the worship cannot commence according to the intention of the testator until the image has been consecrated and established, but in no way can the dedication fail on the ground that the donee was not in existence at the death of the testator. It is quite possible that cases may be found where the dedication clause is not very happily worded, but we must look to the substance of the thing with a view to give effect to the intention of the testator and not to defeat it by drawing metaphysical distinctions too subtle to grasp.

Other conditions of a valid gift.

Having gone so far, I shall next proceed to consider the remaining conditions of a valid gift, and in doing so it will not perhaps be out of place to follow the Hindu Law-givers in the distinctions drawn by them between देय (what is fit to be given), अदेय (what is unfit to be given), दत्त (what has been irrevocably given), and अदत्त (what, although given, is, in contemplation of law, not

Deya : Things fit to be given.

Adeya : Things not fit to be given.

given). Following these divisions, we find that a thing is regarded as fit to be given when it is the property of the donor, and there is no prohibition in the Sastras to make a gift of it. Conversely, unfitness to be the object of a gift may arise from either want of title in the donor or existence of prohibition in the Sastras. As examples of things which are not fit to be given by reason of want of title in the donor, mention is made of pledges, deposits and things borrowed or otherwise obtained on trust; in these cases, the person in possession is not the owner of the thing, and a gift made by him will not only be infructuous, but will also render him liable to punishment. As regards sons and wives, they are also declared unfit to be given away by their fathers and husbands respectively, but there is a difference of opinion as to whether this is so by reason of want of ownership in the father and the husband or on account of the Sastric prohibition, which, in spite of ownership, condemns the gift as improper. I abstain from entering into the details of the controversy at this place, as I propose to deal with it in my lectures dealing with parental and marital relationships. Barring these, there are certain other instances in which a gift is prohibited although there can be no question of absence of ownership; they are these: (1) gift of a thing which is the common property of the donor and other persons, (2) gift of property without keeping enough for the maintenance of the family, (3) gift of entire property when there are children to be provided for, and (4) gift to one, of a thing which has been previously promised to another.

As regards things which do not belong exclusively to the donor, it is clear that although the donor has ownership in them, his ownership is not absolute, but is limited by the co-equal ownership of others; hence he alone cannot have the right to give them away, and if he does, it cannot operate to the prejudice of the other owners. It may, however, be asked whether in such a case the donee may not step into the shoes of the donor and claim, not the entire property, which the donor had certainly no power to give, but a share which the donor might have claimed as his own ; the answer to this question will depend upon the conception of co-ownership in each case, and as there is a well-known difference about this matter between the Dayabhaga and the Mitakshara Schools, I reserve the point for a future lecture in which I shall try to explain this difference and deduce the necessary consequences therefrom.

As regards the rule that the extent of a person's gift should not be such as to deprive his family of the means of subsistence, it seems to be nothing more than a moral or religious injunction and the excess of the limit thus laid down cannot be a ground for holding the gift invalid. Jimutavahana expressly says so, and the opinion seems to be in consonance with the reason of the rule.

A similar interpretation should also be placed upon the prohibition of the gift of the entire property when there are sons to be provided for, unless we follow Apararka in maintaining that the prohibition is meant to apply to cases where there are sons who compose an undivided family with their father and are thus co-owners with him.

Lastly, the direction that a thing which has been promised to one should not be given to another seems also to belong to the same class and not to affect the validity of a transaction.

On the whole, therefore, the conclusion at which we arrive is that it is only when a thing is declared unfit to be given by reason of want of title in the donor, that the gift, if made, does not pass any title, because the donor himself had none to convey. Where, however, the donor is the owner of the property, a gift of it will convey a valid title in spite of any prohibition that the Sastras may have laid down. It is true that there are certain texts which lay down that both the giver and the acceptor of a thing declared unfit to be given render themselves liable to punishment, and some commentators argue therefrom that such a gift is liable to be revoked and the thing restored; but having regard to the general principles of transfer of ownership, I think it will be going too far to say that although the owner makes a gift of his own property, no title will pass, simply because the Sastras have condemned such a gift as improper. It is therefore important to distinguish between the two classes of objects unfit to be given, the unfitness being due either to want of title in the donor or to a mere prohibition in the Sastras; in the former case, the gift, if made will be invalid and infructuous; in the latter case, the gift will be legally operative, but the act will be regarded as sinful and the parties to it will also render themselves liable to punishment from the king. Jagannatha seems to support this view. 'That a thing may not be given,' says he, 'denotes that the gift is attended with sin, for this form of speech bears the sense of the imperative. It does not denote that the gift is a void act; were it so, it would not differ from a void donation; and full dominion would not be noticed under this title of 'what may not be given'. If it be said this title is intended to show punishment for such gifts it is answered, this form of prohibition implying offence, the offender should be punished. Thus the gift of things which are enumerated among those which may not be given is punishable; gifts enumerated among those which are void are utterly null'. The same conclusion will follow from the following considerations; acquisition of ownership, as has been explained in the last lecture, follows, according to the more widely recognised view, the popular usage; and gift and sale being among the means recognised by popular usage as causing a transfer of ownership, all that can be legitimately required from the legal stand point to create a valid transfer are that the transferor should have full dominion over the property, that he should otherwise have full capacity to enter into a legal transaction, and that the transaction itself should be properly and legally performed; these conditions being fulfilled, the title will pass, notwithstanding any prohibition laid down in the Sastras which can only operate upon the will of the transferor and the transferee by reason of the sanction attached to it in the form of punishment from the king, or at any rate, of misery in the life to come which is the inevitable result of the transgression of Sastric injunctions; beyond this the force of the prohibition cannot go according to the well-known canon of construction tersely summed up by Jimutavahana in the dictum 'a fact cannot be altered by a hundred texts.'

Datta: **Irrevocable gifts.**

Having thus discussed what are and what are not fit to be given, let us now pass on to what the Hindu Law considers as irrevocably given. These are indicated in the following text of Narada[1]: they who know the law of gifts declare that things once delivered as the price of goods sold, as wages, for the pleasure (of hearing poets, musicians or the like), from natural affection, as a return for a benefaction, as a nuptial gift to a bride or her family, and through regard for religious merit, cannot be resumed. It will be observed that in each of these cases there is some sort of consideration, whether valuable or not, to support the

[1] पण्यमूल्यं भृति स्तुष्ट्या स्नेहात् प्रत्युपकारतः ।
स्त्रीशुल्कानुग्रहार्थं च दत्तं दानविदो विदुः ॥

gift, and a gift once made under these circumstances cannot be revoked.

Adatta: **Void gifts.**

Last of all let us consider those gifts which are absolutely void and are treated as if they were not made. Narada gives sixteen instances of void gifts : 'what has been given by men oppressed with fear, anger, or intense grief; or as a bribe, or in jest, or by mistake, or through any fraudulent practice; what has been bestowed by a minor, an idiot, a person under duress, one whose mind is unsettled by disease, one intoxicated, or insane; what has been given in consideration that the donee will do some service in return (which, however, he has not performed); what has been given through ignorance to a bad man who pretended to be good, or for a righteous undertaking (where none was really contemplated); these (though given) are declared as not given.[1] A consideration of these instances will shew that the grounds on which the gifts fail are reducible to two main heads, (1) want of capacity of the donor, and (2) want of reality and freedom of the act of gift. Under the first head will come such temporary disabilities as minority, insanity, or want of freedom; under the second head we may consider the case where there is no real intention to make a gift, as when it is made in jest, and the cases where the gift is induced by coercion, fraud, mistake or misrepresentation. In all these cases the law declares that there is no real gift, but

[1] अदत्तं तु भय क्रोध शोकवेगरुगन्वितैः।
तथोत्कोच परीहास व्यत्यासच्छल योगतः॥
बालमूढा स्वतन्त्रार्त मत्तोन्मत्तापवर्जितम्।
कर्त्ता ममायं कर्मेति प्रतिलाभेच्छया च यत्॥
अपात्रे पात्रमित्युक्ते कार्ये वा धर्मसंहिते।
यद्दत्तं स्यादविज्ञानाददत्तमिति तत्स्मृतम्॥

only a semblance of gift ; and therefore the transaction is void of legal effect and the donor is entitled to revoke the gift and get the things given restored to him. The operation of the rules laid down above is not limited to the case of a gift, but they have a wider application; thus Manu delares that 'a gift induced by force, possession taken by force, and document obtained by force, in short everything brought about by force should be regarded as null and void[1]'; similarly, 'a pledge, a sale and a gift and acceptance induced by fraud, and wherever there is a condition which comes to light; in all these cases the transaction is to be rescinded'.[2] The last portion of the above text as explained by Mitakshara lays down the law about contingent and conditional transfers; it says that 'wherever a pledge, a sale, or a gift and acceptance is made subject to a future condition as its adjunct, there, on the disappearance of that adjunct, the pledge, the sale, or the gift, as the case may be, shall be liable to be rescinded,[3] which means that where the operation of a transfer is made dependent upon the continued accompaniment of a certain condition, there the condition disappearing the operation of the transaction shall also cease to exist. For instance, if I give my property to you on condition of your supporting a certain religious institution, the gift will be rescinded on your ceasing to do so, inasmuch as the gift was not absolute, but subject

---

[1] बलाहृतं बलाद्भुक्तं बलाद् यदपि लेखितम् ।
सर्व्वान् बलकृतानर्थान् अकृतान् मनुरब्रवीत् ॥

[2] योगाधमन विक्रीतं योगदान प्रतिग्रहम् ।
यत्र वाप्युपधिं पश्येत् तत्सर्वं विनिवर्त्तयेत् ॥

[3] येनागामिनोपाधिविशेषेणाधिविक्रयदान प्रतिग्रहाः
कृतास्तदुपाधिविगमे तान् क्रयादीन् विनिवर्त्तयेत् ।

to a condition as the auxiliary cause of its continued operation, which being gone, it could no longer continue to operate. I do not know how it may strike you, but it seems to me that these rules and the distinctions on which they are based exhibit a deep logical insight, a marked development of juristic ideas, and a high moral standard of which we, as the distant descendants of those who laid them down, may justly be proud.

On the whole the conclusion seems to be that where the gift is made by a person without the ownership or without the requisite capacity to make a gift by reason of some disability whether of a temporary or of a more enduring character, or where the act of gift is not a real act, having been made in jest, or is not a free act by reason of its having been induced by coercion, fraud, misrepresentation or mistake, there the gift will be invalid and inoperative; otherwise, a gift, when made, will be valid and operative, although in certain cases a gift made in contravention of Sastric prohibitions based on grounds other than those enumerated above will render the parties to the transaction liable to punishment from the king, apart from misery in the life to come which is the general sanction attached to Sastric prohibitions.

I have stated that a gift made by a person suffering from disease is generally regarded as invalid on the ground that such a man is not in a proper frame of mind to weigh his act and come to a right decision about it; this is, however, subject to an exception in favour of pious gifts, for Katyayana says 'What a man has given or promised for a religious purpose, whether in health or in sickness, must be given; and if he has died without giving it, his son shall doubtless be compelled to deliver it.'[1] So we see that not only will a gift actually made for pious purposes be supported as valid, but even a promise made for such purposes will be enforced against the promisor, if he be living, and against his sons, if he be dead. The obligation thus cast upon the son to carry out the promise made by the father before his death has been supposed to contain the germ of a testamentary bequest and on the basis of such texts M. Gibelin has maintained that the Hindu will was of indigenous growth and not an European invention. However that may be, it is at any rate clear that the obligation so imposed upon the son was not regarded as a mere moral obligation, but as a legal obligation specifically enforceable by the king.

Is a voluntary promise of gift enforceable?

This brings us, by a natural transition to the question, How far is a voluntary promise enforceable against the promisor himself? Mr. Mayne says that it is a general principle common to all systems of law that a voluntary promise cannot be enforced, though the voluntary act when completed is irrevocable; it seems that this statement is not stictly accurate so far as the Hindu Law is concerned, for according to that system a promise made with a view to help the promisee in the performance of some religious or pious act which he has already begun is binding and enforceable as a debt due by the promisor. Thus Harita says 'whatever has been promised in words, but not performed in deed with a view to help the promisee in the performance of some meritorious act is a debt both in this world and in the

[1] स्वस्थेनार्त्तेनवा दत्तं श्रावितं धर्म्मकारणात् ।
अदत्त्वा तु मृते दाप्यस्तत्सुतो नात्र संशयः ।
दत्तमित्यत्र देयमित्यपरार्कधृतः पाठः ।

next.[1] So also Katyayana says that 'whoever having voluntarily promised a gift to a Brahmana for religious merit afterwards refuses to give, shall be made to carry out his promise as if it were a debt, and shall also be liable to punishment.'[2] It is therefore clear that according to the Hindu Law, the promise of a gift, though voluntarily made, was enforceable as a debt when it was made either to a Brahmana for religious merit or with a view to help the performance of some meritorious act. Mr. Mayne says that 'it is quite certain that no promise to confer a future benefit upon a priest, however holy, would be enforced by the secular courts'. That may be so, but then the courts would not be administering the Hindu Law as it is, but merely giving effect to a doctrine of the English courts of Equity erroneously supposed to involve a principle common to all systems of law. It will be seen that the Hindu Law does not lay down that every voluntary promise of a gift is enforceable; it is when the gift is voluntarily promised to a pious Brahmana who counts upon such gifts for his subsistence, or when it is promised in furtherance of a pious act in which the promisee is engaged, that the promise is declared enforceable by the court as if it were a debt incurred by the promisor; and Gautama expressly enjoins that 'a gift, though promised, should not be made to an unrighteous man.'[3] It seems to me that understood in this limited sense, the rule of

---

1 वाचैव यत्प्रतिज्ञातं कर्म्मणानोपपादितम् ।
ऋणन्तद्धर्म्म संयुक्तमिहलोके परत्र च ॥

In the above translation, I have followed the explanation given in Viramitrodaya.

2 स्वेच्छया यः प्रतिश्रुत्य ब्राह्मणाय प्रतिग्रहं ।
न दद्याद्दृणवद्दाप्यः प्राप्नुयात् पूर्व्वसाहसम् ॥

3 प्रतिश्रुत्याप्यधर्म्मसंयुक्ताय न दद्यात् ।

Hindu Law is not unreasonable or unjust; on the other hand, to allow a man to create expectations without incurring any obligation to fulfil them can hardly be regarded as just and proper, especially when the person who is lured by such false hopes is a pious Brahmana, or a person engaged in the performance of some meritorious act, who would naturally adjust his expenses with reference to the assurance received. There can be no doubt that such a conduct would, everywhere, be regarded as morally reprehensible, and the Hindu Law only made the legal rule conform to the moral in recognising certain exceptions to the general rule that 'a voluntary promise can never be enforced'.

Validity of a gift to one after promise to another.

You will remember that I have already pointed out that according to the Hindu sages, a thing promised to one is not fit to be given to another; you now see that in certain cases a voluntary promise may be legally enforced; but you must not understand that a mere promise does, in any case, confer a title upon the promisee without an actual gift. Hence if a man gives to a person what he has promised another, the gift will not be invalid, and the thing cannot be recovered from the donee: although, under certain circumstances, the first promisee may pursue his remedy personally against his promisor and recover the equivalent of the gift from him on the principle already explained. This is not only clear on the general principle of transfer of ownership which I have already explained, but is also supported by the fact that even in those cases where a promise is declared to be binding, the obligation is likened to a debt, which indicates that the promisee has no title to the thing itself, but merely a personal right against the promisor.

I have so long dealt with the principles applicable to the case of a gift, and you will easily understand how most of

Principles common to sale and gift.

them are equally applicable to the case of a sale. Thus, in order that a sale may be valid, it is necessary that the vendor should have full dominion over the property sold, that he should have full legal capacity to enter into the transaction, and that the transaction itself should be real, and not brought about by fraud, or coercion, or the like. It is needless to reiterate these principles which have been fully explained in relation to a gift, and it is also needless to impress upon you that such prohibitions, as are to be found in the Sastras but are not based upon any of the grounds indicated above, would generally be so interpreted as to make out that their violation would not affect the validity of the transaction. In these respects, the rules laid down, and the distinctions set forth in the case of a gift would *mutatis mutandis* hold good in the case of a sale. I shall now proceed to discuss some supplementary rules having special reference to the Law of Sale.

Effect of purchase from a person who is not the real owner.

I have stated that a purchaser from a person who is not the owner cannot confer any title upon the purchaser although he might have *bonafide* belived that his vendor had a real title to pass. What then is to happen if the real owner comes forward and claims the thing? The procedure to be followed by a Court when a claim of this description, comes before it for adjudication is thus explained by Mitakshara: The claimant must in the first instance establish his title to the thing and explain how it got out of his hands. On his succeeding to prove a subsisting title, the purchaser will be called upon to produce his vendor, and when the vendor appears, the contest will go on between him and the claimant; thereupon if the claimant succeeds in establishing his claim, then he will recover the property, and the purchaser will get back his price from his vendor who will also render himself liable to punishment from the king; in the converse case, the unsuccessful claimant will not only fail to get the property, but will himself be punished for bringing forward a false claim. If, however, the purchaser fails to produce his vendor, then he will not only lose the property, but shall also be required to prove the *bonafides* of his purchase in order to exculpate himself. This rule, however, is subject to certain exceptions; for, as Katyayana has laid down, if the purchaser proves that he purchased the property from market overt or to the knowledge of King's officers, or openly from a place where the vendor cannot be traced, or the vendor is dead, then, the claimant, although he is the real owner, shall get back the property on payment of half its price to the purchaser.[1] These exceptions are justified on the ground that the owner loses half the price because somehow or other the property got out of his hands, and the purchaser loses half as he had the misfortune to purchase from one whom he cannot trace or produce before the court, although there could be no question about the *bonafides* of his purchase, so that both being equally blameless and equally unfortunate, it is but meet that the loss should be equally distributed between the two. On the other hand, where the purchaser fails to prove the *bonafides* of his purchase, for instance, where he purchased in secret, without publicity, from doubtful character, at an inadequate price, or at an improper time, there he shall be liable to punishment as if he were a thief, the presumption being that he must have purchased with the knowledge that there was something wrong about it. I need not dilate upon this subject any further, as I believe I have stated enough to show that the rules of the Hindu

Purchase in the market overt and in the presence of King's officers.

Purchaser when liable to punishment.

---

[1] वणिग्वीथीपरिगतं विज्ञातं राजपुरुषैः ।
अविज्ञाताश्रयात् क्रीतं विक्रेता यत्रवा मृतः ।
स्वामीदत्त्वार्धमूल्यं तु प्रगृह्णीयात् स्वकं धनम् ।

Law upon the subject are on the whole well-considered and reasonable. I should, however, add that it was considered to be the duty of the owner to bring a theft to the knowledge of the king, and if he remained satisfied on merely getting back the property without bringing the matter to the notice of the king, he would render himself liable to be punished with a fine,[1] a rule which is based upon the recognition of the interest of the community as something distinct from the interest of the individual which it is the duty of every individual to subserve.

Owner's duty to bring a thief to the notice of the king.

Rescission of sale.

The next topic that deserves a brief consideration is the rescission of sale. It often happens that after a purchase we begin to repent of the bargain either because the thing purchased proves to be worse than what we took it to be or because the price we paid appears to be too high; the question is whether there ought not to be any remedy for it. On the one hand, it may be said that one ought to take proper care before the transaction is completed and that once the bargain is struck there can no longer be any help for it; on the other hand, it seems to be very hard that in no case should the purchaser be allowed to cancel the purchase and get out of the transaction which he had concluded under a misconception about its nature and advantages.

There can be no doubt that much may be said in support of the former view that a purchaser makes the purchase at his risk and should not be allowed to complain after the bargain is once concluded, but at the same time it must be observed that commercialism need not be the sole guiding principle of a community and an actual hardship

---

[1] हृतं प्रनष्टं यो द्रव्यं परहस्तादवाप्नुयात् ।
अनिवेद्य नृपे दण्ड्यः स तु षण्णवतिंपणान् ॥ याज्ञवल्क्यः ।

should be relieved in so far as it can be done without unjustly entailing equal or greater injury to others. It is therefore highly interesting to find that the Hindu Law attempted to reconcile the interest of private purchasers with the interest of trade by laying down certain rules which without sacrificing the certainty of trade by allowing excessive and belated interference with concluded transactions provided some protection against being entrapped into and held fast by hasty and inconsiderate bargains. The rules were these: in every case the purchaser, unless he had previously examined the thing purchased with a view to ascertain their quality and approved of them upon such examination, was entitled to a certain period to examine them, and if within that period it was found that the thing was defective he could return it to the vendor and recover the price from him. The period allowed for examination was viewed according to the nature of the object sold; thus three days were allowed for the examination of a milch-cow, five days for the examination of a horse, and seven days for that of precious stones such as pearls, diamonds and the like. If however, the purchaser had before the purchase examined the thing to be purchased, and approved of it, then he could not afterwards complain and have the sale rescinded on the ground that there was a defect which had escaped his examination.[1] You will observe that what has been stated above related to the rescission on the ground of discovery of defect after the completion of the purchase without previous examination, and the rule upon the subject does not seem to me to be at all unreasonable or unjust; those of you who have any doubt upon it will I hope think otherwise, when

Conditions of rescission.

---

[1] क्रेतापण्यं परीक्षेत प्राक्स्वयं गुणदोषतः ।
परीक्ष्याभिमतं क्रीतं विक्रेतुर्नभवेत्पुनः ॥ नारदः ।

you will have more frequent occasions to purchase things like those mentioned above. Apart, however, from any examination or discovery of defect, the Hindu Law allowed a further indulgence to the purchaser; it granted him a period of grace within which to return the thing purchased, a sort of *locus penitentiæ,* so to say, if he repented of the bargain and desired to rescind the sale; the period allowed was, however, very short, being the first day to get back the full purchase money, and the second and third days to recover.[1] It should also be mentioned that the right to return could not be availed of if the article sold had been soiled or otherwise injured by use, although it might appear to have been defective.[2] Considering, then, all these rules together subject to the limitations indicated above, it seems to me impossible to say that they do not deserve serious consideration, although I do not know of any other system of law in which similar rules have prevailed.

Time of completion of sale: non-delivery of articles sold.

I shall now say a few words about the completion of sale and the effect of non-delivery of articles sold. A purchase ordinarily becomes completed on the payment of the price, unless the payment is deferred by a special contract between the parties, the result, therefore, is that where the price has not been paid, the vendor is free to sell to another in the absence of a special contract to the

---

[1] क्रीत्वा मूल्येन यः पण्यं दुष्क्रीतं मन्यतेक्रयी ।
विक्रेतुः प्रतिदेयं तत्तस्मिन्नेवाह्न्यविक्षतम् ॥
द्वितीयेऽह्नि ददत्क्रेता मूल्यात् त्रिंशांशमाहरेत् ।
द्विगुणं तु तृतीयेऽह्निपरतः क्रेतुरेवतत् ॥

[2] परिभुक्तन्तु यद्वासः क्लिष्टरूपं मलीमसं ।
सदोषमपितत् क्रीतं विक्रेतुर्नभवेत्पुनः ॥

contrary.[1] When the sale has been completed by the payment of the price, the seller is bound to deliver the article sold to the purchaser, and on refusal will be compelled to deliver together with proper compensation. Various rules have been laid down for measuring the compensation in each case, of which the following may be specially noticed; if the price of the article has fallen down in the interval, then the seller shall be compelled to deliver the articles sold together with such compensation as will make up for the reduction in the price; where, the price has remained constant, there nothing more than ordinary interest will be charged; where, however, the price has gone up there the compensation will be measured by the profit which the seller has reaped after this improper refusal to deliver. These rules are to be understood to refer to the case of a purchaser belonging to the same locality as the vendor; where the purchaser has come from a different country with a view to send the article there, in that case the price that prevails in that country must be taken into account in measuring the compensation.

Compensation for non-delivery.

As regards loss or deterioration of the articles sold while lying in the hands of the seller the law stands thus: If the seller did not deliver the articles although the purchaser asked for their delivery, then any subsequent loss or deterioration, even if it arises from an act of King or an act of God over which the seller has no control, must fall upon him for the non-delivery was due to his default.[2] Conversely if the purchaser did not take delivery

Liability for deterioration or loss after demand.

दत्तमूल्यस्य पण्यस्यविधिरेष प्रकीर्त्तितः।
अदत्तेऽन्यत्रसमयान्नविक्रेतुरतिक्रमः।
राजदैवोपघातेन पण्ये दोषमुपागते।
हानिर्विक्रेतुरेवासौ याचितस्याप्रयच्छतः॥ याज्ञवल्क्यः।

although the seller expressed his readiness to deliver, then any loss arising from an act of King or an act of God must be suffered by the purchaser, for it was he who defaulted in taking the delivery.[1] Of course, if the loss arises from some wilful act of the seller, this rule will not apply and he will be responsible for the same. It may be mentioned that when a thing is burnt by fire or stolen by thieves the loss is generally regarded as one due to an act of God. So far the position is quite clear : the loss will fall upon the party owing to whose default the thing remained in the hands of the seller, except of course where the loss itself was caused by one of the parties to the transaction. A doubt, however, arises as to what should be the rule, when previous to the loss, there had been neither any demand for delivery on the part of the purchaser, nor any offer to deliver on the part of the seller. Viramitrodaya

Viramitrodaya.

says that the text of Yajnavalkya, referred to above, makes the seller responsible when he had failed to deliver the thing sold upon demand from the purchaser, which indicates that in the absence of such previous demand, the seller cannot be held responsible for any loss or deterioration arising from an act of King or an act of God, but it then proceeds to quote without any apparent disapproval the

Smriti Chandrika.

opinion of the author of Smriti Chandrika to the effect that where after the completion of purchase, neither the purchaser has asked for delivery nor the seller has offered to deliver the thing sold and it is lost or injured under those circumstances, there the loss will be equally divided between the seller and the purchaser in as much as owing to the negligence of the one to offer and of the other to

---

दीयमानंन ग्टह्णाति क्रीतम्पण्यञ्चय: क्रयी ।
स एवास्य भवेद्दोषो विक्रेतुर्योऽप्रयच्छत: ॥ नारद: ।

demand delivery, there has been default on both the sides.[1]

It may be interesting to compare with these provisions some of the provisions of the Roman Law bearing upon similar questions. According to the Roman Law also, a sale does not become complete and the property does not pass from the seller to the buyer, until the buyer has paid the price to the seller, or satisfied him in some way or other, except where the seller has accepted the credit of the buyer in which case, the property becomes immediately the property of the buyer. You will find that so far, the Roman Law is in complete accord with the Hindu Law. The Roman Law however recognises a contract of sale, as distinguished from a completed sale and lays down that the contract is formed as soon as the price is agreed upon, although the title may not be transferred until the payment of the price; as a corollary from this, it further lays down, that from the moment of the completion of the contract on the parties having agreed on the price, all the risks attaching to the thing contracted to be sold falls upon the purchaser, although the thing has not yet been delivered to him; and similarly, he also becomes entitled to all the advantages which may accrue and be attached to that thing. Now, looking at these provisions as a whole, it does not seem to me that either in point of subtlety, or in point of reasonableness or logical consistency, the Hindu Law suffers from a comparison with Roman Law.

Hindu and Roman Law compared.

I have stated that according to the Hindu Law, a mere verbal agreement does not, in the absence of a special contract, preclude the owner from dealing with some other intending purchaser. It is, however, otherwise, where the

[1] क्रयानन्तरं क्रेता न याचितं विक्रेता च न समर्पितं जातश्चौराद्युपद्रवस्तद्द्वयोः समाहानिः। क्रेतृविक्रेत्रोरुभयोरपि याचनार्पणयोः शैथिल्येन सापराधत्वात्।

Effect of payment of earnest money.

verbal agreement has been followed by payment of earnest money; for, in that case, it has been laid down, that 'if the intending purchaser refuse to complete the purchase within proper time, he shall forfeit the earnest money; while on the other hand, if the seller refuse to complete the sale, he shall have to return not only the earnest money, but also to pay an equal sum as compensation.[1] Curiously enough, these provisions completely coincide with those of the Roman Law as modified by Justinian. It is stated in the Institutes of Justinian that 'if earnest has been given, then, whether the contract was written or unwritten, the purchaser, if he refuse to fulfil it, loses what he has given as earnest, and the seller, if he refuse, has to restore double'; and on this Mr. Sandars comments that 'the arræ were either signs of a bargain having been struck, or consisted of an advance of a portion of the purchase money. Justinian gave these deposits a new character by making them the measures of a foreit in case either party wished to recede from this bargain, it being open to either party to retract if he chose to incur his foreit.'

Priority in cases of gift and sale.

It now remains to me to close this lecture by pointing out that both in cases of gift and sale, the prior in time prevails for it has been said that 'in all litigious disputes the subsequent act prevails, but in case of pledge, acceptance (of a gift) and purchase, the prior act is more forcible'.[2] The reason of this is quite plain, for once a transfer has been made the transferor has lost his interest and is quite incompetent to interfere with the right of the transferee.

---

[1] सत्यकारं चयोदत्वा यथाकालं न दृश्यते ।
पण्यं भवेन्निसृष्टं तद्दीयमानमगृह्णतः ॥ व्यासः
सत्यङ्कारकृतं द्रव्यं द्विगुणं प्रतिदापयेत् । याज्ञवल्क्यः
अलपण्यद्रव्यस्योत्सर्गः सत्यङ्कार द्रव्यस्योत्सर्गोऽभिमतः इतिवीरमित्रोदयः ।

[2] सर्वेष्वर्थविवादेषु बलवत्युत्तराक्रिया ।
आधौ प्रतिग्रहेक्रीते पूर्वातुबलवत्तरा॰

LECTURE IV.

THE LAW OF PRESCRIPTION.

Prescription adverse possession.

In this lecture, I propose to deal with the Hindu Law of Prescription, or the effect of long possession without any opposition from the true owner. The plain meaning of the text of Yajnavalkya bearing upon this question seems to be that 'he who sees his land being enjoyed by a stranger for twenty years, and his personal chattel for ten years without asserting his own right, loses them'.[1] You will observe that in order to have the effect mentioned by this text, the possession must have been held by the stranger to the knowledge of the owner, but without any protest or opposition from him; it is the concurrence of the presence of knowledge with the absence of opposition on the part of the owner that attaches to the adverse possession when it has continued for a certain length of time, the effect of extinguishing the right of the previous owner; and either of these elements being wanting, the resulting consequence will not arise. It therefore follows that, whatever the length of possession may be, it will be of no avail if the owner was not aware of it, or being aware, asserted his title, and opposed the possession of the stranger. You will also notice that the period required for ripening the prescription is longer in the case of immovable property than in the case of movables, being twenty years in the former case, and ten in the latter, a difference evidently due to the greater value and importance of land. These elements in the constitution of the

Text of Yajnavalkya.

Elements of prescription.

[1] पश्यतोऽब्रुवतो भूमेर्हानिर्विंशतिवार्षिकी ।
परेण भुज्यमानाया धनस्य दशवार्षिकी ॥

rule being understood, the question arises, what is the effect? One thing seems to be clear, *viz.*, that the effect spoken of is extinctive in its character as indicated by the word हानि which means loss or deprivation; words used in the texts of other lawgivers to which I may have occasion to refer are also of similar import; we may therefore take it, that by adverse possession of the requisite character, the owner loses, or, in other words, is deprived of something; but the question is, what that something is. I may tell you at once that our jurists are not all agreed upon this point, and a remarkable controversy full of subtle distinctions, has clustered around it. I shall try to give you some idea of this controversy and of the different opinions that were maintained by the different jurists.

Controversy.

Mitakshara view.

The author of Mitakshara seeks to place a very narrow construction upon the text cited above, and the effect of prescription, according to him, is very limited in its character; he argues that omission to assert one's title cannot legitimately be regarded as a cause of the extinction of that title; similarly, mere enjoyment, whatever its duration may be, cannot be regarded as a source of title, since it is not recognised as such in popular usage, and a text of Narada has declared that 'the king shall punnish a person who enjoys another's property without any title as if he were a thief, although he may have done so for hundred years'; [1] he therefore concludes that the loss (हानि) spoken of in the text means not the loss of the property itself, but of the usufruct enjoyed by the person in adverse possession, so that the owner shall not be entitled, after the prescribed period, to recover the

Usufruct is lost but not title.

[1] अनागमन्तु यो भुङ्क्ते बहून्यब्दशतान्यपि
चौरदण्डेन तं पापं दण्डयेत् पृथिवीपतिः

profits already appropriated by the person in possession whom he has allowed to do so with his eyes open and without any opposition; but that the title to the property itself and the right to recover the same shall remain intact, since title cannot be lost by mere lapse of time in asserting it.

Kalpasutra; Ratnakara; Smrititatwa and Smritichandrika.

On the other hand, the authors of Kalpasutra, Ratnakara, Smrititatwa and Smritichandrika maintain that adverse possession for the prescribed period and fulfilling the required conditions does extinguish the title of the owner so kept out of possession, not only to the usufruct but also to the property itself; they argue that there is no sufficient ground to limit the scope of the text by putting an unnatural and strained meaning upon its words in the way indicated above; when Mitakshara admits that after the prescribed period the usufruct is lost to the owner, it may be asked—why is it so lost? To this question, there are two possible answers, for it may either be said that the loss is the condign consequence of the owner's own fault in omitting to protest against the possession which was being enjoyed before his eyes or it may be advanced, that the text of the Sastra being there, it is unnecessary to grope for any other basis than that furnished by the text itself; now, as regards the former alternative, it may be observed that it does not sufficiently explain the rule, for, if the loss of the usufruct was the natural consequence of the owner's own default in omitting to oppose the possession of the stranger, what is the reason for fixing upon twenty years or ten years to entail that consequence? Did not the fault due to the owner's own default exist even before the completion of the prescribed period, and, if so, how can the prescription be sufficiently explained from the reason of the rule without recourse to the authority of the text? It being then

Extinctive prescription: title also is lost.

conceded that ultimately there can be no escape from falling back upon the authority of the text, the question arises whether we should interpret that text according to its obvious and natural import, or turn and twist it with a view to make it fit in with a preconceived idea that property cannot be lost by mere non-enjoyment, whatever its duration may be. The authors mentioned above therefore maintain that adverse possession of the nature described in the text already explained extinguished the title of the owner kept out of possession not only to the usufruct but also to the property itself.

Bhavadeva's view.

Between these two extreme views there are certain intermediate positions which may now be briefly indicated and explained. Bhavadeva maintains that adverse possession for the prescribed period to the knowledge of and without any opposition from the owner has the effect of raising a presumption that the owner must have abandoned the property, which being taken up by the possessor, he acquires a title to it by a sort of appropriation (परिग्रह) of a thing which is for the time without an owner. His conclusion, therefore, practically coincides with the last mentioned view, but it is arrived at in a somewhat roundabout way; for, according to his contention, the extinction of title of the previous owner is not the direct result of adverse possession for the prescribed period suffered by him without opposition, but is the result of abandonment which is presumed from that adverse possession; the loss of title, therefore, is, according to this view, inferential, the inference being propped up by the presumption of abandonment which, as it arises from the text quoted above, must be taken to be irrebuttable in its character.

Doctrine of presumption.

Pradipakara's emendation.

Pradipakara also accepts this view, but with a little emendation; he says that the presumption arises from adverse possession extending over the prescribed period coupled with the impossibility of ascribing non-resistance to mere indifference or good-naturedness of the owner, and the character of the presumption is that the owner has either transferred the thing to the person in possession or has abandoned it in his favour, it being unnecessary to select between the two. The real difficulties of this doctrine of irrebuttable presumption are why should the presumption at all arise, and at all events, why should it be irrebuttable? As Viramitrodaya very pertinently points out, ten years or twenty years is not too long a time to be beyond all human recollection, and when no body recollects any transfer in favour of the possessor, or any abandonment by the previous owner, the inference arises that no such thing took place, since otherwise, it would have been remembered; hence the presumptions, on which reliance has been sought to be placed by Bhavadeva and the author of Pradipa, do not really arise and their doctrines cannot be seriously sustained.[1] If in order to escape from these difficulties, it becomes necessary to say that the presumptions do arise, and they cannot be rebutted by reason of the text cited above, then is it not better to avoid the circumlocution, and say plainly that the loss of title rests solely on the authority of that text? The doctrine of presumption, therefore, seems to be either untenable or unnecessary, and it can only serve as a specimen of the ingenuity displayed by Hindu jurists, in drawing fine distinctions in order to arrive at a desired conclusion.

Criticism of the doctrine of presumption.

The real difficulty in the way of accepting the doctrine of extinctive or translative prescription arises from the view which seems to have been widely recognised that title

Criticism of the doctrine of extinctive prescription.

---

[1] आगमकाले अर्थव्याकरणरूपया योग्यानुपलब्ध्या भोक्तुरागमाभाव निश्चये पूर्वस्वामिनश्च त्यागाभावनिश्चये तदीय परिग्रहज्ञात स्वत्वोत्पत्ति पूर्वस्वामित्व ध्वंसानु-भावपि कल्पयितुमशक्यावित मतद्वयमपीदमत्ययुक्तं। इति वीरमित्रोदयः।

cannot be extinguished by mere adverse possession . without the consent or concurrence of the real owner; hence Vijnaneswara attempted to explain the text of Yajnavalkya by arguing that the loss (हानि) spoken of there referred to the loss of the usufruct already enjoyed, but he does so, as I have alredy pointed out, by putting a somewhat strained interpretation upon the words of the text. Vachaspati

Vachaspati's view.

endeavoured to dispose of the question in a somewhat different way; the text of Yajnavalkya and similar other texts, he contended, were designed to point out the risk of indifference in asserting one's title to a property which is being enjoyed by another, and hence to impress upon the owner the duty of preserving with care the evidence of his title by asserting it in proper time; this view reduces the rule of prescription to a rule of evidence, but the obvious objection to it is that it renders the prescription of definite periods (ten years and twenty years) superfluous, since it cannot be said that the risk is any the less before the completion of those periods.

Aparārka's solution.

Aparārka seeks to escape from these difficulties by maintaining that what has been laid down in the texts about the loss of property has been stated from the standpoint of positive law administered by the Courts, but it does not indicate the real direction which the property takes under those circumstances. This, he says, is supported by the text of Manu declaring that 'if a person, not being an idiot or a minor, allows his property to be enjoyed by another, then his title to it breaks down and the person in enjoyment succeeds in litigation'; [1] hence all that can be said is that after the lapse of the prescribed period the court will not help the owner in getting back the property

---

[1] अजडश्चेदपोगण्डो विषयेचास्यभुज्यते ।
भग्नंतद्व्यवहारेण भोक्ता तद्द्रव्यमर्हति ॥ मनुः ॥

from the person in possession, but his title is not lost; and if the person in possession, out of conscientious scruples or moral compunction, returns the property, title and possession again meet in the same individual, and the original condition is restored. It will appear that Apararka thus reduces the rule into a rule of limitation of action, but he also has not consistently maintained the distinction between a rule of limitation which is meant for the guidance of the court, and a rule of prescription which operates by extinguishing the title itself.

Viramitrodaya reconciles the texts of Brihaspati and Yajnavalkya.

There is a text of Brihaspati which lays down that 'when a person has been in possession continuously for thirty years without any interruption that possession will not be afterwards disturbed'.[1] Viramitrodaya reconciles this with the text of Yajnavalkya by holding that the rule of twenty years applies where the owner has not asserted his title in opposition to the person in possession, but the thirty years' rule applies where in spite of verbal protest, the adverse possession has been continuously maintained.

Comments upon the controversy.

On a perusal of the discussions which have centred round this remarkable controversy, one cannot but be struck by the splendid development of juristic ideas which they evince; the arguments advanced display a clear conception of the problem, great logical acumen in drawing distinctions and dealing with them, and a high moral standard which hesitates to invest the man in possession with ownership when that possession had its origin in wrong. Sir William Markby therefore betrays a very insufficient knowledge of the Hindu Law of Prescription when in a footnote in the chapter on Prescription in his Elements of Law, he somewhat superciliously observes—

---

[1] अध्यासनात् समारभ्य भुक्तिर्यस्या विघातिनी ।
त्रिंशद्वर्षाण्यविच्छिन्ना तस्य तां न विचालयेत् ॥

'Even in a system so little advanced as the ancient Hindu Law, the advantages of a just title are recognised. The Mitakshara lawyers would allow a right to be gained in twenty years, but only if the party already held under a title which though defective was just.' It is apparent that Sir William Markby knew very little of the Hindu Law of Prescription, and that little not correctly, and yet we are sorry to observe that he could not introduce his casual observations without a fling upon the ancient Hindu Law. For this, however, we ourselves are partly responsible; since, while foreign jurists, in spite of their many disadvantages, have out of a pure spirit of research directed their attention to these subjects, no matter with what success, we ourselves have simply looked on.

As regards the controversy itself, it seems to me that the texts themselves laid down not merely a rule of limitation or a rule of evidence, but a rule of extinction of title by operation of law. The text prescribing punishment for wrongful possession, although that possession may have continued for a very long time, is not really in conflict with the other texts laying down definite periods for extinction of title by prescription, for a man may be punishable for the original trespass even after a long lapse of time apart from any question regarding the civil rights of the parties and the civil remedies of the original owner. When, however, in course of time, the constructive period was followed by the critical period of Hindu Jurisprudence, and the Philosophical Jurists who took up the discussions began to enquire into the theoretical basis of prescription, they were beset with doubts and difficulties and in the result, different jurists tried to solve them in different ways. The foundation of this difficulty is not far to seek, for, theoretically, one might find it difficult to understand why an existing right should be destroyed by mere non-assertion of it for a certain length of time, or how possession, which was wrongful, could, by mere continuance, change its character and become rightful after a certain period. It is remarkable that a study of the modern European Jurisprudence discloses a similar controversy and a similar disinclination to regard title as capable of being totally lost through dispossession. Sir Henry Maine's remarks on this question are so instructive and interesting that I can not resist the temptation of quoting them here *in extenso*. "Prescriptions," says he, "were viewed by the modern lawyers, first with repugnance, afterwards with reluctant approval.* * * This tardiness in copying one of the most famous chapters of Roman Law, which was no doubt constantly read by the majority of European lawyers, the modern world owes to the influence of Canon Law. The ecclesiastical customs out of which the Common Law grew, concerned as they were with sacred or quasi-sacred interests, very naturally regarded the privileges which they conferred, as incapable of being lost through disuse however prolonged; and in accordance with this view, the spiritual jurisprudence when afterwards consolidated, was distinguished by a marked leaning against Prescriptions. It was the fate of the Canon Law, when held up by the clerical lawyers, as a pattern to secular legislature, to have a peculiar influence on first principles. It gave to the bodies of custom which were formed throughout Europe far fewer express rules than did the Roman Law, but then it seeems to have communicated a bias to professional opinion on a surprising number of fundamental points and the tendencies thus produced progressively gained strength as each system was developed. One of the dispositions it produced was a disrelish for presumptions, but I do not think that this prejudice would have operated as powerfully as it has done, if it had not fallen in with the

Similar controversy in European Jurisprudence. Sir Henry Maine.

Influence of Canon Law.

doctrine of the scholastic jurists of the realist sect, who taught that, whatever turn actual legislation might take, a *right,* how long so ever neglected, was in point of fact indestructible. The remains of this state of feeling still exist. Wherever the philosophy of law is earnestly discussed, questions respecting the speculative basis of prescription are always hotly disputed; and it is still a point of the greatest interest in France and Germany, whether a person who has been out of possession for a series of years is deprived of his ownership as a penalty for his neglect, or loses it through the summary interposition of the law in its desire to have a *finis litum*". English lawyers do not seem to have been much perplexed by these theoretical difficulties; the bent of English mind has always been practical and not speculative; they make the law, and leave the philosophy of law to take care of itself.

The speculative basis of prescription: a point of interset in France and Germany even now; not so in England.

I may wind up this part of the discussion by saying a few words upon the Roman Law of Prescription. Before Justinian's time, the operation of possession in perfecting one's title was known as usucapion; the periods provided for the operation of usucapion were very shout, being one year in the case of movables and two years in the case of immovables within *solum Italicum;* moreover, to have this effect, possession must have commenced *bonâ fide,* and *ex justa causa, i.e.,* in some recognised method of acquiring property insufficient to create title by reason of some defect in form under the peculiar rules of Roman Law which required the peculiar ceremonies of mancipation for the transfer of Res Mancipi. The necessity of showing *justa causa* and the shortness of the periods prescribed for the operation of usucapion clearly prove that it was at first used as a rude device to escape from the embarrasments created by a crude system of conveyance; and hence when under Justinian's legislation, tradition took up the place of mancipation, usucapion was also superseded by prescription with the periods for its operation considerably lengthened: from one year to three years in the case of movables, and from two years to twenty years or ten years in the case of lands wherever situate, according as the adverse possession was held against a person present in the province or absent therefrom. Thus modified, the prescription under the Roman Law very much approached the prescription under the Hindu Law. There were, however, a few points of difference; in the first place, the period laid down for the operation of prescription in the case of movables was shorter under the Roman Law than under the Hindu Law; in the second place, the Hindu Law does not seem to have allowed the rule of prescription to operate against an absent owner who knew nothing about the adverse possession; in the third place, where the possession had no *bona fide* beginning, a still longer period, *viz.*, thirty years, seems to have been required under the Roman Law to ripen the prescription which went under the name of *prescriptio longissimi temporis*, a provision with which we may compare the rule of the Hindu Law that when the adverse possession was not free from verbal protest, a period of three years was necessary to put a stop to future disturbance of that possession. On the whole, the two systems exhibit accidental resemblances of a striking character, and where they differ, I can not say that the Hindu Law suffers from the comparison. As regards the theoretical difficulties of prescription, they do not seem to have perplexed the Roman Jurists who allowed usucapion to be transferred into prescription by the mandate of the legislator when the cumbrous formalities of transfer were swept away to make room for simpler methods.

The Hindu and Roman systems compared.

Exceptions to the applicability of prescription

I shall now pass on to consider some of the exceptions to the applicability of the rule of prescription. They are their principle. Similar exceptions in other systems.

mostly summed up in the text of Yajnavalkya which lays down that the rule applies except in the cases of pledges, boundaries, trust deposits, the wealth of idiots and infants, sealed deposits, and the property of a king, a woman, or a priest versed in the Vedas.[1] The principles on which these exceptions are based are not peculiar to the Hindu Law and similar exceptions are also to be found in other systems of Jurisprudence. Thus with regard to property entrusted to another by way of a pledge or a trust, so long as the pledge or trust continues there can be no prescription against the owner; this is on the principle that derivative possession does not induce prescription, and although in the case of a pledge for custody (and not for use) and a trust deposit the pledges and the bailee exceed their power in using or enjoying those things, still such enjoyment or use does not make their possession a verse against the owner who entrusted the things with them, the only difference that it makes being that he becomes entitled to compensation for the unauthorised use of his things in violation of the agreement under which possession was derived. There can be no prescription against a minor or an idiot because he is unable to protect his own interest and should, therefore, be protected by the law; similar protection is also afforded to women by reason, as Mitakshara puts it of their ignorance and want of forwardness (अज्ञात्वादप्रागल्भ्यात्) with the exceptions made in favour of a King and a learned Brahmin we may, compare the maxim 'nullum tempus occurrit regi aut ecclesiæ,' and the Mitakshara justifies them on the ground that the King by reason of his numerous avocations, and the learned Brahmin by reason of his absorption in spiritual studies and consequent inattention to secular concerns of life may be

---

[1] आधिसीमोपनिक्षेप जड़बालधनैर्विना
तथोपनिधिराजस्त्री श्रोत्रियाणां धनैरपि ।

unmindful of the possession held adversely against them, and should, therefore, be exempted from the operation of prescription. As regards the exception in the case of encroachment overstepping intermediate boundary, the Mitakshara says that in as much as boundaries are easily ascertainable by reference to permanent boundary marks it is not unlikely that one may look with indifference upon an encroachment by the neighbour, and hence omission to protest should not entail the consequence which attaches itself to unexplained negligence in asserting one's claim; you will understand that this explanation proceeds upon the view held by the Mitakshara that what the owner loses by adverse possession is not the property itself, but the usufruct, and that the loss is a sort of penalty for the owner's laches in opposing the possession in proper time, so that any excuse for non-opposition will furnish a ground for not enforcing the penalty; the explanation, however, may not seem to be adequate on the view that prescription is a cause of loss of title in the property itself, and it may be suggested that the real explanation may be that encroachment in a neighbouring field by overstepping the intermediate boundary is calculated to be of such a fitful character that it may not often attract attention and is not always capable of prevention, so that such acts ought to be regarded as isolated acts of tresspass and should not be allowed to ripen into a prescriptive title. Besides these exceptions, it was also laid down that there could be no prescription when the possession was permissive, being allowed through affection for a kindred or the like:[1] the reason is that in a case like this, possession cannot be regarded as adverse. On the whole it may be safely asserted that the exceptions are all eminently reasonable,

---

[1] सम्प्रीत्याभुज्यमानानि न नश्यन्ति कदाचन । मनु ।

and they are founded on principles which have been adopted more or less in all systems of Jurisprudence.

There is another question discussed in Hindu Law relating to the effect of long possession which is so very similar to the question so long discussed that it is not impossible for one to overlook the distinction between the two and confuse them with each other. The question is this: possession, as far as it goes, is evidence of title, for in the absence of evidence to the contrary, it should be presumed that the man in possession is the owner of the thing possesesd; but in as much as it is not unusual to find possession without title, and title without possession, bare proof of possession does not ordinarily exclude an enquiry into the question of title: and if it can be shown by independent evidence that the possession is not founded on title, then ordinarily the title will prevail over such possession. The question, therefore, arises whether under any circumstances evidence of possession can supersede the necessity of an enquiry, so as to entitle the person in possession to rely upon it alone as evidence of his title without recourse to any other evidence. This question has been answered by our lawgivers, and I shall attempt to explain their position as briefly as I can.

Possession as evidence of title.

Yajnavalkya. Hereditary possession: what it means.

Yajnavalkya declares that 'title preponderates over possession unless the latter be hereditary.'[1] This means that if a person proves his possession over a property, but cannot show how he acquired it, and another, although not in possession, proves his title by showing that he acquired the property in some recognised way of acquiring ownership, such as sale, gift, etc., then the title so proved must prevail over possession unless such possession is shown to be hereditary, being in fact a continuation of

---

[1] आगमोऽभ्यधिको भोगद्विनापूर्व्वं क्रमागतात् ।

ancestral possession. The exception made in favour of hereditary possession indicates that such possession supersedes an enquiry into title, but it raises the question what hereditary possession means. Now there are texts to the effect that in order to have the desired effect, possession must have continued through three generations in the past. So Narada says, that where possession has continued through three generations in the past including the father, it cannot be disturbed even if it was wrongful;[1] and according to a text of Vyasa, possession extending over one generation means possession for twenty years, so that possession for three generation means possession for at least sixty years.[2] Apararka however cites an anonymous text which lays down that possession for one generation should be taken to extend over thirty-five years.[3] The real significance of these texts is thus sought to be explained by the author of the Mitakshara; he says that the crucial distinction is between possession which had its beginning within living human memory, and possession which extends beyond that, so that possession extending over three previous generations really imports possession from time immemorial; he argues that when possession had its beginning within living memory, it may not be impossible to show that it was not founded on any valid title, whereas in a case of immemorial use, you connot say that it had no valid origin, since that origin is not within living human recollection, and that being so in this latter case all

Narada

Vyasa

Apararka

Mitakshara

---

1 अन्यायेनापि यदभुक्तं पित्रा पूर्व्वतरैस्त्रिभिः ।
न तच्छक्यमपाहर्तुं क्रमात्त्रिपुरुषागतम् ॥

2 वर्षाणि विंशति भुक्ता स्वामिना व्याहता सती ।
भुक्तिः सा पौरुषी भूमेर्द्विगुणा च द्विपौरुषी ॥

3 त्रिपौरुषी च त्रिगुणा न तत्रान्विष्य आगमः ।
वर्षाणि पञ्चविंशान्तु पौरुषो भोगउच्यते ॥

further enquiry into the question of title is practically superseded, and nothing remains to be done but to support the existing possession as incontestable and incapable of being lawfully disturbed. This position is supported by the text of Katyayana which clearly explains the ground of the rule; it says that in a case of dispute about land, where possession had its beginning within living memory possession, accompanied by title has to be sought after, but where it is extended beyond human memory, there in as much as it is impossible to be certain about absence of title, possession descending through three generations must prevail.[1] That mere continuance of possession through three generations is not conclusive and is really meant to stand for a period beyond human recollection appears from the fact that under extraordinary circumstances this may be compassed within a much shorter period so as to take the case out of the reason of the rule as explained in the text of Katyayana cited above. The utmost extent of human life, and therefore the extreme range of human memory is said by Mitakshara, according to a text of the Veda, to be hundred years, but the real test must be understood to be furnished by the limits of living human memory which must be regarded in each particular case.

Conclusion

The conclusion therefore seems to be this: under ordinary circumtances, mere possession does not exclude an enquiry into title, for possession may lie with one person and title with another; where, however, that possession has descended through three previous ancestors, it was thought that to render proof of title was superfluous, and some lawyers laid down that such possession, even if shown to be wrongful, could not be disturbed; this period was

---

आगमकाले क्रियाभूमेः सागमाभुक्ति रिष्यते ।
अस्मार्त्तेऽनुगमाभावात् क्रमात् त्रिपुरुषागता ॥

stated by some sages to cover sixty years, and there is one text, which, if genuine, would make it cover one hundred and five years. It was perhaps considered, as the text of Katyayana would seem to indicate, that when possession continued through three successive generations, it could very well be regarded as having its origin beyond living human memory. The Mitakshara then takes its stand upon the reason of the rule, and contends that mere passing through three generations is not necessarily conclusive, for it is not inconceivable that under extraordinary circumstances such a thing may happen within a comparatively short time; hence it concludes that it is only when the origin of possession is lost in obscurity by reason of its having commenced beyond living human recollection that enquiry into the question of title is superseded and possession, standing alone, justifies itself; for in such a case the presumption is that possession has, as a matter of fact, followed title.

Even then it allows that such presumption is not absolutely irrebuttable, a qualification which flows logically from the doctrine that possession is never an equivalent of title, but only presumptive evidence thereof; but this concession to logical consistency seems to be inconsistent with the text of Narada cited above, which shows that in such a case, the existing possession cannot be disturbed even it shown to be wrongful. On any view, the practical result is almost indentical; in a case where possession has come down from time immemorial, it is not merely nine points, but ten points of title, and even when it had its origin within living recollection and enquiry into title is not therefore superseded, evidence of title being equally balanced, possession must prevail.

I hope you will now understand why I have kept this discussion into the effect of enjoyment from time immemorial quite apart from the discussion into the effect of enjoyment of a particular character and for a certain definite period in extinguishing the title of the real owner. Apart from the doctrine of the Mitakshara School that in no case can possession for a definite period having its beginning within living recollection extinguish the real owner's right to any thing more than the usufruct already enjoyed, there is, even on a thorough recognition of the doctrine of extinctive prescription, this difference in principle between the two doctrines that enjoyment from time immemorial supersedes an enquiry into title by raising an almost irrebuttable (if not absolutely irrebuttable) presumption of lawful origin, while adverse possession for the prescribed period when its fulfils certain conditions operates by extinguishing the old title and thereby substituting a new title in its place.

Similar doctrines in other systems.

It will now be interesting to compare with this doctrine of Hindu Law, similar doctrines in other systems of Jurisprudence. Thus it will be found that the doctrine of immemorial enjoyment has been recognised in public law, and is thus stated by Savigny :—'when a condition of things has lasted so long that the present generation never knew any other, and their forefathers knew no other, then it must be assumed that this condition of things is so bound up with the convictions, feelings, and interests of the nation that it cannot be disturbed.' Vattel in his Law of Nations subscribes to the same doctrine, when he says that in addition to ordinary prescription 'there is another called immemorial, because it is founded on immomorial possession, the origin of which is unknown or so deeply involved in obscurity as to allow no possibility of proving whether the possessor has really derived his right from the original proprietor or received the possession from another.'

Savigny.

Vattel.

As regards the Roman Law, Sir William Markby points out that 'Savigny considers that in the Roman Law the principle of time immemorial applied only to three kinds of rights—*viae vicinales*; rights connected with the prevention of floods; and rights connected with the supply of water. He seems to think that it was as being matters of public concern that the principle of time immemorial was applied to these rights. The notion of the Roman lawyers seems to have been that in regard to a thing '*cujus memoriam retustes excedit*,' if the public were interested in it, they ought to treat the case in the same way as if a *lex* had authorised it. As regards the length of time which would be considered time immemorial, '*cujus contrarii non extat memoria*.' The '*contrarii memoria*' seems to mean a recollection of the time when no such right existed. If there is a *memoria* of this, any presumption in favour of the right is excluded. And the result of two passages in the Digest upon the subject appears to be that if any person comes forward and can say, either from his own recollection or from the information of others speaking from their own recollection that the thing was at one time illegal, the presumption will be excluded. But more ancient information than this as to any illegality would not be sufficient. One may ask why in the Roman Law, the doctrine of immemorial enjoyment was not applied to corporeal things; I cannot answer the question with any amount of confidence, but I may be permitted to suggest that it was perhaps so, because the rule of *prescriptio longissimi temporis* would, on thirty year's possession, make the possessor completely secure against any future disturbance by the previous owner, so that recourse to the doctrine of 'immemorial enjoyment' would hardly be necessary in such a case, while under the Hindu Law by reason of the doubt which has existed regarding the recognition of the doctrine of extinctive prescription and also by reason of the limitation under which alone it can be applied, the doctrine of 'immemorial enjoyment' cannot be regarded as similarly superfluous. I may, however, venture to observe that the question of necessity or superfluity does not necessarily exclude considerations of logical consistency, and the foundation of the doctrine of 'immemorial enjoyment' being what it is, I do not quite see how the Roman Lawyers could, with a strict regard for the underlying principle, limit its application to a few incorporeal rights.

English Law

Turning now to the English Law, we find that it was very early recognised that long continued enjoyment of an incorporeal right *nec vi* (peaceably), *nec clam* (openly), and *nec precario* (as of right) would establish the right. In explaining long enjoyment, Lord Coke says that it has reference to 'the time given by law, which in England is the time whereof there is no memory of man to the contrary.' Sir William Markby points out that Littleton identified prescription and enjoyment from time immemorial, that he did not base its operation upon the presumption of a legal title, and that he assumed time immemorial to mean the time whereof there was no memory of man to the contrary.

Littleton

The English lawyers following Littleton also adopted time immemorial as the basis of their law; but they at the same time (in this respect not following Littleton) adopted the principle that enjoyment from time immemorial was not a mode of acquisition, but only afforded a presumption of legal origin; but it so happened that shortly after the enactment of the statute of Westminister in 1275, the English lawyers came to hold that nothing was beyond human memory which had its beginning since the time of Richard I, A.D. 1189. The result was that the protection afforded by English Law to long enjoyment was very slender, and gradually as the

Introduction of the presumtion of legal origin.

The first year of the reign of Richard I.

Inconvenience of the rule.

time which had elapsed since the time of Richard I became longer and longer, the protection so afforded became almost shadowy and ineffectual. Hence the Judges, about the end of the eighteenth century, tried, by a sort of fiction, to afford an ample protection to long enjoyment, by introducing the presumption of a modern lost grant; but it was, at all events, as Sir William Markby calls it, a clumsy legal fiction which has now been almost, though not altogether, superseded by the provisions of the Prescription Act, also called Lord Tenterden's Act, making the presumption of legal origin conclusive after an enjoyment of twenty years, provided the enjoyment fulfils certain conditions which I need not here explain. "The Act", says Sir William Markby, "does not make the prescription or the English Law any thing different from what it was before. It does not do away with the presumption of a legal origin. Nor does it even apply to all kinds of *jura in re aliena,* but only to those mentioned in the Act. The protection of other rights remains as before, and juries are still often gravely asked to presume that grants have been lost which no one believes ever to have existed."

Presumption of a modern lost grant.

Hindu and English Law compared,

This, then, is the condition of the English Law, and if we compare with this the doctrine of the Hindu Law, which I have tried to explain above, it seems to me quite clear that the Hindu Law will not suffer from the comparison. It bases the protection afforded to long possession or enjoyment on a presumption of its legal origin, and then correctly traces the real foundation of the presumption in the continuity of the possession from time immemorial, then, in determining what 'time immemorial' means, it does not fall into the error, if not the folly, of the English Law, of fixing upon a fixed point of time as the limit of living human recollection, although time flows, as it has always done and the distance from that fixed point increases every day, so that the protection sought to be afforded gradually dwindles away; then, again, in as much as the principle on which the rule is based is of universal application, the Hindu Law does not limit its application to this or that right, but allows it to have its full scope and operation wherever the reason of the rule applies. After this short comparative review I leave it to others to say whether the Hindu Law of Prescription does not deserve the serious attention of every student of historical and comparative jurisprudence; and whether, in many of its features, it does not compare very favourably with some of the most advanced systems of western law; it is unfortunate that the subject has not, up to the present moment, been studied with the proper amount of care; otherwise, I doubt not, it would have demonstrated how wonderfully the influence of universal reason permeating human institutions bridges over the gulf of time and space, and produces similarity of the most extraordinary kind.

LECTURE V.

THE LAW OF SUCCESSION.

The scope of the present lecture.

The subject of the present lecture is the Law of Succession. It will be readily understood that I do not propose to enter into a discussion of the details of the subject; my only aim is to explain some of the fundamental principles which furnish the key to the understanding of the law of succession as unfolded by the Mitakshara and the Dayabhaga Schools; these principles when properly understood, will elucidate how and in what respects the Mitakshara and the Dayabhaga Schools differ from each other, and the elucidation of these differences will, I hope, clear up much that seems to be obscure to a student who, without being initiated into the secret which gives, as it were, an entrance into the interior of the shrine, merely tries to gather as much information as he can by peeping from outside. Knowledge of isolated details so long as they are not deduced from and connected with their underlying principles is, however, as slippery as it is confusing, and it is better to have a firm grasp over a few fundamental principles than to collect mechanically a mass of disjointed details.

I have used the word 'succession' to describe the subject matter of the present lecture, but, I am afraid, that the word has been somewhat loosely used, since, as you will see, we shall have to deal not only with acquisition of ownership through kinship after the cessation of the interest of the last holder, but also with acquisition of ownership through the same source along with the last holder. Speaking generally, therefore, we may say that the scope of the present lecture is to deal with acquisition of ownership through kinship to the last holder independently of any voluntary act on his part designed to have this effect.

दाय what it means? According to the Mitakshara.

The word used to denote property which has devolved upon a person in this manner is दाय. The Mitakshara explains this term as signifying 'the wealth which becomes the property of another solely by reason of his kinship to the owner'[1] and the word 'solely' (एव) is intended to exclude the co-operation of any other cause such as a gift or a sale on the part of the owner and to lay stress on the fact that it is the relationship alone that determines the accrual of ownership.

According to the Dayabhaga.

The Dayabhaga, on the other hand, defines the term as signifying 'the wealth in which property, dependent on kinship to the former owner, arises upon the cessation of his ownership thereof.'

The two definitions compared.

On a comparison of the two definitions, you will observe that according to the Mitakshara, it is not absolutely necessary that the ownership of a person must cease in order that his kinsmen may step into his shoes and acquire ownership in his property, but that, according to the Dayabhaga, the cessation of the ownership of a person is a condition precedent to the acquisition of ownership by his kinsman by virtue of the relationship that exists between them.

This furnishes one of the fundamental distinctions between the two schools.

The difference between the Dayabhaga and the Mitakshara doctrines, which forms one of the fundamental distinctions between the two shools governed by those two works, therefore, consists in this: according to the Dayabhaga, ownership to a person's property by virtue of kinship to that individual arises only when that person's ownership comes to an end which happens usually on his death, so that before this, no one, however close his

[1] दायशब्देन यद्धनं स्वायिसम्बन्धादेव निमित्तादन्यस्य स्वं भवति तदुच्यते ।
मिताक्षरा । दायभाग प्रकरणम् ।

relationship to the owner may be, can claim to have acquired an owner's right to the property which still belongs to his relation; heirship, according to the Dayabhaga, is, therefore, succession in the strict sense of the term by reason of kinship to the former owner, or to be more precise, of kinship to and survival of the former owner; according to the Mitakshara, on the other hand, there are certain relations who, at the moment of their birth, acquire ownership in the property of their relations, so that the accrual of ownership does not, in their case, depend upon the cessation of the ownership of the previous owners, but they, along with their relations, the previous owners, become co-owners in the same property, thus, in their case, it may be said that it is their birth that is the cause of the accrual of their ownership, and hence this doctrine has been designated as जन्मस्वत्ववाद or the doctrine of acquisition of property by birth, as distinguished from the Dayabhaga doctrine which, for contrast, may be characterised as उपरम स्वत्ववाद or the doctrine of the acquisition of ownership upon the demise of the last owner.

जन्मस्वत्ववाद contrasted to उपरमस्वत्ववाद

Acquisition of ownership by birth how far it extends.

You must, however, remember that even, according to the Mitakshara, the acquisition of property by birth is limited only to a very few relations, *viz.*, the son and other direct male descendants of the owner. The Mitakshara in speaking of the relations who thus acquire a co-ownership by their very birth makes mention of sons and grandsons, but the Viramitrodaya explains that the great-grandsons also are included in the same category; beyond these the principle of acquisition of co-ownership by birth does not extend; as regards other relations they succeed in the same ways as heirs under the Dayabhaga School upon the demise of the previous owner. Upon this distinction between the two classes of relations is founded the Mitakshara classification of दाय into the two

The distinction between unobstructed and obstructed heritage.

divisions of अप्रतिबन्ध (unobstructed) and सप्रतिबन्ध (obstructed). The classification is thus explained in the Mitakshara: 'The wealth of the father or the paternal grand-father becomes the property of his sons or grandsons, in right of their being his sons or grandsons; and that is a devolution of property not subject to obstruction. But property devolves upon parents, (or uncles) brothers and the rest, upon the demise of the owner, if there be no male issue; and thus the actual existence of a son and the survival of the owner, are impediments to the succession; and on their ceasing, the property devolves upon the successor in right of his being uncle or brother. This is an inheritance subject to obstruction.[1] The characteristic difference between the two classes is therefore this, that in a case falling under the former class title arises immediately upon the birth of the kinsman so that nothing can impede its accrual, while, in a case falling under the latter class the accrual of title is merely contingent upon the non-existence of an heir belonging to a superior class and the survival of the claimant on the demise of the previous owner; so that there being these impediments to the succession it cannot be said until the demise of the last owner whether the title in question will or will not arise.

The distinction has no place in the Dayabhaga.

You will at once understand that this distinction between devolution of property 'subject to obstruction' and 'not subject to obstruction' has no place in the doctrine of the Dayabhaga School, for according to it neither the son nor any other kinsman acquires any title by birth, so that until an owner dies no one can say who will succeed to his property and, therefore, even the succession of the son is liable to be obstructed by the survival of the father; thus the result is, that if you choose to employ the expression

---

[1] Mitakshara Chap. I. Sec. 1, 3.

'succession' under the Dayabhaga School, it must always be regarded as सप्रतिबन्ध (liable to obstruction.)

To what kinds of father's property does the peculiar Mitakshara doctrine apply?

I have explained that according to the Mitakshara, the son acquires co-ownership with the father from the moment of his birth. It may, however, be asked whether this is limited to the ancestral property in the hands of the father which has devolved upon him as unobstructed property from his paternal ancestors or also extends over other kinds of property of the father including property inherited by him from persons other than his paternal ancestors and his self-acquisition.

Mayne's view.

Mr. Mayne says 'that all property which a man inherits from a direct male ancestor, not exceeding three degrees higher than himself, is ancestral property, and is at once held by himself in coparcenary with his own issue. But where he has inherited from a collateral relation, as for instance from a brother, nephew, cousin, or uncle, it is not ancestral property; consequently his own descendants are not coparceners with him'.[1] Similarly he maintains, that property inherited by a man from a female or through female, not being ancestral property as explained above, partakes of the same character as property inherited from a collateral; and with regard to father's self-acquisition he says that *ex-vi-termini* it does not belong to the co-heirs.[2]

The opinion criticised.

Now, it seems to me that this statement of the Mitakshara law is not strictly accurate, although the inaccuracy, such as it is, may not make much difference in the result. As I understand the Mitakshara, the right acquired by a son by birth in the property of his father is not limited to any particular kind of property, but extends over all the property of the father, however, acquired.

---

[1] Mayne's Hindu Law p. 344.

[2] Mayne's Hindu Law p. 451.

Nature of son's interest in father's ancestral property and in father's own acquisitions.

Thus after an elaborate discussion on the maintainability of the doctrine that property arises by birth, the Mitakshara concludes that therefore (*i.e.*, on the grounds already set forth) it is certain that property in the paternal as well as grand paternal (पैतामह) estate arises by birth ;[1] now in this passage the separate mention of paternal and grand-paternal (*i.e.*, ancestral) estates as being both subject to the accrual of son's right by birth implies, that the son acquires his right by birth in all the properties of his father whether it be ancestral or not, and this conclusion is further strengthened by the fact, that in winding up the discussion, the Mitakshara says that 'although property arises by birth in paternal as well as grand-paternal (ancestral) estate, we shall mention a distinctive peculiarity in dealing with the text "land acquired by grand-father etc.," the peculiarity so promised to be subsequently stated being, that in regard to property derived from the grand-father, the father's right of free alienation is restrained by the co-equal co-ownership of the son, while in regard to the properties acquired by the father himself (whether by collateral succession or any other mode of acquisition) the son has no right to object to the father's alienation but must acquiesce therein. The distinction thus stated does not, as Mr. Mayne seems to think, indicate that the son's right by birth is limited only to the ancestral property in the hands of the father, but it only shows that although the right extends over all the properties of the father, yet the son cannot oppose an alienation by the father except in the case of ancestral property. This is made quite clear by the following passage in the Mitakshara ; "consequently the difference

---

[1] तथापैतृके पैतामहे च द्रव्ये जन्मनैव स्वत्वम् ।

The translation of this passage by Mr. Colebrooke 'therefore it is a settled point, that property in the *paternal or ancestral* estate is by birth' may be misleading.

is this : although he has a right by birth in his father's and in grand father's property, still, since he is dependent on his father in regard to the paternal estate and since the father has a predominant interest as it was acquired by himself, the son must acquiesce in the father's disposal of his own acquired property ; but since, both have indiscriminately a right in the grand father's estate, the son has a power of interdiction (if the father be dissipating the property)." It may be that this recognition of ownership in the son while he has no power to control the action of the father either by restraining him from alienating the property or by forcing him to come to a partition is not of much value ; still it is none the less important to have a clear and correct idea of the scope of the doctrine which I am so long seeking to explain, together with such qualifications as it may be subject to. My conclusion, then, is, that the right which a son acquires by birth in his father's property is not limited to ancestral property alone, but extends over the entire property of the father, although the extent of the right is not everywhere the same but depends on the nature of the property.

Father's power of alienation without the concurrence of the sons—how far it extends :

What has been stated above with regard to the father's power of alienation without the concurrence of the son may suggest that the father is absolutely free to dispose of his self-acquired property in any way he likes, and that so far as the ancestral property is concerned he has no power of alienation except with the consent of the son. Both these propositions, however, seem to require qualification, the first with regard to self-acquired immovables, and the second with regard to ancestral movables. As regards the self-acquired immovable property of the father, you have observed that in a passage which I have cited from Mitakshara it is stated generally that "since he is dependent on his father in regard to the paternal estate, and since the

Self acquired immovable property : Can the father alienate it at

his pleasure without the concurrence of the sons ?

father has a predominant interest as it was acquired by himself, the son must acquiesce in the father's disposal of his own acquired property ;"[1] this would seem to indicate that the father can dispose of his self-acquired property, whether it be movable or immovable, in any way he likes, and the son must acquiesce in it ; there is however an earlier passage which seems to lay down a different rule, for it is there stated that 'the father is subject to the control of his sons and the rest in regard to the immovable estate, whether acquired by himself or inherited from his father or other predecessor, since it is ordained. 'Though immovable or bipeds have been acquired by a man himself, a gift or sale of them should not be made without convening all the sons. They who are born, and they who are yet unbegotten, and they who are still in the womb, require the means of support, no gift or sale should, therefore, be made."[2] There is thus an apparent conflict between these two passages, and the question is how to reconcile them; the most obvious way of reconciling them is to read the special rule having relation to the father's immovable property as an exception to the general rule regarding the father's acquired property of all kinds, so that the father's uncontrolled right of alienation will, on this interpretation, be restricted to properties other than immovable. This view seems to find support from the Viramitrodaya, it says that 'although the ownership of the sons and grandsons in the property of the father and the grandfather arises by birth alone, still by reason of the texts previously stated, the sons being dependent on the father, with respect to the father's self-acquired property, and the father being entitled to superiority on account of his being the acquirer, the sons must give their assent to the disposal

Conflicting texts : how they can be reconciled.

[1] Mitakshara Chap. I. Sec. V. 10.

[2] Mitakshara Chap. I. Sec. I. 27.

by the father of his self-acquired property excepting land and slaves, by reason of the previously cited text, namely —'immovables and bipeds, etc.'[1] and in another passage it is pronounced that "of immovable property, whether ancestral or self-acquired, the father may make gift and the like only with the consent of the sons by reason of the text previously cited, *viz.*—'Immovable and bipeds, although acquired by a man himself, shall not be gifted away or sold without the consent of all the sons.'[2] It has, however, been decided by the Privy Council in the case of Rao Balwant Singh *vs.* Rani Kishori[3] that the passage in which the Mitakshara prohibits the alienation of his self-acquired immovable property by the father without the assent of the sons merely lays down a rule, founded on moral and religious considerations, which carries with it no legal obligation. Referring to the apparent conflict in the Mitakshara, their Lordships observe that 'all these old text-books and commentaries are apt to mingle religious and moral considerations, not being positive laws with rules intended for positive laws.' It is, as their Lordships think, the most reasonable inference that the precepts in Mita. I Sec. 1, belong to the former class of precepts, and of sections 4 and 5 to the latter. Now I am quite free to admit that the text 'Immovable bipeds etc.' on which the Mitakshara relies in support of its position that a father should not dispose of his self-acquired immovable property without the assent of his sons has the appearance of being a moral or religious injunction, since the maintenance of children born and unborn which is brought forward as a ground for the prohibition seems to suggest that the precept is directory and not mandatory in its character;

Decision of the Privy Council in Rao Balwant Singh *vs.* Rani Kishori.

The decision considered.

[1] Viramitrodaya Chap. II, Pt. 1, 17.

[2] Viramitrodaya Chap. II, Pt. 1, 22.

[3] 25 I.A. 54; S.C. 26 All 267.

at the same time it may be pointed out that in Chapter I, Sec. I, the Mitakshara specially refers to several directions relating to alienation of property and expressly declares that any violation of them will not in any way affect the validity of the transaction and explains the purposes for which they were introduced ; this will appear from paragraphs 31 and 32 where the Mitakshara discusses the formalities of alienation of immovable property to which I have already referred in my last lecture, and from paragraph 30 which deals with the requirement of the consent of separated kinsmen and points out that 'among separated kindred, the consent of all tends to the facility of the transaction, by obviating any future doubt whether they be separate or united ; it is not required on account of sufficient power in the single owner ; and the transaction is consequently valid even without the consent of the separated kinsmen' ; so it is abundantly clear that in writing Chapter I, Sec. I, the author of the Mitakshara was not unmindful of the distinction that exists between the rules 'intended for positive laws' and the rules not so intended, and in the very section he points out how several rules deducible from the texts of the Dharmasastras should not be treated as 'intended for positive laws,' and would not, if not complied with, affect the validity of the transaction : that being so, is it at all unreasonable to presume that if he had not considered it essential for the validity of the transaction that the sons should consent to the alienation of father's self-acquired immovable property, he would have expressly said so, just as he did in relation to the consent of separated kinsmen, co-villagers, and neighbours ? Moreover, the expression used in the Mitakshara *viz.*, 'subjection to the control of the son and the rest (पुत्रादिपारतन्त्र्य) to denote the limitation of the father's power of alienation does not seem to indicate a mere moral rule but a real limitation of power intended to have a legal bearing. It is, therefore, not at all clear that the way in which their Lordships of the Privy Council have attempted to reconcile the apparent conflict between the two passages in the Mitakshara is correct, and I am not sure that they have not departed from the strict Mitakshara law under a misconception that the distinction between a legal rule and a moral or religious recommendation was not quite familiar to it, a misconception which is all the more inexplicable because in the very section with which they were concerned (*viz.*, Chap. I, Sec. I) there is ample evidence to show that the distinction was fully recognised and its importance clearly appreciated by the author. It may, however, be asked that if the consent of separated kinsmen, co-villagers, and neighbours be regarded as non-essential, why should the consent of the son with reference to the present question be not treated in the same light? It seems to me that there is a very reasonable answer to this question and it is this; the consent of separated kinsmen, co-villagers and neighbours could not be required on account of any sort or ownership that they could claim in the property to be transferred, for in fact they had none, and as the transferor had thus full dominion over the property an alienation by him would on the principles explained by me in the last lecture, pass a good title without that consent; the Mitakshara, therefore, explains the requirement of the consent in these cases on the ground that it was either required to give a greater publicity to the transaction or to prevent the possibility of a future dispute; the son, however, acquires by birth an interest in the property of the father, and this, as I have explained above, is not limited to ancestral property but also extends over the self-acquired property of the father apparently, therefore, in the absence of any special ground the father cannot be said to have absolute dominion over his self-acquired property in as much as the son has, also, acquired an interest therein from the moment of his brith; hence, the consent of the latter to an alienation by the father of such property cannot, on ordinary principles, be regarded as non-essential, unless it be possible to assign some special ground for considering otherwise; the Mitakshara however, says that in the case of self-acquired proprety of the father such a special ground does exist since by reason of the dependence of the son on him, and also in view of the predominant interest which he has in his self-acquired property, the son cannot oppose an alienation by him of such porperty, but should rather acquiesce therein; now, it may be, here, observed that the Mitakshara does not say that the consent of the son is not at all necessary, but points out that in as much as it is the duty of the son to give his consent in such a case, he cannot oppose the transaction on the ground that his consent has not been obtained; with regard to immovable property, however, a distinction may very well be drawn, and it may be fairly contended that in as much as the Sastras prohibit an alienation by the father without the son's consent, the latter may legitimately withhold his consent to a dissipation by the father of his immovable property although he may have acquired it himself, and by the reason of co-ownership which the son has acquired from his birth this consent cannot be regarded as non-essential to the validity of the transaction. This position is further strengthened by the fact that in the Mitakshara as well as in the Viramitrodaya the dependence of the father in making an alienation of immovable property, whether ancestral or self-acquired, is laid down in one and the same sentence [1] and it would be opposed to the well-known

[1] स्थावरेतु स्वार्ज्जिते पित्रादि प्राप्ते च पुत्रादि पारतन्त्र्यमेव ।
Mitakshara. Chap. I. Sec. I. 27.

canon of construction that a word once pronounced can convey only one meaning [1] to maintain that it means one thing when the property is ancestral, and another when it is self-acquired, nay, the Viramitrodaya expressly declares that 'with regard to immovable property, whether self-acquired or inherited from the father or the ancestor, the dependence on the sons &c., is alike.' [2] It should not be considered that the acceptance of this position would obliterate all distinction between self-acquired and ancestral immovable property in the hands of the father, for, apart from anything else, the son has a right to call upon the father to come to a partition with regard to the latter property and not with regard to the former.

Power of the father over ancestral movables.

Let us now turn to the case of ancestral movables in regard to which the proposition that the father has no right to alienate ancestral property without the consent of the son seems to require qualification. The qualification is founded upon the text of Narada declaring that 'the father is master, even of all gems, pearls, and corals; but neither the father nor the grandfather is so of the entire immovable property.' [3] This seems to indicate that the power of the father over ancestral movables is only limited as Mr. Colebrooke said, by his own discretion and by a sense of spiritual responsibility; it has, however, been suggested that since Vijnaneswara, referring to the father's power of alienating such property says that although property in the paternal as well as grand-paternal (ancestral)

---

1 सकृदुच्चारित: शब्द: सकृदर्थं गमयति ।

2 स्थावरादौतु स्वार्ज्जितं पित्रादि परम्पराप्राप्तं च पुत्रादिपारतन्त्र्यं तुल्यमेव ।
Viramitrodaya. Chap I. 30.

मणिमुक्ता प्रवालानां सर्व्वस्यैव पिता प्रभु: ।
स्थावरस्य तु सर्व्वस्य न पिता न पितामह: ॥

estate arises by birth, still the father has an independent power in the disposal of effects other than immovables for necessary acts of duty, and for purposes prescribed by texts of the Sastras such as gifts through affection, support of the family, relief from distress, and so forth,'[1] it should be taken that the father has no absolute power of disposing of movables at his own discretion, but only for the purposes, indicated in the above passage. The question is not free from difficulty; it may be said, on the one hand, that this would be putting a narrow construction upon the passage cited from the Mitakshara, for, the purposes enumerated in that passage are merely illustrative, and they refer, as the passage stands, to self-acquired movables also, in relation to which the father's power of free disposal cannot be possibly gainsaid; moreover, it may be pointed out that the text of Narada does not impose any limitation upon the father's control over movables, and no limitation can possibly be deduced from it; and the Viramitrodaya in one place says without any qualification that as regards gems, pearls, etc., though inherited from the grand-father, the father alone has independence by reason of the previously cited texts, *viz.*, the father is master of all the gems, pearls and corals, &c.[2] On the other hand, the text of Yajnavalkya that the ownership of father and son is similar in land which was acquired by the grand-father, in a corrody, and in chattels (which belonged to him), and the commentary of the Mitakshara based on this text that since both (*i.e.*, father and son) have indiscriminately a right in the grand-father's estate the son has a power of interdiction created a difficulty in adopting the above view. Under the circumstances the best way of reconciling these conflicting considerations is

[1] Mita. Chap. I. Sec. 1. 27.

[2] Viramitrodaya, Chap. II, part 1, Sec. 17.

to hold that the father has the power of alienating ancestral movables at his discretion, but if he begins to dissipate them the son has the right to object on the basis of his co-equal ownership. The explanation of Nilakanta that the independence of the father in relation to gems, pearls, and corals, &c., relates only to 'the wearing and other use of ear-rings, etc., but does not extend to gift or other alienation '[1] is opposed to the Mitakshara, and cannot be held to contain a correct exposition of the Mitakshara view.

The Dayabhaga brushes all these distinctions aside.

The Dayabhaga, however, brushes all these distinctions aside by holding that the father, so long as he is alive, is the absolute owner of all his property whether ancestral or self-acquired, and the son does not acquire any ownership by his birth but only upon the extinction of the father's ownership either by his death or in any other way. The absolute ownership of the father being thus established it follows, on the principles which I have explained in the last lecture, that he can alienate his property at his discretion, and the texts which seem to require the concurrence of the sons or of anybody else in certain cases are all explained as laying down mere moral or religious injunctions. Thus after maintaining that the consent of divided or undivided kinsmen required by the text of Vyasa in the alienation of immovable property is merely directory and its absence does not invalidate the transaction, Jimūtavāhana goes on to say "so likewise other texts such as 'Though immovables and bipeds have been acquired by a man himself a gift or sale of them *should* not *be made* by him without convening all the sons' must be interpreted in the same manner. For here the words 'should be made' must be understood.

Father's power of alienation under the Dayabhaga.

Prohibitory texts do not affect the validity of the transaction.

[1] V. May Chap. V. Sec. 1.

Therefore, since it is denied that a gift or sale should be made, the precept is infringed by making one. But the gift or transfer is not well; for a fact cannot be altered by a hundred texts."[1]

The positions summarised: Mitakshara

To sum up the discussion, we find that according to the Mitakshara the son, upon his birth, acquires an interest in the property of his father, whether it be ancestral or self-acquired; with regard to ancestral property, the interest so acquired is so far equal to that of the father, that it entitles him to call upon the father to come to a partition, and with regard to immovable property it gives him the further right to control an alienation by the father without his consent.

Dayabhaga

According to the Dayabhaga, on the other hand, the son does not become co-owner with the father during his lifetime, since his ownership arises only upon the extinction of the father's ownership; he, therefore, can not compel the father to partition the property with him, and the latter is free to give or sell the property without his consent.

Is there any recognition of righ fath prop rty duri ng his lifet the Dayabhaga?

Does the Dayabhaga, then, recognise no interest whatsoever in the son in the father's property before succession opens out to him on the extinction of the father's ownership either upon his demise or otherwise? It appears that, even according to the Dayabhaga, the father may, at his option, divide his property among himself and his sons, and in doing so, although he may distribute his self-acquired property in any way he likes, he cannot make an unequal distribution among the sons, of the ancestral immovable property, corrody and slaves, and he cannot also withhold them altogether from the sons by refusing to give them any share whatsoever or by retaining more than a double share for himself. Thus referring to the text of Yajnavalkya, "The ownership of father and son is

[1] Dayabhaga. Chapter II. Secs. 29 and 30.

similar in land which was acquired by his father, and in a corrody and in chattels," Jimūtavāhana explains that chattels must mean slaves, and goes on to say that "the meaning of the text may be as set forth by Dhareswara, "a father, occupied in giving allotments at his pleasure, has equal ownership with his sons in the paternal grand-father's estate. He is not privileged to make an unequal distribution of it, at his choice, as he is in regard to his own acquired wealth. So Vishnu says, "When a father separates his sons from himself, his will regulates the division of his own acquired wealth. But, in the estate inherited from the grand-father, the ownership of father and son is equal. This is very clear. When the father separates his son himself he may, by his own choice, give them greater or less allotments, if the wealth were acquired by himself; but not so, if it were property inherited from the grand-father; because they have an equal right to it. The father has not in such case an unlimited discretion." From these and other passages it is perfectly clear that although Jimūtavāhana repudiated the theory that property arose from birth, he allowed to the sons at least so much interest in ancestral property as would place a restraint upon the unlimited discretion of the father in distributing that property, if he, at his option, chose to distribute it. Referring to this restraint Mr. Mayne observes that "in the very chapter in which he (Jimūtavāhana) lays down that the absolute ownership of the father enables him to deal with his ancestral property as he likes, he also lays down that if he chooses to distribute it, he must do so upon general principles of equity, and cannot even for himself, reserve more than a double share. He affirms for one purpose the very ownership by birth which he denies for another." It may, perhaps, be going too far to say that the recognition of this restraint upon the father's absolute discretion in distributing ancestral property amounts to the admission of a qualified ownership in the son in respect of such property even during the lifetime of the father, for to speak of ownership without the least *right* of enjoying the usufruct except at the option of another may seem to involve a contradiction in terms; it may, however, be said without any impropriety that the limits imposed upon the absolute discretion of the father in distributing the ancestral property in any way he likes to the prejudice of the sons show that the Dayabhaga admitted that they had an interest in that class of father's property even during his lifetime which might be of importance under certain contingencies. The position thus accorded to the sons may be compared to that of *sui heredes* under the Roman Law; they were children and grand-children in the power of the deceased who on his death became *sui juris*, and with regard to them, it is stated, in the Institutes of Justinian, that they are *sui heredes* "because they are family heirs, and even in the lifetime of their father, are considered owners of the inheritance in a certain degree."[1] It may also be remarked that just as under the Roman Law grand-children cannot be regarded as *sui heredes* unless their father has ceased to be *suus heres*, in the lifetime of his father, having been either cut off by death, or otherwise freed from paternal authority, so, under the Dayabhaga law also, the grand-sons cannot claim to share the inheritance with their uncles unless their father has died or otherwise become incapable of inheriting during the lifetime of his father. Resemblances like these are so startling and there are so many of them to be found in almost all the different branches of jurisprudence that one often wonders how they came about, unless the ancestors of the two people (the

The position of the son compared to that of *sui heredes* in the Roman Law.

Striking resemblances: What they seem to indicate.

[1] Institutes Lib. II, Tit. XIX, 2.

Romans and the Hindus) had at one time, inhabited the same country and been governed by the same institutions which they carried with them in their migrations to shape the further development of their legal ideas. Comparative Jurisprudence, when properly studied, thus supports the conclusions of Comparative Philology, and it is because the Hindu Jurisprudence has not been studied with that amount of care which has been bestowed upon the study of the Sanskrit language, that we do not as yet possess sufficient materials to guide our researches and help us in our conclusions.

Distinction regarding the devolution of property on the death of a member of a joint family between the Dayabhaga and the Mitakshara Schools. Dayabhaga.

I will now turn to the next great distinction between the Mitakshara and the Dayabhaga Schools. This relates to the devolution of property on the death of a member of a joint family. According to the Dayabhaga the position of a deceased owner as the member of a joint family does not make any difference whatsoever for the purposes of succession to the property left by him as a part of the joint family property; the person who is entitled to succeed will be determined in the usual way, and as regards that it would have made no difference if instead of being a member of an undivided joint family he had been separated from his coparceners before his death.

Mitakshara.

The Mitakshara law, however, proceeds upon entirely different principles; according to that system to quote the words of Mr. Mayne 'there is no such thing as succession, properly so called, in an undivided family. The whole body of such a family, consisting of males and females, constitutes a sort of corporation, some of the members of which are coparceners, that is, persons who on partition would be entitled to demand a share, while others are only entitled to maintenance. In Malabar and Canara, where partition is not allowed, the idea of heirship would never present itself to the mind of any member of the family.

Each person is simply entitled to reside and be maintained in the family house, and to enjoy that amount of affluence and consideration which arises from his belonging to a family possessed of greater or less wealth. As he dies out his claims cease, and as others are born their claims arise. But the claims of each spring from the mere fact of their entrance into the family, not from their taking the place of any particular individual. Deaths may enlarge the beneficial interest of the survivors, by diminishing the number who have a claim upon the common fund, just as birth may diminish their interests by increasing the number of claimants. But although the fact that A is the child of B introduces him into the family, it does not give him any definite share in the property, for B himself has none. Nor upon the death of B does he succeed to anything, for B has left nothing behind to succeed to. Now in every part of India where the Mitakshara prevails the position of an undivided family is exactly the same, except that within certain limits each male member has a right to claim a partition, if he likes. But until they elect to do so, the property continues to devolve upon the members of the family for the time being by survivorship and not by succession. The position of any particular person as son, grand-son, or the like, or one of many sons or grand-sons, will be very important when the time for partition arrives; because it will determine the share to which he is then entitled. But until that time arrives he can never say, I am entitled to such a definite portion of the property; because the next year the proportion in which he would have a right to claim on a division might be much smaller, and the year after much larger, as births or deaths supervene'.[1] The above extract contains a clear exposition of the devolution of joint family property

[1] Mayne's Hindu Law, page 333.

under the Mitakshara law upon the death of one of its members. The difference between the Dayabhaga and the Mitakshara on this question being thus understood, let us see how far it can be deduced as the logical result of the corresponding difference between the Dayabhaga and the Mitakshara conceptions of co-ownership in undivided property. This difference will be made evident from a comparison of the definitions of partition or severence of co-ownership (विभाग) as given in the Dayabhaga and Mitakshara respectively.

How far the difference can be deduced from the corresponding difference regarding the conception of co-ownership in an undivided family.

Severence of co-ownership as defined in the Dayabhaga.

The Dayabhaga defines partition in the following manner: "Partition consists in manifesting (or in particularising) by the casting of lots or otherwise, a property which had arisen in lands or chattels, but which extended only to a portion of them, and which was previously unascertained, being unfit for exclusive appropriation, because no evidence of any ground of discrimination existed. Or partition is a special ascertainment of property, or making of it known (as inhering in a particular share with reference to a particular person)" [1].

The Mitakshara definition.

The Mitakshara, on the other hand, says that "Partition (or severence of co-ownership) is the adjustment of divers rights regarding the whole, by distributing them or particular portions of the aggregate." [2]

The defference explained.

प्रादेशिकस्वत्ववाद

The difference between the two views, therefore, consists in this: according to the Dayabhaga, each of the undivided coparceners has ownership, not over the entire joint property, but only over particular portions thereof which becomes

---

[1] Dayabhaga Chap. 1. Secs 8 & 9. एकदेशोपात्तस्यैव भूहिरण्यादावुत्पन्नस्य स्वत्वस्य विनिगमनाप्रमाणाभावेन वैशेषिकव्यवहारानर्हतया अव्यवस्थितस्य गुटिकापातादिना व्यञ्जनं विभागः। विशेषेण भजनं स्वत्वज्ञापनं वा विभागः (पुरुष विशेष निरूपितांश विशेषनिष्ठत्वेन इत्यर्थः इति श्रीकृष्णः)।

[2] Mitakshara Chap. 1. Secs. 1, 4. विभागोनाम द्रव्य समुदाय विषयानामनेक स्वाम्यानां तदेकदेशेषु द्रव्यस्य व्यवस्थापनम्।

manifest when upon partition these several portions are specifically allotted to the several coparceners, so that at no time does the ownership of one among several coparceners extends over the whole of the joint property but it always extends over a part, unascertained and undefined before partition, and ascertained and particularised after it. This doctrine, is therefore known as प्रादेशिकस्वत्ववाद or the doctrine of ownership in a part.

सामुदायिक स्वत्ववाद

According to Mitakshara, on the other hand, the ownership of each coparcener in an undivided family extends over the whole of the joint property, and each part thereof, although to borrow the words of Lord Westbury in Appovier's case, 'no individual member of that family, while it remains undivided can predicate of the joint and undivided property that he, that particular member, has a certain definite share.' [1] The result is that each co-owner is deemed to be the owner of the whole, in the same manner as other co-owners are also owners of the whole, the ownership of the one without excluding the co-ownership of the others. This view is known as सामुदायिक स्वत्ववाद or the doctrine of ownership in the whole.

The difference between the conceptions of ownership indicated above, has sometimes been expressed by saying that a Dayabhaga coparcener holds the property in quasi-severalty as if he were a tenant in common, whereas a Mitakshara coparcener holds the entire property and every part of it as if he were a joint tenant. It is unnecessary to pause and consider how far these descriptions are strictly accurate, for the analogies, as far as they go, are not likely to be misleading. What I am at present concerned with is to consider how far the difference between the Dayabhaga and the Mitakshara as regards

---

1 Appovier vs. Ram Subba Aiyar 11 Moo. I. A. 89.

the devolution of joint property upon the demise of one of the co-owners can be said to be a legitimate deduction from the difference in the conception of co-ownership explained above. Giving the matter my best consideration I am inclined to think that although it cannot be said that the doctrine of survivorship is necessarily bound up with the peculiar conception of co-ownership maintained by the Mitakshara School in as much as that conception is not necessarily inconsistent with the course of succession laid down by the Dayabhaga, yet it must be admitted that there is a very close affinity between the Mitakshara conception of co-ownership and the dotrine of survivorship as well as between the Dayabhaga conceptions of co-ownership and the devolution of property by succession. The reasons why I say so are these: you will remember that according to the Mitakshara conception of co-ownership each undivided co-parcener is the owner of the whole joint property. So that if one of them dies out while others remain, it does not create, if I may use the expression, a void to be filled up by a successor; the surviving co-parceners were from before the owners of the entire property, and no change is created by the death beyond the disappearance of a co-owner, who, when alive, was entitled to be maintained out of the family funds and to claim a share on partition. The doctrine of survivorship therefore, readily chimes in with a conception of co-ownership of this description, and I may almost say that it is incompatible with the conception of co-ownership as explained in the Dāyabhāga, for if the co-owners held the property in quasi-severalty, the most natural consequence would be that one of them being dead he would be followed by a successor as heir who would step into his shoes and occupy the same position as he did and if by a coincidence another co-owner becomes entitled to the

Relation of the doctrine of survivorship with the Mitakshara and the Dayabhaga conceptions of co-ownership.

inheritance he would come in as a successor and not as a survivor. The natural transition from the conception of co-ownership to the course of devolution laid down in each school is therefore abundantly clear; still I cannot say that the transition, though natural, is absolutely necessary, and my reasons are these. You are aware that Raghunandana, the author of Dāyatatta, is one of the most celebrated exponents of the Dāyabhāga doctrine; similarly, Nilakaṇṭha, the author of Vyavahara Mayukha, is in the main a follower of the Mitākṣara School; yet, although they do not depart from the course of devolution laid down by the leading authorities of the School to which they belong, they do differ from their masters as regards the conception of the interest of a co-parcener in an undivided family, for in this point Raghunandana controverts the position of Jimūtavāhana while Nilakaṇṭha supports the same. Thus referring to the Dāyabhāga definitions of partition Raghunandan objects that 'the definition is not accurate for how may it be certainly known since no text declares it, that the lot for each person, falls precisely on the article which was already his?' and gives his own definition of partition as 'a distributive adjustment, by lot or otherwise, of the property of relatives vested in them over the whole wealth, in right of the same relation, upon the extinction of the former owner's property.' S'rīkṛishṇa Tarkālankāra also, after making a faint attempt to repel the objections of Raghunandana, proceeds to observe without any comment that Harinath, Vijñanes'vara, Vachaspati Misra and their followers controvert the doctrine of Dāyabhāga and summarise their reasons for doing so, and hence Jagannātha has inferred that Raghunandana's opinion is indirectly admitted even by S'rīkṛishṇa. On the other hand Nilakaṇṭha observes that the prior undefined ownership of

The transition from the conception of co-ownership to the course of devolution laid down in each school is natural; but is it absolutely necessary?

Raghunandan's criticism of the Dayabhaga conceptions of co-ownership and partition.

Srikrishna Tarkalankara's view.

many brothers, &c., is defined (and made known) by partition. According to some, by the extinction of prior joint ownership extending over the whole property, a particular ownership is created in portions of it; but, the idea of extinction of a prior ownership and the creation of a new one, involves (the logical fault of) cumbrousness; (it is better, therefore, to conclude) that the particular ownership which was created in a portion was (only) made known by partition as inhering in a particular thing.[1] You will understand that I am not here concerned to consider the logical merit of these conflicting opinions, for the conclusion which I wish to deduce from their existence is, as I have already indicated, that although the doctrine of survivorship flows naturally from the Mitākshara conception of co-ownership it is not impossible for a supporter of the Dāyabhāga succession to adopt that conception, and that one who adopts the Dāyabhāga conception of co-ownership may also on the basis of specific authority, acknowledge the line of devolution pointed by the Mitākshara in the case of the demise of a co-parcener of an undivided family. It cannot however, be gainsaid that in the fitness of things the Mitākshara conception of co-ownership in an undivided family paves the ground if I may use the expression, for the doctrine of survivorship, while the Dāyabhāga conception is naturally antagonistic to it.

Nilakantha adopts the Dayabhaga conception of co-ownership

Conclusions deduced from the above.

The next question that I propose to discuss is the power of alienation of joint property by an undivided co-parcener. You may anticipate from the difference that I have pointed out between the Mitākshara and the Dāyabhāga conceptions of co-parcenery property, that the power of an undivided co-parcener in a Mitākshara family

Power of alienation undivid[illegible] co-parcen[illegible] difference between th[illegible] Dayabhaga and the Mitakshara Schools.

[1] Vyavahara Mayukha, Chap. IV, Sec. 1.

to alienate joint family property is not likely to be the same as that of an undivided co-parcener in a Dāyabhāga family. So long as the family continues joint no Mitākshara co-parcener can say that he has got a definite share in the joint property; it is true that he has got an interest in the whole of the joint property, but his interest is limited by the co-equal interest of the other co-parceners. That being so, it follows that one co-parcener cannot alienate either the whole or any portion of the joint property without infringing the rights of the other co-parcener, for there is not a single item of property in which one co-parcener can claim title to the exclusion of the others. Therefore, according to the strict Mitākshara

The Mitakshara view.

doctrine an undivided co-parcener has no right to alienate any portion of the joint property without the concurrence of the others, and if he does, it will be invalid in toto for the alienor cannot say that he has got a definite share to the extent of which the alienation may hold good, although it may be invalid as to the rest. Thus in the chapter dealing with the rescission of gifts, the Mitākshara lays down that joint property has been declared unfit to be given in the same way as pledges, trusts, deposits, etc., on the ground that it is not the property of the donor, meaning thereby that the donor has not got absolute dominion over it,[1] and it will follow from the principles explained by me in the last lecture that an alienation of such property must be treated as invalid; the matter is also made quite clear where the Mitākshara referring to the text 'separated kinsmen as those who are unseparared are equal in respect of immovables' goes on to

---

[1] स्वंदद्यादित्यनेन चास्वभूतानामन्वाहित याचितकाधि साधारण निक्षेपाणां पञ्चानामप्यदेयत्वं व्यतिरेकतो दर्शितम् ।

मिताक्षरादत्ता प्रदानिक प्रकरणम् ।

explain that 'among unseparated kinsmen the consent of all is indispensably requisite, because no one is fully empowered to make an alienation since the estate is common; but among separated kindred the consent of all tends to the facility of the transaction, by obviating any future doubt whether they be separate or re-united; it is not required on account of any want of suffiicient power in the single owner; and the transaction is consequently valid even without the consent of the seperated kinsmen;'[1] and commenting upon the same text the Viramitrodaya observes that 'although the incompetency without the consent of the others, is settled by reason of the co-equality of ownership, in joint property of undivided co-parceners, still the same is here particularly mentioned in respect of immovable property for the purpose of extolling its worth; but as regards the separated co-parceners what is said in this text is for the purpose of facility of proof in case of dispute." The position is, therefore fully established that an alienation by an undivided co-parcener without the consent of the other co-parceners is not valid. To this limitation upon the power of a single co-parcener there is an exception based upon the text 'even a single individual may conclude a donation, mortgage, or sale of immovable property during a season of distress, for the sake of the family, and specially for pious purposes,' which is explained by the Mitākshara to mean that 'while the sons and grand-sons are minors and incapable of giving their consent to a gift and the like or while brothers are so and continue unseparated; even one person who is capable, may conclude a gift, hypothecation, or sale of immovable property, if a calamity affecting the whole family require it, or the support of the family render it necessary or indispensable

Exception to the restriction on alienation.

[1] Mitāksara, Chap. I, Sec. I, 30.

duties, such as the obsequies of the father or the like, make it unavoidable."[1]

Judicial departure from the strict Mitakshara view.

What has been stated above represents the strict Mitākshara Law, but our courts have departed from it to various extents principally on equitable considerations although all the High Courts have not proceeded to the same extent. On such considerations, all the High Courts have held that the interest of an undivided co-parcener may be seized and sold in execution of a decree, obtained against him and the purchaser may enforce his right by coming to a partition and obtaining definite properties to the exclusion of the other co-parcener. As regards the position of an alienee for valuable consideration, where the purchase was made without the aid of the Court, all the Courts are not similarly agreed. Thus, the Bombay and Madras High Courts have held that an alienation for valuable consideration should be held valid to the extent of the share which the alienor would have received on partition, so that the alienee may sue for partition, and thus obtain possession of the share to which he had become entitled by his purchase. On the other hand, the Calcutta and the Allahabad High Courts seem to stick to the strict doctrine of the Mitākshara Law and maintain that a voluntary alienation of joint property by an undivided co-parcener whether for valuable consideration or not is invalid, but even there, in some cases, the Court, in setting aside the alienation, has enforced the equities in favour of the alienee in such a manner as to bring about exactly the same result as is worked out by the Bombay and Madras doctrine. As regards alienations without consideration all the Courts seem to be agreed that an undivided co-parcener can not dispose of the joint property even to the extent of the share

[1] Mitāksara, Chap. I, Section I, 28 & 29.

which he would receive on partition, and as the alienee, being a volunteer, can not put forward any equitable considerations, no indulgence should be shown to him. It is not within the province of these lectures to discuss the various decisions in so far as they are based upon principles extraneous to the Hindu Law, and I may point out that it has been acknowledged by their Lordships of the Judicial Committee in the case of Suraj Bunsi Koer *v.* Sheopersad Singh[1] that 'there can be little doubt that all such alienations, whether voluntary or compulsory are inconsistent with the strict theory of a joint and undivided Hindu family; and the law as established in Madras and Bombay has been one of gradual growth, founded upon the equity which a purchase for value has, to be allowed to stand in his vendor's shoes, and to work out his rights by means of a partition and these observations have been repeated by them in the subsequent case of Laksman Dada Naik *v.* Ramchandra Dada Naik.[2] I may, however, observe that it is somewhat difficult to understand how a person, who knowingly purchases a property inalienable under the law, can have much reason to complain when he finds that he can not reap any benefit under it, and the difficulty of allowing him any relief on strict principles of the Hindu law becomes almost insuperable when it is remembered that Manu declares that he who gives property declared unfit to be given and he who receives it are both liable to punishment as if they were thieves,"[3] and a purchase, with full knowledge of the circumstances, is as

---

[1] I. L. R. 5 Cal. 148 (166.)

[2] I. L. R. 5 Bom. 61 S. C. 7 I.A. 181.

अदेयं यश्च गृह्णाति यश्चादेयं प्रयच्छति ।

तावुभौ चौरवच्छास्यौ दाप्यौ चोत्तमसाहसम् ॥

वीरमित्रोदय दत्त प्रदानिक प्रकरण धृत वचनम् ।

much within the reason of the condemnation as the acceptance of a gift; our Courts have, however, thought fit to hold otherwise, and thus lent a helping hand to the diverse influences already at work in undermining the integrity of a joint family under the Mitakshara law.

The right of a Dayabhaga co-parcener to alienate his own share explained.

The position of an undivided co-parcener under the Dāyabhāga is, as already explained somewhat different, for his interest, according to the peculiar doctrine of Jimūtavāhana, does not extend over the whole joint property but only over a part which is only defined and made manifest by a subsequent partition; therefore, it is possible for a Dāyabhāga co-parcener to say, even before partition, that he has got a definite share in the joint property although it cannot be allocated before a partition actually takes place. This being the Dāyabhāga conception of co-ownership in an undivided family it follows that it is open to a Dāyabhāga co-parcener to transfer his own share in the joint property, and such a transfer will be valid even without the concurrence of the other co-parceners who cannot legitimately interdict an alienation of what is not their own. Thus Jimūtvāhana expressly says that 'It should not be alleged, that by the text of Vyāsa (A single co-parcener may not without consent of the rest, make a sale or gift of the whole immovable estate, nor of what is common to the family. Separated kinsmen, as those who are unseparated are equal in respect of immovables for one has not power over the whole, to give, mortgage or sell it) one person has no power to make a sale or other transfer of such property. For here also (in the very instance of land held in common) as in the case of other goods, there equally exists a property consisting in the power of disposal at pleasure. But the texts of Vyasa, exhibiting a prohibition, are intended to show a moral offence, since the family is distressed by a sale, gift or

Texts to the contrary how reconciled.

other transfer which argues a disposition in the person to make an ill use of his power as owner. They are not meant to invalidate the sale or other transfer.[1] The position of the Dāyabhāga upon this point is clearly explained by Śrīkṛiṣṇa Tarkālaṅkār in the 11th Chapter of his Dāyacrama Saṃgraha headed 'the discussion whether common property is or is not fit to be given by one.' In this chapter he first of all points out that there are certain lawyers who contend that one co-parcener has no right to dispose of any portion of the joint property and then explains that this view is founded upon the doctrine of co-equal right in the whole according to which all co-parceners have property in the entire property and hence a gift, a sale or any other sort of transfer made by one would be invalid. But says he 'this cannot be correct since the author of Dāyabhāga has refuted the doctrine of co-equal right in the whole for want of sufficient basis. Hence the author of Dāyabhāga after quoting the text of Vyāsa and raising the dispute on the authority of that text that one has no right to make a gift or sale, &c., resolves that dispute by maintaining that even here (*i.e.*, in the case of common property) property which consists in the fitness of free disposal exists just as well as in the case of other goods, so that the text (of Vyāsa) merely exhibits a prohibition for the purpose of indicating a moral offence, since the family is distressed by a sale which argues a disposition in the person to make an ill use of his power as owner, but is not meant to invalidate the sale or other transfer. Since there is nothing like common property in the sense that it is common to several owners, such a thing being unreal, commonness means no more than undividedness, and, therefore, in as much as property exists in the so-called common property even before partition, there is

Srikrishna's exposition of the Dayabhaga view.

[1] Dāyabhāga, Chapter II, 27 and 28.

nothing to hinder a person from giving or otherwise transfering his own share, and this is the intention of the author of the Dāyabhāga who maintains the doctrine of property in parts. The whole of this discussion furnishes a striking specimen of the way in which the peculiar doctrine of the Dāyabhāga School concerning the conception of co-ownership in an undivided property is carried to its logical consequence, and the basis of the difference regarding the right of alienation of an undivided co-parcener between the Dāyabhāga and the Mitākṣara Schools is clearly explained. It shows that the decision of the question really hinges upon the existence or non-existence of full dominion over the property to be transferred, and where it exists no amount of prohibition in the Sāstras can invalidate the transfer since as Jimūtavāhana asserts 'a fact cannot be altered by a hundred texts' a dictum which is not a peculiar text of the Dāyabhāga School, but is a recognised principle of Hindu Jurisprudence founded upon strict logic and good sense and practically adopted by the Mitākshara in dealing with the requirement of the consent of divided kinsmen and the like.

Ground of the distiction between the two schools.

Can a Dāyabhāga co-parcener alienate the entire joint property, or one entire undivided property out of the joint property?

Having thus shown that according to the Dāyabhāga School an undivided co-parcener can alienate his own share in the joint property, we are called upon to consider how far he can alienate the entire joint family property or one entire undivided property out of the joint family property. Now in dealing with the question we can at once say that such a transaction cannot be entirely valid, since no one can transfer what was not his own. This follows from the general principles already explained by me and is also cofirmed by the following passage in the Dāyabhāga. "Donation is complete then only when the owner, conscious that the thing is his, relinquishes it with a view to its becoming the property of another person, and that other person is sensible of the property apprehending 'this is become mine'; but that cannot occur in respect to common goods, and therefore common property is pronounced unfit to be given."[1] It must be understood that the above criticism applies to an attempted alienation of the entire joint property since an individual co-parcener cannot possibly deal with it as his own, and also of one entire property since it can be ascertained before a partition actually takes place that it will be allotted to the share of the alienor; hence, in such a case, it is impossible for the alienee to be conscious that the property sought to be transferred is his to the exclusion of the other co-parceners, and the alienee also cannot appropriate it with the consciousness that it is become his simply by the act of the alienor without the concurrence of those co-parceners. The conclusion, therefore, is that such an alienation cannot be valid as it stands and the only question that remains to be considered is whether some effect should not be given to it by holding it effectual to the extent of the share of the alienor. Jagannāth in his Digest quotes the opinion of Vāchaspati Bhaṭṭāchāryya to the effect that if the whole of the joint property be sold by one of the parceners, the sale is not valid so far as regards the shares of the other parceners, but is valid so far as regards the seller's own share, and he says that this opinion may be admitted upon the reason of the law.[2]

Can such an alienation be regarded as partially valid? Answer suggested by Vachaspati Bhaṭṭacharyya quoted by Jagannāth.

The position of cognates: Difference between the Mitakshara and the Dayabhāga Schools. The Mitakshara.

Turning next to the question of succession proper the most noticeable distinction between the Mitākshara and the Dāyabhāga Schools relates to the position of cognates in the order of succession. According to the Mitākshara, all agnates *i.e.* relations who trace their connection exclusively through males are entitled to inherit in preference

[1] Dayabhāga, Chap. XIII. 8.

[2] Colebrook's Digest, Vol. II, p. 58.

to cognates or relations through a female, with the only exception of a daughter's son, who although a cognate, occupies a very high position in the order of succession coming just after the daughter and before the parents. It may also be remarked that the peculiar favour shown to a daughter's son has been considered to be a somewhat later introduction. If we look to the Dharma-Sāstras we find that the peculiar position of a daughter's son is not recognised by all, and even in the text of Yājñavalkya enumerating the heirs of a man dying without a male issue he is not specially mentioned, so that Vijñāneśvara is constrained to fall back upon the particle (च) and argue that by the import of the particle 'also' (च) the daughter's son succeeds to the estate on failure of daughters;[1] among the Commentators also Apararka does not accord any special position to a daughter's son, so that he can only come in as a bandhu after all the agnates, however remote, are exhausted. Mr. Mayne, therefore, suggests that the explanation for the peculiar favour shown to a daughter's son "is to be found in the old practice of appointing a daughter to raise up issue for a man who had none. The daughter so appointed was herself considered as equal to a son. Naturally her son was equivalent to a grand-son, and as the merits of son and grand-son are equal, he ranked as a son. Consequently, we find him enumerated among the subsidiary sons, and taking a very high rank among them, generally second or third. Subsequently the appoinment of a daughter to raise up issue for the father became obsolete, but the fact of the nearness of daughter and daughter's son remained, and their natural claim to succession on the ground of mere consanguinity recommended itself for general acceptance."[2] The expla-

The position of a daughter's son.

Suggested explanation for the peculiar favour shown to him.

---

[1] Mitākṣara, Chap. II, Sec. II. 6.

[2] Mayne's Hindu Law p. 764.

nation is very plausible and, in all probability furnishes a correct account of the way in which the exceptional position came to be accorded to a daughter's son; but however that may be, it is certain that with this single exception no cognate can ever succeed in preference to an agnate to the property of his deceased relation. Jimūtavāhana, however, does not recognise the rule that agnates must always succeed in preference to cognates, and settles the order of succession by the application of a new principle, *viz.*, the principle of spiritual benefit; the result of the application of this principle is that apart from a daughter's son who has a peculiar position accorded to him by specific texts in the Dharma Sāstras, other cognates are, to borrow Mr. Mayne's expression, 'sifted in and out among the agnates, heirs in the female line frequently taking before very near sapindas in the direct male line, on the principle of superior religious efficacy'.[1] This result is attained mainly on the interpretation which Jimūtavāhana puts upon two texts of Manu which run as follows :—'To three must libations of water be made, to three must offerings of food (pinda) be presented, the fourth in descent is the giver, but the fifth has no concern with them : To the nearest sapinda the inheritance belongs; after that the distant kinsman (sakulya) shall be the heir, or the vedic preceptor, or the pupil.' Relying on these texts, Jimūtavāhana argues that in as much as at the time of the Pārvana Srāddha a person presents funeral cakes not only to his three paternal ancestors, but also to his three maternal ancestors, therefore in addition to the agnatic sapindas a person may also have certain cognatic sapindas being allied with them by the presentation of a common funeral cake, and these sapindas, although cognates, will succeed in preference to sakulyas including

The Dayabhaga: the principle of spiritual benefit.

Result of its application.

Manu's text: how explained and applied by Jimūtavāhana.

[1] Mayne's Hindu Law, p. 689.

agnates beyond three degrees according to the Hindu mode of computation and some of them, *viz.*, the daughter's sons of the three paternal ancestors will, on the analogy of the succession of one's own daughter's son, succeed even in preference to some agnatic sapindas the father's daughter's son succeeding before the paternal grand-father and the rest, and so on. Thus after laying down that 'on failure of the descendants of the father down to the great-grand-son, it must be understood that the succession devolves on the father's daughter's son in like manner as it descends to the owner's daughter's son' and that 'the succession of the grand-father's and great-grand-father's lineal descendant including the daughter's son must be understood in a similar manner according to the proximity of the funeral offering, since the reasons stated in the text 'for even the son of a daughter delivers him in the next world like the son of a son' is equally applicable and the daughter's sons of his father and the rest transport his manes over the abyss by offering oblations in which he may participate',[1] Jimūtavāhana goes on to observe that on failure of these persons since the maternal uncle and the rest present oblations to these maternal ancestors of the deceased beginning with his maternal grand-father which the deceased himself was bound to offer, therefore the property should devolve on the maternal uncle and the rest, for it is by means of wealth that a person may become giver of oblations[2] and he ultimately sums up the discussion by saying that a kinsman whether sprung from the family of the deceased though of different male descent as his own daughter's son or his father's daughter's son or sprung from a different family as his maternal uncle or the like being allied by a common funeral cake on account of their presenting offerings to

---

[1] Dāyabhāga, Chap. XI, Sec. vi. 9.

[2] Dāyabhāga, Chap. XI, Sec. vi. 13.

the three ancestors in the paternal and the maternal family of the deceased owner, is a sapinda; and the text (To them must libations of water be made &c.) is intended to propound the succession of such kinsmen, and the subsequent passage (To the nearest sapinda etc.) must be explained as discriminating them according to their degrees of proximity. But on failure of kin in this degree, the distant kinsman (Sakulya) is successor.[1]

Difference between the two schools summarised.

In this way by the application of the doctrine of spiritual benefit, as interpreted by him, Jimūtavāhana makes room for a number of cognates to succeed even in preference to many agnates, while, according to the Mitakshara, none of them excepting the daughter's son of the deceased owner, would have any place until all the agnates however remote, are completely exhausted.

How far the principle of spiritual benefit is a guiding principle in the Dayabhaga law of succession — explained.

The principle of spiritual benefit is therefore a characteristic guiding principle in the Dayabhaga law of succession, although it cannot be said to be the sole guiding principle in as much as it is introduced apparently with the object of interpreting and corroborating specific texts of the Dharma Sastras, and supplementing them where necessary, but not with the design of subverting the authority by substituting an independent principle in their stead; otherwise, as Srikrishna Tarkalankar points out, a stranger who throws the bones of the deceased into the Ganges, or presents funeral cakes to his departed spirit at the holly shrine of Gaya might, on the ground of superior spiritual benefit, claim his property even in preference to his relations.[2]

The principle of propinquity, the guiding principle of the Mitakshara law of succession.

On the other hand, the characteristic principle of the Mitakshara law of succession is the principle of propinquity with this most important

---

[1] Dāyabhāga, Chap. XI, Sec. vi. 19 & 21.

[2] अथैतासां स्मृतीनां न्यायमूलत्व सत्यपि तद्भोग्यपार्वणदातरि तस्य गङ्गाया-मस्थिप्रक्षेप्तुर्गयायां पिण्डदातुर्वा उदासीनस्याधिकारापत्तिः।

Srikrishna's Commentary on Dayabhaga Chap. XI. Sec. vi. 33.

* *

qualification that no cognate excepting a daugher's son can succeed in preference to an agnate; and even this qualification may be regarded not as an exception to the principle of propinquity, but rather as an illustration thereof in as much as under the peculiar organisation of the ancient Aryan family it was natural to regard an agnate as a nearer kinsman than a cognate, although on a mere computation of the degrees it might appear to be otherwise.

Is the principle of spiritual benefit ever recognised in the Mitakshara School?

The principle of spiritual benefit is not even mentioned by the Mitakshara in determining the order of succession, although the Viramitrodaya formulates and makes use of it in finding a position for the great-grandson among the direct male descendants of the deceased on whom the property devolves before the widow and the rest can claim the succession.[1] At all events, it is never brought forward to abrogate the superior position undoubtedly accorded by the ancient lawgivers to the agnates in preference to the cognates with the single exception of a daughter's son. We may, therefore, say that the main distinction between the Dayabhaga and the Mitakshara lies in the fact that the Mitakshara does not depart from the ancient rule which gives preference to an agnate in the order of succession except in the case of a daughter's son, while the Dayabhaga by introducing the principle of spiritual benefit and putting a novel interpretation upon it makes room for a large number of cognates and sifts them in and out among the agnates, so that many agnates who under the Mitakshara would have an undoubtedly superior position, are postponed to them.

Preference of agnates in other systems of Jurisprudence. The Roman Law.

This preference of agnates over cognates in the scheme of succession had its parallel in other systems of Jurisprudence. If we look to the history of the Roman law, we find that the law of the Twelve Tables recognised only

[1] Viramitrodaya, Chap. XVII. Pt. 1. Sec. iii.

the succession of (1) *Sui heredes*, (2) Agnates, (3) gentiles; cognates had no place under this scheme, so that if there were no gentiles, the inheritance would lapse to the state rather than go to the cognates. This law appears all the more peculiar when we take into account the complication due to emancipation being regarded as a *Capitis deminutio* and hence involving a severance of the tie of agnation, so that even emancipated sons were looked upon as strangers to the family and had thus no share in the inheritance. This resulted in such a disparity between the line of succession laid down by the rules of the civil law and the direction of the natural affection of the owner, that the Praetor had to intervene to remove some of the glaring anomalies by granting what was called *Bonorum possessio* to various classes of relatives who could not be the heirs under the strict civil law. To this divergence between the law of succession and the promptings of natural affection, Sir Henry Maine attributes the horror of intestacy that prevailed among the Romans. 'Every dominant sentiment,' says he, 'of the primitive Romans was entwined with the relations of the family. But what was the family? The law defined it one way—natural affection another. In the conflict between the two, the feeling we would analyse grew up, taking the form of an enthusiasm for the institution by which the dictates of affection were permitted to determine the fortunes of its objects;'[1] and he explains that the feeling did not die out with the improvements introduced by the Praetors, for, 'every body conversant with the philosophy of opinion is aware that the sentiment by no means dies out, of necessity, with the passing out of the circumstance which produced it.'[2]

[1] Maine's Ancient Law, p. 222.

[2] Maine's Ancient Law, p. 222.

However that may be, even in the time of Gaius the order of succession was (1) sui heredes, (2) agnates and (3) cognates, so that cognates could not inherit before the agnates. At last Justinian by his 118th and 127th Novels completely modelled the laws of intestate succession by abolishing the difference between agnates and cog ates and creating a new order of succession under which speaking broadly the descendants succeeded first, the ascendants next, and last of all the collaterals according to nearness of kinship. It will appear from the above review that the preference of agnates in the Mitākshara law of succession has nothing unusual or extraordinary in it. Indeed, as Sir Henry Maine observes, 'there are few indigenous bodies of law belonging to the Communities of the Indo-European Stock, which do not exhibit peculiarities in the most ancient part of their structure which are clearly referable to agnation.'[1] The Mitākshara law was, however, free from the peculiar anomalies of the early Roman Law due to emancipation being regarded as a capitis deminutio involving the severance of the tie of agnation. In this respect the Mitākshara law was less unnatural or anomalous than the early Roman law, for it cannot be supposed that the result ascribed to emancipation by what Sir Henry Maine calls 'legal pedantry' had its counterpart in the natural affection of the parents, for as he truly points out 'enfranchisement from the father's power was a demonstration, rather than a severance, of affection—a mark of grace and favour accorded to the best beloved and the most esteemed of children.'[2] As for the general preference of agnates over cognates in the scheme of succession it seems that there were reasons why the seeming anomaly involved in this was not very keenly felt by the Mitākshara Hindus.

Why the seeming anomaly involved in the general preference of agnates

[1] Maine's Ancient Law, p. 150.

[2] Maine's Ancient Law, p. 222.

was not keenly felt by the Mitakshara Hindus.

In the first place, the rule that in the case of joint undivided property the interest of a deceased co-percener passes not by succession but by survivorship would in many cases prevent the question of precedence from arising and striking the sensibility of the persons concerned as something very unnatural; in the second place, even where the question did arise, as in the case of a divided family, the close ties created by living under the peculiar organisation of the Hindu family system which was mainly agnatic would take away the point from the exclusion of the cognates by the agnates; and lastly in the very few cases where a result would ensue from the operation of the rule of succession altogether inconsistent with the natural affection of the owner of the property, the system of adoption would serve the very same purpose as the system of making a testament under the Roman law. In Bengal, the Dāyabhāga practically obliterated the distinction between divided and undivided property by maintaining a a conception of joint ownership which was very much laxer than that of the Mitākshara; the idea that co-owners hold their shares in quasi-severalty which they can dispose of at their pleasure bespeaks a disruption of the close ties of the old joint family system, and this, in the fitness of things, had its concomitant in the altered course of succession abandoning the almost unqualified preference given to agnates over cognates. Mr. Mayne, therefore, seems to have struck the true note when referring to the difference between the Mitākshara and the Dāyabhāga, he observed that 'much was of course due to the natural progress of Society. A race so full of commercial activity as the Hindus who were settled along the lower course of the Ganges would find their growth crampled by the Procustean bed of ancient traditions'[1] but I am not prepared

I[nn]ovation [of t]he Bengal [sch]ool explained.

Mr. Mayne's explanation considered.

[1] Mayne's Hindu Law, p. 326.

The influence of Brahmanism: how far it furnishes an explanation for the altered course of succession laid down by the Dayabhaga.

to go along with him when he says that 'Brahmanism was rampant among the law writers of Bengal,' and that 'it was this influence which completely remodelled the law of inheritance in that Province by applying tests of religious efficacy which were of absolutely modern introduction.'[1] It is true that in Bengal the law of inheritance was remodelled by giving a better position to a certain number of cognates in the scheme of succession; it is also true that this result was achieved by applying the doctrine of religious efficacy measured in a peculiar way which seems to have been an innovation; but I do not think that the formulation of the doctrine of religious efficacy, the peculiar interpretation put upon it, and its application to determine the order of succession were at all dictated by the influence of Brahmanism; on the other hand, I agree with Babu Golapchandra Sarkar when he says that 'the doctrine appears to have been introduced by the author of the Dāyabhāgha as a mere pretext for assigning in the order of succession a higher possition to some dear and near cognates who, under the Mitākshara, are all postponed even to the most distant agnates,—a pretext similar to that under which the Praetor Urbanus of Rome recognised the heritable rights of the cognates'; otherwise there is no reason for supposing that the influence of Brahmanism was more keenly felt in Bengal than in the sister provinces of Mithilā and enares. Mr. Mayne himself says that while the influence of Brahmanism was more powerful in Bengal than in Southern and Western India, it must have been less powerful than in Benares which he characterises as the very hot-bed of Brahmanism; assuming that to be so, does it not follow that neither the decay nor the vigour of Brahmanical influence could determine a peculiar development of the law of succession as that which took place in

[1] Mayne's Hindu Law, p. 328.

The gradual disruption of the old family system: how it explains altered cause of sucession.

Bengal, but that other influences were at work which differentiated Bengal from the other Provinces? I am convinced that it was the gradual disruption of the old joint family system in Bengal owing to the operation of social and economical influences that diverted the natural affection of the people into new channels, and when this took place it became difficult to stick to the old scheme of succession which directed the devolution of property in a way inconsistent with it. The altered direction of the popular feeling, therefore, demanded that there should be a corresponding alteration in the law; and when Jimūtavāhana took the matter up, he found that there was only one way of doing it; he could not legislate, but had only to interpret the existing law, and the expedient hit upon by him to get a number of cognates interspersed among the agnates in the line of succession was to bring forward the doctrine of spiritual benefit on the authority of Manu's text, 'To three must libations of water be made etc.' by putting upon it an interpretation which would suit his purpose, and when the doctrine was once introduced, he could not but carry it to some thing like its logical consequences, for a Hindu jurist was nothing if not logical. It is, therefore, a mistake to suppose that a sister's son, for example, was introduced before a paternal uncle in the order of succession because the Brahmanical influence that prevailed in Bengal assigned to the former superior religious merit than to the latter, but it was because owing to the disintegration of the old family system a sister's son came to occupy a better position in the affection of his maternal uncles than he formerly did that it became necessary to re-adjust the old order of succession in order to give him a higher place therein; and when this had to be done, the doctrine of spiritual benefit was availed of as a means to an end, because it furnished a consistent theory, had a chance of standing the test of criticism and controversy and was at the same time, not repulsive to the sentiments of the people. The highly artificial character of the arguments which Jimūtavāhana was forced to use to establish that the maternal uncle and other relatives connected through the mother confer spirtiual benefit upon the deceased owner in order to make room for them before the Sakalyas (or distant agnates) at once demonstrates that he was not so much anxious for the repayment of actual religious merit as for giving a better place in the line of succession to a class of cognates whose claims, for other reasons, he wanted some how to advance; otherwise, it would have been the easiest thing for him to show that agnates, although they may belong to the class of sakulyas, conferred more spiritual benefit upon the deceased than a maternal relation could possibly do.

Principles common to both the schools.

The exclusion of females unless admitted by virtue of special texts.

The principles to which I now wish to draw your attention are common to both the Dāyabhānga and the Mitākshara Schools, although here and there there may be differences in detail. The first of these principles to which I will advert is the exclusion of females unless admitted by virtue of special texts. The Dāyabhāga expressly recognises the principle on the authority of the text of Baudhayana, and explains that the succession of the widow and certain other women does not contradict this rule in as much as they take under special texts.[1] It is true that the Mitāksara does not in so many words lay down this principle, but the general outline of the Mitāksara scheme of succession clearly indicates its recognition and the Viromitrodaya and the Smriti Chandrikā both expressly lay down the rule in unhesitating terms. It appears from the authorities relied on in support of this position, that it is as old as the Vedas, and it is even

[1] Dāyabhāga Chap. XI, Sec. 6-11.

doubtful whether in ancient times it was not even more stringently exclusive than we at present find it to be. Thus in dealing with succession to males, the Viramitrodaya says, "As for the text of the Smriti, namely,—'Therefore women are devoid of the senses and incompetent to inherit,' and for the text of Manu beased upon it, namely—'Indeed the rule is that women are always devoid of the senses and incompetent to inherit,'—these are both to be interpreted to mean to refer to those women whose might of inheritance has not been expressly declared. Haradatta also has explained (those texts) in this very way, in his Commentary on the Institutes of Gautama called Mitākshara. But some (Commentators) say that the term 'incompetent to inherit' implies censure only, by reason of its association with the term 'devoid of the senses'. This is not tenable, because it cannot but be admitted that the portion, namely, 'incompetent to inherit' is prohibitory and not condemnatory,"[1] and in another passage dealing with succession to Stridhana property he reiterates the same opinion and says: 'But the daughter-in-law and others (of the same sex) are entitled to food and raiment only; for the nearness as a Sapinda is of no force when it is opposed by express texts.' Since a text of the Sruti declares,—'Therefore women are devoid of the senses and incompetent to inherit',—and a text of Manu, founded upon it, says—'Indeed the rule is that, devoid of the senses, and incompetent to inherit, women are useless'—the conclusion arrived at by the author of Smriti Candrikā Haradatta, and other Southern Commentators, as well as by all the Oriental commentators such as Jimutavāhana, is that those women only are entitled to inherit whose right of succession has been expressly mentioned in such texts as —'The wife and the daughters also etc.' but that others are

[1] Viramitrodaya Chap. III, Pt. 1, Sec. 13.

certainly excluded from taking heritages by the texts of the Sruti and of Manu.'[1] This makes it perfectly clear that the principle of the exclusion of females was recognised on all hands, and had been so recognised from a very ancient time. It was indeed a corollary from the position of a female in the organisation of the ancient Aryan Society; there her position was one of life long dependence. So Manu says:—'The father protects a woman in her childhood, the husband during her youth, the son in old age; a woman has no right to independence;' that being her position, it was quite natural that she could not take the inheritance, and the few cases in which she was called to do so seem to have been subsequent concessions made for special reasons in favour of a few very near relations such as wife, daughter, mother and the like. I do not here propose to enter into a discussion as to how the right of each of these female relatives grew up, as the point has been elaborately discussed by Mr. Mayne in Chapter XVII of his valuable work on Hindu Law, but I may point out in passing as it may be interesting to you that even the right of the widow to inherit her deceased husband's property was not for a long time clearly recognised and that the celebrated dramma Abhijnāna Sakuntalam of Kālidāsa contains an indication of this where the king, being reported that a certain merchant was dead without any issue so that his estate should escheat to the Crown, directs an enquiry as to whether any of his widows was enciente, an enquiry which would have been unnecessary if a widow could take the property in her own right.[2]

A corollary from the position of a female in the organisation of the ancient Aryan Society.

Admission of sister in the line of

The Vyavahāra Mayukha which is recognised as an authority in Bombay admits the claim of a sister, and gives

[1] Viramitrodaya Chap. V, Pt. II, 15.

[2] Abhijnāna Sakuntalam, Act VI.

her a very nigh position in the line of succession, viz., after the grand-mother and before the grand-father. This it does on the ground that she is a gotraja being born in the family of the propositus, although she may be transferred to another gotra by marriage, and as such entitled to inherit in order of propinquity. The way in which the Bombay High Court has admitted other females into the line of succession does not seem to me to be based on any intelligible principle but must be rested on special custom and the analogy of the reasoning employed by the Mayukha in admitting the sister's right. The Madras High Court, also while professing to follow the Mitākṣhara has admitted the claim of a number of females to inherit as bandhus, but this position is hardly justified by the Mitākṣhara and clearly contrary to Smṛiti Chandrikā which is an undoubted authority of the southern school ; these decisions, therefore, exhibit a clear departure from the law as originally laid down by the sages and interpreted by the authoritative commentators.

succession by the Vyavahara Mayukha.

How the Bombay High Court has made room for other females

The course adopted by the Madras High Court Is it justified by the Mitākṣara ?

The conclusion, therefore, at which we arrive is that both the Dāyabhāga and the Mitākṣara recognise the principle of the exclusion of females from inheritance unless admitted by special texts with this diference that in the case of the property of an undivided co-parcener no question of succession can properly arise under the Mitākṣara Law by reason of the operation of the rule of suvivorship and hence women who can only take by way of succession cannot claim the same, while under the Dāyabhāga Law which makes no distinction between the properties of divided and undivided co-parceners for the purposes of inheritance, women inherit both kinds of property in exactly the same way, a difference which as I have already sought to explain, is connected with a corresponding difference in the conception of co-ownership, the

The conclusion.

The difference between the two schools

result, perhaps of a disintegration of the ancient joint family system in Bengal owing to the operation of social and economic causes to which I need not here advert.

Exclusion from inheritance Grounds of exclusion classified.

Exclussion from inheritance :—Under the Hindu Law there are several grounds for exclussion from inheritance, and they may be broadly divided into three classes : (1) Physical disease or deformity of a certain type, (2) Mental incapacity, and (3) Moral or religious disqualification. Under the first division may be mentioned, congenital blindness and deafness, dumbness, lameness, impotency, leprosy and other incurable virulent diseases ; insanity and idiocy are causes of exclusion coming under the second division of mental incapacity ; commission of a vice leading to excommunication, being born of a father who has been so excommunicated, assumption of the order of ascetics and unchastity in the case of a widow are moral and religious disqualifications which exclude a person from inheritance. As regards physical deformity the text of Manu clearly shows that blindness and deafness must be congenital to be a bar to inheritance, and that being so it is difficult to see why the same condition should not be attached to other physical deformities such as dumbness and lameness. As regards moral or religious disqualifications they are sometimes expiable, and when so expiated cannot be a ground for disinherison. The disqualification, however, is in any case personal, so that the son of a disqualified person may inherit the property although the father cannot, and moreover, the persons so excluded from inheritance become entitled to maintenance except when the exclusion is due to the commission of a sin leading to excommunication, or to being born of a father so excommunicated. Having thus indicated the causes of exclusion from inheritance the next question is what is the point of time at which the cause must exist in order that the effect

The point of time at which

may follow. As regards the Dāyabhāga, there can be no difficulty for succession opens out, according to it, on the extinction of the ownership of the previous owner and that is the moment at which the disability must exist in order to shut out a person otherwise entitled to inheritance.

the ground of exclusion must exist in order to load to the exclusion The position according to the Dāyabhāga According to the Mitākṣhara.

The Mitākṣhara, however, lays down that it is the existence of the disqualification at the moment of the division of the property that excludes a person from getting his share, but one already separated from his co-heirs is not deprived of his allotments by the subsequent accrual of any disqualifying defect and what is more, it goes on to say that the removal of the defect, even after the partition, will entitle the person so freed from the disqualifying cause to have the partition re-opened and get his share in the property.[1] It does not seem that according to the Dāyabhāga the devolution of inheritance can be disturbed by reason of the subsequent removal of the disqualifying defect, for in the absence of express authority an inheritance must remain where it has fallen.

Subsequent removal of disqualification: its effect.

This brings us to the consideration of two principles which have often been pronounced to be principles of Hindu Law, *viz.*, (1) that succession can never remain in abeyance and (2) that an estate once vested cannot be divested.

Two other principles often pronounced to be principles of Hindu Law.

As regards the principle that succession can never remain in abeyance, it is not a principle founded upon any special text, but is a logical deduction from the conception of succession. According to the Hindu Law title by succession arises without any reference to the volition of any individual by the operation of a rule of law, and since this rule comes into operation at once on the extinction of the previous ownership, it follows that there cannot

Succession can never remain in abeyance. A logical deduction from the conception of succession.

---

[1] Mitākṣhara Chap. II, Sec. X. 6 and 7.

be any interval between the extinction of the interest of the predecessor and the accrual of the interest of the successor, for, were it otherwise, then during the interval the property would be reduced to the condition of a *res nullius*. In this respect, therefore, it differs from the Roman Law according to which acceptance of the inheritance by the heir, except in the case of a *suus heres* who was on that account called *heres necessarius*, was a condition of the estate being vested in him; the result of this was, as Sir William Markby points out, that 'there was a space of time, very often a considerable one, during which, whatever the theory might be the interitance did in fact belong to no one. This difficulty was partly got over by the doctrine of 'relation back' as it is called, that is to say, the heir, though he was not really heir before he accepted, yet, when he accepted, was treated exactly as if he had succeeded immediately on the death of the owner. Still the difficulty remained, that in the interval the inheritance was vacant, which might give rise to practical inconveniences which no fiction could remedy."[1]

Difference from the Roman Law.

An estate once vested cannot be divested. Not a special principle of the Hindu Law.

As regards the other principle that an estate once vested cannot be divested, I do not see why it should be regarded as a special principle of the Hindu Law. When an estate once vests in a person, it must follow from the universal principle of reason that there cannot be an effect without a cause, that it cannot be divested unless a sufficient ground for it supervene, and it may be observed that under the Hindu Law there are occasions on which an estate once vested is actually divested, although, it must be admitted, that such occasions are exceptional in their character.

Nor of universal application.

Exceptions

Thus the birth of a posthumous son, the adoption of

[1] Markby's Elements of Law, Chap. XVIII.

a son by a widow after the death of her husband, and the removal of disqualification of an heir even alter the distribution of property under the Mitākshara Law furnish instances where property once vested in one person is divested and passes to another. Of course, when no such ground exists the property must remain where it lies, simply because there is nothing to remove it, so that the high-sounding proposition that 'an estate once vested cannot be divested' really amounts to nothing more than this, that a person who acquires an ownership remains owner until for some sufficient reason he ceases to be an owner.

The basis of the principle explained.

The lecture has already become too long, and here I close it with the hope that although the details of the subject can only be gathered from text-books specially dealing with the same, the principles explained above will place them in their true light and afford a rational basis for taking a connected view of the whole.

LECTURE VI

THE LAW OF PLEDGE.

Pledge treated as a security for the re-payment of a debt.

Two modes of ensuring the confidence of a creditor.

Pledge creates a real right.

In the last four lectures I have dealt with ownership and the various modes of its acquisition whether original or derivative. In the present lecture I propose to discuss the Hindu Law of Pledge. The Hindu lawyers deal with this subject in connection with recovery of debt, for a giving of pledge, according to them, is a form of furnishing security for the repayment of debt, or, in other words, it is a mode of ensuring the confidence of the creditor. So Narada says, 'surety and pledge, these are the two sources of ensuring the confidence of the creditor.'[1] Among the two I propose to deal with the law of pledge at this place, because the giving of a pledge involves, as you will find, the transfer of an interest in property in favour of the creditor which under certain circumstances matures into full ownership, and thus creates a real right as distinguished from a right corresponding to a mere personal obligation, so that in logical order of sequence the discussion of this subject should come immediatly after the discussion of the transfer of full ownership with which I was busy so long.

Pledge (आधि) defined.

Division of pledges.

The ordinary Sanskrit equivalent of the word pledge is आधि which is thus defined in the Mitakshara : "Whatever is placed under the control of the creditor by the debtor as a security for the thing lent to him is called, an adhi."[2] If may be of various kinds : So

[1] विश्रम्भ हेतु द्वावत्र प्रतिभूराधि रेवच ।

[2] आधिर्नाम गृहीतस्य द्रव्यस्योपरि विश्वासार्थमधमर्णे नोत्तमर्णेऽधिक्रियते— आधीयते इति आधिः । मिताक्षरा । ऋणादान प्रकरणम् ।

Four-fold division by Narada.

Narada first divides it into two classes viz., (i) that redeemable within a definite time and (ii) that given for an indefinite period until the repayment of the debt, and these two classes are again divided into two, in as much as they may be either for custody or for use.[1] Brihaspati gives a somewhat different classification; he begins by saying that a pledge is of four kinds, and then goes on to specify an eight-fold division viz, (1) movable, (2) immovable, (3) for custody, (4) for use, (5) discretionary (i. e. without a time limit) (6) with a fixed time limit, (7) evidenced by a document, and (8) evidenced merely by witnesses.[2] This apparent inconsistency is reconciled by Smriti Chandrika by saying that although the divisions actually enumerated are eight yet the principal divisions are four as enumerated in the text of Narada, in as much as they are productive of important consequences, while the remainder of the classification, being of minor importance, may safely be ignored; on the other hand, the Kritya-Kalpataru makes a very ingenious suggestion which, to my mind, affords a more acceptable solution of the puzzle: it says, that although the divisions enumerated are eight in number, yet the classification is really four-fold since the principles of classification are four viz, (1) nature of the property pledged, (2) form of the pledge, (3) time relation and (4) nature of the evidence by which the pledge is supported (स्वरूप प्रकार काल प्रमाणैश्चतुर्विधत्वम्). According to the nature of the property a pledge is either movable or immovable; according to the form

Eight-fold division by Brihaspati.

The two classifications how reconciled by Smriti Chandrika.

By Kritya-Kalpataru.

The principles of classification.

[1] आधिर्नियत इत्यादि—सविशेषी विलक्षणः। कृतकालापनेयश्च यावद्देयोद्यतस्तथा।

[2] स पुनर्द्विविधः प्रोक्तः गोप्यो भोग्यस्तथैव च। आधिर्बन्धः समाख्यातः स च प्रोक्तश्चतुर्विधः। जङ्गमःस्थावरश्चैव गोप्यो भोग्यस्तथैव च। याद्दच्छिकः सावधिश्च लेख्यारूढोऽथ साक्षिमान्।

it is either for custody or for use; according to time-relation it is either with or without a time-limit; and according to the nature of the evidence it is either supported by a document or merely by witnesses. The way in which the differences indicated by these divisions affect the incidents of the pledge will be pointed out later on.

Could there be a pledge without delivery of possession?

It will be seen from the classification given above that although a pledge is distinguished into a pledge for custody and a pledge for use, there is no suggestion of a third class, viz., a pledge which is not accompanied by possession. This raises the question whether under the Hindu Law there could be a pledge without the accompaniment of delivery of possession, or, in other words whether the very nature of the transaction did not involve the transfer of possession from the pledgor to the pledgee as an element in its constitution. The question was raised before the late Supreme Court of Calcutta in the case of Shibachandra Ghosh *v.* Russickchandra Neoghy[1] and the majority of the court held that whatever might have been the case in early times, the later Hindu Law recognised the validity of a pledge although unaccompanied by possession, and they relied in support of this conclusion upon some of the texts of Hindu Law as well as upon the general usage of the country. Mr. Justice Grant, however, was of a different opinion, and held that delivery of possession was necessary to the validity of a pledge in Hindu Law and that this was also in conformity with the general principles of natural law. The argument of Mr. Justice Grant, in so far as it is based upon a consideration of the so-called law of nature, is somewhat difficult to follow, for, as Dr. Ghosh points out, "if it were not for the peculiar views about the law of nature so widely prevalent at the time, Mr. Justice

Shibchandra Ghosh *v.* Russick-chandra Neoghy.

Mr. Justice Grant's judgment.

Dr. Ghosh's criticism.

[1] Fult. 36.

Grant could hardly have failed to perceive that the Hindu Law might have been developed in course of time in the same manner as the Roman Law was developed by the introduction of hypothecation".

Element of truth in the aforesaid judgment.

The element of truth which it probably contains, although expressed in a somewhat obscure language, is that having regard to the purpose for which a pledge was required, viz., ensuring the confidence of the creditor, it was not likely that a pledge unaccompanied by possession would, in the early stages of society, meet that end so that in the order of evolution, the recognition of hypothecation is a later juridical phenomenon than the prevalence of pledges accompanied by possession.

The question discussed: arguments pro and contra.

Arguments for an answer in the negative:

But, then, just as in the later Roman Law, the altered conditions of the time led to the recognition of hypothecation unaccompanied by possession as a valid transaction, so it is not at all unlikely in the nature of things, that a similar transition should also take place in the later Hindu Law; on the other hand, if the growth of hypothecation was a natural growth determined by circumstances which might appear anywhere, it would be only reasonable to expect that its recognition would not be confined to a particular system of laws, but find a place in other systems as well. *Prima facie*, therefore, we cannot attach much importance to this sort of *a priori* speculation, and the real question is whether upon the evidence available to us we can say that the Hindu Law did recognise the validity of a pledge unaccompained by possession. On giving the matter my best consideration I have come to the conclusion that our Dharma Sastras do not contain much evidence of the prevalence of a hypothecation; on the other hand the scheme of the law bearing upon the subject and the rights and obligations arising under it all go to show that a pledge involved the placing of a property of the debtor under the control of the creditor as a security for the payment of the debt. In support of this position, I may begin by referring to the definition of 'adhi' which I have already placed before you, for it shows that the term denotes a thing placed under the control of the creditor in order to ensure his confidence, and indeed the etymology of the word (:आधीयते इत्याधि:), supports this definition; in the second place the division of a pledge into two classes, e.g., गोप्य (for custody) and भोग्य (for use) suggests the same conclusion, for the recognition of hypothecation will require the admission of a third class of pledge which is neither for custody गोप्य nor for use भोग्य; in the third place the various rights and obligations of the pledgor and pledgee to which I will presently advert contemplate the pledgor parting with his possession at the time of creating the pledge. It seems to me that it is but natural that this should be so, for what is hypothecation but an agreement on the part of the debtor to hold his property as a security for the fulfilment of his engagement to repay the loan, and could it under ordinary circumstances be sufficient to ensure the confidence of the creditor? It is practically one promise (viz., to hold the property as a security) on the top of another (viz., to repay the loan) and if it could be relied on, why not the bare promise to repay? It may be said that a hypothecation creates a qualified right in the property hypothecated in as much as it gives you a right to sell the property under certain circumstances; that is quite true, but it must be remembered that the right can only be exercised if the debtor retains the property, for, if he sells it off to a *bona fide* purchaser, the situation will be this, that if you allow the hypothecation to prevail, the honest purchaser is defrauded and deprived of his property without any fault of his own; while if you do not, the hypothecation practically loses the whole of its value. These

Etymological meaning of the word आधि.

The division of a pledge into two classes गोप्य and भोग्य.

Nature of the rights and obligations.

Was hypothecation likely to be regarded as a sufficient security? Disadvantages of hypothecation:

disadvantages of hypothecation are so palpable that I am not quite sure that a Hindu creditor would not have reposed more confidence in a solemn promise exacted from the debtor, such as is involved in what is called a pledge of religious merit चरित्र बन्धक according to one of its interpretations, whereby the debtor, for instance, says to his creditor "until I repay the loan I will not bathe in the Ganges" or "the benefit of my ablution in the Ganges shall accrue to you," than in a security like this, and to this stage of feeling are to be attributed the text of Yajnavalkya, "By the acceptance of a pledge is its validity maintained"[1] and the text of Narada attributed by Jagannatha to Vyasa, "Pledges are declared to be of two sorts, immoveable and moveable, and both are valid when there is actual enjoyment, and not otherwise"[2]. All these considerations, therefore, combine to show that in the early Hindu Law a pledge without the accompaniment of delivery of possession was not usually recognised. Let us now consider the evidence which has been supposed to indicate the existence and recognition of a hypothecation under the Hindu Law. In his work on the Law of Mortgage, Dr. Ghosh quotes a passage from the Mitakshara in support of the position that in the mature Hindu Law the rule requiring tradition had fallen into disuse, and that a real right, whether by mortgage or sale, could be created by a mere expression of the intention of the parties. The passage cited is one to which I have already had occasion to draw your attention in another connection. It is this: "The acceptance of gold, cloths, etc. being completed by

Yajnavalkya's text.

Narada's text

Arguments in favour of an answer in the affirmative considered.

A passage from Mitakshara cited by Dr. Ghosh.

---

[1] आधेः स्वीकरणात् सिद्धिः ।

[2] आधिस्तु द्विविधः प्रोक्तः स्थावरो जङ्गम स्तथा ।
सिद्धिरस्योभयस्यापि भोगो यद्यास्ति नान्यथा ।
गोप्याधौ भोगः स्वीकारः भोग्याधौ फलभोग इति वीरमित्रोदयः ।

the ceremony of bestowing water, and falling therefore under either of the means, may be designated as a three-fold acceptance; but in the case of land as there can be no corporeal acceptance without enjoyment of the produce, it must be accompanied by some little possession; otherwise the gift, sale, or other transfer is not complete. A title, therefore, without corporeal acceptance, consisting of the enjoyment of the produce, is weaker than a title accompanied by it or with such corporeal acceptance. But such is the case only, when of these two the priority is undistinguishable, but when it is ascertained which is first in point of time and which is posterior, then the simple prior title affords the stronger evidence."[1] I am afraid that this passage does not support the conclusion for which it is sought to be used. It is true that it shows that tradition is not necessary to complete a transfer of property, but that it is of importance only when a question of relative superiority arises between two transactions where priority in time cannot be ascertained and it does not affect the other question whether from the very nature of a pledge delivery of possession by the debtor to the creditor is not one of its constituent elements. The fact is that the above observations were made by Vijnaneswara in connection with the question of acceptance; acceptance, he says, may take either of three forms; it may be mental, verbal or corporeal, and in order that the acceptance of a transfer may be complete it is not absolutely necessary that it should take the corporeal form; although, in so far

True import of the passage.

The passage does not solve the question.

[1] Ghoshe on Mortgage, p. 46. The first part of the translation is somewhat inaccurate; it should run thus: Since in the case of gold cloths etc., it it possible to take hold of the thing immediately after the ceremony of bestowing water, acceptance in all the three forms (*i.e.*, mental verbal and corporeal) completely takes place; but in the case of land &c.

as corporeal acceptance, which involves an assumption of possession, and in the casé of land, some enjoyment of usufruct, is more tangible and easily demonstrable, it determines the relative superiority between two transfers where priority in point of time cannot be clearly ascertained. It therefore follows that in so far as assumption of possession may be regarded as a part of acceptance, it is not really indispensable; but it does not follow that delivery of possession can be dispensed with even when the very nature of the transaction involves it as one of its constituent elements. I am, therefore, of opinion that the above observations were made by Vijnaneswara in connection with a transfer of ownership such as a gift or a sale, and not in relation to a pledge, and that so far as this latter transaction is concerned, the question whether it does not involve delivery of possession by the debtor to the creditor as one of its constituent elements is not at all affected by it. To put the same matter in another form: suppose a debtor offers a pledge and the creditor accepts it; the contract is complete without any delivery of possession, since acceptance is not necessarily corporeal, but the question remains whether the creditor is not entitled to demand possession: if a pledge involve delivery of possession as one of its constituent elements, he is; but if it do not, the pledge is a mere hypothecation of the Roman Law, and he is not. The question whether the Hindu Law recognised a transaction of the latter kind does not find any solution from the passage quoted above, nor is there any other passage in the Mitakshara to show that it did. There is a text attributed by Jágannatha to Brihaspati which is sometimes cited in support of the recognition of a pledge without possession. It runs thus: "Of him who does not enjoy a pledge, nor possess it, nor claim it on evidence, the written contract for that pledge is nugatory,

What the question really amounts to.

No trace of hypothecation in the Mitakshara.

A text of Brihaspati quoted by Jagannatha.

like a bond when the debtor and witnessess have deceased." This seems to me to lay down a rule of evidence, and is besides of such a doubtful import that it does not lead to a definite conclusion as to whether there could be a pledge without possession. It must also be remembered that Brihaspati divides a pledge with reference to its form into two classes, viz., pledge for custody and pledge for use, and, that being so, it becomes difficult to infer that in the text quoted above he recognises a third class of pledge which is neither for custody nor for use. Referring to the use of the word *bandhaka* to designate a pledge, Dr. Ghosh suggests that "change from *adhi* to *bandhaka* marks the progress from a pledge with possession to a pledge not followed by delivery or in other words to hypothecation." This suggestion is based by him upon the etymology of the two words for he says that while the word *ādhi* signifies bailment, *bandhaka*, the word now in familiar use among the Hindus, like lien in the English law, imports merely a tie or nexus.[1] There may be a good deal in this suggestion, but, with all deference, I am bound to point out that an argument upon the etymology of a Sanskrit word is seldom conclusive, for it is often quite possible for a Sanskritist to give it a different turn. Thus with reference to the etymology of the word *bandhaka* Jagannatha says: '*bandha*' is derived in the passive form, "that which is bound or pledged (*badhyate*)". A male slave or the like, being bound or confined is then unable to perform service for his master; a horse also being bound or tied, is then unfit for his owner's use. By acceptation, the sense of the word '*bandha*' is a thing remaining in the creditor's possession by an agreement on the part of the debtor in this form, 'this chattel shall remain in

This also does not lead to any definite conclusion.

Dr. Ghose's argument based on the etymology of the word *bandhaka*.

The argument not conclusive.

A different etymological meaning attributed to the word by Jagannātha.

---

[1] Ghosh on Mortgage, p. 42.

thy possession so long as I do not repay the money'. Accordingly it is said by eminent logicians that 'the meaning of words is apprehended by grammar, by analogy, by dictionaries, by original instruction, and by practice or acceptation'.[1] It is plain that if this interpretation be accepted, the etymology of the word *bandha* instead of supporting Dr. Ghose's theory really goes against it. It must also be remembered that Brihaspati begins his discussion of the law of pledge by saying that "an *ādhi* is also called a *bandha* and it is of four different kinds"[2] and in many texts of Hindu Law the two words are used as synonymous. I am, however, disposed to think, on other grounds, that the suggestion that "the change from *ādhi* to *bandhaka* marks the progress from a pledge with possession to a pledge not followed by delivery or in other words to hypothecation" is not without foundation, and what is more, it also helps us to mark out the several stages in the transition from the former to the latter, and this I shall presently try to show. In doing this I shall first place before you indisputable evidence to show that a pledge without possession was recognised by the later Hindu Law, and I shall then try to explain the causes which determined its recognition and reconstruct the several stages through which the transition, in all probability, came about. There is a text of Kātyāyana which dealing with the priority between two pledges says, "If a pledge, a sale, or a gift of the same thing be made before witnesses to one man, and by a written instrument to another, the writing shall prevail, because one transaction only can be maintained".[3] Commenting

The two words 'ādhi' and 'bandha' sometimes used as synonymous.

How the suggested transition can be worked out.

Evidence to show that a pledge without delivery of possession was recognised by later Hindu Law.

---

1 Colebrook's Digest, vol. 1, p 145.

2 आधिर्बन्धः समाख्यातः स च प्रोक्तश्चतुर्विधः।

3 आधानं विक्रयो दानं लेख्यं साक्षिकृतं तथा।
एकक्रिया विरुद्धन्तु लेख्यस्तत्रापहारकं।

Jagannātha's comments on Katyāyana's text. Halāyudha's

upon this Jagannātha observes that "Halāyudha says if there be no occupancy but a writing exists duly attested and so forth, the writing shall prevail because it is the best evidence of a transaction; it shall establish the mortgage. It is hereby intimated that if there be written and verbal contracts, a mortgage is not of course invalid for want of occupancy."[1] Now Halāyudha, as you are perhaps aware, was the chief judge in the reign of Lakshmana Sen, one of the Sen Kings of Bengal, and his opinion may be regarded as quite conclusive regarding the prevalence of hypothecation at least in Bengal.[2] A few centuries after this, Raghunandan, who is known as the Smarta Bhattacharyya in Bengal and whose work known as *Ashtavinsati-tattva* at present regulates the ceremonial law of that Province, writes in his Dāyatattva: "Thus also if the pledge be not redeemed by reason of death or the like of the seller or donor, it may be redeemed by the buyer or donee, because a right equal to that of the former owner has been generated by the sale or gift. In such a case if a dispute arise as to the source of the right, then the buyer or other donee "(who is admitted as such) is required to prove his possession, and not the commencement of his title."[3] This passage among other things clearly shows that according to Raghunandana there could be a pledge without possession and that such a pledge was prevalent in his days. We

The value of this opinion to show that hopothecation prevailed in Bengal.

A passage from Raghunandana's Dāyatattva supports the conclusion.

[1] Colebrooke's Digest, p. 221.

[2] Halāyudha thus described the successive offices held by him under Lakshmana Sen in his Brahmana Sarvasva:—

बाल्येख्यापित राज पण्डित पदः श्वितांशुबिम्बोज्ज्वल-
च्छत्रोत्सिक्त महामह-त्तकपदं दत्वानवे यौवने ।
यस्मिन् यौवन शेष योग्यमखिलक्ष्मापाल नारायणः ।
श्रीमांल्लक्ष्मणसेन देवनृपतिर्धर्माधिकारं ददौ ।

[3] Dayatattva translated by Babu Golapchandra Sarkar, p. 32.

may, therefore, safely conclude that the system of hypothecating property without delivering possession of it to the creditor was prevalent in Bengal at least from the time of the Sen kings, and it seems to me that there are reasons why such a form of mortgage should find a readier acceptance in Bengal than anywhere else. A pledge, as you have seen, may either be movable or immovable; now, in the case of movable property the transfer of possession from the debtor to the creditor may not cause much inconvenience, but in the case of immovable property it may often prove to be a source of inconvenience to both the parties; for the creditor, on the one hand, may often be unwilling to undertake the trouble of cultivating or making other profitable use of the land, and the debtor also may, on the other hand, be diffident regarding the honesty or capacity of the creditor; it is, therefore, quite natural that in a province where pledges of immovable property frequently take place, the people should, sooner or later, hit upon the expedient of introducing a system of mortgage which would not require the debtor to part with possession of the property; now, as I have already explained in another place, transfers of immovable property were likely to be more frequent in Bengal than anywhere else where the Mitākshara law with its peculiar restraints on alienation especially of immovable property prevailed, and the necessity for raising a loan and that speedily, would also be more frequent there by reason of the commercial activity of the people who settled along the lower course of the Ganges; it is, therefore quite natural that these circumstances should combine to produce a modification of the original law under which a pledge necessarily involved delivery of possession of the property pledged by the debtor to the creditor. I must not, however, be understood to say that hypothecation was unknown

Why hypothecation should find a readier acceptance in Bengal?

Evidence of prevalence of hypothecation outside Bengal.

outside the province of Bengal; on the other hand there is clear evidence of its prevalence to be found in works regarded as authoritative in other provinces: thus in Vyāvahāra Mayūkha Nīlakantha referring to a text of Brihaspati in which the two words *ādhi* and *bandha* are used together so as to signify that different meanings must be attached to them says that the word *bandha* may be taken to mean an agreement of this form, *viz.*, "I shall not make a gift, sale, pledge, or other disposition of this house or field, or other property until the debt I owe you is cleared off;"[1] and this is an explanation which clearly marks off a hypothecation from a pledge accompained by possession, and supports the suggestion of Dr. Ghose that the word *bandhaka* as distinguished from *ādhi* was taken hold of to introduce a new kind of mortgage which gradually did away with the requirements of delivery of possession without which there could be no pledge under the older law.

Vyāvahāra Mayūkha.

Successive stages in the transition to hypothecation.

Having thus shown that the later Hindu Law discloses the recognition of a form of mortgage which did not involve transfer of possession, I shall now attempt to trace the successive stages which led to this transition. I have stated that the word *bandhaka* has in many texts been used in the same way as *ādhi* to denote a pledge with the accompaniment of delivery of possession so that the two words may be taken as synonymous expressions; there is, however, a text of Brihaspati in which distinction seems to have been drawn between them in so far as it says that "a creditor should give a loan either attested by a document or in the presence of witnesses after obtaining an *ādhi* or a

A text of Brihaspati distinguishing between *ādhi* and *bandha*.

---

[1] यावत्तावदृणं न शोध्यते तावदेतद्गृहक्षेत्रादि दानविक्रयाधिकरणादिकं न करिष्यामीति निर्बन्धो बन्धः ।

bandhaka of adequate value or a reliable surety."[1] Here the use of the two words *ādhi* and *bandha* conjunctively suggests that they are employed in different senses, and the Viramitrodaya in explaining this quotes a text of Nārada which says that the word *bandha* signifies a property placed in the hands of a friend for the confidence of the creditor.[2] Now, it seems to me that this marks off the first stage in the transition from a pledge with delivery of possession to the creditor to a hypothecation in which the debtor retains the possession of the property for, here, although the debtor parts with his possession, it is not the creditor but somebody else in whose hands the property is placed in order that he may produce it in case the debtor cannot fulfil his engagement to pay off the debt. The next stage in the transition is reached when the third party who played the part of a stake-holder, so to say, is transformed into a surety for the production of the pledge when the creditor becomes entitled to demand its production. That this transformation did actually take place appears from the fact that while Yājnavalkya describes three classes of sureties, *viz.*, for appearance, for trust, and for payment,[3] other lawgivers have noticed a distinct class of surety, *viz.*, a surety for the production of the pledge who is sometimes described as a surety for the production of the debtor's property (ऋणिद्रव्यार्पण प्रतिभू) and sometimes, more precisely, as a surety for the production of the pledge taken (गृहीत बन्धोपस्थान प्रतिभू). I shall deal with these classifications more fully in a future lecture, but I simply mention them here to show that when a

A text of Nārada to explain the distinction quoted by Viramitrodaya.

The first stage in the transition; property placed in the hands of a third party.

The second stage: the stake-holder transformed into a surety for the production of the pledge.

---

[1] परिपूर्णं गृहीत्वाधिं बन्धं वा साधुलग्नकं ।
लेख्यारूढं साक्षिमद्वा ऋणं दद्याद्धनी तथा ।

[2] निक्षेपो मित्रहस्तस्थो बन्धो विश्वासकः स्मृतः

[3] दर्शने प्रत्यये दाने प्रातिभाव्यं विधीयते ।

pledge was allowed to be placed in the possession of a third person instead of the creditor nothing was more natural than that that person should gradually be permitted to exercise his discretion to keep it in the possession of the debtor provided he took upon himself the responsibility and risk of standing a surety for its production at the proper time and this was what actually took place in the Hindu Law. When we have reached this stage, it is not at all difficult to conceive that there should be a further relaxation and that ultimately the debtor should be allowed to retain the pledge in his possession on his own undertaking not to alienate it in any way without being required to procure a surety to ensure the production of the pledge in case he failed to discharge his debt in proper time; when we arrive at this stage we get what is called hypothecation, and I have already shown that the later Hindu Law furnishes ample evidence of its recognition.

The last stage in the transition: The intervention of a third party dispensed with.

Importance of the transition: what it demonstrates.

The above account of the way in which the necessity of making over the property pledged to the creditor was gradually shaken off furnishes a curious instance of the manner in which old order slowly changes yielding place to the new without abruptness and without any seeming compulsion, but moved and guided along the line of least resistance by the impetus supplied by the altered conditions of the society and the exigencies created thereby, and it is only one among numerous instances of gradual modifications introduced into the Hindu Law in response to the demands of time and the growing necessities of the society. I therefore, venture to affirm that the critic who pretends to see nothing in the Hindu Law but a stagnant mass of archaic rules knows not what he says, and shows that he himself has got a stagnant mind.

Having thus explained to you the nature of a pledge under the Hindu Law, I shall now shortly discuss the rights and obligations arising from the transaction. You will remember that a pledge may either be for a definite period or without any period previously fixed, and it may again be either for custody or for use. The incidents of a pledge vary according to its nature with reference to these distinctions. Thus, in the case of a pledge given upon the definite understanding that it must be redeemed within a definite time, the pledgor loses his right to redeem if he fails to carry out his undertaking, and in this respect it does not make any difference whether the pledge was one for mere custody or for use. Where, however, no such period is fixed by contract, there if the pledge be merely for custody so that the pledgee cannot get anything out of it in satisfaction of his debt, the pledgor loses his right to redeem when the amount of interest accruing due reaches its extreme limit allowable under the Hindu Law, which usually happens when the debt doubles itself; for the Hindu Law does not ordinarily allow accummulation of interest exceeding the principal. The principle underlying this seems to be that a creditor should not be compelled to stay his hands when the debt ceases to carry interest while the pledge being merely for custody does not bring any satisfaction. In either case, however, the law allows a period of grace which usually extends to two weeks, so that the debtor can get his property released by paying off the debt within that time, although he has failed to pay off the debt within the period fixed by the contract, or allowed the interest to accummulate up to the maximum limit.[1] On the other hand, where the pledge is for use and no period is fixed by

Rights of the pledgee.

Pledge for a definite period: no redemption after the expiry of the period.

Pledge without a period fixed.

When the right of redemption ceases, if the pledge be for mere custody.

Period of grace.

Pledge for use without a definite period fixed: no forfeiture.

हिरण्ये द्विगुणीभूते पूर्णे काले कृतेऽवधौ ।
बन्धकस्य धनी स्वामी द्विसप्ताहं प्रतीक्ष्यतु ।
तदन्तरा धनं दत्वा ऋणी बन्धमवाप्नुयात् ।

A further distinction in regard to a pledge for

The usufruct may be enjoyed in lieu of interest; or it may go to satisfy the principal as well.

The duty of the pledgor in the former case.

No forfeiture in the latter case.

contract upon the expiry of which the pledge shall be forfeited, there no forfeiture can take place, and the pledgor is free to redeem and get back the property at any time he likes.[1] Then, again, there is a further distinction to be observed in regard to a pledge for use, for the pledgee may be let into possession either on the understanding that the usufruct shall be enjoyed in lieu of interest, or on the understanding that besides the interest the principal also shall be satisfied out of the usufruct. In the former case where the usufruct is enjoyed in lieu of interest, it will be the duty of the pledgor to pay off the principal either within the time limited by the contract, if there be any, or at any time he chooses, if there be no fixed time limit, in order to get back the property in his possession. In the latter case where the principal also is to be satisfied out of the usufruct it follows from the very nature of the contract that there cannot be any forfeiture, and the pledgor shall get back his property on the expiry of the term fixed by the contract, if there be any, or on the principal with interest being satisfied out of the usufruct, if there be none.

A pledge of this latter class is known as चयाधि and resembles the *vivum vadium* of the old English Law.

Improvement or deterioration of the pledge: its effect.

This latter class of usufructuary mortgage in which the debt is liquidated from the usufruct was popularly known as चयाधि or a pledge that exhausts the debt, and, as Dr. Ghose points out, it resembled in many points the *vivum vadium* of the old English law. The Mitakshara, however, lays down a special rule on the authority of a text of Brihaspati that if in such a case after the pledgee has been let into possession of the property, it unexpectedly acquires an additional value or deteriorates from its previous condition

---

आधि: प्रणश्येद्द्विगुणे धने यदि न मोक्ष्यते।

काले काल कृतोनश्येत् फलभोग्यो ननश्यति।

then the increase or the decrease in the usufruct shall, in the absence of a contract to the contrary, be taken into account in estimating the amount payable to redeem the property, so that the debtor shall have to pay less than the principal in the one case and more than the principal in the other. Those, then, being the conditions for foreclosure, it follows that the pledgor is entitled to get back his property on the satisfaction of the amount payable by him at any time before the foreclosure becomes absolute on the expiry of the period of grace allowed by the law, and it is laid down that if the pledgee refuse to release the property in such a case he shall be liable to punishment as if he were a thief. There is, however, one exception to this rule, *viz.*, that where a usufructuary mortgage is given upon the definite understanding that it will be redeemed at a particular time there it cannot be redeemed before the close of the term even if the debtor wishes to get back the property on paying the amount due to the creditor without waiting till the end of the term unless the creditor agrees to forego his strict rights to retain the property in his possession for the full period originally agreed upon. It, thus, appears that the Hindu Law, while protecting with care the rights of the mortgagor to get back his property at the proper time, cannot be accused of showing an undue indulgence to him so as to enable him to get out of the terms of the contract into which he entered with open eyes.

When the pledgor gets back his property.

Pledgee bound to release the property upon satisfaction of the debt before the foreclosure becomes absolute.

An exception to the rule in the case of a usufructuary mortgage for a definite period.

Those, then, being the conditions of foreclosure under the Hindu Law, it remains to be considered whether under that law, the creditor, could under any circumstances sell the property pledged in order to obtain satisfaction of his debt. It appears that under the Hindu Law, the right of sale was given to the pledgee as an exception to the right of foreclosure, that is to say, where, except in the case of

When can the creditor sell the property pledged?

The right of sale given as an exception to the right of foreclosure.

a usufructuary mortgage without a fixed time limit which is incompatible with both a foreclosure and a sale, the creditor would otherwise be entitled to foreclose the mortgage, it would be open to him to sell the property mortgaged, if he were prevented from exercising the right of foreclosure by reason of a contract to that effect or some rule of law prohibiting a foreclosure and entitling the creditor to his money. There are two special kinds of pledges in which the law lays down that there can be no foreclosure and the creditor must take his money including such interest as he is entitled to. Those pledges are known as चरित्र बन्धक (pledges of good faith or according to another interpretation, pledges of religious merit) and सत्यङ्कारकृत (pledges of solemn promise). A pledge is said to be a pledge of good faith when there is a great difference between the value of the pledge and the money borrowed whether it be in favour of the creditor or in favour of the debtor, since such a pledge must be taken to have been given or taken in reliance upon the good faith of the creditor in the one case and of the debtor in the other. In a case of this description there will be no foreclosure, but the creditor will be entitled to sell the property pledged to recover his money at the proper time. The expression चरित्र बन्धक may also mean a pledge of religious merit whereby the debtor stipulates that he shall not perform a particular act of religious merit or if he performs it the benefit of it shall accrue to the creditor until he repays the debt. In such a case also there will be no forfeiture since a forfeiture does not amount to a fulfilment of the stipulation and the creditor shall take the money by the sale of the pledge, if any, given along with the stipulation. A pledge of solemn promise is a pledge given by the debtor with a solemn promise to repay the debt and not to allow the pledge to be taken

Two special kinds of pledge: चरित्र बन्धक and सत्यङ्कार कृत.

in satisfaction of the debt. Here, also, there will be no foreclosure since the solemn promise mentioned above implies a contract that there will be no foreclosure; in consequence, the creditor will be entitled to sell the pledge in case he cannot otherwise obtain satisfaction. The practical result of these rules, therefore is, that the right of sale arises, when in a case otherwise, fit for foreclosure, the right to foreclose is expressly or impliedly debarred by a contract between the parties, or where there is such a difference between the value of the pledge and the amount due to the creditor that it would entail great hardship either upon the creditor or upon the debtor to have the debt wiped off by the forfeiture of the pledge. It need hardly be said that it is laid down that where the pledge is sold and there remains a surplus after the satisfaction of the debt the debtor becomes entitled to the surplus, but it may be observed that our lawgivers do not expressly say anything about the liability of the debtor to make good the deficiency if the sale-proceeds do not fully satisfy the debt. With reference to this omission, Dr. Ghose remarks, with his usual raciness, that "like a similar omission in the English Pawn Brokers Act, it may be regarded as an indirect compliment to the proverbial shrewdness which establishes the kinship of the worthy brotherhood of money-lenders all the world over." As regards the method of carrying out the sale, the creditor must of course give due notice of his intention to the debtor, but if he is dead or cannot be found then the creditor has the power to sell the pledge even in his absence, in the presence of witnesses, or may keep it at a public place for ten days after having fixed the price; if within that time the debtor does not come forward and discharge the debt, then the creditor shall have his debt satisfied out of it and the surplus if any, shall be made over to the debtor's kindreds or in their

The rules summarised.

If upon a sale, there remains a surplus, the debtor becomes entitled to it.

But what if the price falls short?

Method of carrying out the sale.

absence to the king.[1] Kātyāyana, however, says that in such a case the creditor should sell the pledge after producing the pledge before the king and obtaining his permission and the surplus sale-proceeds will remain with the king for the benefit of the debtor.[2] You will thus see that the Hindu Law does not omit to lay down rules for the proper conduct of the sale to ensure that the interest of the debtor may not be unjustly sacrificed to serve the purpose of the creditor. As regards the time when the right of sale becomes capable of being exercised, it is the same as in the case of foreclosure and I need not repeat the rules which I have already explained in that connection.

A pledge created a real right.

You will observe from the rights of the mortgagee noticed above that the giving of a pledge created a real right and also furnished what is called a real security. It created a real right because the creditor when a pledge was given became invested with an interest in the property pledged which under certain conditions and on the expiry of a certain period would either ripen into full ownership or entitle him to sell the property without the concurrence of the debtor; this right, therefore, is a right in the property itself as distinguished from the right corresponding to the debtor's personal liability to pay.

The Mitākshara supports this position.

The Mitākshara expressly supports this position when it says that "the giving of a pledge is well-recognised among the people as a conditional

---

1 हिरण्ये द्विगुणीभूते मृते नष्टेऽधमर्णिके :
द्रव्य तदीयं तदीयं संगृह्य विक्रीणीयात् ससाक्षिकं ।
रक्षेद्वा कृतमूल्यन्तु दशाऽहान संसादि ।
कृत्वानुरूपमूल्यतो गृहीताव्यन्तु वर्जयेत् । बृहस्पतिः ।

2 आधाता यत्रैव न स्यात्तु धनी बन्धं निवेदयेत् ।
राज्ञस्ततः स विख्यातो विक्रेय इति धारणा ।
सवृद्धिकं गृहीत्वातु शेषं राजन्यथार्पयेत् ।

cause of extinction of property, and the acceptance of a pledge as a conditional cause of acquisition of property, so that after the debt has doubled or the stipulated time has arrived the right to satisfy the debt ceased, and by virtue of the text of Yājnavalkya which is being commented upon the debtor's right is extinguished for ever, and the creditor's ownership becomes absolute." So also the security furnished by a pledge under the Hindu Law was what is called a real security, for it not only operated upon the will of the debtor to induce him to pay off the debt in so far as he was kept out of possession of the property given in pledge, or at all events restrained from making free dispositions of it so long as the debt was not discharged, but it, at the same time, placed in the hands of the creditor sufficient tangible means of obtaining satisfaction quite independent of the wishes or ability of the debtor. A security, as far as one can see, may become a real or substantial security to the creditor in three ways:—(1) through authority to enjoy, (2) through authority to foreclose, and (3) through authority to sell, and it has been shown that all these authorities were recognised and conferred by the Hindu Law upon pledges in proper cases according to the intention of the parties and the nature of the pledge.

The security furnished by a pledge was a real security.

That this was the state of the Hindu Law in its more developed form admits of no doubt whatsoever, but it has been supposed that in the days of Manu the pledgee had no more than a bare right of detention, and reliance is placed in support of this position upon the text of Manu, "However long the time may be neither an assignment nor a sale of pledge can be made."[1] This, however, is explained by the Mitākshara with reference to the context to refer to a pledge for use, and I

Was it so in the days of Manu?

* न चाधेः कालसंरोधान्निसर्गोऽस्ति न विक्रयः ;

cannot say that the interpretation is far-fetched and unreasonable.

Power to create a sub-mortgage: How far limited according to Viramitrodaya.

It appears that the pledgee had also a right to create a sub-mortgage, and the Viramitrodaya says that this would follow *a fortiori* from the existence of the right to sell, for a creditor having a right to sell would only be acting with leniency if he were to realise his money by creating a sub-mortgage. It, however, lays down on the authority of a text of Prajāpati that a sub-mortgage cannot be created for more than the principal money due by the debtor; the reason of this rule seems to be that otherwise the sub-mortgagee might become entitled to demand more upon his mortgage than what the mortgagee could demand from the mortgagor by reason of the rule and the Hindu Law prohibiting accummulation of interest beyond a certain limit bearing a certain proportion to the principal, usually equal to it, so that there would arise a conflict between the rights of the mortgagor and the sub-mortgagee.

Doubts thrown by Medhātithi and Govindarāya.

I may however, mention that Medhātithi and Govindarāya in their commentaries on the Institutes of Manu seem to throw a doubt on the right of the mortgagee to create a sub-mortgage on the authority of the text of Manu quoted above.

How met by the Mitākshara.

I have already cited the interpretation put by the Mitākshara upon that text which gets rid of the objection by limiting its application to the case of a usufructuary mortgage.

Kullūka Bhatta's criticism.

I may also mention that Kullūkabhatta, another principal commentator on the Institutes of Manu, observes that the interpretation of Medhātithi and Govindarāya is contrary to the approved usage in all the provinces, since it is usual to mortgage land and other properties mortgaged at another place.[1] It may be noticed that the

Power to demand fresh security or payment of the money in certain cases.

[1] अत्र तु सर्व्वदेशीय शिष्टाचार विरोधः बन्धकी कृत भूम्यादेर् बन्धाधीकरण समाचारात् ।

pledgee has the right to demand fresh security or in the alternative, payment of the mortgage debt on the determination, loss or destruction of the pledge without the fault of the pledgee owing, as our lawgivers put it, to an act of the king or an act of God,[1] and the Viramitrodaya here puts a note to explain that an act of the king means a wanton act of oppression proceeding from the king not due to any fault of the creditor. As Dr. Ghose remarks, our lawgivers appear to "speak somewhat bluntly of the acts of the king and not of the king's enemies, probably because the casuistry which treats the king's own acts as those of his enemies was too subtle for the unsophisticated Hindu Jurists," and he compares this rule with that to be found in Article 2131 of the French Code which says: "In like manner in case the present movables or immovables, subjected to mortgage, have perished or sustained deterioration in such manner that they have become insufficient for the security of the creditor, the latter shall be permitted either to sue immediately for repayment or to obtain an additional mortgage." It may also be compared with the provisions of Section 68 of the Transfer of Property Act which lays down: 'Where by any cause other than the wrongful act or default of the mortgagor or mortgagee, the mortgaged property has been wholly or partially destroyed, or the security is rendered insufficient as defined in Section 66, the mortgagee may require the mortgagor to give him within a reasonable time another sufficient security for his debt, and if the mortgagor fails so to do, may sue him for the mortgage-money." The wonder is how the human reason bridges over the gulf of time and

Similar rule in the French Code.

Compared to Sec. 68 of the T. P. Act.

---

[1] राज दैवोपघातेन यत्राधिर्नाशमाप्नुयात्
तत्रान्यद्दापयितव्यं धनभागी धनी भवेत् । बृहस्पति ।

space and arrives at similar results by a process which is entirely its own.

Rights of the pledgor, and consequent duties of the pledgee.

Having passed under review the various rights of the pledgee under the Hindu Law I shall now say a few words about his duties towards the pledgor. Shortly stated they may be described as (1) duty to use proper care in keeping and using the pledge, (2) duty not to use or enjoy the pledge when it has been given merely for custody, and (3) duty to return the pledge on satisfaction of the debt either out of the usufruct or from payment made by the pledgor.

Duty to use proper care.

If the pledgee out of negligence spoils or destroys the thing placed under his care, then it will be his duty to make good the loss by restoring the thing to its former condition in the first case and by returning its price in the second, and if the pledge were for use so that the interest were to be satisfied out of it, then the pledgee would not be able to claim any interest from the pledgor by reason of the deterioration or destruction of the pledge, for he was himself responsible for it. Then, again, when the pledge has been totally destroyed, the pledgee cannot claim the principal without paying the price of the pledge as a compensation, and in a case where the pledge is very valuable, so as to be more precious than the principal and the interest payable to the pledgee put together, the pledgor may even claim the balance.

Duty not to use a pledge for custody.

When the pledgee in violation of the compact uses a pledge placed in his hands merely for custody it will work a forfeiture of the interest, and the Mitākshara takes care to note that this will happen although the interest may exceed the usufruct because the pledgee has infringed the compact.[1]

Duty to return the pledge when the debt has been paid off.

As regards the duty to return the pledge

---

1 गोप्याधिभोगे नो वृद्धिः सोपकारेऽथ हापिते
नष्टो देयो विनष्टश्च दैवराजकृतादृते । याज्ञवल्क्यः ।
अत्र मिताक्षरा—गोप्याधेरुपभोगे महत्यापि वृद्धिर्हातव्या समयातिक्रमात् ।

Payment how to be made if the pledgee be absent.

when the debt has been paid off, I dealt with it before; I may here add that if the pledgee be absent then the debtor is to pay the money to the members of his family, and take back the pledge from them; if, however, no person be available who can return the pledge, then the money being tendered, the interest will cease to run.

Right of the pledgor to sell or mortgage the property pledged.

His ownership not affected by the pledge.

The next question to which I will advert relates to the right of the pledgor to sell or mortgage the pledge. As the ownership of the pledgor is not affected by his giving the property in pledge, it follows that he can sell it subject to the rights of the pledgee. On such a sale the purchaser steps into the shoes of the pledgor and can redeem the pledge as his vendor could have done. If any authority were needed, the passage I have quoted from the Dayatattva is an express authority on this point. As regards the right to create a second mortgage, it seems to me that it did not exist at least under the earlier Hindu Law, and that would be so, because as I have already pointed out, the earlier Hindu Law did not recognise a pledge which did not involve delivery of possession, and one thing could not be placed in possession of two persons. Hence Katyayana declares, that if a person pledges a property to two individuals, then the first transaction shall prevail, and the pledgor shall be punishable like a thief[1] and a text of Vishnu prescribes the nature of punishment to be inflicted on the offending pledgor. Referring to the latter test Dr. Ghosh observes that the test seems only to point to a fraudulent second mortgage executed by the debtor without disclosing the first mortgage, and that no exception could be taken to

Could he create a second mortgage? The question discussed.

Dr. Ghosh's view.

[1] आधिमेकं द्वयोर्यस्तु कुर्य्यात् का प्रतिपद भवेत्।
तयोः पूर्वं कृतं ग्राह्यं तत्कर्त्ता चौरदण्डभाक्।

the second mortgage honestly created by the debtor. It must, however, be observed that under the Hindu Law so long as it required possession to be delivered to the pledgee, a debtor could not possibly create a second mortgage with honesty except with the connivance and consent of the first mortgagee and hence the texts penalising the creation of a second mortgage are found to be general in their terms, without any qualification and thus indicate the invalidity of such a transaction. That this was the Mitakshara view appears from a passage in which the author commenting upon the text of Yajnavalkya, "In the case of a pledge, an acceptance of a gift, or a purchase, the prior in time prevails"[1] says "If it be said that this text is superfluous because when a property has been pledged, the owner's right in it (to pledge it again) being wanting a second pledge is impossible, and that similarly of a property either given or sold, no second gift or sale can be validly made, it is answered that this is no real objection because the text is really founded upon reason to show that if a person by reason of a clouded intellect or greed create a second mortgage, etc., although he has no right to do so, then the first shall prevail." This shows that, according to the Mitakshara, since after the creation of the first mortgage the mortgagor ceases to have the right to create a second, the second mortgage created, without the right, cannot be valid. It may, however, be that when in course of time the necessity of delivery of possession came to be dispensed with, the creation of a second mortgage ceased to be amenable to the same objections as before and gradually came to be regarded as valid subject to the superior rights of the first mortgagee, and it may be contended, that when a gift

This is doubtful.

The Mitakshara view.

It may be that a second mortgage was gradually recognised as valid.

---

[1] आधौ प्रतिग्रहक्रीते पूर्व्वातु बलवत्तरा।

or a sale of mortgaged property subject to the mortgage was regarded as valid, as appears from the passage quoted from the Dayatattva of Raghunandana, it would follow *a fortiori* that a second mortgage could not be treated as invalid. I feel that these considerations raise a presumption that a second mortgage was gradually recognised as valid under the Hindu Law, but I must confess that I can not be quite sure about this when I find that the Viramitrodaya which is a comparatively modern work says, "Where a person having pledged a field to one, on taking a loan from him, again takes a loan from another on pledging the same property there the field shall be held (under mortgage) by the first person, and not by the second; and a similar rule shall apply to an acceptance of a gift and a purchase, the reason being the obstruction of ownership (in the case of a pledge) and the removal of ownership (in the other cases) due to the completion of the previous transaction." It is, therefore, not unlikely that the difficulties of adjusting the rights of successive mortgagees which prove so embarassing to an English lawyer was unknown to the Hindu lawyers who insisted on the much simpler rule that a second mortgage created without redeeming the first could not be valid. Of course, if the first mortgagee were to be paid off out of the money raised on the second mortgage, there would be no difficulty, since in that case the second mortgage would practically be the first, but if the debtor were not so disposed there would not be much injustice in debarring him from creating a second mortgage at all; at all events it would save the court from a good deal of confusion if not prevent a good deal of fraud. I shall now turn to the rules laid down in the Hindu law to determine which among several mortgages shonld prevail. The general rule of course is that in the case of pledges just as in other transfers, the

Even this is doubtful.

Cf. Viramitrodaya.

Priority of mortgages.

The general rule: prior in point of time prevails.

first in time prevails. But then there is this peculiarity in the case of pledges, that the priority in point of time is of no avail if the prior mortgagee has not obtained possession while the subsequent mortgagee has done. So the Viramitrodaya says: 'If an unrighteous debtor obtains loans from two creditors by pledging the same property, then the priority shall be determined by reference to possession. So says Vishnu: "If two men to whom the same property has been pledged enter into a contest, he shall win who has obtained possession if it were not obtained by force."[1] Dr. Ghose, however, supposes that in the Mitakshara 'priority is determined not by possession, but by the order in which the mortgages have been made, possession by the mortgagee being material only when it cannot be ascertained which of two competing mortgages was prior in order of time'.[2] I venture to presume that he says so on the authority of the passage in the Mitakshara which I have already quoted from his book in a previous part of my discussion, and as I have there attempted to show that the passage had reference to a transfer of ownership, by a gift or a sale, and not to a pledge at all. I hope I shall be able to settle this point by referring you to the passage in the Mitakshara which directly deals with the question of priority of pledges and appears to be in agreement with the rule quoted by me from Viramitrodaya. Commenting upon the text of Yajnavalkya "By the acceptance of a pledge is its validity maintained," Vijnaneswara observes as follows:—"The taking of a pledge becomes complete by its acceptance which means enjoyment, whether it be a pledge for use or for custody not

But prior from what standpoint?

Priority by reference to possession; see Viramitrodaya.

Dr. Ghose's view doubted

Mitakshara in agreement with Viramitrodaya.

---

1 ययोर्निक्षिप्त आधि स्तौ विवदेतां यदा नरौ ।
यस्यभुक्तिर्जयस्तस्य बलात्कारं विनाकृता ॥

Ghose on Mortgage, p. 58.

by mere witnesses or document nor by mere intention. Thus Narada says 'Pledges are declared to be of two sorts, immovable and movable, and both are valid when there is actual enjoyment, and not otherwise. The result of this is as follows :—it has been said that, 'in the case of a pledge, an acceptance or a purchase, the prior prevails,' here the transaction ending in acceptance (as explained above) being prior, prevails, but if it be wanting in acceptance then although prior, it does not prevail." To obviate possible mistakes I should mention that the word enjoyment used in this connection is explained by the Viramitrodaya to mean bringing under one's own control in the case of a pledge for custody and enjoyment of the usufruct in the case of a pledge for use. [1] Similarly Aparарka explains the word acceptance in the text of Yajnavalkya by saying that it extends to the enjoyment of the usufruct in the case of a pledge for use and to putting it into the store-room in the case of a pledge for custody. [2]

Cf. Apararka.

Conclusion.

It is, therefore, clear that according to the Mitakshara, priority of the mortgage without possession is of no avail if the subsequent mortgage succeeds first in getting possession provided it was obtained without force or fraud. The fact is that the Hindu lawyers of the Mitakshara School never went so far as to hold that in the case of a pledge the delivery of possession was immaterial even for the purpose of determining priority between two transactions.

Priority when the transactions are contemporaneous.

It is also laid down that when two pledges are created contemporaneously then he who first obtains possession secures the better title.

Similar rule in the Roman Law.

This is similar to the rule of the Roman Law noticed by Dr. Ghose under which if a debtor pledge his property to two persons at

---

1 गोप्याधौ भोगः स्वीकार भोग्याधौ फलभोगः ।

2 स्वीकारश्च भोग्याधौ भोग पर्यन्तं गोप्याधौ तु भाण्डागार प्रवेश पर्यन्तं ।

the same time and one of them happened to be in possession he could claim preference over the others. If, however, in such a case both come to take possession during the same day, then they must divide the pledge among them. When these considerations do not arise, there are certain special rules laid down to determine the priority between two transactions. Thus a mortgage created by a document is declared fit to prevail over a parol mortgage merely supported by witnesses, and even among mortgages created by documents, the document in which the mortgaged property is clearly defined prevails over one in which it is not so defined and is consquently left as imperceptible as the subtle element. If these special considerations do not apply, the general rule will, of course, hold good and the mortgage which is prior in point of time must prevail.

What if possession is sought at the same time?

Special rules when the above considerations do not apply.

I will, now, conclude my review of the Hindu Law of pledge. It would no doubt be interesting to compare with this the Law of Mortgage in some of the western systems, but as the lecture has already become long I cannot permit myself any such lengthy digression at this place. I may, however, venture to affirm that the Hindu law of pledge is on the whole eminently logical and reasonable, and I hope that whoever will study it with care, and without prejudice due to preconceived ideas which often blur the vision of able but unsympathetic readers, will be disposed to agree with Dr. Ghose that it is "a model of good sense and logical consistency." Nay I may go further and say that whatever its imperfections may be, we need not be ashamed to place it side by side with any system of law bearing upon the subject.

The Hindu Law of pledge logical and reasonable.

'A Model of good sense and logical consistency.'

LECTURE VII

THE LAW OF BAILMENTS AND OTHER INCORPOREAL RIGHTS.

How a bailment differs from a pledge.

Why the subject is treated here as a part of the law of things.

In the present lecture I propose to deal with the Hindu law of bailments and other incorporeal rights not already discussed. A bailment differs from a pledge in so far as in the case of a bailment property belonging to a person is placed under the control of another out of trust reposed in that person and not as a security for the performance of any obligation cast upon the owner. It follows from this that the rights of a bailee over the thing bailed are much more limited than the rights of a pledgee over the pledge, since those peculiar rights which arise from the relation of creditor and debtor in the latter case cannot arise in the former. Still it cannot be denied that the bailee does, by the act of bailment, acquire certain rights over the thing placed under his custody, and it is because these rights constitute what a Hindu lawyer would call qualified property appropriate for keeping the thing in safe custody (रक्षणोपयोगिस्वत्व) that I propose to discuss the subject at this place as a part of the law of things instead of postponing its discussion to give it a place in the law of contract.

Sir William Jones on the Hindu law of bailments.

Speaking of the Hindu law of bailments, Sir William Jones, who being an accomplished lawyer as well as a Sanskritist, was competent to express an opinion on the subject, has said : "It is pleasing to remark the similarity, or rather identity, of those conclusions, which pure unbiassed reason in all ages and nations seldom fails to draw, in such judicial enquiries as are not fettered and manacled by *positive* institution; and although the rules of the *pundits* concerning *succession* to *property*, the *punishment* of *offences*, and the *ceremonies* of *religion* are widely different from ours, yet in the great system of *contracts*, and the common intercourse between man and man, the *Pootee* of the Indians and the Digest of the Romans are by no means dissimilar." The truth of these remarks will, I hope, appear from the following short account of the Hindu law of bailments.

Different kinds of bailments.

There are several different kinds of bailments mentioned by our lawgivers, but their incidents are almost identical. The words निक्षेप (nikshepa) and न्यास (nyása) are often used to denote bailments in general, but they have also been used to denote special kinds of deposits. Thus the word निक्षेप (nikshepa) in its special sense means an open deposit made in the presence of the bailee after showing him the nature and quantity of the thing deposited; the word न्यास (nyása) signifies an open and ascertained deposit entrusted in the absence of the bailee with the members of his family; the word उपनिधि (upanidhi), on the other hand, means a deposit under a sealed cover of which the nature is consequently not disclosed to the bailee; besides these, there is the term अन्वाहित (anváhita) which means a bailment for delivery, that is to say, a deposit made over by the depository to another saying 'a certain person deposited this with me, and you shall deliver it to him,' याचितक (yáchitaka) which means a loan for use, शिल्पिन्यास (silpinyása) which means a deposit with an artist, for instance, of gold with a goldsmith in order that he may make ornaments with it for the depositor, and प्रतिन्यास (pratinyása) which means a mutual bailment, that is, a deposit made in return for a deposit received. Out of these, the distinctions, which it may be useful to remember, are those between open and ascertained deposits and sealed deposits, and between deposits for safe custody, loans for use, and deposits with an artist, because these distinctions are based on real differences in the character of bailments, and they also give rise to some differences in the rights and liabilities of the parties. In the main, however, the incidents of these various kinds of bailments are very much the same.

The acceptance of a bailment is always an onerous undertaking; and it seldom brings benefit to the bailee, for except in the cases of a loan for use where the bailee gets the benefit of using the thing for his own purposes, and perhaps also of a deposit with an artist where the bailment is a part of an entire transaction which is profitable to the artist, the bailee accepts the risk of keeping the deposit safe without getting any tangible benefit in return. Brihaspati, therefore, extols such an act as an act of merit, and says that whoever accepts a trust-deposit and keeps it with care does as meritorious an act as one who gives shelter to a person seeking protection, but, at the same time, he gives the warning that the destruction of a deposit out of negligence or greed is sinful as well as a source of disgrace, and one should, therefore, either refuse to accept a bailment, or having accepted it preserve it with care and return it as soon as asked to do so.[1] But apart from these religious and moral considerations, the acceptance of a trust-deposit

Grounds of bailee's obligations.

---

[1] ददतो यद्भवेत् पुण्यं हेमरूप्याम्बरादिकम् ।
तत्स्यात् पालयतो न्यासं यथैव शरणागतम् ॥
भर्तृद्रोहे यथा नार्याः पुंसः पुत्रसुहृद्वधे ।
दोषो भवेत्तथा न्यासे भक्षितोपेक्षिते नृणाम् ॥
न्यासद्रव्यं न गृह्णीयात्तन्नाशक्षयकारकः ।
गृहीतं पालयेद्यत्नात् सकृद्याचितमर्पयेत् ॥
वीरमित्रोदये निक्षेपाख्य व्यवहारपदधृत—बृहस्पति वचनम् ।

creates certain legal obligations supported by legal sanctions. It is not necessary for a Hindu lawyer to try to resolve this simple fact, *viz.*, the accrual of legal obligations on the acceptance of a trust-deposit, into something finer than that, for he has not got to meet the difficulty of squaring it with the doctrine of consideration by bringing forward an artificial explanation such as that of an eminent English judge who had to contend that even in a gratuitous bailment there is a consideration, because the owner's trusting the bailee with the goods is a sufficient consideration to oblige him to a careful management. It is much simpler to say, as Brihaspati does, that you may not accept a bailment at all, but if you do, the very fact of your acceptance places you under certain responsibilities, for then, you must preserve it with care and return it on the first demand. Stated shortly, it is the trust accepted by the bailee which is the ground of his obligations, and not any consideration proceeding from the bailor in reposing the trust in him.

Duties of the bailee.

Duty to take proper care.

I shall now proceed to explain the duties of the bailee on accepting the bailment and the penalties for their breach. The first duty of the bailee is to preserve the property placed in his hands with proper care, and if the property, while in his hands, is lost or destroyed for want of such care, he must compensate the bailor.

Measure of proper care according to the Hindu law.

The usual test.

The measure of proper care which the Hindu law requires from the bailee is the care which he exercises for his own goods, so that the usual test is, that if along with the goods entrusted with the bailee, his own goods are also lost or destroyed, then the loss must be suffered by the bailor without complaint, for he ought not to expect more care from a gratuitous bailee than what that person exercises for his own goods. Similarly, the bailee cannot be held responsible when the loss or destruction of the

Bailee not responsible for loss

property entrusted to his care happens through an agency over which he had no control, that is to say, as our lawgivers succinctly put it, through an act of the king or an act of God. I have had occasion to refer to these two expressions in dealing with the law of pledge; an act of God means such unforeseen accidents as fire, flood, etc.; an act of the king means a wanton act of oppression proceeding from the king; our lawgivers, you will thus observe, did not pretend to think that the king could do no wrong, and they had not learnt the sophistry of describing the king's own acts, when they were wrong, as the acts of his enemy. I should also mention that in regard to a bailment, theft was placed by our lawgivers in the same category as an act of God, so that if the property deposited was lost by theft, the bailee was exempted from liability in the same way as if the property had been destroyed by fire or carried away by flood. It may, however, be observed that while exonerating the bailee from responsibility when along with the property deposited, the property of the bailee was lost or destroyed, or when the loss or destruction resulted from an act of the king or an act of God including theft, the Hindu lawgivers were acute enough to perceive that a dishonest bailee, if so disposed, could create, an apparent excuse with an eye to his own benefit by fraudulent means. Hence, Narada, when saying that the loss falls upon the bailor when his goods are lost or destroyed along with the goods of the bailee, or when it arises from an act of the king or an act of God, in the same breath adds the qualification: "provided it does not arise from the tortuousness of the bailee."[1] It

arising from an act of the king or an act of God.

Theft placed in the same category as an act of God.

Bailee not exonerated when apparent excuse was created by him by fraudulent device.

1 ग्रहीतुः सह योऽर्थेन नष्ट एव स दायिनः ।
दैवराजकृते तद्वन्न चेत्तज्जिह्मकारितम् ।
चौरमिश्रोदयं निषेध प्रकरणस्थत नारद वचनम् ।

will thus appear that the bailee is relieved from responsibility on account of loss or destruction of the thing deposited when it happens in spite of his exercising the proper amount of care, or through what we may call, adopting an expression from the Roman Law, a *vis major*; therefore, if charged for the loss or destruction of the deposit, it will be a sufficient defence for the bailee if he can show that he exercised as much care over it as over his own things, or that the loss or destruction was due to an extraneous agency over which he had no control.

As regards the quantum of care required, it made no difference whether the bailment was gratuitous or it was a loan for use.

A special rule applicable to a bailment for mere custody.

As regards the quantum of care required, it does not appear that it made any difference in the Hindu Law whether it was a case of a gratuitous bailment for mere custody or of a loan for use, for in each case the measure of proper care was the same, being the amount of care which the bailee used to bestow upon his own property. In the case of a bailment for mere custody in which the benefit was entirely on the side of the bailor, there was a special rule, which, I think, did not apply to the case of a loan for use, to the effect that if a bailor, being aware that the bailee used to lose his own goods from carelessness, still chose to entrust him with his own goods, then he could not hold the bailee responsible even if he lost them out of carelessness, for in such a case it should be presumed that the bailor knowingly accepted the risk of the goods deposited being lost by the carelessness of the bailee. The text of Katyayana on which this rule is based,[1] although cited by the Viramitrodaya, is not noticed by the author of the Mitakshara and some other commentators, but I do not think that this can be regarded as

---

1 ज्ञात्वा द्रव्यवियोगन्तु दाता यत्र विनिक्षिपेत् ।
सर्व्वोपायविनाशेऽपि ग्रहीता नैव दाप्यते ॥
वीरमित्रोदये निक्षेप प्रकरण धृत कात्यायन वचनम् ।

a sufficient ground for regarding it as spurious, for it is not unusual to find some commentators citing more texts than others; and, moreover, the text itself is not only not inconsistent with the general rule that one should use as much care in protecting things entrusted to him as he does in relation to his own property, but may, in one sense, be said to be almost a deduction from that rule, since, a person, who is, to the knowledge of the bailor, careless about his own property, may be excused if he proves no better about the property of the bailor placed in his hands, and the bailor himself cannot complain, for he ought to have expected as much. However that may be, the general rule seems to be that the Hindu law requires that the bailee should exercise as much care in protecting things entrusted to him as he does in relation to his own property, and he cannot be held responsible for the loss or destruction of the thing deposited simply because some one more careful than himself might have avoided or averted it.

The general rule summarised.

Some distinction drawn by the Roman law not recognised by the Hindu law.

Comparing these provisions, then, with those of the Roman law, we find that according to that system the extent of responsibilty was not the same in the cases of a loan for use and a bailment for mere custody. Thus, with reference to a loan for use, which is known as *commodatum* under the Roman law, it is stated in the Institutes of Justinian that "he who has received a thing lent for his use, is indeed bound to employ his utmost diligence in keeping and preserving it; nor will it suffice that he should take the same care of it, which he was accustomed to take of his own property, if it appear that a more careful person might have preserved it in safety; but he has not to answer for loss occasioned by superior force or extraordinary accident, provided the accident is not due to any fault of his;" on the other hand, with reference to a deposit, by which is meant a gratuitous bailment for mere custody, it is there stated that "a person with whom a thing is deposited............is only answerable if he is guilty of fraud, and not for a mere fault, such as carelessness or negligence; and he cannot, therefore, be called to account if the thing deposited, being carelessly kept, is stolen. For he who commits his property to the care of a negligent friend should impute the loss to his own want of caution."[1] It will thus appear that in the case of a loan for use the Roman Law seems to require more care to be exercised by the bailee than the Hindu Law, whereas in the case of a gratuitous deposit it seems to require less. The provisions of the Roman Law seem to have been based on the following considerations: a person who takes a loan of a thing for use (*commodatum*) derives some benefit from the loan, while the lender does not get any, for the transaction is entirely gratuitous; hence the Roman Law ordains that in such a case the borrower must use extreme care to keep the thing safe; on the other hand, in the case of a bailment for mere custody (*depositum*), the benefit is entirely on the side of the depositor, and hence the bailee should not be held responsible unless he is guilty of fraud. Turning now to the Hindu law, we find that the standard of care required is not an abstract standard, but a concrete and relative standard which makes allowance for the differences in human capacities provided there is no wilful default. It may be pointed out that in the case of partnership (*societas*), the Roman law allows that the fault of a partner in dealing with partnership properties 'is not to be measured by a standard of the most perfect carefulness possible, and that it is sufficient that he should be as careful of things belonging to the partnership as he is of his own

Rules of the Hindu law compared with the provisions of the Roman law, and the former sought to be justified.

---

[1] Institutes Lib: III. Tit: XIV.

property, for he who accepts as partner a person of careless habits has only himself to blame.'[1] Now, having regard to this argument, may we not say that a person does not usually lend his property gratuitously for use to another man unless there exists some sort of friendship or close acquaintance between them, and, that being so, the lender ought to know whether the borrower is ordinarily of careful habits or not, and, if knowing that, he thinks it fit to accommodate his friend, he ought not to complain if his friend takes as much care of the articles lent as he does of his own things, and no more? I cannot, therefore, say that the standard laid down by the Hindu law is unfair or unjust, and if any body be not satisfied with it, there is nothing to prevent him from entering into a special contract before he lends his things. As regards a mere deposit, the Roman Law holds the depositary liable only for fraud, and any amount of carelessness on his part is excused on the ground that 'he who commits his property to the care of a negligent friend should impute the loss to his own want of caution.' It seems to me that the rule of the Hindu law is on this point more reasonable and just. The ground set forth above to justify the rule of the Roman law assumes that the depositor is aware of the careless habits of the depositary, but he could only be aware of this, if the depositary had, on previous occasions, been found careless about his own things; in such a case, Katyayana's text quoted by me shows that even the Hindu law made an exception to the general rule. But in other cases, where the depositor, judging from the previous habits of the depositary, could not know that the latter was peculiarly careless about his own things, it would not be unreasonable to require that having accepted a deposit the depositary should take as

[1] Institutes Lib. III. Tit. XXV.

much care of it as he did of his own things; at all events, in a case like this, the ground that 'he who commits his property to the care of a negligent friend should impute the loss to his own want of caution' cannot apply, and the rule of the Roman law must be defended, if possible, on some other ground than what the Institutes suggest. The idea which really pervades the rule of the Roman law seems to be that whoever takes charge of another's property without any remuneration or other kind of benefit need not take as much care of it as he does of his own, or, at any rate, he ought not to be held accountable if he does not; nay, the rule goes to the length of absolving the depositary altogether from all responsibility for mere carelessness, for he cannot be held responsible for anything short of fraud. It seems to me that the standard laid down by the Hindu law that a person should take as much care of things entrusted to him as he does of his own is more consonant with our moral sense than the rule of the Roman law; as the Hindu lawgivers point out, you may not accept a bailment if you like, but if you do, you should not make any distinction between your own property and the property so committed to your care. A person, who after taking charge of another's property without demur afterwards bestows very little care upon it simply because it is not his own, may be absolved from responsibility by the technical rule of the Roman law, but will, I hope, be not similarly absolved by the moral consciousness of any civilised community. It may be said that legality and morality do not often agree; that may be true but there can be no harm, if, in a case like this they do. As regards the rule that a bailee cannot be held accountable if the loss or destruction of the property results from some uncontrollable external agency, both the Hindu and the Roman systems agree, and, as

I shall show, there are resemblances in other respects also.

Provisions of the English Common Law compared.

Turning, now, to the Common Law of England, it appears from the luminous account given by Mr. Justice Holmes that the liability of the bailee was originally much more rigorous than under either the Hindu law or the Roman law. The old Common Law rule was that when the bailor's goods were placed in the bailee's hands, the latter was bound to hold the former harmless, and if the goods were lost, it was no excuse to say that they were stolen without his (the bailee's) fault. Thus, it was laid down in the case of Southcote v. Bennet that delivery to a bailee chargeth him to keep at his peril, and it was no plea that he was robbed, and Lord Coke added "That *to keep* and to keep safely are one and the same thing." It should be observed that Southcote's case did not recognise any distinction between a paid and an unpaid bailee, although in a subsequent case Popham C. J. sought to draw a distinction between the two, and differentiate the extents of their liability. Gradually, however, the rigour of the old Common Law has been relaxed, but a remnant of it still lingers in the special liability of the inn-keepers and common carriers, which is now supposed to be an exception introduced by the custom of the realm, but is regarded by Mr. Justice Holmes to be a survival of ancient law regarding the general liability of the bailee. However that may be, the overthrow of the rule deducible from Southcote's case may be said to date from the decision in Coggs v. Bernand, in which Lord Holt, being under the impression that the common law of bailment was derived from the Roman law, assimilated it, as far as possible, to the rules laid down by that system. In that case Lord Holt distinguished between bailees for reward exercising a common calling and other bailees, and held that the bailees of the former class incurred a special liability by reason of their exercising a common calling for remuneration, but, at the present day, the principle of common employment has been given up, and the special liability is only confined to common carriers and innkeepers, which remains, as Mr. Justice Holmes puts it, as a merely empirical exception from the general doctrine, in so far as they cannot claim any immunity unless they can make out that the loss or damage was due to an act of God or an act of the public enemy. That being the history of the English Common Law, it seems to me that the ancient Hindu law regarding the liability of the bailee was much more reasonable than the ancient Common Law. Indeed, as Mr. Justice Holmes points out, the peculiarity of the old English law upon the point was due to a peculiarity of procedure under which the remedy for wrongful appropriation by a third person of property committed to the care of a bailee was exclusively in his hands, and hence he was held responsible to the bailor whether the loss or destruction of the property was due to his fault or not; in course of time, the right to sue was extended to the bailor, but the old view regarding the strict liability of the bailee still lingered, until the law was gradually changed and assimilated to the Roman law.

Different degrees of blame-worthiness and different standards of compensation based thereon.

Let us now revert to the main subject of our discussion. I have explained the grounds on which a bailee may claim immunity from liability on account of loss or destruction of the property placed in his hands. Where these grounds do not exist, the bailee is liable to compensate the bailor for his loss; but it ought to be mentioned that the Hindu law recognises that the bailee may not be equally blamable in every case. Thus the loss or destruction of the property committed to the care of the bailee for which he is accountable may arise in either of three ways : (1) The bailee may have consumed the property himself ; (2) he may have allowed it to be lost or destroyed through his negligence ; or (3) the loss or destruction may have happened through a mistake on his part which ought not to have occurred. In the first case, the property is said to have been भक्षित (consumed), in the second, उपेक्षित (neglected), and in the third अज्ञाननाशित (destroyed through mistake). It is apparent that you cannot impute the same amount of blame to the bailee in these cases, and, taking this into consideration, the Hindu law has adjudged that the measure of compensation payable by the bailee should vary according to the extent of blame imputable to him. Thus, it has been laid down that where the bailee has himself consumed the property placed in his hands, he shall have to pay its price together with interest ; where it has been lost or destroyed through his negligence, he shall have to pay a sum equal to its price (without interest) ; and where the loss is attributable to a culpable mistake on his part the compensation shall amount to a little less than its proper value,[1] allowing, according to the Mitakshara, a deduction of one fourth. Apart from this, a person who consumes a property committed to his care, or uses it for his own profit without the permission of the owner renders himself liable to punishment. It may be added that in the case of a doposit delivered under a sealed cover, the bailee is not at all responsible if somehow or other it becomes spoiled within the cover, but he becomes liable if he breaks the seal and uses any part of the deposit for his own purpose.

Measure of compensation in each case.

Punishment for breach of trust.

[1] भक्षितं सोदयन्दाप्यः समन्दाप्यमुपेक्षितम् ।
किञ्चिदूनं प्रदाप्यः स्याद्द्रव्यमज्ञाननाशितम् ॥
मिताक्षरा उपनिधि प्रकरणधृत कात्यायनवचनम् ।

Duty to return the deposit on demand.

After demand, bailee responsible for loss however it may arise.

The next duty of the depositary is to return the thing deposited as soon as asked to do so; if he fails to do so, then he becomes answerable for any subsequent loss of the deposit even if it happens from an act of the King or an act of God;[1] in other words, although a depositary cannot ordinarily be held liable for the loss of the deposit if it be due to some uncontrollable agency, yet this defence ceases to be available to him if at the time when the demand was made for the return of the deposit he could have returned it but did not do so without any excuse; in such a case it was the duty of the depositary to return the deposit as soon as he was asked to do so, and if he omitted to do it, he did so at his peril, so that no excuse based upon any subsequent accident could be listened to. Vyasa, however, remarks that if the loss arises from an act of the king or act of God, the depositary should not be called upon to pay more than the price as compensation, and this, as the Viramitrodaya observes, is proper, since it would be hard to force him to pay more when his only fault was the delay in returning the deposit after demand.

Exception to the obligation to return on demand.

To this rule requiring the bailee to return the thing committed to his care as soon as a demand is made, the Hindu Law recognises an exception in the case of a loan for use, for it lays down that if a person obtains a thing from another for using it on a particular occasion, or for a particular period of time, then he cannot be held guilty if he does not return the thing before that particular occasion or within that particular period of time, when his work is half-finished although the lender asks

---

[1] याचनान्तरं नष्टो दैवराजकृतेऽपि सः।
तर्हीता प्रतिदाप्यः स्यात् मूल्यमात्रं न संशयः। व्यासः
प्रत्यर्पण विलम्बमात्रापराधे सर्वस्वदापनस्यान्याय्यत्वात्।
इति वीरमित्रोदयः। निक्षेपाख्य व्यवहारपदम्।

for its return.[1] Curiously enough, the Roman Law also recognises a similar distinction, for while it lays down that a depositor may reclaim the deposit whenever he pleases, a *commodans* (*i.e.*, a lender for use) must wait for the expiration of the time agreed on. The Hindu Law, however, attaches an exception to the above exception, for it says that if it so happens that some work of the lender will suffer if he has to wait till the expiration of the time agreed on, then the borrower should return the thing borrowed although his work has only been half finished.[2] This seems reasonable, since in the case of a gratuitous loan it is but fair that the work of the lender should not suffer even at the cost of some inconvenience to the borrower. In the case of articles deposited with an artist in order that he may exercise his workmanship upon it, the artist should complete his work within the appointed time; if he does not, then he shall be responsible for a subsequent loss however it may arise; moreover, if the article is damaged during the progress of the work, then, if it happens owing to some defect in the article, the artist shall not be responsible for it; but it will be otherwise, if the damage is due to some fault on the part of the artist.

A similar rule in the Roman Law.

An exception to the exception.

Special rules regarding a deposit with an artist.

As regards the manner of returning a deposit, it is laid down that it should be returned in the same way as it was taken. Thus, when a property has been deposited by a certain person, it is the duty of the bailee to return it to him, and Brihaspati takes care to add that the bailee

The manner of returning a deposit.

Duty to return to the bailor, and not to any other claimant.

---

1 यदि तत्कार्य्यमुद्दिश्य कालम्परिनियम्यवा ।
याचितोऽर्थंकृती यस्मिन्प्राप्ते नतु दास्यति ॥
वीरमित्रोदय—निक्षेप प्रकरण धृत कात्यायन वचनम् ।

2 यत्र कार्य्यविपत्तिस्तु तत्रैव स्वामिनो भवेत् ।
अर्धान्ते वै समाप्तेतु दाप्यस्त्वर्धकृतेऽपितत् ॥
वीरमित्रोदये—निक्षेपप्रकरण धृत कात्यायन वचनम् ।

should not make it over to any person other than the bailor, although he may claim to be the owner of the thing, nor even to the sons or other close relations of the bailor, so long as he is alive.[1] This corresponds to the principle of estoppel applicable to the case of a bailment as laid down in sec. 116 of the Indian Evidence Act. Then, again, where there has been a mutual deposit, the return should also be mutual.[2] When, however, the bailor is dead, the bailee should return the deposit to the heirs of the deceased bailor, but if there be several such heirs, the return should be made in the presence of all of them.

Compare bailor's estoppel.

Bailor being dead, the thing may be returned to his heirs

Ordinarily the bailee may return the deposit whenever he chooses.

Exception to this rule.

As in the case of a gratuitous bailment, the bailee does not derive any benefit from the task undertaken by him, he is ordinarily free to return the thing deposited at any time he pleases, even before the bailor asks for it; but then, where the deposit was made out of fear for some anticipated danger, the bailee should not, if he were aware of the motive which induced the deposit, return it until the danger was over. Such a return is called premature (कालहीन) and the bailee who makes such a return against the wishes of the bailor renders himself liable to be punished with a fine, if, in consequence, the bailor suffers any loss.

Duties how enforced by the king.

In a proper case, and at the proper time, the king will enforce the return of the deposit, if the bailee do not return it of his own accord, and, furthermore, he who denies a deposit made with him and he who falsely claims to have

---

1 स्थापितं येन विधिना येन यत्र यथाविधि ।
तथैव तस्मात्तद्देयं न देयं प्रत्यनन्तरे ॥

स्थापयितै तरस्य यस्य स्थापित द्रव्यस्वत्वमस्ति स एव प्रत्यनन्तर उच्यते इति स्मृति-चन्द्रिकायां, प्रत्यनन्तरे पुत्रादाविति कल्पतरौ । वीरमित्रोदये निक्षेप प्रकरणम् ।

2 मिथोदायः कृतो येन गृहीतो मिथ एव वा ।
मिथ एव प्रदातव्यो यथादाय तथागमः ॥

made a deposit with another and demands its return should both be punished by the king.

Some incorporeal rights.

I shall now give a short account of some incorporeal rights recognised by the Hindu Law which have not found a place in the discussions contained in this and the previous lectures, and with this I shall conclude this lecture as well as the Part dealing with the Law of Things. We do not find any lengthy discussion about these rights in the Hindu Law, and I shall, therefore, content myself with merely indicating their nature as disclosed in the works on Hindu Law.

Right of pasturage.

The first right of this kind to which I may advert is the right of pasturage. The importance of this right to an agricultural people can hardly be denied, and hence we find our lawgivers making provisions for the maintenance of pasture-grounds in or around every village which may be used by the villagers in general for grazing their cattle on. So Yājñavalkya declares that in every village there should be land set apart for pasturage either by the common consent of the villagers, or by a special order of the king.[1] This seems to imply that if the villagers could not agree among themselves, then the king should interfere and compel the villagers to make proper provision for pasturage by setting apart sufficient land for that purpose. The proper measure of the land which ought to be set apart for this purpose is also stated by Yājñavalkya, for he says, that between a village and the culturable fields a space measuring four hundred cubits should be reserved for grazing purpose; in the case of a '*Kharvata*' (which according to one interpretation means a village inhabited

Land set apart for pasturage by the common consent of the villagers or by a special order of the king.

Extent of pasturage-ground.

---

[1] ग्रामेच्छया गोप्रचारोभूमी राजवशेनवा ।
याज्ञवल्क्यः व्यवहाराध्यायः ।
स्वामिपाल विवाद प्रकरणम्।

It was kept in the form of a belt or enclosure around the village.

by many artificers and husbandmen, and according to another interpretation means a village abounding in thorny shrubs) the space left should measure eight hundred cubits, and in the case of a city, sixteen hundred cubits.[1] From a text of Manu bearing upon this point, it seems that the space for pasturage used to be kept in the from of a belt or enclosure around the village on all sides which separated the inhabited portion of the village from the cultivated lands attached to it;[2] and it was utilised by all the villagers for grazing their cattle on.

Sir Henry Maine's view that it furnishes an indication of communal ownership.

Those who have read Sir Henry Maine's 'Village Communities' will remember how he makes use of the custom of setting apart pasture-lands for the common use of all the villagers in support of his theory that individual ownership has gradually grown out of communal ownership or joint ownership of the whole community.

The explanation given by Yajñavalkya presupposes individual ownership.

I cannot say that there may not be a good deal in this argument, but I should point out that the explanation given by Yājña-valkya presupposes *individual ownership* as distinguished from joint ownership of all the villagers over all the lands of the village; for he says that 'lands are set apart for pasturage by the wish of the whole village or by the control exercised by the king,'[3] a position which seems to me to be incompatible with the supposition that all the lands in and around the village belonged jointly to all the villagers, for, if it were so, it would be unnecessary to

---

1 धनु:शतं परीणाहो ग्रामक्षेत्रान्तरं भवेत्
द्वेशते खर्वटस्य स्यात् नगरस्य चतु:शतम् ॥
याज्ञवल्क्य: । स्वामिपालविवाद प्रकरणम् ।

2 धनु:शतं परीहारो ग्रामस्य स्यात् समन्तत: ।
मनु: । ८।२३७

3 ग्रामेच्छया गोप्रचारो भूमी राजवशेन वा ।

specialise the fact that a common pasture-ground was set apart by the common consent of all the villagers, or, when that could not be secured, by the special interference of he king. Of course, it may be said, and I consider this to be a very plausible hypothesis, that originally the custom of setting apart some lands for pasturage at the outskirts of the village had its basis on communal ownership, but that when in Yājñavalkya's time that kind of ownership had been superseded by individual or rather family ownership, the only explanation which he could put forward to account for the existence of these common pasture-grounds was that they must have been set apart either by the common consent of the villagers or by an order from the king; but what I wish to impress upon you is that our Dharma Sastras had long out-grown the stage of communal ownership, so that even in explaining phenomena which might be considered to be relics of the old system, they proceeded upon the assumption of a new order of things based upon a new system of holding lands.

Conclusion.

Right of way

Let us now turn our attention to the right of way. The primary distinction which we have got to consider with reference to this subject is between public way and private way. The right of way over private lands is recognised in a text of Sāmkha and Likhita which is thus explained and amplified by the Vīramitrodaya: "whoever constantly passes through a field or by its side should not be obstructed." It is not stated how long this user must continue in order to render its obstruction improper, but I take it that the user must be long enough and frequent enough to be considered a constant and customary user in order to make it improper on the part of the owner to interfere with it. A public way is divided into three classes: संसरण (highway), चतुष्पथ (public

Private way and public way.

Evidence of the recognition of private right of way.

There kinds of public way.

thoroughfare), and राजमार्ग (king's highway). A संसरण (highway) is defined as the way over which men and beasts pass and repass without interruption, and it is declared that no one should obstruct it in any way.[1] A public thoroughfare (चतुष्पथ) is described as the way over which all people without any distinction pass and repass at all times, and a king's highway (राजमार्ग) is said to be a way which is ordinarily open to the public at particular hours, but may be closed by the king's officers at other times.[2] It, however, appears from a text of Sāmkha and Likhita that a king's highway should not be so closed as not to leave room enough for the turning of a chariot. It is not unlikely that the power reserved for the king's officers to stop a king's highway at certain periods was intended to enable them to collect tolls from the frequenters of the way at those times, but this is a mere guess and I cannot lay much stress upon it. It is declared that 'no one should by throwing filth or making a platform, a ditch, an aqueduct, or eaves of a house obstruct a public thoroughfare, a place of worship, and a king's highway',[3] and whoever does so renders himself liable to punishment. It may be curious to notice that Manu declares that whoever discharges excrement on a highway save under extreme necessity shall be liable to pay a fine, and also to remove the filth, but in the case of a person under distress, an old or a pregnant woman, and

Duty not to obstruct a public way.

---

[1] यान्त्यायान्ति जना येन पशवश्चानिवारिताः ।
तदुच्यते संसरणं न रोद्धव्यन्तु केनचित् ॥ बृहस्पतिः

[2] सर्व्वेजना सदा येन प्रयान्ति स चतुष्पथः ।
अनिषिद्धा यथाकालं स राजमार्ग उच्यते ॥ कात्यायनः

[3] अवस्करस्थलश्वभ्र भ्रमस्यन्दनिकादिभिः ।
चतुष्पथ सुरस्थान राजमार्गान् न रोधयेत् ॥

a boy, it is directed that the fine should be remitted for a warning.

Some other incorporeal rights appurtenant to a tenement, and regulating relations between owners of adjacent lands.

Besides these, there are certain other incorporeal rights, chiefly appurtenant to the tenement occupied by a person, which, according to the Hindu Law, must not be interfered with. Thus, it has been declared that the particular mode of enjoyment of a house and its doors, and of a market, or the like, dating from the first entry by the enjoyer must not be disturbed; so also, a window, an aqueduct, a raised platform, and the eaves of a house must be allowed to remain as they have existed from the very beginning, but an intermediate structure interfering with another person's enjoyment of his own lands may be objected to. Similarly, a right of support for one's existing structure seems to have been recognised in the direction that no one should so act as to endanger the foundation of another's house. It is also laid down that no one should open a window overlooking, or a new water-course discharging its water into, another's house; of course, when they have existed from before they may remain as they are. The prohibition to open a new window overlooking another's house seems to have been based on the right of privacy of the owner of an adjacent house.

Certain peculiar interferences with another's proprietary right allowed by the Hindu Law.

I think I have said enough to give you an idea of the variety of rights recognised by the Hindu Law regulating the relations between owners of adjacent lands. I shall now give you some instances where certain interferences with another's proprietary right are permitted by the Hindu Law in consideration of greater benefit expected to arise therefrom both to the owner and to his neighbours. Thus Yājñavalkya says: 'an embankment which is beneficial to the people should not be prohibited by the owner of the soil, where the

Digging well and raising enbankment on another's field.

inconvenience is slight, and similarly, a well which occupies a little space, and supplies abundance of water.'[1] To the same effect is the text of Narada which runs as follows: 'a reservoir in the middle of another man's field shall not be objected to by the owner, if the benefit is great and the damage small, since profit is to be desired even at the cost of a trifling loss.'[2] It is, however, directed that before raising the embankment or excavating the well the permission of the owner of the soil should, if possible, be obtained.

Cultivation of another's land, the owner being dead, long absent, or otherwise unable to till it.

I shall now conclude this lecture by mentioning to you some peculiar rights recognised by the Hindu Law which may seem to us strange, but were allowed in ancient time as being suitable to the condition of the people in those days, and not opposed to their feelings and sentiments. Thus, if the owner of a field was dead, long absent, or otherwise incapable of cultivating it, then a stranger might, unless prohibited from doing so, till the field and appropriate the produce; if, in the meantime, the owner returned or otherwise recovered his capacity, and demanded the land back, then he was required to pay to the stranger the expenses incurred by him for preserving the land from turning into a waste; and, if he were unable to pay the same, then the stranger could keep the land in his possession until he could recoup himself from the usufruct; but even during this time the owner was to recieve a certain portion of the produce as his share, and the remainder was to be taken by the cultivator in satisfaction of the expenses incurred and labour bestowed by him. It may be said

---

[1] न निषेध्योऽल्पबाधस्तु सेतुः कल्याण कारकः ।
परभूमिं हरन् कूपः स्वल्पक्षेत्रो बहूदकः ॥

[2] परक्षेत्रस्य मध्येतु सेतुर्न प्रतिषिध्यते ।
महागुणोऽल्पदोषश्चे वृद्धिरिष्टाक्षयेसति ॥

that if I allow my land to lie waste, it is no body else's business to interfere with it; that may, indeed, be our modern idea, but having regard to the condition of the people in ancient time, I cannot say that the legalisation of this sort of action, which was not prejudicial to the interest of the owner, but was rather beneficial to him was improper or unreasonable. The last right which I shall mention was the right accorded to a person belonging to the twice-born classes to take fuel and fruits and flowers for the performance of religious rites from another person's land; but in the case of fruits there was this limitation that they could not be taken from trees which were enclosed by the owner within fences. These minor rules may not have much value to a student of modern law, but I mention them here, in order to show the spirit in which they were conceived by the sages and obeyed by the people.

Right to take fuel and fruit from trees not enclosed.

LECTURE VIII

LAW RELATING TO PARENTAL AND QUASI-PARENTAL RELATIONSHIP.

The subject-matter of this and the two following lectures indicated.

In this and the two following lectures I propose to deal with the various rights and obligations which arise between two persons by reason of their being related to each other, the relationship being of a more or less durable character and giving rise to what has been described as status or legal condition, as distinguished from rights and obligations entirely regulated by mutual agreement which exhausts itself as soon as those rights and obligations are fulfilled. The present lecture will be confined to the discussion of the law relating to parental and quasi-parental relationship.

Different kinds of sons primary and secondary.

Our Dharma-Sastras make mention of various descriptions of sons. One of them is called the primary (मुख्य), and the others secondary (गौण). It is unnecessary to enter into anything like a detailed examination of the various kinds of sons so described, since most of these classes of secondary sonship, excepting one or two, have long become obsolete. It may, however, be not altogether useless to try to explain the principles on which these various classes of persons were given the positions of a son under the ancient Hindu law, for, it seems to me that the somewhat peculiar rules bearing upon the subject must appear anomalous to those who do not appreciate those principles.

Twelve kinds of sons.

The persons who were accorded the position of a son were chiefly the following: (1) a son begotten by the father upon his lawfully wedded wife औरस; (2) the son of an appointed daughter, or, according to another view, the daughter herself treated by special appointment as a son (पुत्रिका पुत्र); (3) the son begotten by a stranger upon a man's wife through appointment (क्षेत्रज); (4) the son secretly conceived in the husband's house from a man other than the husband (गूढज); (5) the son of a damsel (कानीन); (6) the son taken with the bride being in his mother's womb at the time of her marriage (सहोढ); (7) the son of a twice-married woman (पौनर्भव); (8) the son given in adoption by his father or mother (दत्तक); (9) the son bought from his parents (क्रीत); (10) the son, who, being an orphan, is taken in adoption with his own consent (कृत्रिम); (11) the son who, being bereft of parents or abandoned by them, presents himself to another saying, 'Let me become they son' (स्वयं दत्त); and (12) the son cast off by his natural parents and taken by another (अपविद्ध). Of these the first alone was recognised as the son in the proper sense of the term, and the second also was regarded as almost equal to him in rank having no stain in blood, and being, at the same time, an offspring of the person regarded as the father; besides these two, the others were sons only in a secondary sense, and were more or less held in disfavour.

Recognition of sonship in all these cases did not imply equality of status.

It would be a mistake to suppose that the recognition of sonship in all these cases implied an equality of status or that they were supposed to confer an equal amount of spiritual benefit upon their so-called father wlth the 'aurasa' son, for Manu himself declares; "A person who wishes to cross the darkness of the future would through sons of an inferior class obtains the same sort of result as a person who wishes to cross a stream by an ill-constructed vessel."[1] I do not, of course, deny that in the absence of a son of the primary kind,

---

[1] यादृशं फलमाप्नोति कुप्लवैः सन्तरन् जलम् ।
तादृशं फलमाप्नोति कुपुत्रैः सन्तरंस्तमः । मनुः ।

these inferior sons could, to some extent, occupy his place, and stand as a substitute for him, 'just as,' to quote the words of Brihaspati, 'in the absence of clarified butter, oil often takes its place'; but, it seems to be absurd to suppose that the recognition of all these persons as sons was solely due to the intense desire of an ancient householder to have a son at any cost. Such an explanation may possibly account for the recognition of sonship in a case of adoption, whether it be in the *dattaka*, *kritrima*, or *krita* form, and also in a case of appointment to raise an issue upon another's wife, but in the other cases, I can scarcely conceive that the recognition of sonship was due to an anxiety which prevailed in ancient time to have a son in any shape and at any cost. Who can ever think that the affiliation, for instance, of a damsel's son either to her father, or after her marriage to her husband, or of a son begotten upon a woman either before or after her marriage by a stranger to the husband of that woman was guided by considerations of benefit, secular or spiritual, to be conferred upon the so-called father, although he had no connection with the paternity of the child? I can not, therefore, agree with Mr. Mayne when he says that the true solution of the problem, how these came to be regarded as his sons, is to be found in the indispensableness of a son to an ancient Aryan householder which would lead to every contrivance being exhausted to procure one, and that the relations between the sexes in early times were such that neither delicacy nor sentiment would stand in the way.[1] No doubt the customs of adoption and appointment had their origin in the desire to have a male child to perpetuate the lineage and offer

Principles underlying the recognition.

Mr. Mayne's view criticised.

[1] Mayne's Hindu law, 8th Ed. p. 83.

funeral oblations, but, even then, the practice of appointment was condemned by Manu in no doubtful terms. Thus, he says, ' no widow should be authorised by regenerate men to beget children by other persons, for those that authorise her to conceive by other men violate the eternal law ; such appointment is nowhere mentioned in the Vedic texts on marriage, nor is the remarriage, of widows mentioned in the law relating to marriage ; this practice, fit only for brutes, and condemned by learned regenerate men, was introduced among men while Vena held the sovereign sway ; he, ruling the whole world and eminent among the royal saints, produced confusion of tribes while his intellect was perverted by passion ; since then, the virtuous censure him, who, through clouded intellect, authorises a widow to have intercourse with a man for the sake of progeny.' As regards the duty of a woman to remain faithful to her lord even after his death, the same sage has declared, ' Let her rather emaciate her body by living upon pure flowers, roots, and friuts, but let her not, when the husband is dead, even pronounce the name of another man ';[1] and again : ' Longing for the unparalleled virtue of those who are constant to one husband, she should continue till death, forgiving all injuries, observing strictly the rules of continence, and foregoing all sensual pleasure ; many thousand bachelor Brahmins have ascended the celestial regions without leaving any issue ; like those lifelong students, a chaste woman leading a life of austerities after the death of her husband, goes to heaven though destitute of sons ; a woman who being covetous for offspring proves faithless to her husband, brings disgrace on herself in this world, and becomes excluded from the regions of her lord in the next.'[2] I should like

[1] Manu, V 157.
[2] Manu, V 158.

to know where fidelity to the husband is enjoined in stronger terms, and its violation more severly condemned than in the texts quoted above, and I am not prepared to hold that, if the anxiety to have a son were the only motive, the recognition of sonship in some of the instances noticed above would not have been condemned by Manu on these grounds alone. The problem suggested by Mr. Mayne must, therefore, at least in part be susceptible of another explanation, and it seems to me that he himself comes very near to it when, in the next paragraph, he proceeds to explain the theory of paternity among the Hindus. According to the ancient conception of family relationship among the Aryans, a child must be under the *patria potestas* of some individual, and this was not confined to the case of a legitimate child, born in lawful wedlock and lawfully begotten upon its mother by her husband; the question, therefore, arose: how, in any other case, should it be determined as to who was the person under whose *patria potestas* a particular child stood? The answer to this question was furnished by the enumeration of subsidiary sons indicated above. It will be found from an examination of the different descriptions of sonship given above, that it arose in either of two ways: (1) through dominion over the mother of the child; and (2) through transfer of *patria potestas* from the natural parents either by gift or sale, or by the consent of the child when freed from the *patria potestas* of the parents either by reason of their being dead, or by reason of their having cast him off. I have no leisure to dwell individually upon each of the cases of secondary sonship enumerated above, but, I hope, it will not be at all difficult for you to see that my explanations meet every one of them. That the husband of a woman becomes invested with *patria potestas* over the son of that woman although

The theory of paternity according to the ancient Hindu Law: principles regulating the determination of patria potestas as indicated by the enumeration of subsidiary sons.

Paternity through dominion over the mother of the child.

he may not have been the real procreator of the child is supported by Manu on the analogy of ownership over the produce of a field, when the field belonged to one and the seed was sown by another. "Unless there be a special agreement," says he, "between the owners of the land and of the seed, the crop belongs clearly to the land-owner, for the receptacle is more important than the seed," and he concludes that a similar rule should apply in the case of a child, and it should belong to him who had marital property in the mother and not to the actual procreator when he happened to be a stranger. As regards the system of adoption in its various forms, you will observe that it was essential that some how or other the *patria potestas* of the natural father should cease, and this condition being satisfied it made no difference whether the adoption was due to a desire on the part of the adopter to perpetuate his lineage, as in *dattaka*, *kritrima*, and *krita* forms of adoption, or on the part of the child to obtain protection from danger or destitution due to the death of or abandonment by the natural father, as in *swayamdatta* and *apaviddha* forms of adoption. It, therefore, seems to me that the problem suggested above as to how the various kinds of sonship came to be recognised by the *Dharma-sastras* admits of an easy solution, if we remember that they really exemplified the rules by which the question of *patria potestas* had to be determined under the earlier Hindu law, and this becomes all the more clear from the fact that a son born of an unmarried woman was regarded as the son of the father of that woman so long as she continued unmarried, but of her husband when she passed under his control upon marriage, a position which can be rationally explained only upon the view already indicated that sonship, in such a case, meant no more than subjection to the *patria potestas* of an

Paternity through transfer of *patria potestas*.

individual although paternity, in the strict sense of the term, could not be predicated of him.

Gradual curtailment of this wider conception of paternity and the consequent curtailment in the list of irregular sons.

In course of time, however, this wider and somewhat peculier conception of paternity gradually dwindled away, and in consequence, most of these kinds of irregular sons, if I may use the expression, became obsoleute. So Parasara who professes to lay down the law for the *Kali Yuga* in particular recognises only four kinds of sons, *viz.*, *aurasa* (the truly legitimate son), *kshetraja* (the son of a wife by appointment), *datta* (the son given), and *kritrima* (the son made).[1] In the *Pauranic* age this list was further curtailed, and it was declared that the wise men had, in the beginning of the *Kali Yuga*, solemly prohibited certain practices, including among them the recognition of various classes of sons besides *Aurasa* and *Dattaka*, for the protection of the people, and that such a resolution arrived at by the virtuous carried as much authority as a text of the Veda itself.[2] The result, therefore, is that at the present day there are only two kinds of sons recognised by the Hindu law, *viz.*, *Aurasa* and *Dattaka*, save that in Mithila, in deference to old established usage, the kritrima form of adoption is also regarded as valid, and this is reconciled with the above rule by construing the word 'datta', to include *Kritrima* as well.[3]

At present only two descriptions of sons are generally recognised : aurasa and dattaka.

Kritrima form of adoption still prevails in Mithila.

---

[1] औरसः क्षेत्रजश्चैव दत्तः कृत्रिमकः सुतः ।

[2] दत्तौरसेतरेषान्तु पुत्रत्वेन परिग्रहः ।

* * *

एतानि लोकगुप्त्यर्थं कलेरादौ महात्मभिः ।
निवर्त्तितानि कर्म्माणि व्यवस्थापूर्व्वकं बुधैः ।
समयश्चापि साधूनां प्रमाणं वेदवद्भवेत् ॥

दत्तपदं कृत्रिमस्याप्युपलक्षणम् । दत्तकमीमांसा ।

An important change in the conception of sonship: adopted son assimilated to *aurasa* by a legal fiction.

Along with the limitations thus introduced, the conception of sonship has undergone an important change, and now a son means primarily a truly legitimate son begotten by the father upon his lawfully wedded wife, and an adopted son is assimilated to him by a legal fiction that upon the ceremonies of adoption having taken place, he is, by reason of the mysterious force of those ceremonies, to be treated as if reborn in the family of the adopter, a fiction, which, as you are aware, has given rise to certain rules limiting the choice of an adopted son so as to prevent that fiction from appearing unnatural.

***Legitimatio per subsequens matrimonium* not recognised.**

From this altered conception of sonship it follows that *legitimatio per subsequens matrimonium*, which was recognised by the Roman Law, can no longer be recognised in the Hindu law, for he alone is an *aurasa* (or truly legetimate) son who is begotten by the father upon his lawfully wedded wife.[1] It may, however, be remarked that the necessity for such a rule can hardly be felt among the Hindus, because among them a girl is ordinarily married at an age when she cannot have the physical capacity for child-bearing, and the *Sastras* enjoin upon the guardians to see that she is given in marriage at such an age.

Turning now to adoption, I may remind you that I have already explained the difference between the dattaka and the kritrima forms of adoption, and pointed out that the kritrima form prevails only in Mithila, and nowhere else. The really important form of adoption from the stand point of the modern Hindu law is, therefore, the dattaka, and I shall say only a few words about it as the scope of my subject will not permit a fuller discussion.

[1] स्वे चेत्रे संस्कृतायान्तु स्वयमुत्पादयेद्धि यम् ।
तमौरसं विजानीयात् पुत्रं प्रथमकल्पितम् ॥

Dattaka form of adoption: necessity of religious ceremonies.

Difference of opinion traced to its root.

It has often been asked, can there be a valid adoption without the performance of religious ceremonies? The answer to this question must depend upon the conception of subsidiary sonship according to the Hindu law, and as this conception has, as I have already indicated, undergone an important change, it is not at all surprising that different opinions have been entertained about it. I have stated that originally the recognition of a person as a subsidiary son meant no more than that the person was treated as subject to the *patria potestas* of his so-called father, and an act of adoption took effect by transferring the *patria potestas* from the natural to the adoptive father; viewed from this standpoint it would follow that the formalities of adoption would not require anything more than gift and acceptance, the gift by the natural father extinguishing his *patria potestas*, and the acceptance by the adoptive father investing him with it. Hence, at that stage of the Hindu law, the performance of any religious ceremony could not be treated as absolutely essential for the change of status involved in an act of adoption, and we, therefore, find that in the definition of an adopted son, as given in the Institutes of Manu, hardly any stress is laid on the performance of any religious ceremony such as datta-homa.[1] This conception of sonship has, however, been now substantially given up, so that according to the orthodox view, an act of adoption is no longer regarded as mere transference of the *patria potestas* to the adoptive father, but is supposed to involve the creation of a certain non-sensuous relation by virtue of the mysterious force attached to the performance of the sastric ceremony.

[1] माता पिता वा दद्यातां यमद्भिः पुत्रमापदि ।
सदृशं प्रीतिसंयुक्तं स ज्ञेयो दत्त्रिमः सुतः ॥ मनुः

A physical act carries with it certain physical consequences; a secular transaction produces certain secular effects; but beyond these, they cannot go; so that if you want to maintain that the creation of sonship by an act of adoption involves something more than the mere production of certain secular rights and obligations, it becomes incumbent upon you to admit that the transaction itself must be somehow more than secular, and as it is the performance of the accompanying religious ceremonies which alone can stamp it with a higher character, they become an essential part of the entire transaction. You will perhaps understand this position better, if I try to elucidate the distinction by an illustration. Take, for instance, the ceremony of consecrating an image, and contrast with it that of consecrating the site of a building; in the former case, so long as the ceremony is not duly performed, the super-sensuous attribute ascribed to the image does not arise, and the idol cannot be regarded as anything more than a block of wood or a slab of stone which has taken a certain shape; but in the latter case, the main purpose of building a house being physical, the non-performance of the ceremony of consecrating its site cannot possibly affect the fulfilment of that purpose, the only object of performing the ceremony being to invoke the blessing of God on the eve of occupying the house. It is, therefore, natural that when sonship created by an act of adoption came to be regarded as having a higher than secular aspect, the Brahmanical writers, such as the authors of Dattaka Chandrika and Dattaka Mîmansa, who adopted this standpoint, could no longer treat the performance of Datta-homa as non-essential. With them an act of adoption had too aspects: in its secular aspect, it consisted of gift and acceptance which could only result in transferring the boy from the parental

Two aspects of an act of adoption.

dominion of the donor to that of the donee; but, in so far as adoption was supposed to establish a certain non-sensuous religious relation carrying with it certain religious and juristic consequences, it could only be reached by the due performance of the religious ceremonies prescribed. According to this view, therefore, the father by giving his son to another without the accompaniment of religious ceremonies can perhaps make the son a slave to the latter, provided he has got the necessary authority to make such a gift, but in order to create filial relation with a person who is not the natural father, so as to make the boy competent to take part in the religious ceremonies in his adoptive family as a member thereof, the religious rites, prescribed by the Sastras, for adoption must be duly performed. I am aware that this question has given rise to a good deal of controversy in our courts, and decisions of a more or less conflicting character have been passed; I am not here concerned to deal with those dicisions in detail, but I may be permitted to point out that if the standpoint of the later Hindu law be not brushed aside as an innovation, it seems to me difficult to escape from the logical consequences of that position which would make the performance of religious ceremonies an essential part of an act of adoption.

Standpoint of the later Hindu Law.

Other consequences of the altered standpoint.

The acceptance of the view that adoption is an act which depends for its effectiveness on *Sastric* sanction must also give rise to certain other important consequences, for the construction of negative or prohibitory precepts depends mainly upon the character of the act to which those precepts are attached. The rules bearing upon the subject and the distinctions on which they are based have been fully explained by me in a series of articles which I contributed sometime ago to the Calcutta Law Journal 'On

Construction of negative precepts in Hindu Law.

the interpretation of negative precepts in Hindu law,'[1] and I must refer you for fuller information to those articles. A negative precept, by which I mean a precept contained in the Sastras calculated to dissuade people from following a particular course of action, is, as I have there explained, capable of being differently construed, and the interpretation has, in each case, to be selected with great care in accordance with recognised principles of logic laid down and explained by the Mîmánsakas. Following these principles, we find that sometimes a negative precept amounts to nothing more than a mere prudential admonition designed to emphasise the pernicious character of the prohibited course of action by reason of its natural visible consequences which prudence, apart from any sastric injunction, would induce us to avoid; sometimes it is construed as laying down a sastric prohibition (प्रतिषेध), in the proper sense of the term, supported by the sastric sanction indicating that its violation is sinful, and therefore calculated to bring about misery either in this life or in the life to come, through an invisible force appertaining to a forbidden action, unless expiated by the performance of proper penance; and, sometimes, it has to be read as limiting the scope of some positive injunction to which it is attached, and thereby defining the conditions under which alone the latter can be validly fulfilled, so that the performance of the act enjoined without regard to and in violation of the negative precept so construed would import such an essential defect or imperfection as would render the whole thing infructuous and incompetent to produce the desired effect. A negative precept of the first kind is said to import a prohibition having a visible end in view (दृष्टार्थ प्रतिषेध); when it belongs to the second kind, it is said to contain a prohibition having a non-visible

Different modes of construing negative precepts, and the principles governing the same.

[1] Calcutta Law Journal, Vol. IV, pp. 21, 27, 35, 63, and 75.

end in view (अदृष्टार्थ प्रतिषेध), or a prohibition based upon the sastras in the strict sense (शास्त्रीय प्रतिषेध); when, however, it falls under the third class, it is said to be an excluding clause limiting the scope of the positive injunction to which it is related or attached (पर्य्युदास). It is apparent, that from the standpoint of positive law, a negative precept of this last class has the most important consequences, and, therefore, whenever we come across a negative precept it behoves us to enquire whether or not it belongs to this class. Now, on this enquiry the nature of the act or ceremony to which the negative precept relates has a very important bearing, and a little consideration will enable you to see why this should be so. In the case of an act having a merely secular object, the attainment of that object depends upon the fulfilment of its secular conditions, and any rule laid down in the sastras in such a case must either be a reiteration of those secular conditions (अनुवाद) which does not lend any additional weight to them beyond what they otherwise possess, or amount to a sastric prohibition (प्रतिषेध) implying that its violation is sinful but does not affect the validity of the transaction. It is, however, otherwise with a religious act or ceremony which depends for its effectiveness on a sastric injunction, for in such a case the validity of the transaction rests on the fulfilment of that injunction, and here the question at once arises whether a negative precept laid down in the *Sāstras* should be construed as a mere prohibition (प्रतिषेध) as explained above, or as a qualifying clause limiting the scope of the injunction (पर्य्युदास), for, in the latter case, the infringement of the precept will entail the consequence of invalidating the transaction itself. Take for instance, the performance of a *srāddha* which is a ceremony of this character; there is a positive precept that it should be performed at the new moon; on the other hand, there is a negative precept that it should not be performed at night; now reading these together, what is the inference? It may either be that the performance of the *sraddha* at night, provided the other conditions are satisfied, is not infructuous, but the performer becomes a sinner by transgressing the prohibition; or, it may be, that such a performance is to be treated as void, because the negative precept curtails the scope of the positive injunction, so that it is no performance of the ceremony according to the true import of the *Sāstras*. Now, as I have elsewhere explained, the latter interpretation should, according to the rules of construction, be accepted, as correct, and, in fact, in the absence of clear and insuperable objections to the contrary, a negative precept attached to a positive precept, where both are based on the *Sāstras*, should, as far as possible, be so construed as to make the former limit the scope of the latter, so that both may have equal effect given to them. It will be difficult, at this place, to give an exposition of the grounds on which this conclusion has been arrived at, and I must refer you for fuller information to my articles in the Calcutta Law Journal to which I have already referred. You will thus see that the construction of negative precepts bearing on the law of adoption must, to a great extent, turn upon our conception of the nature of an act of adoption; if it be regarded as a secular act having only certain secular consequences, we shall have to apply one set of principles to construe those precepts; whereas, if it be treated as a religious ceremony bringing in its train, among other consequences, the creation of an invisible property (संस्कार) by which the son of one man becomes converted, as it were, into the son of the adopter, and invested with the right of performing religious ceremonies in the adopter's family, a consequence which could not possibly be reached by a mere secular

Their bearing on some of the questions relating to the law of adoption.

act unaided by the mysterious force belonging to the fulfilment of a Sāstric injunction according to the mode prescribed by the Sastras, the question of construing those precepts will be governed by a different set of principles guided by different considerations. Bearing these distinctions in mind, and remembering the altered conception of an act of adoption noticed above according to which it depends for its effectiveness on the Sastric injunction, let us consider how far some of the precepts bearing upon the subject affect the validity of an adoption.

Authority to give and authority to receive a son in adoption in the case of a woman.

Let us take the text of Vasishtha: 'A woman should neither give nor accept a son in adoption except with the permission of her husband'.[1] This raises two questions: (1) Can a woman take an adopted son to her husband without his permission? (2) Can she give her son in adoption without her husband's permission?

Can a woman take an adopted son without her husband's permission? Different ways of answering the question indicated.

As regards the first question, a little consideration will show that there are several different ways of looking at the precept. (*a*) For instance, you may say that the text indicates that a woman has ordinarily no power to take a son in adoption, but that authority given by her husband entitles her to act on his behalf, so that, where that authority is wanting, the power to adopt does not at all arise. The result of adopting this view would be to make an adoption hy a woman without her husband's permission absolutely invalid. (*b*) From another standpoint, you may say that a woman has the right to take a son in adoption, and that the text of Vasishtha does not impose a new limitation upon it, but merely expresses the ordinary limitation upon woman's power of free action by reason of the control exercised upon her by her husband so long as he is alive. According to this view,

---

1. न स्त्री पुत्रं दद्यात् प्रतिगृह्णीयात् वा अन्यत्रानुज्ञानात् भर्तुः ।

an adoption by a woman without her husband's assent so long as he is alive and capable of giving consent may be invalid, but when he is dead, his control over her being withdrawn, she can make an adoption, and the utmost that can be required of her is that she should obtain the assent of the male relative on whom she is then dependent. This explanation reduces the precept to a mere reiteration (अनुवाद) of the secular rule deducible from the general dependence of a woman, and has been virtually adopted by the Viramitrodaya when it says: "The meaning of the words 'except with the assent of her husband' is that while the husband is alive, a son should not be adopted by the wife acting independently in the absence of the husband's permission; but when the husband is dead, the assent of those alone is required on whom she is then dependent. On this view, the prohibition appears to have a merely visible (secular) basis. Therefore, although the husband be dead without giving permission to adopt, still an adoption by the widow is not invalid."[1] (c) Yet another way of construing the precept is to hold that the prohibition it contains is a Sastric prohibition, in the proper sense of the term, deriving its authority from the Sāstra, and then the question will be on what is the authority of a woman to take a son in adoption based? If you say, it is also based upon the Sāstra, then the affirmative rule granting the power, and the negative rule curtailing its scope, being both derived from the same

---

[1] भर्त्तरि जीवति भार्य्याया स्वातन्त्र्येण तदनुमती न
पुत्त्रीकरणीय इति भर्त्तुरनुज्ञानादन्यत्वेत्यस्यार्थः।
मृते तु तस्मिन् यत्पारतन्त्र्यन्तदनुमतिरेवापेक्षिता।
एवं सतिदृष्टार्थता भवति प्रतिषेधस्य।
दत्तानुज्ञे मृतेपि भर्त्तरि भार्य्याया दत्तकादिकरणः सविकल्पम ।

source, the negative precept must be construed as पर्युदास, and an adoption in violation thereof must be treated as invalid. If, on the other hand, you maintain that a woman has got the power to take a son in adoption independently of any Sastric sanction, then the prohibition must be treated as a प्रतिषेध indicating that its violation is sinful but does not affect the validity of the adoption.

These, then, being the possible standpoints, I do not think myself called upon to discuss which of them represents the correct view; in fact, the object with which I have indicated them is not so much to enable you to come to a definite conclusion regarding the question, but to illustrate the manner in which the interpretation of a precept varies with a slight alteration in the standpoint from which one approached the question. As the law now stands, it is agreed on all hands that during the life time of the husband the wife cannot adopt to him without his express sanction, but differences have arisen regarding the power of a widow who seeks to adopt a son to her deceased husband.

Different views held by the different schools.

According to the Bengal School, authority given by the husband is operative even after his death, and an adoption by the widow in pursuance of such authority is valid; when no such authority exists, no adoption can be validly made.

The Bengal doctrine has been applied to cases governed by the Benares School, although the Viramitrodaya which is regarded as an authority in Benares maintains a different position.

In Mithila, the assent of the husband must be given contemporaneously with the adoption by the wife, which being impossible in the case of an adoption by a widow, no such adoption can be validly made.

In Southern India, the assent of the kinsmen may take the place of that of the husband according to the decision of the Judicial Committee in the Ramnad case.[1]

According to the Mahárástra School, the text requiring the sanction of the husband applies only to an adoption made in the husband's life time, and is not to be taken to restrict the widow's power to do that which the general law prescribes as beneficial to her husband's soul.

Can a woman give her son in adoption without authority from her husband?

Next, let us consider whether a woman can give her son in adoption without authority from her husband. It seems to be clear that she cannot do so, so long as the husband is alive and capable of according sanction. The prohibition contained in Vasishtha's text should be construed as imperative, and the sanction of the husband takes the case out of it, being what may be called a प्रतिप्रसव (remedy), so that in the absence of such sanction the adoption falling within the scope of the prohibition must be deemed as invalid. But, then, how far does this prohibition extend? Does it apply also in the case of a widow giving her son in adoption? It has been held by our courts that it does not, so that a widow is free to give her son in adoption, unless, of course, she was distinctly prohibited by the husband to do so.[2] There is no doubt that both Dattaka Chandrika and Dattaká Mimánsá which are recognised as authoritative treatises on the law of adoption support this view; and, although, as observed by their Lordships of the Judicial Committee in Balusu Gurulingaswami *v.* Balusu Ramalakshmamma,[3] caution is required in accepting their glosses where they deviate from or add to the Smritis, it is very much doubtful whether

Calcutta decision on the point.

[1] Collector of Madura *v.* Mootoo Ramalinga, 12 Moo. I. A. 440.

[2] Jogeshchandra Bandyopadhyay *v.* Nonabali Bepari, 7 C.W.N. 871.

[3] 3 C.W.N. 439.

our courts will be prepared, in any future case, to reconsider the question and reject the opinion supported by them as incompatible with a correct and logical interpretation of the text bearing upon the point, for the authority of these two works was not, in their Lordships' opinion, open to examination, explanation, criticism, adoption, or rejection like a scientific treatise on European Jurisprudence. I must, however, confess that I find it difficult to reconcile this view with the view which prevails in Bengal and Benares Schools that a widow cannot make a valid adoption to her deceased husband without an authority given by him during his life time, or with the Mithila doctrine that she cannot make any such adoption at all, for I fail to understand how the text of Vasishtha 'Let not a woman give or accept a son without her husband's sanction' can be interpreted in one way in the case of a gift and in another way in the case of an acceptance; it seems that if the aforesaid text does not apply to a widow with regard to a gift, it should receive a similar interpretation with regard to an acceptance also, for the two portions of the text are so collocated, that they should be held to have an exactly similar scope. Dattaka Mimānsā tries to get over this difficulty by arguing that the text of Manu—'A son equal (in caste) and affectionately disposed whom his father or mother (or both) give with water at a time of distress is known as the dattaka son,'[1] indicates that both parents are equally competent to give a son in adoption; but it is open to the comment that the above text only contains a definition of the adopted son, and does not negative the position that the power of the mother should be held to be limited by the conditions imposed by the text

Difficulties of the view.

---

[1] माता पिता वा दद्यातां यमद्भिः पुत्रमापदि।
सदृशं प्रीतिसंयुक्तं स ज्ञेयो दत्त्रिमः सुतः। मनुः

of Vasishtha referred to above. Dattaka Chandrikā adopts a somewhat curious argument in support of the widow's power of gift when it says that an absence of prohibition is tantamount to a sanction; it may not be altogether illogical for the author of Dattaka Chandrikā to maintain this position seeing that he does not say that a widow has no power to accept a son in adoption without express authority from her husband; but for one who maintains that express authority from the husband is requisite in order to empower a widow to take a son in adoption, that position is absolutely impossible, for it can scarcely be argued that husband's sanction should be implied when his widow is giving his son away although it cannot be held to exist when she is taking a son in adoption for the benefit of his soul. It is, however, useless to dilate upon this topic any further, for positive law does not always develop itself in a strictly logical way, and our Courts are not likely to retrace their steps when a particular point has been settled by judicial decisions on the basis of authoritative treatises dealing with the same.

Adoption of an only son.

Vasistha's text: how it should be construed.

The next point on which I may say a few words is the validity of the adoption of an only son. Vasishtha's text prohibiting such an adoption runs as follows: 'But let not a person give or accept an only son, for he is for the continuance of the line of his forefather.'[1] Now in order to determine the correct import of this precept, one has to remember what I have explained more fully in my articles 'On the interpretation of negative precepts in Hindu Law,' that the construction of a negative precept depends principally on the character of the act or ceremony to which it relates; whatever might have been the real character of an act of adoption in ancient time,

न त्वेकं पुत्रं दद्यात् प्रतिगृह्णीयाद्वा स हि सन्तानाय पूर्वेषां

there can be little doubt that now-a-days it is looked upon as an act which takes effect by virtue of a Sastric injunction (शास्त्रप्राप्त) and not merely in pursuance of a secular inclination (रागप्राप्त), and if this conception be accepted as correct, I think the prohibition contained in Vasishtha's text must, on the acknowledged principles of construction, be construed as (पर्य्युदास) curtailing the scope of the injunction authorising gift or acceptance of a son, in order to avoid the eightfold defects incidental to the admission of an option (विकल्प) which would result from the adoption of a different construction. It would be tiresome to go through the grounds on which these principles of construction are based, and it would not also be possible for me to repeat the reasons which have induced me not to accept the proposition that a negative precept supported by the assignment of a reason must be construed as a mere (अर्थवाद) having no obligatory force. Those who are curious to know more about the subject will, I hope, find fuller information from my articles in the Calcutta Law Journal to which I have already referred. However that may be, the validity of the adoption of an only son has been firmly established by the decision of the Privy Council in the case of Balusu Gurulingaswami v. Balusu Ramalakshmamma,[1] and any further discussion can only have an academic interest.

A decision of the Privy Council has settled the law in a different way.

As regards the adoption of the eldest son, the prohibition against it is merely inferntial, being deduced by the commentators from the superior merits of such a son as described by Manu. It, therefore, stands to reason that such a prohibition should be treated as merely recommendatory, its purpose being to dissuade the parents from giving away the most meritorious of all the sons; if, however, the parents choose to disregard the admonition

Adoption of the eldest son: prohibition should be treated as merely recommendatory.

---

[1] L. R. 26, I.A. 113 : I. L. R., 22 M 398.

and give the eldest son in adoption, the adoption will undoubtedly be valid, for the Dharmasastras have not the same, and the scope of a Sastric 'vidhi' can only be curtailed by a Sastric prohibition.

Extent of the *patria potestas* under the Hindu Law

Referring you for fuller information about the details of the law of adoption to treatises specially dealing with the subject, I now pass on to consider the extent of *patria potestas* under the Hindu Law, and compare the same with that under the Roman Law.

Power over the person of the son under the Roman Law.

Speaking of the Roman Law, Mr. Sandars says: 'The *patria potestas* differed originally little, if at all, from the *dominica potestas*. If the sense of the ownership was not so complete in the former, it was probably limited more by natural feeling than by law. The father could sell, expose, or put to death his children. Time, however, ameliorated the position of the child, and all that was left was a power to inflict moderate chastisement, and to sell at the time of birth in cases of extreme necessity. Constantine condemned the father who killed his child to the punishment of a parricide. The sale of a child was in general fictitious, and only formed the mode by which the child was released from the father's power.'[1] Turning, now to the Hindu Law, we find that Manu says that a father had no right to do any thing more than inflict moderate chastisement upon his son only as a punishment for an offence using a string or a light rattan, and taking care to strike on the back and never on the head;[2] and Gautama says

The Hindu Law compared: limited power of chastisement.

---

[1] Institutes, Lib: I: Tit. IX:

[2] भार्य्यापुत्रश्च दासश्च शिष्यो भ्राता च सोदरः ।
प्राप्तापराधास्ताड्याः स्यू रज्ज्वा वेणुदलेन वा ॥
पृष्ठतश्च शरीरस्य नोत्तमाङ्गे कथञ्चन । मनुः । ८ ।

that chastisement should not ordinarily be corporeal, and infliction of bodily punishment in the mode mentioned above should only be resorted to in extreme cases, and even then light string or rattan should be used, any violation whereof would be punishable by the king.[1] These minute rules and the prescription of punishment for their infringement show that from very early times the power of a Hindu father over the person of the son was circumscribed within very narrow and reasonable limits. He did not posses anything like the power of life and death at least from Manu's time, and it is doubtful if he ever had it. We need not, therefore, grudge the pride which Justinian seems to feel when he says: "The power which we have over our children is peculiar to the citizens of Rome; for no other people have a power over their children such as we have over ours."[2] As regards the power of gift and sale, the authorities seem to be somewhat in conflict, indicating, as I think, a gradual change in the law restricting the power of the father within very narrow limits. Thus, Vasishtha says that in as much as the son springs from the corporeal particles of the parents, they are the causes of his being, and so they have the power to give, sell, or cast him away.[3] On the other hand, both Yājnavalkya and Nārada include a son among objects unfit to be given[4] and the latter adds that these should not be given even under

Power of gift and sale: different views indicated.

Among the text-writers.

---

1 शिष्यशिष्टिरवधेनाशक्तौ रज्जुवेणुविदलाभ्यां तनुभ्यामन्येन घ्नन् राज्ञा शास्यः ।

2 Institutes, Lib. I: Tit. IX. 2.

3 शुक्रशोणितसम्भवः पुत्रः मातापितृनिमित्तकः ।
तस्य च प्रदान विक्रयत्यागेषु मातापितरौ प्रभवतः ।

4 स्वं कुटुम्बाविरोधेन देयं दारसुतादृते ।
याज्ञवल्क्यः दत्ताप्रदानिक प्रकरणम् ।

extreme distress.[1] Kātyāyana takes an intermediate position and says that no gift or sale should be made of sons against their wishes, but at a time of distress this may be done, otherwise not.[2] There being thus an evident conflict among the text-writers, it is not at all surprising that there should be a similar diversity of opinion among the commentators. Thus, commenting on the text of Yājnavalkya declaring that a son and certain other objects are unfit to be given, Vijnāneswara observes that this does not indicate absence of ownership, since ownership does exist over a son, a wife, the entire property, or what has been promised to another, although these have been declared as unfit to be given.[3] On the other hand, Nilakantha says that the father cannot claim ownership over the son in the same way as he claims ownership over the offspring of his cattle, since his wife is not his property in the same way as the cattle is; moreover, it apears from the sixth chapter of the Pūrva Mīmānsā that although in a Viswajit sacrifice the sacrificer should give his whole property away, yet the daughter, the son, and the like should not be given, which indicates that the father has no ownership over his son; and, therefore, it has been concluded by Misra in Tantravarttaka that the gift of a son in adoption is a gift only in a secondary

Among the Commentators.

---

1 निक्षेपं पुत्रदारांश्च सर्व्वस्वं चान्वयेसति ।
आपत्स्वपि च कष्टासु वर्त्तमानेन देहिना ।
अदेयान्याहुराचार्य्या यच्चान्यस्मै प्रतिश्रुतम् । नारदः

2 विक्रयश्चैव दानञ्च न नेयाः स्युरनिच्छवः ।
दाराःपुत्राश्च सर्व्वस्वमात्मन्येव च योजयेत् ।
आपत्काले प्रकर्त्तव्यं दानं विक्रय एव च ।
अन्यथा न प्रवर्त्तेत इति शास्त्रेषुधारणा । कात्यायनः ।

3 मिताक्षरा दत्ताप्रदानिक प्रकरणम् ।

sense.[1] Jīmūtavāhana also seems to hold this opinion, when he says: "Neither is it true that the son is the property of his father, for the contrary has been shown under the head of gift of a whole estate. The term 'acquistion' would, therefore, be metaphorical in regard to son."[2] Commenting upon this passage, Raghunandana argues that the father has no property in the son, but that a gift in adoption is allowable in as much as it is not a real gift, but a mere semblance of it entitling the son to perform the funeral ceremonies of the adopter, and this indicates that gift in no other form could be made. On the other hand, Śrīkṛishṇa Tarkalamkāra suggests that the father has property in the son, but his power of making a gift or a sale is limited in the way stated in the text of Kātyāyaṇa, and fettered by conditions prescribed therein. The Vīramitrodaya suggests a somewhat different solution, for it says that the texts prohibiting the gift of a son were meant to refer to the gift of an only son, as such a gift would result in the extinction of lineage of the donor, but when he had more sons than one the conditions under which a gift or a sale of a son may be made are laid down in the text of Kātyāyṇa referred to above.[3]

Conclusions summarised.

What, then, are the conclusions that we can derive from these conflicting opinions? It seems that a gift in adoption has always been regarded as valid except in the case of an only son, and that although at first, there might not have been much difference between it and any other form of gift, gradually there grew up the idea that it was a gift of a peculiar kind, and strictly speaking a gift only in a secondary sense. It also appears that just

[1] Vyavahāramayūkha, Ch.N., Sec. 1.

[2] Dāyabhāga. Ch. II, Sec. 67.

[3] वीरमित्रोदयः, दत्तप्रदानिक प्रकरणम् ।

as a gift in adoption began to be looked upon as something different in kind from an ordinary gift, the gift of a son for any other purpose, and the sale of a son, both came to be regarded as improper acts on the part of the father, if not absolutely beyond his authority. So it has come to pass that although originally a gift or a sale of a son had, in all probability, been allowed as an exercise of paternal authority, gradually it has fallen into disuse, and all that is now left to him is the right to give his son in adoption when he has more sons than one, and many commentators even deny that he has ownership over the son. In other words, although in remote past a gift or a sale of a son was not perhaps regarded as beyond the scope of paternal authority, that state of the law has long been changed, and it is no longer regarded as permissible either on the ground that it is condemned by the *Sāstras* or on the ground, as some commentators put it, that this condemnation presupposes that the father has no such ownership over the son as would entitle the former to give or sell the latter away, barring, of course, a gift in adoption which is supposed to stand on a different footing. That there was a time when a gift or a sale of a son was not regarded as beyond the power of the father may be shown by quoting one or two instances from our ancient books. The sale of a son is illustrated by the story of Sunahsepha whom king Harischandra bought from his father Ajīgartha for the completion of a certain sacrifice; he was saved from the peril by the sage Visvāmitra whose protection he begged by offering himself as a son. This story indicates that originally the father had a right to sell his son although the practice came subsequently to be disapproved. Similarly, the right of a father to make a gift of his son otherwise than in adoption finds some support from the story of Nachiketas related in the Kathopaniṣad; there it is

Indications that there was a time when a gift or a sale of a son was not regarded as beyond the power of the father.

recited that Vājasravasa performed the Visvajit sacrifice and gave away his entire property, but this did not satisfy his son Nachiketas who thought that gift of half-starved cattle and the like could not be an act of much merit; so he asked his father, 'Father, to whom art thou going to give me?' The father at first did not give any reply, but being irritated by his repeated importunities said, 'I give you to death.' The son acting upon this sought the abode of Death, and obtained from him spiritual instruction. This, no doubt, is a sort of introduction to the main theme of the Upanisad, and we are not called upon to treat it as an authentic record of actual facts, but, at all events, it indicates that the gift of a son was not, perhaps, conceived to be altogether beyond the power of the father. However that may be, you have seen how these practices snbsequently came to be eschewed, no matter whether this was due to a Sāstric prohibition in the proper sense of the term, or to an alteration in the conception about the extent of the father's rights over the son, so that under the later Hindu Law a father could not ordinarily sell his son or give him away except in adoption.

Subsequently these practices came to be eschewed.

Extent of *patria potestas* in other respects. Rights to control son's marriage under the Roman Law.

Having dealt with the rights of the father over the person of his son, let us now turn to the extent of *patria potestas* in other respects. We find that under the Roman Law, the marriage of a son under power was completely under the control of his father. Thus, the consent of the *pater familias* was a condition precedent to the validity of such a marriage, and the absence of such consent rendered the marriage absolutely void, so that not even subsequent consent could ratify it.[1] Under the Hindu Law, I am not aware of any text requiring the consent of the father for the validity of the marriage of his son; on the

No such right seems to exist under the Hindu Law.

[1] Institutes, Lib v. Tit x.

other hand, in as much as it is the bridegroom who accepts the gift of the bride, it is his consent that is essential for the completion of the gift and the creation of the marital relationship. Of course, now-a-days it is not unusual to find that the father really controls his son's marriage, and the latter signifies his consent, and accepts the bride almost as a matter of course following the wishes of the former; but I do not think that the law casts upon the son any obligation to be guided entirely and exclusively by the wishes of the father in a matter like this beyond the general moral obligation to obey the parents. Moreover, even so early a lawgiver as Apastamba clearly saw that the free consent of the bridegroom was not a negligible factor when he laid down that marriage becomes propitious when both the mind and the eyes of the bridegroom become attached to the bride.[1] No doubt, besides this there are other considerations which ought to regulate the selection of a bride, and these cannot always be properly weighed by a young man who cannot often be expected to take a cool and sober view of the whole situation, so that the practice which now prevails in many parts of India, of the father selecting the bride for his son cannot be condemned as absolutely unreasonable or unsuitable to the condition of the society in which we live, but it is a matter for sincere regret that in the selection of a bridegroom or a bride, we do not often pay much heed to the rules laid down in the Sāstras, and allow ourselves to be led away by sordid and unworthy considerations. This, however, is a mere digression, and what I really want to impress upon you is that the power of the father, under the Roman Law, to control the marrige of his son was more extensive than under the Hindu Law.

[1] यस्यां मनश्चक्षुषोर्निबन्धस्तस्यामृद्धिः ।

Right of holding separate property.

Under the early Roman Law.

It also appears that as regards the right of holding separate property during the lifetime of the father. The provisions of the Hindu Law were much more favourable to the son than those of the Roman Law. The *filius familias* could not, under the strict Roman Law as it originally stood, hold any property as his own, and the father was entitled to take the whole of the son's acquisition without any exception. This state of the law continued unaltered for a pretty long time, and the changes that have been subsequently introduced have been slow in coming and gradual in their character. The first exception was that introduced in the early years of the Empire in favour of acquisitions of soldiers in service, which were withdrawn from the control of the father under the name of *castrense peculium*, doubtless as a reward for military service and an incentive for martial enterprise. The next stage was the extension of a similar privilege to acquisitions made by certain civil functionaries by virtue of their office which were called *quasi-castrense peculium*. Shortly after this Constantine introduced another kind of *peculium* called *peculium adventitium* by which the father's absolute control over property which his son had inherited from his mother was taken away. The furthest point in these modifications was reached when Justinian included under *peculium adventitium* acquisitions from other sources as well, and enacted that unless the acquisitions of the son were derived from the father's own property, 'the father shall have the usufruct but the son shall retain the ownership, so that another may not reap the profit of that which the son has gained by his labour or good fortune.'[1] Even in this final form, we find that the property which the son acquired with the help of his father's fortune

Exceptions gradually introduced.

Castrense peculium.

Quasi-castrense peculium.

Peculium adventitium.

[1] Institutes Lib. II, Tit. IX.

became absolutely the property of the father, and as to the rest, with the exception of *castrense peculium* and *quasi-castrense peculium*, the usufruct belonged to the father, though the ownership was left to the son. Sir Henry Maine, therefore, truly observes that 'even this, the utmost relaxation of the Roman *patria potestas* left it for ampler and severer than any analogous institution of the modern world.' I shall now attempt to show that the Hindu Law has long been much more favourable to the rights and privileges of the son than the Roman Law in its maturest shape. The only text which seems to deny to the son the right to hold separate property during the lifetime of the father is the text of Manu which says: "three persens, *viz.*, a wife, a son, and a slave are declared to have no wealth of their own; the wealth which they earn is of the man to whom they belong."[1] It is true that later commentators have almost unanimously explained this text as implying not want of ownership in regard to property acquired, but merely want of free and unfettered control over the property so acquired by reason of the dependent condition of the acquirers, in order to make it consistent with other texts recognising their separate ownership.[2] I am not, however, quite certain that it might not really be an echo of a still more ancient rule under which the head of the family had almost an absolute control over property acquired by its subordinate members. However that may be, it is quite clear that under the Hindu Law the power of a son to acquire property for himself was very early recognised, although other members of the family, and

The Hindu Law much more favourable to the son.

---

[1] भार्य्यापुत्रश्च दासश्च त्रय एवाधनाः स्मृताः ।
यत्ते समधिगच्छन्ति यस्यैते तस्य तद्धनम् ।

[2] See Dāyabhāga, Chap. 1, 16; Vyāvahāra Mayūkha, Chap. III, 49.

especially the father, had under certain circumstances a right to claim a share in the property so acquired. The right of other members of the family to a share was limited to the property which was acquired with the aid of joint funds; but the father according to Jīmūtavāhana, was entitled to a share in every case, however the property might have been acquired. Jīmūtavāhana sums up his opinion in these words: "The father has a moiety of the goods acquired by the son at the charge of his estate; the son who made the acquisition has two shares; and the rest take one a piece. But, if the father's estate have not been used, he has two shares; the acquirer as many; and the rest are excluded from participation."[1] The text on which Jīmūtavāhana bases his view that the father takes a share in property acquired by his son without the aid of paternal estate is explained in the Vīramitrodaya in a different way, so as to make it applicable only to cases where the paternal estate is used in the acquisition of the property by the son,[2] so that in this respect the Dayabhaga seems to extend the father's right even further than the Mitakshara School. Besides, as you are aware, the son, according to the Mitakshara School, acquires from the very moment of his birth an interest in the property of his father, which gives him, in the case of ancestral property, a right to demand a partition and obtain a separate allotment free from any control which the father might otherwise exercise. It, therefore, follows that as regards proprietary privileges the position of a son under the Hindu Law is much more advantageous than under the Roman Law even in its most advanced form.

Father's right according to Jīmūtavāhana

According to the Mitakshara School.

Reciprocal duties of the father and the son.

From the rights, let us now turn to the duties. It is the duty of the father to maintain the son so long as he is

---

[1] Dayabhaga, Chapter II, 71.

[2] Vīramitrodaya (Sarkar's Edition) Chapter II, part 1, section 12.

young and incapable of supporting himself; he is not, however, bound to pay off his son's debts unless they were incurred according to his direction, or for family purposes under extreme necessity; he may also render himself liable by subsequent ratification of the debt by a promise to pay it himself.[1] On the other side, the son must maintain his parents when they become old and infirm;[2] the mother also gets a share on partition among her sons in lieu of her maintenance. The son lies under an obligation to pay the debts incurred by the father, when the latter is dead or absent from the country for twenty years, or otherwise permanently incapacitated to pay them himself; in such a case it is the duty of the son to clear off the debts with interest, even if he has not got from the father assets sufficient for the purpose. The duty extends to the grandson, but in the absence of assets he need not pay more than the principal; the great grandson need not pay anything unless of course he is in possession of assets which belonged to the great grandfather who had contracted the debt. There are, however, certain well-known exceptions to the liability of the son to discharge his father's debts; these are based upon the character of the debt and the way in which it was incurred. Thus it has been laid down that "the son is not compellable to pay sums due by his father for spirituous liquors, for losses at play, for promises made to unrighteous persons without consideration, or under the

Duty to maintain.

Duty to pay off father's debts.

Exception.

ऋणं पुत्रकृतं पिता न देयमिति धर्मतः।
देयं प्रतिश्रुतं यत्स्यादथवा स्यादनुमोदितम्। कात्यायन:
पितुरेवनियोगाद्वा कुटुम्बभरणाय वा।
कृतं वा यदृणं कृच्छ्रे दद्यात् पुत्रस्य तत्पिता। नारद:।

वृद्धौच मातापितरौ साध्वीभार्य्या सुत: शिशु:।
अप्यकार्य्यशतं कृत्वा भर्त्तव्या मनुरब्रवीत्।

influence of lust or wrath or sums for which he was liable as a surety, or a fine, or a toll, or the balance of either."[1] The principle underlying these exceptions seems to be that when the claim of the creditor is so devoid of merit as to have no moral consideration to support it, or when it is founded upon a ground which was entirely personal to the deceased debtor, the law does not cast any obligation upon the son to satisfy the same. In some of these cases, as, for instance, in the case of a promise made to an unrighteous person without any legal or moral consideration, even the promisor himself may not incur any legal obligation; in others, as for instance in the case of a fine, or an obligation incurred by reason of having stood a surety for the appearance of another, the liability is of such a personal character that it dies with the death of the person so liable, and does not extend to his heirs; and in the rest as for instance in the case of sums payable for wine or women, the immoral character of the debt justifies the immunity of the son from liability. It should be mentioned that the duty to pay off the father's debt does not create an enforceable obligation until the son attains majority, and so the creditor's right to sue him is till then postponed.[2] This indulgence shown to the infant children of a deceased debtor might, sometimes, cause a little inconvenience to the creditor, but it was calculated to save many families from utter ruin against which our modern law makes no provision whatsoever, and

Duty to pay off father's debt when enforceable.

---

1 सौराचिकं वृथादानं कामक्रोध प्रतिश्रुतम् ।
प्रातिभाव्यं दण्डशुल्कशेषं पुत्रोनदापयेत् । बृहस्पति ।

2 नाप्राप्तव्यवहारश्च पितर्य्युपरते क्वचित् ।
कालेतु विधिना देयं वसेयुर्नरकेऽन्यथा ।
अपरार्क वीरमित्रोदयधृत कात्यायन वचनम् ।

there was the compensating advantage that the son was required, on attaining majority, to pay off the debt irrespective of the amouut of assets left by the father.

Duty towards daughters.

In regard to daughters, it was the duty of the father to maintain and educate them, and give them in marriage before they attain puberty to suitable bridegrooms.[1] On the death of the father the duty devolves upon the brother or the then head of the family whoever he may be.

Persons authorised to dispose of a girl in marriage.

As regards the persons who are authorised to dispose of a girl in marriage, Yājñavalkya says : "The father, the paternal grandfather, the brother, a sakulya or member of the same family, and the mother ; in default of one previously mentioned the next in order, if *sui juris*, is to give a damsel in marriage."[2] Vishnu introduces the maternal grandfather before the mother ; in other respects his list agrees with that given above.

When the girl may seek a husband for herself.

Where no su h person is alive, the girl must seek a husband for herself ; if, however, there is a guardian whose duty it is to give her in marriage, but he neglects to do so, then the girl is to wait for three years after attainment of puberty, and then may choose a husband for herself ; it is, however, laid down that when a girl acts in this way, she must not take away with her ornaments which she had received from her parents or brother. It must not, however, be supposed that because the Sastras enjoin the father to give his daughter in marriage before she attains puberty, it must be done at any cost without any regard for proper qualification in the bridegroom to be

---

1 कन्याप्येवं पालनीयाशिक्षणीयातियत्नतः :
देयावराय विदुषे धनरत्न समन्विता।

2 पिता पितामहोभ्राता सकुल्यो जननी तथा।
कन्याप्रदः पूर्वनाशे प्रकृतिस्थः परःपरः।

selected; "it is far better," says Manu, "that the girl should remain unmarried in her father's house until she dies, than that she should anywise be given in marriage to a worthless man."[1]

Litigation between father and son.

There is a text which seems to prohibit litigation between a father and his son,[2] but the Mitakshara explains this to mean that such a litigation should be discouraged as far as possible, but points out that there may be occasions on which it may be allowed in order to secure them in the proper enjoyment of their mutual rights and obligations. Wherever a person is molested or a right is infringed in contravention of the written law or established usage, there arises a cause of action which the court cannot refuse to entertain whatever the relationship between the parties may be, although between close relations such as father and son, preceptor and pupil, master and slave, and husband and wife, such a litigation should be discouraged, and attempt should be made to bring about an amicable settlement as far as possible. It seems that under the Roman Law, a father and the son under his power laboured under a mutual incapacity to sue each other, and I am not quite sure that the text referred to above does not indicate that at one time the Hindu Law also imposed a somewhat similar limitation.

Son's delicts.

As regards delicts, there was a peculiar rule in the Roman Law by which the father was made liable for the wrongful acts of his children, but he could escape from the liability by surrendering the person of the delinquent to

---

[1] काममामरणात्तिष्ठेत् गृहे कन्यर्त्तुमत्यपि ।
नत्वेवेनां प्रयच्छेत्तु गुणहीनाय कर्हिचित् ।

[2] गुरोःशिष्ये पितुः पुत्रे दम्पत्योः स्वामिभृत्ययोः ।
विरोधेऽपि मिथस्तेषां व्यवहारो न सिध्यति ।

the injured party. The practice had become obsolete in Justinian's time, and he disapproved its application to children, although in the case of slaves a similar rule still applied.[1] No trace of this primitive conception of delinquency and its retribution is to found in the Hindu Law.

Preceptor and pupil.

The relation between the Vedic preceptor and his pupil was very close in ancient time. In default of kinsmen, one could inherit the property left by the other. Besides, during the period of instruction, whatever the pupil acquired by his own exertions had to be offered to the preceptor who, in his turn, imparted the instruction without any pecuniary remuneration and also maintained the pupil at his own house. The pupil had also to render implicit obedience to the preceptor, and do his good in every possible way.[2] As regards the power of chastisement, it was limited in the same way as in the case of father and son.

Instructor and apprentice.

The relation between an instructor and his apprentice was almost contractual, but on account of its peculiar character I have thought it fit to deal with it here. An apprentice is a person who, with the consent of his relations, enters into an engagement for a fixed term to learn a particular art from the instructor, and lives with him for that purpose. He cannot desert the instructor without his fault within the period agreed upon, and, if he does so, may be forced to go back to the instructor and reside with him according to the engagement to the end of the term. On his part,

---

[1] Institutes Lib. IV. Tit. VIII.

[2] गुरुं चैवाप्युपासीत स्वाध्यायार्थं समाहितः।
आहूतश्चाप्यधीयीत लब्धं तस्मै निवेदयेत्।
हितं तस्याचरेन्नित्यं मनोवाक्कायकर्मभिः॥ याज्ञवल्क्यः।
ब्रह्मचारिप्रकरणम्।

it is the duty of the instructor to treat the apprentice with affection as it he were his own son, and to train him in the art by supplying him with food. The instructor must not make the apprentice do any work other than the one which the latter was seeking to learn; otherwise, the apprenticeship is cancelled, the apprentice becomes free, and the instructor becomes liable to punishment for infringement of the compact. The apprentice must serve out the term agreed upon, even if he has completely mastered the art before the expiry of the period, and any profit that may accrue from his work during this period goes to the instructor; he may, however, take the wages which his instructor may choose to allow on account of his skill, but must not enter into any body else's service without his sanction. These rules are so reasonable and well considered that I can scarcely conceive how they can be improved.

LECTURE IX.

LAW RELATING TO MARITAL AND QUASI-MARITAL RELATIONSHIP.

Different kinds of marriage.

There are eight different forms of marriage mentioned in the Dharmashastras of which all but two have now become obsolete. It is not, therefore, necessary to enter into any lengthy discussion about these obsolete varieties of marriage and I do not propose to give anything more than a bare outline of their nature and the way in which they differed from one another. In the *Brahma* form of marriage, the girl is given by the father with such ornaments as he can afford to a man whom he voluntarily invites and respectfully receives without taking anything in return. In the *Daiva* form, the girl is given by the father to a priest who officiates at a sacrifice commenced by him, so that although there is no pecuniary return, the performance of the sacrifice may be regarded as some consideration for the gift. In the *Arsha* form, the father received from the bridegroom one pair kine or two pairs for uses prescribed by law such as the performance of some sacrifice, and not as bride's price, and thus there is some consideration for the gift though the father does not want to make a profit out of it. In the *Prajapatya* form, the father gives away his daughter to a suitor on the distinct understanding that they should both perform their civil and religious duties together, so that here the father obtains some sort of undertaking from the bridegroom who himself comes forward as the suitor for marriage. In the *Gandharva* form, it is not the father of the girl who settles the marriage, but the bridegroom and the bride arrange it among themselves out of sensual inclination. In the *Asura* form, the father of the girl accepts money from the bridegroom so that it approaches a sale of the girl in consideration of the amount so received. In the *Rakshasa* form, the bridegroom does not wait for the consent of the father or of the girl herself, but takes her away by force. In the *Paishacha* form, the bridegroom fraudulently gets possession of the person of the girl, and it is therefore characterised as the basest of all forms of marriage. It goes without saying that the first four forms of marriage are the most approved, among which the first, *i.e.*, the Brahma form is the best; the Gandharva and the Rakshasa forms were tolerated among the Kshatriyas, and the Asura also prevailed among the Vaisyas and the Sudras although it was much condemned as savouring of a sale. The last form, as its very name indicates, was condemned in unqualified terms as fit for filthy devils and not for men. The ideal type of marriage is therefore, the one in which the father of the girl does not desire to reap any advantage for himself out of the marriage but gives her away freely in pursuance of a sacred duty which devolves upon him with such ornaments etc., as his means can afford; in this there is no sordid motive on either side, and neither lust nor avarice holds its sway. Hence, the Gandharva and the Asura were among the disapproved forms of marriage which were tolerated among certain people but at the same time condemned. Mr. Mayne, however, observes that "no part of the Hindu law is more anomalous than that which governs their family relations," for he says that here "we find a law of inheritance, which assumes the possibility of tracing male ancestors in an unbroken pedigree extending to fourteen generations, while coupled with it is a family law, in which several admitted forms of marriage

Mr. Mayne's comments.

are only euphemisms for seduction and rape, and in which twelve sorts of sons are recognised, the majority of whom have no blood relationship to their own father."[1] As regards the recognition of twelve sorts of sons, I have dealt with its significance in my last lecture, and pointed out the fallacy of Mr. Mayne's assumptions. Turning now to the recognition of eight kinds of marriage, it seems to me that here also Mr. Mayne has failed to appreciate the real meaning and purpose of this recognition. His remark seems to convey that he understood that the recognition of the inferior kinds of marriage amounted to a sort of legalisation of the use of force or fraud which did not involve the creation of any permanent relationship between the man and his so-called wife; otherwise, the difficulties suggested by him of reconciling it with the possibility of tracing male ancestors in an unbroken pedigree extending to fourteen generations becomes difficult to understand. This, however, was not really so, for a marriage according to the Hindu idea always involved the creation of a permanent tie in whatever manner it might come to take place. Therefore Madhavacharya points out: "It must not be supposed that in these disapproved forms of marriage beginning with Gandharva, the relationship of husband and wife does not arise for want of the ceremonies of marriage including the taking of seven steps, because although they do not take place at the outset before acceptance afterwards they are invariably performed. Hence Devala says: "In the forms of marriage beginning with Gandharva, the marital rites have again to be duly performed in the presence of the fire." It is therefore clear that there is no reason to suppose that these disapproved forms of marriage involved nothing more than a temporary connection which would make

Criticism of his view.

Religious ceremonies how far essential.

[1] Mayne's Hindu law, p. 73.

them incompatible with the tracing of male ancestors in an unbroken line. The only question that may be asked is, why did not our lawgivers at once declare that no one who gets hold of a girl by the use of force or fraud should be able to take advantage of his wrong and why did they make it possible for such wrongdoers to become the husbands of the girls whom they had thus wronged? To this question an answer would at once suggest itself to those who understand anything about the Hindu sentiments regarding female chastity; a woman should not only be free from stain but free from all suspicion of any stain; a suspicion that she may have known another man even against her inclination might dissuade many people from afterwards marrying her; hence the requirement that the wrong-doer should in such a case, afterwards duly perform the marital rites and take her as his wife. So Madhavacharya points out that "if the ceremonies are not performed, the marital relationship does not arise." So Vasistha and Baudhayana have declared: "When a damsel is carried away by force, but is not solemnly married according to the religious rite. She may be duly given in marriage to another, for there she remains a virgin as before."[1] After this, if any body says that the recognition

---

[1] होमाकरणे तु न भार्य्यात्वं । अतएव वशिष्ठ बौधायनौ बलादपहृता कन्या मन्त्रैर्यदि न संस्कृता ।

अन्यस्मै विधिवद्देया यथा कन्या तथैव सा । I may mention that Kamala Kara explains this text in a somewhat different way. He says that the possibility of giving a girl in marriage to another before the performance of the religious rites is common to all kinds of marriages; hence it would be futile to say so specifically in regard to the Rakshasa and the Paishacha forms; therefore, the text should be interpreted distributively to mean that in regard to these two forms, in the absence of the consent of the girl, she may be given in marriage to another whether the ceremonies have been performed or not.

Nirnaya Sindhu p. 227.

these of marriages gives a premium to the use of force or fraud, I shall recommend him to read the severe penalties precribed by the Hindu Law against the culprit who becomes guilty of such transgressions, a subject to which I shall advert in my lecture upon the Hindu Law of Crimes.

Two kinds of marriage that are now in use : how they differ.

The only two kinds of marriage that are now in use are the *Brahma* and *Asura* forms. In the first the father of the girl gives her away to a person whom he invites for the purpose without taking from him anything in return in any shape, and in the second, the father does accept money from the bride-groom as a consideration for the gift. It will be noticed that our lawgivers do not at all contemplate a third contingency in which the intending bridegroom may put pressure upon the father of the girl to pay him handsomely for the favour of marrying her, no matter whether his means allows him to do so or not; therefore, our law givers declared that the father should give away his daughter with such ornaments as he can afford (अलंकृता). As regards presents to the bridegroom the practice which has unfortunately become only too frequent now-a-days of extorting money from the father of the bride on the occasion of the marriage does not seem to have prevailed in those days.

Two stages in the marriage ceremony (1) gift an acceptance (2) performance of certain religious cremonies.

Turning now to the two forms of marriage that are now prevalent, we find that it consists of two stages, *viz.*, gift and acceptance of the bride in marriage, and the performance of certain religious ceremonies. It will follow from the very nature of the marital relationship according to the Hindu conception that it can not become complete until the religious ceremonies prescribed by the sastras are duly performed, for the production of a peculiar non-secular condition involving the creation of a sort of spiritual union between the husband and the wife must depend upon the mysterious force of the sastric ceremonies prescribed for the purpose and these cannot be possibly dispensed with without affecting the validity of the transaction. I need not, however, labour upon this point at this place as I have dealt with it more fully when discussing the necessity of the performance of religious ceremonies in connection with an act of adoption ; moreover, there is express authority in support of this position for it has been dec'ared by Manu : " The recital of holy text in connection with the joining of the hands of the bride-groom and the bride determines the growth of marital relationship. These should be deemed by the learned to attain finality in the taking of the seven steps.[1]

Conditions of a valid marriage.

I may now briefly refer to some of the conditions of a valid marriage besides gift and acceptance and the performance of the religious ceremonies. You are aware that our Dharmasastras contain various rules for the selection of a suitable bride-groom or a bride. Most of these should be regarded as what I have called prudential admonitions having certain visible ends in view ; a violation of any of these rules cannot possibly affect the validity of the marriage. Take, for instance, the following text of manu : 'In taking a wife, let him avoid the following ten families, be they ever so great or rich in kine, goats, asses, money, or grain, *viz.*, one which neglects the sacred rites, one in which no male children (are born), one in which the veda is not studied, one the members of which have thick hair on their body, and those which are afflicted by hemorrhords, phthisis, dyspepsia or white or black leprosy'[2] It cannot be

---

[1] पाणिग्रहणिका मन्त्रा नियतं दारलक्षणं ।
तेषां निष्ठातु विज्ञेया विद्वद्भिः सप्तमेपदे: । मनु: ८।२२७ ।

[2] महान्त्यपि समृद्धानि गोऽजाविधनधान्यत: ।
स्त्री सम्बन्धे दशैतानि कुलानि परिवर्ज्जयेत् ।
हीनक्रियं निष्पुरुषं निश्छन्दोरोमशार्शसं ।
क्षय्यामयाव्यपस्मारिश्वित्रिकुष्ठि कुलानिच । मनु: ।

possibly supposed that a marriage in any of these families will be invalid and it must be taken that the sole intention of these prohibitions is to warn against the evil consequences of such marriages. Hence, Kullûka says "where the enunciations of injunction and prohibition have their root in visible good and evil consequences as for instance in the text 'one which neglects the sacred rite' and so forth, there the contravention of the rule does not entail the negation of marital relationship."[1] Leaving these aside as well as those prohibitions which import nothing more than sinfulness of their violation, let us see if there are rules which when contravened, affect the validity of the marriage for they alone are important from a juristic standpoint.

Gotras and pravaras: prohibitions based thereon

Marriage within the same *gotra* or between families having the same *pravaras* is prohibited, and the text of Vishnu, "one should not marry a wife within the same *gotra* or having the same *pravara*"[2] has been interpreted by the authoritative commentators as a *paryudâsa* (excluding clause), the consequence being that a marriage taking place in violation of this text is considered as invalid. It should, however, be mentioned that this restrictive rule applies only to the twice-born classes, the sudras having no *gotras* of their own, although in Bengal, where traces of rigid Brahmanical influence are more visible than anywhere else, they profess to have *gotras* and usually shun intermarriage within their limits. On the other hand, it may be that in provinces where the influence of Brahmanism has waned to a considerable extent instances may be

[1] येषां पुनर्दृष्ट गुणदोषमूलकौ,
विधि-निषेधाभिधाने यथा हीनक्रियमिति
न तदतिक्रमे भार्यात्वाभावः।

[2] न सगोत्रां समान प्रवरां भार्यां विन्देत

found even among twice-born castes of marriages solemnised in violation of the prohibition referred to above, and Mr. Mandlik seems to suggest that such practices do prevail in his part of the country.[1] To us in Bengal some of his statements seem to be somewhat startling; but however that may be, an orthodox Hindu Lawyer cannot allow the prevalence of such transgressions to derogate from the authority of sastric injunction, although it is quite probable that the existence of a full-grown usage in violation of a distinct sastric injunction may make our courts reluctant to declare that a marriage solemnised in conformity to such usage is invalid in view of the very serious consequences which such a declaration would involve.

Prohibited degrees in marriage.

Different sages have laid down different rules on the subject of prohibited degrees for marriage. I do not propose to discuss these apparently divergent texts and to try to reconcile them if possible. Babu Golapchandra Sarkar observes that there is so much divergence between the sages as well as between the commentators on this subject that it would not be safe to enforce their views as binding rules of conduct. The observation is no doubt forcible, and as he points out different usages prevail among different classes and in different localities in respect of this matter. I may, however, be permitted to observe that prohibitions on this head cannot absolutely melt into the air, and there is perhaps everywhere a well-understood narrower limit which furnishes, so to say, an irreducible minimum and must not be transgressed; if this limit be overstepped, it will not only lower the position of the transgressing parties, but the marriage itself will be invalid according to the general principle of construction which I have elsewhere explained.

---

[1] Mandlik's Vyavahara Mayukha Appendix IV.

Dependence of women.

Turning now to the general condition of women, we find it stated that it is one of dependence. 'While young she remains under the control of her father, after marriage under the control of her husband and, on his death under the control of her sons; she does not deserve complete independence at any time'.[1] It may be mentioned that if she becomes a widow without sons, her husband's kinsmen are preferred over her father's kinsmen to watch after her interest and protect her in every way; if there be no one to look after her in either line, the duty then devolves upon the king.

Nature and extent of husband's control.

Let us now consider the nature and extent of the husband's control over his wife. I have already stated that Nilkantha denies that the husband has ownership over the wife, though Vijnaneswar allows that he has. It is, however, universally recognised that his rights are limited in several particulars. As regards the power of chastisement, it is limited in the same way as the power of the father in relation to his son, moreover, Manu has declared, "Divine blessing abides in that household where female members receive due honour; where they are not honoured, no act or ceremony bears its proper fruit; that family perishes in no time where the female members pass their days in sorrow, it prospers all along the line where they do not. Blessed is that family without fail in which the husband is always

Limited power over the person of the wife.

Dependence of women does not import any degradation.

पिता रक्षति कौमारे भर्त्तारक्षति यौवने ।

पुत्रास्तुस्थविरेभावे न स्त्री स्वातन्त्र्यमर्हति ।

रक्षन्ति स्थविरे पुत्रा इत्यापि पाठः । मनु ।९।३

रक्षेत् कन्यां पिता विन्नां पतिः पुत्रास्तु वार्द्धके

अभावेज्ञातयस्तेषां न स्वातन्त्र्यं क्वचित्-स्त्रियाः ।

याज्ञवल्क्य ।८४।

pleased with his wife and the wife with her husband."[1] "The good fortune of the family rests in them for they keep up the line, all honour is due to them; they are the lights of the household, the females and the fortune of the household--there is no distinction between the two."[2] It is, therefore, a great mistake to suppose that the declaraion of the perpetual dependence of women imports any degradation; it is only meant as a measure for their protection, for they are by nature weak and unable to bear the turmoils of the world and stand against its terrors and temptations without guidance and control.

Power of gift and sale: how far it existed.

As regards the power of the husband to dispose of the wife by gift or sale, you have already seen that Yajnavalkya and other sages enumerate a wife among objects unfit to be given; whether this is so because the husband is not the owner of the wife as Nilkantha maintains, or because the sastras, in spite of his ownership prohibit such an act, is not of much consequence. Manu has also declared that a wife cannot be detached from her husband either by sale or by abandonment, implying that the marital tie cannot be severed in any way being inalienable by its very nature.[3] It also follows from the above that the Hindu Law does not recognise a divorce

No divorce allowed.

---

1 यत्र नार्य्यस्तु पूज्यन्ते रमन्ते तत्र देवताः ।
यत्रैतास्तु न पूज्यन्ते सर्व्वास्तत्राफलाः क्रियाः ।
शोचन्ति जामयो यत्र विनश्यत्याशु तत्कुलम् ।
न शोचन्ति तु यत्रैता वर्द्धते तद्धि सर्व्वदा ।
सन्तुष्टो भार्य्यया भर्त्ता भर्त्रा भार्य्या तथैव च ।
यस्मिन्नेव कुले नित्यं कल्याणं तत्र वै ध्रुवम् । मनुः ।३।५६।५७।६०।

2 प्रजनार्थं महाभागाः पूजार्हा गृहदीप्तयः ।
स्त्रियः श्रियश्च गेहेषु न विशेषोऽस्ति कश्चन ।

3 न निष्क्रय विसर्गाभ्यां भर्त्तुर्भार्य्या विमुच्यते । मनुः ।९।४६ मनुः ९।२६ ।

meaning thereby the severance of a marriage already completed under the law. Then, again, it is laid down that the abandonment of a guiltless wife is punishable by the King. She is entitled to be properly maintained by the husband so long as she remains faithful to him and even in a case of faithlessness, the law declares that she should be provided with a bare pittance for her subsistence. In a case where the husband abandons his wife without any fault on her part he should be directed to take her back, and on non-compliance should be made to yield a third of his fortune to her; when, however the husband is so poor that deprivation of a third part of his fortune would be extremely hard, he should be made to provide her with proper maintenance.

Abandonment of a guiltless wife punishable.

On her part, it is the duty of the wife to remain faithful and obedient to her husband. Even when the husband dies, the duty is not at an end; 'let her rather emaciate her body by living upon pure flowers, roots, and fruits, but let her not, when the husband is dead, even pronounce the name of another man', so says Manu, 'and longing for the unparalleled virtue of those who remain steadfast to one husband, let her lead a life of austerity observing strictly the rules of continence and foregoing all sensual pleasures until she dies.[1] It would seem to follow from the above, as well as from the distinct text 'a second husband of a good woman is no where prescribed',[2] that Manu did not approve of

Duty of the wife to remain faithful and obedient to her husband.

Duties of a widow.

Controversy about widow re-marriage.

---

1 कामन्तु क्षपयेद्देहं पुष्पमूलफलैः शुभैः
नतु नामापि गृह्णीयात् पत्यौ प्रेते परस्यतु
आसीतामरणात् क्षान्ता नियता ब्रह्मचारिणी
यो धर्म एक पत्नीनां काङ्क्षन्तीतमनुत्तमम् । मनु: ।५।१५७।१५८

2 न द्वितीयश्च साध्वीनां क्वचिद्भर्त्तोपदिश्यते । मनु: ५।१६२
एतच्चसति पुनर्भूत्वमपि प्रतिषिद्धम् इति कुल्लुक भट्टः ।

a widow remarriage; and as the authority of Manu is regarded as supreme among the Hindu law-givers it has been contended that the remarriage of a widow is not sanctioned by the Hindu Law. So commenting upon the above text Kullûka says 'that being so, the second marriage of a woman is also prohibited'. You are, however, aware that this question gave rise to a memorable controversy between Pandit Iswarachandra Vidyasagar who contended mainly on the authority of a text of Parasara that a window marriage was permissible under the Hindu Law and his opponents who controverted that position. The text of Parasara which is also to be found in Narada-Smriti is to the following effect. 'Another husband is ordained of woman in five calamities, namely, if the husband be unheard of, or be dead, or adopt the order of an ascetic, or be impotent, or become an outcast'[1] I need hardly say that the opponents of widow marriage tried to explain this text away by maintaining that it did not refer to the remarriage of a woman who has been duly married to another by the performance of the solemn rites prescribed by the sastras, since, as Manu has declared, 'the remarriage of a widow has never been spoken of in the ordinances about marriage,'[2] but that it referred to a case where there has been a mere bethrothal not followed by the performance of the ceremonies which conclude the marriage and create the marital tie. Then, again, it was contended that even if the above interpretation be not accepted as correct still the prohibition contained in the Adi Purana shows that the practice must, at any rate be eschewed in the

[1] नष्टे, मृते, प्रव्रजिते क्लीवे च पतितेपतौ ।
पञ्चस्वापत्सु नारीणां पतिरन्यो विधीयते ।

[2] न विवाहविधावुक्तं विधवावेदनं पुनः । मनुः ।७।६५

Kali age;[1] and lastly it was asserted that whatever might be the view of Parasara or Narada, their authority could not prevail over that of Manu who prohibited widow remarriage; and that having regard to the fact that Narada expressly concerned himself with laying down the possitive law, his sanction would only show that the practice should not be forbidden and punished by the King and not that it should be regarded as consonant with the sacred law. On the other hand the suppoters of widow-marriage maintained that the text of Parsara did legalise the re-marriage of a woman duly married to another under the circumstances mentioned therein, and that inasmuch as Parasara expressly professed to lay down the law especially for the Kali age, his pronouncement should be regarded as especially authoritative at the present period; as regards the text of Manu, they contended that the laudation of the virtues of a chaste widow simply set forth an ideal, and did not amount to a prohibition of widow re-marriage; otherwise the text 'when a woman being forsaken by her husband, or becoming a widow voluntarily marries again and gives birth to a son, that son is called Paunarbhaba (or the son of re-marriage); if she takes the second husband when her first marriage was not consummated, or really returns to the first husband after having gone over to another, then with him the marital ceremonies may again be solemnised,'[2] would be

---

1 ऊढायाः पुनरुद्वाहं ज्येष्ठांशं गोवधन्तथा ।
कलौ पञ्च नकुर्व्वीत भ्रातृजायां कमण्डलुं ।
यापत्या वा परित्यक्ता विधवा वा स्वयेच्छया ।
उत्पादयेत् पुनर्भूत्वा स पौनर्भव उच्यते ।
सा चेदक्षतयोनिः स्यात् गतप्रत्यागतापि वा ।
पौनर्भवेन भर्त्रा सा पुनः संस्कारमर्हति । मनुः ।९।१७५।१७६।

irreconcibable with that position. I hope from the above statement you will be able to form some idea regarding the nature of the controversy and the arguments advanced on each side; it is not possible for me to proceed further and weigh the arguments on each side for that would entail an amount of discussion which I cannot undertake at the present moment having regard to the limits within which I must confine myself. I may, however, say this without fear of much contradiction that the system of widow re-marriage has never found favour among the Hindus, and it was never in vogue at least among the higher castes.

When the wife becomes liable to pay her husband's debts.

Husband's liability to pay his wife's debts.

As regards the liability of the wife to pay her husband's debts, it only arises when she acknowledges the liability and takes it upon herself, or when she incurs the debt jointly with her husband; otherwise, she is not liable to pay the debt.[1] Similarly the husband also is not liable to pay the wife's debts, unless they were contracted for the family purposes, subject to the exception that certain tradesmen, who cannot carry on their trade without the assistance of their wives are liable to pay off the debt incurred by them, since as Yajnavalkya puts it, their livelihood is dependent on their wives.[2]

Polygamy: how far sanctioned by the Hindu Law.

I have stated above that a wife was directed to remain constant to her husband even after his death, but the husband was not required to stick to a single wife, for

प्रतिपन्नंस्त्रिया देयं पत्या वा सहयत्कृतं ।
स्वयं कृतं वा यदृणं नान्यत् स्त्री दातुमर्हति ।
याज्ञवल्क्यः । ऋणादान प्रकरणम् ।

गोपशौण्डिक शैलुष रजकव्याधयोषितां
ऋणं दद्यात् पतिस्तासां यस्माद्वृत्तिस्तदाश्रयाः । याज्ञवल्क्यः ।

polygamy was not prohibited by the Hindu Law. You may, however, be aware that the late Pandit Isvarachandra Vidyasagara contended that the Hindu law did not make it optional with the husband to take as many wives as he liked, but that his choice in this respect was regulated by certain conditions, such as the first wife proving barren or giving birth to merely female children and so forth.[1] His position was, however, assailed by others, the chief among whom were the late Pandit Taranath Tarkavachaspati, and the late Kaviraj Gangadhar Kaviratna. They pointed out that the grounds for a second marriage prescribed in the texts might be regarded as justifying causes but could not be taken to control the right of a man to contract a second marriage; otherwise the various well known instances of polygamy to be found in the sastras, as Kaviraj Gangadhar Kaviratna pointed out, have to be pronounced as opposed to the sastras, since there is nothing to show that they had been contracted on any of the grounds so specified; it was also shown that there were many indications in the Institutes of Manu, as well as in other Dharma Shastras, the polygamy was permissible under the law apart from the existence of any special cause. Here, also, I don't propose to enter into the details of the controversy but I may say that Pandit Vidyasagara did not seem to have succeeded in establishing his position; moreover, it would scarcely have been of much practical moment even if he had, for, does not Manu say that you may take a second wife at once (सद्य:) if the first be guilty of using towards you unpleasant words?

Second marriage by a man during his wife's life

It is, however, worthy of notice that it is laid down that in case a man marries a second time during the

[1] बन्ध्याष्टमेऽधिवेद्याब्दे दशमेतु मृतप्रजा: ।
एकादशे स्त्री जननी सद्यस्त्वप्रियवादिनी । मनु: ।९।८१

time: husbands duty towards the first wife on such occasion.

life time of his first wife he should pay to the first wife as much as he spends on the second marriage, or, if she has already received some property as her *peculium*, as much as would render this equal to the amount spent over the second marriage;[1] So that she may have no reason to complain that she has been altogether neglected. Moreover, Manu declares that "when the husband marries a second time owing to the ill-health of the first wife, although she is attached to him and is, otherwise, of good character, he should first obtain the assent of that wife and must not slight her in any way;"[2] It is, therefore, apparent that although the Hindu Law sanctioned polygamy, it at the same time took care that it should be attended by as little violence to the feelings of the first wife as possible, and that, she should receive some pecuniary provision on such an occasion. At the same time it was provided that if the first wife being irritated at the second marriage of her husband, leave his house out of anger, then she may either be restrained from doing so or, if the husband so chooses, may be renounced in the presence of the whole family.[3]

The apparent anomaly in permitting polygamy and prohibiting widow-

I am free to admit that one may think it somewhat anomalous that a man should be permitted to have more than one wife while a woman should be enjoined to remain

आधिविन्नस्त्रियैदद्यादाधिवेदनिकं समं।
न दत्तं स्त्रीधनं यस्यैदत्तेत्वर्द्धं प्रकीर्त्तितं।

याज्ञवल्क्यः। दायविभागः।

या रोगिणी स्यात्तु हिता सम्पन्ना चैवशीलतः।
सानुज्ञाप्याधिवेत्तव्या नावमान्या तु कर्हिचित्। मनुः।९।८२

आधिविन्नातु या नारी निर्गच्छेद्रुषितागृहात्।
सा सद्यः सन्निरोधव्या त्याज्या वा कुल सन्निधौ मनुः।९।८२

constant to her husband even after his death, and it may even be suggested that this only shows that how those who had the making of law in their hands turned it to their advantages; the anomaly, however, ceases to be inexplicable if we keep in our mind the peculiar constitution of an ancient Hindu family; whenever a new member entered into it either by adoption or by marriage, he or she became at once so deeply engrafted into the family that the severance of the tie became almost an impossibility; thus when a man married, the wife on her introduction into the family became a limb, as it were, of an orgained whole, and she could not cut herself off simply because her husband, who introduced her into the family, and with whom, of course, she was more closely connected than with any body else, departed from this world; he might be dead but the family did not die and she remained as much a part of it as before. Therefore, during the solemnisation of the marriage ceremony, the husband pointed out to the wife the pole-star, as a symbol of constancy, and she prayed "as this star is constant, so may I be constant in my husband's family." The same considerations, however, did not apply to the case of the husband; he was not, by the marriage, transferred into another family, and if the perpetuation of lineage or other grounds required that he should take another wife, he could do so, and the result would be the introduction of yet another member into the family without in any way involving its disruption. I do not, of course, deny that the possibility for a man to contract more than one marriage was sometimes abused, but that was due to social causes which I cannot, here, stop to discuss; and it cannot also be doubted that this has been followed by a re-action so that now-a-days monogamy is almost the rule and polygamy an exception.

marriage sought to be explained.

Capacity of a wife to hold separate property under the Hindu Law.

Turning now to the capacity of a wife to hold separate property, I may at once say that this is allowed under the Hindu Law. I have already adverted to one kind of such property, *viz.*, that given by the husband to his first wife at the time when he takes another wife as a sort of solatium for her wounded feelings and it is known as आधिवेदनिक. Besides this, she may acquire property in other ways as well, principally through gifts made by the father, the husband, or their relations whether at the time of her marriage or not. It is not necessary for me to refer to the various classes of these properties, for all that I am at present concerned to show is that the Hindu Law does not impose any bar in the way of a wife owning separate property, although a text of Manu to which I have already referred in another connection would seem to show that the husband used at all events to exercise some control over it. I have also shown that she may inherit property from some of her relations, although the right of inheritance in the case of a female is hemmed in by limitations within a very narrow sphere.

Woman's peculuim.

Now, in one sense, all these kinds of property, in so far as they belong to a woman, may be characterised as *stridhana* or woman's property using the expression in its literal non-technical meaning and the Mitakshara has adopted this view ;[1] in other commentaries, however, the word has been used in a more restricted sense denoting only that class of a woman's property which she has the right to give, sell or use independently of her husband's control.[2] However that may be, let us see in what cases and to what extent the Hindu Law allowed the wife to hold and

[1] Mitakshara, Ch. II, Sec. XI, 203.

[2] Dayabhaga—Ch. IV, Sec. 1, 18.

Power to hold property independently of husband's control: how far limited.

enjoy property independently of her husband's control. It appears that in two cases the husband has more complete control over his wife's acquisitions than in the rest; for as laid down in the text of Katyayana, 'the wealth which a woman earns by the exercise of her skill in mechanical arts or receives as affectionate presents from persons not related to her becomes at once subject to her husband's control,'[1] and Jimutavahana explains that he has a right to take it, although there be no distress to compel him to adopt this course. The reason why the Hindu Law allows to the husband an exceptional degree of control over these two kinds of his wife's acquisitions is not perhaps difficult to surmise; to allow a wife to earn wealth for herself by the exercise of mechanical arts is calculated to create in her a desire to devote her time in a way antagonistic to her duty towards her husband for her own special benefit, and to permit her to accept presents from those not related to her and appropriate them herself without any restriction may tend to bring about an undesirable inclination to seek the good graces of those with whom perhaps she ought not to have any concern; hence the Hindu Law very wisely provided by placing the property so acquired absolutely under the control of her husband, that in neither way should the wife be permitted to make any profit for herself.

सौदायिक or gifts from affectionate kindred.

On the other hand, affectionate presents received by a woman from her husband or parents or their relations are known as *saudayika* (सौदायिक) and over those she has absolute control with this exception, *viz.*, that in the case of immovable property received as a gift from the husband she has no right of alienation, not only so long as the husband is alive but even after his death, unless, of course, the husband himself chooses to invest her with the right by express declaration to that effect. It has

---

[1] प्राप्तं शिल्पैस्तु यद्वित्तं प्रीत्याचैवयदन्यतः।
भर्तुःस्वाम्यं भवेत्तत्र शेषन्तु स्त्रीधनं स्मृतं।

been laid down that *sulka*[1] or the gratuity for the receipt of which a girl is given in marriage and लाभ or the profits arising from other properties belonging to her are absolutely at her disposal and thus constitute a part of her *peculium*.

Husband's right over wife's *peculium*.

Having thus indicated the nature of the properties which go to constitute a woman's peculium, let us see in what relation she stands to her husband with regard to them. Ordinarily the husband has no right to take any part of his wife's peculium without her consent; if he does so, by force, then he must be compelled to restore it to the wife together with interest, and shall also be punished for the transgression; if, however, the husband expends his wife's peculium for his own purposes after having obtained her consent, even then he should repay it without interest when he is in a fit position to do so but if he takes another wife in supercession of her, then although the property might have been taken with her consent and duly bestowed out of affection, the King shall and force him to restore the same at once, without any prejudice to her right to obtain from him such maintenance as she is otherwise entitled to.[2] There is, however, this exception to the husband's incapacity to take his wife's property, *viz.*, that if he have no means of subsistence without it as in a famine or other distress, then he may take it even without her consent. So Yajnavalkya declares: "A husband is not liable to make good the property of his wife taken by him in a famine or for the performance of some indispensable duty, or during illness or while under restraint (for payment of a debt or the

---

[1] The word Sulka शुल्क has been variously explained. I have here adopted that meaning which seems to me to give the most important significance of the word.

[2] See Dayabhaga—Chap. IV. Sec. 1. 24.

Alienation by a woman of her peculium.

Is it permissible without her husband's assent?

like)." I have already pointed out that a woman can dispose of her peculium in any way she likes, and except in the case of gifts made by her husband this even includes the right of free alienation. It is, however, doubtful whether an alienation made by the wife without her husband's assent can be regarded as valid; no doubt, her proprietary right includes the power of alienation, but in so far as she herself is not absolutely independent and stands in need of protection, it seems to be required that at least in the case of immovable property, the assent of the husband to the transaction should be obtained. Thus, Katyayana says: "Gift, pledge or sale of fields, houses, or slaves made by dependent persons does not become perfect without the assent of those on whom they are dependent."[1] This may, however, be regarded as controlled by another text in which Katyayana declares that, in regard to *saudayika* property the independent control of women is ever acknowledged both in respect of donation and of sale according to their wishes even in the case of immovables.[2] Reading, therefore, the two texts together the proper conclusion seems to be that with regard to this class of property the husband is not entitled to withhold his consent if the act of alienation is a free act on the part of the wife not induced by force or fraud.

Wife's co-ownership in husband's

Among other legal consequences of a marriage it has sometimes been stated that the wife, by virtue

---

1 न क्षेत्र गृह दासानां दानाधमन विक्रयाः ।
अस्वतन्त्रकृताः सिद्धिं प्राप्नुयुर्नानुवर्णिताः ॥
वीरमित्रोदयधृत कात्यायनवचनं ।

2 सौदायिके सदा स्त्रीणां स्वातन्त्र्यं परिकीर्त्तितम् ।
विक्रये चैव दाने च यथेष्टं स्थावरेष्वपि ॥
दायभागधृत कात्यायन वचनं ।

property: what it

of the marital tie, becomes co-owner with her husband in everything that belongs to him. The question is discussed in several of the commentaries on the Dayabhaga, where it is pointed out that the right of the wife arises without in any way interfering with the full ownership of the husband and ceases with the extinction of that ownership. The recognition of this right has, therefore, very little practical value, in as much as it neither fetters the freedom of the husband to deal with the property according to his pleasure, nor invests the wife with an independent control over it. But still it is not absolutely nominal; hence the Mitakshara points out that the text of Apastamba declaring this co-ownership also indicates the purpose for which it is recognised when it states that by reason of this co-ownership no theft can be imputed to the wife if she expends her husband's property for occasional acts of charity or the like during his absence, and it may also be said that it finds a partial recognition in the direction that when the husband voluntarily distributes his wealth among his sons, the wife should also get an equal share.[1]

Having thus far discussed the position of a wife under the Hindu Law, let us compare this with her position under the Roman Law. Turning to this we find that originally under the Roman law the wife had very little of personal or proprietary independence. This and the way in which she gradually extricated herself out of it are very clearly explained by Sir Henry Maine. He says: "Anciently, there were three modes in which marriage might be contracted according to Roman usage, one involving a religious solemnity, the other two, observance of certain secular formalities. By the religious marriage, or *con-*

मिताक्षरा ऋणादान प्रकरणं ।

ion, by the higher form of civil marriage, which was called *coemptio*, and by the lower form, which was termed *usus*, the husband acquired a number of rights over the person and property of his wife which were on the whole in excess of such as are conferred on him in any system of modern Jurisprudence. But in what capacity did he acquire them? Not as husband, but as father. By the confarreation, coemption, and usus, the woman passed in *manum viri*, that is, in law she became the *daughter* of her husband. She was included in his *patria potestas*. She incurred all the liabilities springing out of it while it subsisted and surviving it when it had expired. All her property became absolutely his, and she was retained in tutelage after his death to the guardian whom he had appointed by will. These three ancient forms of marriage fell, however, gradually into disuse, so that at the most splendid period of Roman greatness, they had almost entirely given plece to a fashion of wedlock old apparently, but not hitherto considered reputable—which was founded on a modification of the lower form of civil marriage. Without explaining the technical mechanism of this institution now generally popular, I may describe it as amounting in law to a little more than a temporary deposit of the woman by her family. The rights of the family remained unimpaired, and the lady continued in the tutelage of guardians whom her parents had appointed and whose privileges of control overrode in many material respects, the inferior authority of her husband. The consequence was that the situation of the Roman female, whether married or unmarried became one of great personal and proprietary independence."

It thus appears that originally the position of a Roman wife was one of complete subordination, involving a very considerable curtailment of personal and proprietary rights, and although subsequently she freed herself from these liabilities, the result was brought about by a relaxation of the marital tie.

Proprietary incapacity imposed upon a married woman by the English Law.

I may also remind you that the proprietary incapacity imposed upon a married woman by the English Common Law was at least equally stringent. It has been thought that this was due to the influence of the Canon Law which introduced the notion that husband and wife constituted, as it were, a single person, so that the very legal existence of the wife, as a distinct person, was almost suspended during her coverture, rendering her incapable of holding any separate property or asserting any right not only against him but also against others without his concurrence. Hence the husband could not make any grant in her favour, because this would involve that she had a separate legal existence, and for the same reason she could not bring any action for redress against any body without the concurrence of her husband Of course, these disabilities were subsequently very much modified by the intervention of the Court of Equity even before the enactment of the Married Women's Property Act, but I am more concerned to point out to you what the state of the pure English Common Law was with reference to this matter, and upon this Sir Henry Maine observes: "I do not know how the operation and nature of the ancient patria potestas can be brought so vividly before the mind as by reflecting on the prerogatives attached to the husband by the pure English Common Law, and by recalling the rigorous consistency with which the view of a complete legal subjection on the part of the wife is carried by it; where it is untouched by Equity or statutes, through every department of rights, duties and remedies."

On the whole, therefore, the position of a wife under the Hindu Law seems to have been much better than under the Roman or the English law. It allowed her greater personal freedom than the Roman Law and larger proprietary rights than either system, while at the same time, care was taken to afford her such protection as her comparative weakness would naturally demand, and it is remarkable that the gradual growth of rights and the removal of her disabilities did not in any way involve any slackening of the marriage tie.

The position of a wife under the Hindu Law seems to have been much better.

As regards litigation between husband and wife, this was allowed by the Hindu Law when requisite, although it was directed that this should be discouraged as much as possible. In this respect also it was more liberal than the English Common Law which disallowed such litigation until it was modified by Statute, 45 and 46 Vict. C. 75.

Litigation between husband and wife.

It need hardly be said that betrothal is quite distinct from marriage, the former being a mere promise to be followed by the latter, which alone produces the marital tie. It is, of course, the duty of father or other guardian of the girl from whom the promise emanates to fulfil it in due course, but our law-givers direct that it is permissible to annul a betrothal if a better suitor becomes available.[1] If, however, the promisor refuses to keep his promise without any excuse, such as the discovery of some defect in the bride-groom, he renders himself liable to be punished by the King.[2] On his turn the bride-groom may even

Betrothal: its effect.

When revocable and when not.

सकृत् प्रदीयते कन्याहरंस्तां चौरदण्डभाक् ।
दत्तामपि हरेत् कन्यां श्रेयांश्चेद्वर आव्रजेत् ।
याज्ञवल्क्यः । विवाह प्रकरणं । ६५

दत्वा न्यायेन य कन्यां वराय न ददाति तां ।
अदुष्टश्चेद्वरो राज्ञा सदण्ड्यस्तत्र चौरवत् । नारद ।

after the betrothal refuse to marry a girl when his consent was obtained by fraud or false pretences or when it is discovered that the girl was suffering from some defect, and it is distinctly declared that when the guardian of the girl secured the consent of the suitor without disclosing some defect to which she was subject, it is only proper that the attempt of that false man should be rendered abortive.[1] In the absence of any justifying cause, a suitor is not free, after the betrothal, to withdraw from his promise to marry, and if he attempted to do so, the King should control him and compel him to marry the girl even against his will.[2] Such then was Hindu Law; but to compel a man to marry a girl against his will must be owned to be a somewhat dangerous experiment, and it is not very much to be regretted that our courts have refused to specifically enforce a contract of marriage holding that the only remedy in such a case is by an action for damages. If may, however, be pointed out that a refusal to marry after betrothal without any just cause casts an unmerited slur upon the girl, and to allow a man, in such a case, to escape by merely paying damages for the breach of the promise for which the guardian of a Hindu girl seldom comes to court seems to let him off rather too easily especially when it is remembered how often such refusals proceed from mere greed for money which is altogether foreign to the sacred character of the Hindu matrimonial relationship. The spirit of commercialism is, however, an incident of our modern material civilisation, and what cannot be cured must, therefore, be endured.

[1] यस्तु दोषवतीं कन्यामनाख्यायोपपादयेत् ।
तस्य तद्वितथं कुर्य्यात् कन्या दातुर्दुरात्मनः । मनुः ।

[2] प्रतिगृह्य तु यः कन्यामदुष्टामुत्सृजेत् नरः ।
स विनेयस्त्वकामोपि कन्यां तामेवचोद्वहेत् ।

LECTURE X.

THE LAW OF DOMINICAL RELATION AND THE LAW OF DEFECTIVE STATUS IN GENERAL.

'Slavery' says Justinian, 'is an institution of the law of nations, by which one man is made the property of another, contrary to natural right.'[1] Whatever this may mean, it is at any rate clear that in the days when this was written there was hardly any nation known to the Romans which did not give any countenance to slavery. In the Hindu Law also we find discussions relating to an institution very similar to it.

Justinian on slavery.

The word दास according to Katyayana, etymologically signifies a person who being free voluntarily gives himself away to another.[2] It is not, therefore, unlikely that originally slavery, or rather what corresponds to it in the Hindu law, arose from a voluntary surrender of oneself to another by a free man with a view to obtain subsistence and protection in lieu of services to be rendered by him. If he offered himself as a son, he became what has been called a son self-given ; if, on the other hand, he could not possibly expect to secure this high status, and yet was in sore need of subsistence and protection, he offered himself unconditionally and thus became a slave. We shall, however, see that this was not the only mode in which a person could become a slave. The difference between a slave and an ordinary servant is thus explained

Meaning of दास

Difference between a slave and an

[1] Institutes, Lib I, Tit III.

[2] स्वतन्त्रस्यात्मनोदानाद्दासत्वं दासवद्भृगुः।

इति कात्यायन।

ordinary servant.

in Smriti Chandrika; both a servant and a slave work for another, but the formef while working for his master also earns an independent livelihood of his own, but the latter works absolutely for the master abandoning all sources of separate and independent earning for himself. The dependenc of the former is, therefore, only partial, while that of the latter is absolute.

Seven kinds of slaves according to Manu.

There is a text of Manu enumerating seven kinds of slaves, or rather seven distinct modes in which slavery could arise; according to this a man could become a slave when he was made a captive in war, or offered himself in slavery for subsistence or was born of a slave woman or transferred by a former master by sale, or gift, or received by inheritance from the former master or made a slave as a punishment by an act of law.[1] Narada gives a longer list mentioning fifteen kinds of slaves; these were: one born in the house (of a slave woman), one purchased, one received in donation, one ved by inheritance, one maintained in a season of dearth, one pledged by the master, one released from some heavy liability, one captured in war, one won at a wager, one who surrenders himself saying I am become thine, one who having become an ascetic breaks the rules of the order, one who surrenders himself in slavery for a fixed term, one who does so in consideration of receiving food and raiment, one who is rendered a slave by attachment to a slave girl, and lastly one who sells himself. Now leaving out of consideration the particular modes that are derivative in their character, we find that at its origin slavery could arise from capture in war or form birth of a slave woman, from attachment to a slave girl, from infraction of the rules of the ascetic order,

Fifteen kinds of slaves according to Narada.

How slavery could be ontracted.

ध्वजाहृतो भक्तदासो गृहजः क्रीतदत्रिमौ।

पैत्रिको दण्डदासश्च सप्तैते दासयोनयः। मनुः। ८।४१५।

from self-surrender to slavery for some sort of consideration, and lastly by way of penalty through an order of court.

Special rules regulating slavery: no Brahmin could be a slave of another.

One belonging to a higher caste could not be held as a slave.

Turning now to the special rules regulating subjection to slavery we find it broadly laid down that a Brahmin could never become a slave of another, and as regards others a person belong to a higher caste could not be a slave of another belonging to a lower caste. Then, again, a person who after having become an ascetic breaks the rules of the order only makes himself a slave of the king by way of punishment for the transgression.

Emancipation from slavery:

As regards emancipation from slavery, it appears that slavery was generally terminable in its character on the fulfilment of certain conditions except when it arose from birth, or from purchase, gift, or succession from the previous master, or when the person had reduced himself to this condition by selling himself for a price.

Conditions of emancipation.

Thus a captive in war could emancipate himself by paying ransom for his release, one who became a slave for subsistence could free himself by repaying the expenses incurred, one who was attracted by attachment to a slave girl became free as soon as he gave her up and subjection to slavery for a definite period ceased upon the expiry of that period. It is not necessary to enter into details, but it seems that slavery was not terminable except at the option of the master only when it arose from birth of a slave-woman, or was contracted voluntarily in consideration of a price received from the master. Nilkantha even doubts whether a person could become a slave from the very moment of his birth so as to be unfit for emancipation except at the option of the master, for according to him his mother could not, and consequently his position could not be worse than hers. This may, however, be a refinement due to advancement of ideas which did not exist in ancient time. Apart from these, all kinds of slaves became free at the option of the master, and there was no limit imposed upon the master's right to emancipate the slave as we find in the Roman Law.

Emancipation at the option of the master: No limit imposed upon such emancipation as in the Roman Law.

Then, again, a slave who saved the life of his master from some impending danger became at once free, and what is more, obtained a share in his property as if he were his son,[1] a provision which shows that with the Hindu, gratefulness was not confined to mere words, but found solid recognition in substantial legal rules.

Saving the life of the master emancipated the slave and entitled him to a share of the master's property.

The formalities of manumission when the master desired to emancipate his slave were very simple, even much simpler than under the Roman Law. All that was required was that the master desiring to emancipate his slave should take from his shoulder a pitcher filled with water and break it down, sprinkle water on his head together with flower and rice, and saying three times 'thou art no longer a slave' let him proceed towards the east. It is impossible to conjecture what these formalities meant unless they were intended to give publicity and add impressiveness to the transaction and invest it with a solemnity preventing future repudiation.

Formalities of manumission.

It was also directed that when a master begets a child upon his female slave he must emancipate her with the issue.

Master begetting a child upon his female slave must emancipate her with the issue.

It may further be mentioned that it was clearly laid down that a person forcibly made a slave or purchased as a slave from a thief who had kidnapped him could not properly be regarded as a slave, so that the king should at once release him from all restraint,[2] a provision

A person forcibly made a slave or purchased from a

[1] यश्चैषां स्वामिनं कश्चिन्मोचयेत् प्राणसंशयात् ।
दासत्वात् स विमुच्यते पुत्रभागं लभेत च । इति नारदः ।

[2] चौरापहृत विक्रीता ये च दासीकृता बलात् ।
राज्ञा मोचयितव्यास्ते दास्यन्तेषु हि नेष्यते । नारदः ।

which shows that the Hindu Law did not tolerate subjection to slavery when it had its beginning in force or fraud.

thief did not really become a slave.

As regards the condition of a slave, I think the provisions of the Hindu Law bearing upon it were on the whole much more humane than under the Roman Law. You are perhaps aware that under the ancient Roman Law the master had the power of life and death over his slaves. 'Slaves' says Justinian, 'are in the power of masters, a power derived from the law of nations: for among all nations it may be remarked that masters have the power of life and death over their slaves, and that everything acquired by the slaves is acquired for the master.'[1] This power of using unrestrained violence was subsequently curtailed, and it is stated that Constantine only permitted moderate corporeal chastisement to be inflicted upon the slave, and Justinian in the Code retains this enactment. Turning to the Hindu Law we do not find any trace of the master having the power of life and death over his slaves; on the other hand Manu distinctly laid down that the master's authority to meet out even moderate chastisement was subject to limitations in the same way as the father's power to chastise his son, and any violation of these limitations was punishable by the king. As regards rights of property, a slave, no doubt, could not acquire any property for himself, during his subjection to slavery, but his former property did not pass to his master and he could buy his emancipation through the same. Then, again, although ordinarily the master had the power of transferring his slave to another, yet it was declared that a master who wanted to sell his female slave devoted to him without any fault on her part and against her wishes

Position of a slave under the Hindu Law

Power of life and death under the ancient Roman Law.

The Hindu Law was much more humane.

A slave could not acquire property for himself, but his former property did not pass to the master.

Limits upon the master's right of selling a female slave.

[1] Institutes Lib I, Tit VIII.

should be punished unless he acted under extreme distress.[1] So, after all, the Hindu Law did not regard a slave as mere chattel but as a human being capable of having feelings and sentiments which should not be needlessly outraged or deliberately ignored.

Transaction entered into by a slave except under direction from the master was void. Not so, if he acted for the protection of his master's family in distress; in such a case the master should ratify the same.

If follows almost as a corollary from the dependent position of a slave that a transaction entered into by him except when he acted under the direction of his master should be treated as void; it was, however, directed that if he did anything for the family of his master at a time of distress, the master should satisfy the same and be bound by the obligation created in that manner.

Other sources of defective status: (1) causing exclusion from inheritance. (2) barring freedom in transactions. Causes that impede freedom in entering into jural transactions, (a) infancy, (b) dependence, (c) mental aberration.

Besides slavery, there are various other sources that give rise to a defective status. Speaking broadly these may perhaps be divided into two classes, viz., (1) those causing exclusion from inheritance, and (2) those barring freedom in transactions. The subject of exclusion from inheritance has already been treated in a previous lecture, and it would be superfluous to revert to it. I, therefore, turn to the second branch of the enquiry relating to the causes that impede a person's freedom in entering into jural transactions. I am inclined to think that speaking generally these may be resolved into infancy, dependence and mental aberration. It will be remembered that in dealing with the law relating to the Transfer of Property I have shown that according to the Hindu Sastras a gift made by a person under the influence of sudden fear, or uncontrollable rage or lust or the like is invalid, because he is not then in a proper frame of mind. Narada says that such people

Mental aberration causing temporary want of freedom.

विक्रोशमानां यो भर्त्ता दासीं विक्रेतुमिच्छति ।
अनापदिस्थः शक्त सन् प्राप्नुयात् त्रिशतं दमं ।[1]

इति कात्यायन:

are for the time being besides themselves, and therefore, although independent, their actions should be regarded as void by reason of the temporary want of freedom.[1] A temporary disability of this sort, cannot, however, be regarded as creating a defective status which implies something more permanent; when this becomes more permanent, we practically get what is called insanity, and a person afflicted with it becomes incapable of entering into any legal transaction. Dependence implies subjection to superior control, the nature of such dependence in the case of sons, wives and slaves has already been explained It goes without saying that there are various degrees of such dependence; it being in fact relative in its character, thus, it has been said that a king is independent, the subjects are dependent on him, the preceptor is independent, his pupils are dependent on him, and the head of the family is independent, and the other members are dependent on him. It would be an unprofitable task to dwell on the exact amount and character of the control exercised in each of these cases; suffice it to say that in every instance there is involved some amount of limitation upon the unfettered freedom of action of the person who occupies the inferior or subordinate position.

Insanity.

Dependence: different grades of dependence.

Turning now to infancy, we find that it is divisible into two sections. Till the eighth year, a boy is, for all legal purposes comparable to a child in its mother's womb; after this till the sixteenth year he is described as adolescent, but by reason of immaturity is regarded as incapable

Infancy; period infancy.

[1] स्वतन्त्रोऽपि हि यत्कार्य्यं कुर्य्यादप्रकृतिंगत:
तदप्यकृतमेवाहुरस्वतन्त्र: स हेतुत: ॥
कांम क्रोधाभिभूतार्त्त भयव्यसन पीड़िता: ।
रागद्वेष परीताश्च ज्ञेयास्त्वप्रकृतिंगता: ॥

of entering into any legal transaction ; when this limit is passed he becomes free and *sui juris* but when his parents are living he is not absolutely free from their control.[1] Minority, therefere, under the Hindu Law extends till the sixteenth year. Mr. Mayne, however, points out that there was a difference of opinion as to whether this age was attained at the begining or at the end of the sixteenth year. 'The Hindu writers', he says, 'seem to take the former view and this was always held to be the law in Bengal. The latter point is stated to be the rule in Mithila and Benares and was followed in Southern India and apparently in Bombay.'[2] The difference of opinion is no doubt attributable to the ambiguity of the particle 'आङ्' which means until and may, therefore, refer to either limit. Having regard to the context, the best interpretation seems to me to lead to the conclusion, that minority extends till the end of the sixteenth year, although Srikrishna Tarkalankara in his commentary on the Dayabhaga appears in one place to take the opposite view.[3] The main point of difference between the position of an infant within his eighth year, and a minor who is above eight but below sixteen years, in age is that the former is even exempted from criminal liability while the latter is not, unless he is incapable of discriminating between right and wrong ; as regards freedom to enter into civil transactions they are both on the same footing.

[1] गर्भस्थैः सदृशोज्ञेय अष्टमा द्वत्सराच्छिशुः ।
बाल आषोड़शाद्वर्षात् पौगःडश्चापि शब्द्यते ।
परतो व्यवहारज्ञः स्वतन्त्र पितरावृते । नारदः ।

[2] Maynes Hindu Law, p. 272.

[3] अप्राप्त व्यवहारा बालका पञ्चदश वर्षानधिक वयस्काः ।
दायभाग टीका ।२।१।१७।

Guardianship of a minor.

As regards the guardianship of a minor, the father, of course, has the first claim, after him comes the mother and if neither be alive, the elder brother takes the place.[1] In the case of a girl, the guardianship, after her marriage, passes to the husband. Ultimately, the King is the guardian of all, and Manu enjoins that when a boy has neither father, nor mother, he should take steps to protect the property of the boy until he attains majority and returns from the house of his preceptor to take charge of it himself.[2]

तयोरपि पिता श्रेयान् बीज प्राधान्य दर्शनात्।
अभावे बीजिनो माता तदभावेतु पूर्व्वजः।
वीरमित्रोदयधृत नारद वचनं।
व्यवहार मातृका प्रकरणं।

बालदायाधिकं रिक्थं तावद्राजानुपालयेत्।
यावत् स स्यात् समावृत्तोयावच्चातीत शैशवः। मनुः।८।२७।

LECTURE XI.

THE LAW OF CONTRACTUAL OBLIGATIONS.

Place of contract in the Hindu Law.

It is remarkable that in the Hindu Law we do not find any distinct treatment of contracts in general as distinguished from the several more important kinds of contract which are separately discussed as giving rise to liabilities enforceable by the court. This is to some extent due to the fact that in our Dharmasastras as well as commentaries and *nibandhas* grounded on them the treatment of the positive law has followed in its order and arrangement the classification given by Manu and other lawgivers of the *topics of litigation or forms of action*; the result was that the different subjects were presented not so much from the standpoint of the positive rights arising from various transactions as from the standpoint of the transgressions furnishing causes of action to be taken cognisance of by the court. The enquiry of the Hindu jurists was, therefore, directed not so much to analyse what a contract in the abstract may be taken to be, as to determine in what ways, the various kinds of contractual obligations may be broken and what are the remedies for the same. This method of treatment may, no doubt, fail to satisfy the theoretical demands of an analytical jurist, but it was sufficient for the purposes of a practical lawyer who is more concerned with decision of disputes than with analysis of abstract conceptions. Yet, it must be confessed that to us who are more conversant with the English Law of Contract in its present shape than with the history of its growth this may seem to be a very conspicuous shortcoming, but if we look back we find that there is not much to be startled at, and that the Hindu Law of Contract was as developed as most other systems of ancient law. 'Taking English Courts', says Sir F. Pollock who is one of the pre-eminent authorities on the subject, 'and the remedies they administered as they were about the middle of the thirteenth century (for it is needless to go further back for our present purpose), we find that what we should call elaborate contracts or covenants, and of sufficiently various kinds, can be annexed to grants of lands and interests in land, but there is very little independent law of contract, and if by a law of contract we mean a law which enforces promises as such, it can hardly be said that there is any at all. Still less there is any theory or system of the law. Bracton, so far as he has a system, copies Azo of Bologna with variations due partly to misunderstanding and partly to the impossibility of contradicting the actual English practice. But the only classification for which the practical English lawyer cares is a classification of forms of action, processes and remedies.[1]' It was, in fact, the modern doctrine of consideration which cemented together the different forms of action, and through the action of assumpsit which was subsequently introduced moulded the different branches of the law of contract into one organic whole. Turning to the Roman Law, as it existed in the days of Justinian, there also we find that the only forms of consensual contracts, in which alone obligation was attached at once to the consensus or mutual consent, were four in number: viz., *emptio venditio* or sale, *locatio conductio* or letting and hiring, *societas* or partnership, and *mandatum* or a particular kind of agency, and every one of these was recognised by the Hindu Law from a very early time. I, therefore, need not make any apology for presenting to you a short account

Development of the law of contract in England.

Character of the Roman Law of contract in the days of Justinian.

[1] Pollock's Law of Contract, p. 135.

of the Hindu Law of contractual obligations in the way in which it was treated by the Hindu lawyers themselves without attempting to clothe it in a foreign mask.

Nonpayment of debt: Debt universally acknowledged to be one of the earliest forms of contract.

Nonpayment of debt is the first among the eighteen topics of litigation mentioned by Manu. Liability to pay a debt is acknowledged on all hands to be one of the earliest forms of contractual obligation. It corresponds to what is called *mutumn* in the Roman Law being a form of real contract in which the obligation is founded upon the delivery of a thing giving rise to a liability to repay. In the English law also, debt with convenant formed the two earliest forms of contract and the enforcement of a mere promise through the intervention of the doctrine of consideration was only a subsequent growth. A loan according to the Hindu Law, may be of two kinds: secured or unsecured; it is said to be secured when the creditor receives a pledge for its satisfaction or when another person stands as a surety for the debtor. An unsecured loan, in its turn, may be evidenced by a written document or merely attested by witnesses. A debt, it will be observed, involves two elements: (1) receipt of a benefit, and (2) existence of an express or implied promise to repay; the primary source of the idea of obligation attached to the taking of a loan was the receipt of the benefit which carried with it the duty to repay; this is indicated by certain texts in which obligations to do certain acts in return for benefits received were assimilated to the conceptions of a debt and its satisfaction even without the accompaniment of any promise on the part of the person who received those benefits. Thus the Taittiriya Sruti declares that a Brahman at the moment of his birth becomes indebted in three ways; he discharges his debt to the gods by the performance of sacrifices, to the ancestors by procreating

A loan may be of two kinds: secured and unsecured.

The latter divisible into two kinds.

A debt involves two elements.

Primary source of the obligation.

children (to continue the line and offer funeral oblations), and to the sages (who went before him) by learning the Vedas.[1] I do not, of course, mean to say that these were debts in the legal sense of the term, or the obligations imposed were legal obligations enforceable by the king; the object with which I mention these is simply to show that the characteristic element which is takon hold of in extending the term 'debt' to these cases is the receipt of benefit which engenders a corresponding duty to make some sort of return, thereby indicating that the receipt of a benefit raises the idea of a moral obligation to repay. This moral obligation is, however, transformed into a legal obligation, when the benefit is conferred on an express or implied undertaking to repay, such an undertaing being presumed when there is nothing to show that the person who conferred the benefit meant to bestow it as a free gift without an eye to a return. Such an obligation was not made to depend upon the accompaniment of any formality as in a Roman *nexum* or stipulation, the receipt of the benefit being itself sufficient to furnish a sufficient foundation for the same, and as such it evinces at least some amount of ethical and juridical advance over that class of archaic rules which attach more importance to the form than to the substance of a legal transaction.

The obligation not dependent on the accompainment of any formaality.

This shows a considerable ethical and juridical advance.

Loan of money and loan of other things.

Difference between a debt and a loan for use:

A debt arose not only from a loan of money but also from a loan of other things. The difference between this and a loan for use corresponds to that between *mutuum* and *commodatum* under the Roman Law. In the case of

[1] जायमानो हि वै ब्राह्मणः
त्रिभिः ऋणै ऋणवान् जायते ।
ब्रह्मचर्य्येण ऋषिभ्यो यज्ञेन
देवेभ्यः, प्रजया पितृभ्यः ।
एष वा अनृणो यः पुत्री,
यज्वा, ब्रह्मचारी च ॥ श्रुतिः ।

Cf. the difference between mutum and commodatum

a debt the thing lent became the property of the debtor and he could use it or consume it just as he liked, being liable to return to the creditor not the exact thing lent, but only an equivalent of it ; while in the case of a loan for use, the property remained with the lender and the borrower was bound to restore the identical thing after having used it for the purpose for which it was lent.

Interest on loan, condemnation of usury.

A debt often carries with it a liability to pay interest upon the amount lent. If we look back, we find that our ancient Dharmasastras severely condemned the practice of taking interest upon a loan. Thus Vasistha says 'Destruction of fœtus and extortion of interest were weighed in the balance ; whereupon the destroyer of the fœtus went upon the scale and the usurer fell down,'[1] and this figuratively expresses the sage's opinion that the extortion of interest which sucks the life blood, so to say, of living men is even more reprehensible than the destruction of fœtus which has not yet seen the light of day ; but even he, while so strongly denouncing the practice as immoral, cannot declare it to be illegal, for, in view perhaps of the prevalent practice, he, with evident regret, concedes its legality by saying apparently with much reluctance 'or let it be paid to that sinner who is lost to all virtuous acts.'[2] Similarly both Manu and Narada disapprove of the practice at least when it becomes extortionate though their disapproval is certainly couched in less severe language ;[3] thus Narada classes it as a means of acquisition of a mixed character being partly white (pure) and partly black (impure), and it is allowed to be a legitimate means of livelihood for a

Still it is not illegal,

वृद्धिं च भ्रूणहत्याञ्च तुलया समतोलयम्
अतिष्ठद्भ्रूणहा कोट्यां वार्धुषिर्न्यक् पपात ह ।
कामं वा परिलुप्तकृत्याय पापीयसे दद्यात् ।
ब्राह्मणः क्षत्रियो वापि वृद्धिं नैव प्रयोजयेत्
कामन्तु खलु धर्मार्थं दद्यात् पापीयसेऽल्पिकाम् । मनुः । १० । ११७ ।

Vaisya belonging to the third or commercial class among the Hindus. The conclusion seems to be that it was tolerated within certain limits, but not regarded as a respectable or a commendable act.

Different kinds of interest. Interest limited by law, and interest fixed by special contract. Simple and compound interest.

There are several different kinds of interest mentioned in the Dharmasastras. In some cases the rate of interest is limited by the law, in others it is fixed by special contract between the parties; such interest may either be simple or compound; and sometimes, the enjoyment of the property pledged represents the interest taken. Leaving out of consideration the last class of cases, we find that ordinarily the rate of interest was fixed by the law; as to this it appears that the rate of interest varied according to the amount of risk incurred by the creditor; thus an unsecured debt carried a higher rate of interest than a secured debt; moreover, the rate of interest also varied according to the caste of the debtor; one belonging to a higher caste being liable to pay at a lower rate than one belonging to a lower caste. Then, again, when the lending of the debt involved exceptional risk as for instance where the debtor intended to undertake a journey through a forest, or a sea-voyage after taking the loan, the creditor was considered entitled to claim interest at a higher rate than was ordinarily allowed in consideration of his incurring the risk of losing even the principal itself. Apart from interest limited by the law, the rate of interest could also be fixed by a special contract made by the parties; but here a rate exceeding the ordinary rate limited by the law would not be valid unless the debtor, in a case of urgency at a time of distress, expressly stipulated to pay it.[1] Jagannatha here

Rate of interest fixed by the law vaired according to the risk incurred;

and also according to the caste of the debtor.

Exceptional risk entitled the creditor to claim special rate of interest.

Interest fixed by special contract.

A rate exceeding the usual rate when allowed.

1 ऋणिकेन तु या वृद्धिरधिका सम्प्रकल्पिता ।
आपत्कालकृता नित्यं दातव्या सा तु कारिता ।
अन्यथाकारिता वृद्धिर्नदातव्या कथञ्चन । बृहस्पतिः ।

remarks that the mention of the time of distress in the text of Katyayana is only illustrative, so that, according to this interpretation Katyayana only declares invalid that interest which has been promised through compulsion: this is an instance of the manner in which commentators bring texts into conformity with the existing practice. It is, however, remarkable that the Hindu Law allowed the creditor to charge interest under certain circumstances even in the absence of a definite contract in that respect. Thus Vishnu laid down that when a person took a loan without interest promising to repay it within a definite period, but did not fulfil that promise within the limited time out of avarice, then the debt would carry interest from after the expiry of that period.[1] Where, however, there was no definite period of repayment fixed by the contract, even there after the expiry of an interval of six months according to Narada, and a year according to Vishnu, the creditor could charge interest at the legal rate; but even then Katyayana said that interest should not run until there had been a previous demand.[2] There are also certain other texts which seem to lay down the following propositions: (1) a person who goes abroad to a different country without returning what he has borrowed shall be liable to pay interest after the expiry of one year; (2) if he does so after the lender has demanded the return of the loan, it will carry interest after the expiry of three months; and (3) when the borrower does not leave the country, but still fails to return the loan

Interest in the absence of a definite contract when allowed.

The question discussed.

---

[1] यो गृहीत्वा ऋणं पूर्व्वं श्रोदास्यामीतिसामकम् ।
न दद्याल्लोभतः पश्चात्तदहर्हाद्वृद्धिमाप्नुयात् । विष्णुः ।

[2] न वृद्धिः प्रीतिदत्तानां स्यादनाकारिता क्वचित् ।
अनाकारितमप्यूर्द्धं वत्सरार्द्धाद्विवर्द्धते । नारदः ।
वृद्धिं दद्युर्वत्सरातिक्रमे यथाभिहितामिति विष्णुः ।
प्रीतिदत्तन्नवर्द्धेत यावन्नप्रतियाचितमिति] कात्यायनः ।

upon demand, he shall be made to pay interest although there is no contract for it from after the date of such demand. Summing up these diverse provisions we find that where there is no contract for the payment of interest but there is a fixed period within which the loan is promised to be repaid, the loan will carry interest after the expiry of that period without payment; this much is perfectly clear; it is, however, open to doubt as to when the creditor becomes entitled to claim interest when there is neither any contract to pay interest, nor any fixed period to repay the debt; with reference to this question we find that there are certain texts which lay down that interest should run after the expiry of certain stated intervals; on the other hand, the text of Katyayana, referred to above, suggests that interest should run on the failure of the debtor to pay on demand whenever that demand may be made. Now, there are two ways of looking at these provisions: you may read these conditions conjunctively so as to require a previous demand as well as the expiry of the given interval of time in order to entitle the creditor to charge interest upon the unsatisfied loan, or you may read them distributively so as to hold that interest commences to run upon non-payment of the debt in either case. Apparently the Mitakshara has adopted the latter construction; and Mr. Justice Chandravarkar acts upon the view in the case of Saunadanappa *vs.* Shivbasawa,[1] where he lays down that it was an incident annexed to every contract of debt by the Hindu Law that interest, though not stipulated for, should run on it in the event of non-payment after demand, from the date of such demand. But there are certain other commentators who, as Jagannath points out, maintain that when a loan is taken without any contract to pay interest, then

[1] (1907) I. L. R. 31 Bom. 354.

if the debt be not paid off upon demand, it shall bear interest if the debtor remains in the country, after one year from the date of the loan and not before, according to the text of Vishnu;[1] Apararka and Kamalakara reduce this period to six months on the authority of the text of Narada referred to above. It is not at all necessary for our purpose to attempt to choose between these different interpretations, but it is undoubtedly interesting to notice how the extreme aversion against the practice of taking interest as disclosed in the text of Vasishtha comparing it with one of the most heinous crimes gradually lost its intensity, until ultimately interest under certain circumstances, came to be allowed even where there had been no previous stipulation to pay the same.

How this illustrates the gradual relaxation of the extreme aversion against the practice of taking interest.

This shows that mere detestation of a practice cannot possibly stop its growth against economical laws based upon the ordinary human impulse of serving one's own interest by taking advantage of the needs and wants of other people; one may admire the man who having money enough to spare lends it to his neighbour who stands in need of it without requiring anything more than a return of the sum lent, but benevolence is not so strong a motive as can be ordinarily counted upon to induce a man to part with his money readily to meet the crying needs of other people even when its return at the proper time may be practically assured. Hence arises the need of some other incentive which is supplied quite naturally by allowing the creditor to claim interest; you cannot, therefore, do away with the practice without causing the greatest inconvenience to the community, and all that the law may and should attempt to do is to regulate it in such a manner as to prevent extortionate and unconscionable bargains. This latter end is, to some extent, subserved by the rules,

Protection against usury:

[1] Colebrooke's Digest, Vol. I, p. 74.

Maximum amount of interest allowed under the law: the rule of Damdupat.

already indicated, limiting the rate of interest within reasonable limits except under special circumstances, but the Hindu Law went further, and prescribed a maximum beyond which interest recoverable at a particular moment could not go. Thus in the case of a loan in cash it was directed that the amount recoverable at a particular moment could not exceed twice the amount of the principal,[1] or in other words, accumulation of interest exceeding the principal could not be allowed; with regard to other objects of loan different limits were similarly prescribed; it must be understood that the creditor could by realising smaller sums as interest on several different occasions collectively recover more than the principal on account of interest; the real mischief against which the rules were directed was the accumulation of interest beyond a certain limit, so as to make it too burdensome for the debtor to clear it off.

It is conceivable that at one time when people were more simple than at present, these measures had the desired effect of saving debtors from the clutches of usurers; but it is very doubtful how far they can be effective against that wily class of present day money-lenders who, with their proverbial shrewdness, may find out various loopholes or invent various devices to evade the restraints imposed by them. As you are perhaps aware, these rules forbidding the accumulation of interest beyond a certain limit are still administered in Bombay as well as by the High Court of Calcutta on its original side under the name of the rule of Damdupat, but I am not aware that this has had any striking effect in stemming the tide of usury in the city of Calcutta or the Province of Bombay. When the debtor tenders payment, interest upon the loan ceases to run, provided the tender is kept good by the debtor by depositing the amount with a third person in case the creditor

Tender stops the running of interest; but the tender must be kept good.

[1] कुसीदवृद्धिर्द्वैगुण्यं नात्येति सकृदाहृता । मनुः ।

refuses to accept the same.[1] It is remarkable that in the case of Jagat Tarini Dasi *v.* Nabagopal Chaki[2] as well as in the judgments of the majority of the Full Bench in the case of Kripasindhu Mukherjee *v.* Annadasundari Devi[3] it has been laid down that a tender must be kept good in order to stop the running of interest. Mr. Justice Mookerjee relied upon a number of English and American authorities to establish this proposition; it is curious to observe that he might as well have pointed out that the rule of the Hindu Law was almost similar in its import.

Debt, if unpaid, how realised:

(1) by recourse to litigation, (2) without recourse to litigation.

The ways in which a debt, when unpaid, was allowed to be recovered were somewhat peculiar. Speaking broadly, these could be brought under two heads: (1) by recourse to litigation, and (2) without recourse to litigation. There was nothing very peculiar in the former of these modes; the creditor having recourse to litigation had to establish his claim before the court if the debtor did not admit the liability of his own accord, whereupon the court passed a decree which was enforced through the agency of the king's officers by compelling the debtor to carry out the directions contained therein; the details of the procedure, being a part of the adjective law, will be discussed in the Lecture dealing with that subject. The means of realising a debt otherwise than by recourse to litigation, that were sanctioned by law in former times, are indicated in the following text of Manu: "By *dharma* (the use of inoffensive persuasion or mediation of friends), by suit in court, by artful management, or by distress, a creditor may recover the pro-

---

[1] तथा च याज्ञवल्क्यः:

दीयमानं न ग्टह्णाति प्रयुक्तं यत्स्वकं धनं।

मध्यस्थ स्थापितं तत् स्याद्वर्धते न ततः परमिति। मध्यस्थ-स्थापितमिति विशेषवे-नाधमर्णो यदि स्वनिकटे स्थापयति तदा भवत्येव वृद्धिरिति वीरमित्रोदयः।

[2] I. L. R. 34 Cal. 305.

[3] I.L.R., 35 Cal. 34.

perty lent, and fifthly, by force."[1] You will observe that in this text besides seeking the assistance of court by bringing a suit, four other means of obtaining satisfaction of a debt are mentioned; these extrajudicial methods involve varying degrees of pressure exercised upon the debtor in order to induce him to pay off the debt; thus in the first which was called *dharma* reliance was placed upon moral persuasion or intervention of friends involving the minimum of external compulsion; in what was called artful management(छल), the creditor had recourse to a little bit of stratagem to get back what was lent by him as for example where with an artful design he borrowed a thing of his debtor or withheld a thing deposited by him and thus compelled payment of the debt; a case like this occupied an intermediate position between mere moral persuasion and forcible coercion to repay the debt; the third method of recovering a debt without litigation was what has been called आचरित and this has been explained by some to mean distress of the chattel belonging to the debtor and by others to signify constant attendance at the house of the debtor without taking any food until the debtor gets rid of the vexation by paying off the debt or, in other words, what is known in common parlance as sitting '*dharna*' at the door of the debtor; the last of these measures was the use of force, as for instance, the forcible confinement of the debtor or the like with a view to enforce the payment of the debt The enumeration of these private or extrajudicial methods of obtaining the repayment of a loan in connection with positive law seems to signify no more than this, that if in a proper case the creditor employs any of these means for the recovery of his debt, he is not to be prohibited or punished by the king;

Extra-judicial methods of obtaining satisfaction.

What the enumeration of these methods implies.

[1] धर्म्मेण व्यवहारेण छलेनाचरितेन च ।
प्रयुक्तं साधयेदर्थं पञ्चमेन बलेन च ॥ मनुः ।

on the other hand, Yajnavalkya says that if the debtor being so treated in a just case complains to the king, he shall not only obtain no relief, but shall also be made to pay off the debt and be even fined for lodging an improper complaint.[1] The law, therefore, sanctions these private methods of enforcing payment of a debt without recourse to litigations but then, there is this important reservation which must not be lost sight of, viz., that the creditor must not take the law into his own hands if the debtor does not admit the creditor's claim, or disputes its amount or character, or, in any way, demands a trial by court, for, in these predicaments, it becomes the duty of the creditor to go to court, obtain its decision, and secure satisfaction through it. A creditor who under such circumstances uses force to compel the debtor to pay, becomes liable to punishment and also loses the debt;[2] for the same law that sanctions the use of force under certain circumstances when the debtor does not dispute the creditor's claim and insists upon judicial determination, also lays down that litigation must be resorted to when the debtor demands the same; but in order to discourage fruitless appeal to litigation it provides that if a debtor compels the creditor to sue by raising false pleas and claiming judicial determination by court knowing that there is no real defence, he should be ordered not only to satisfy the debt established by evidence before the court, but also to pay a penalty

When litigation must be resorted to.

A creditor using force, when law enjoins litigation, becomes liable to punishment and also loses the debt.

Penalty when the debtor compels the creditor to sue by raising false pleas and claiming litigation.

---

[1] प्रपन्नं साधयन्नर्थं न वाच्यो नृपतेर्भवेत्।
साध्यमानो नृपं गच्छन् दण्ड्यो दाप्यश्च तद्धनम्। याज्ञवल्क्यः।

[2] पीडयेद्यो धनी कश्चिद्धणिकं न्यायवादिनम्।
तस्मादर्थात् स हीयेत तत् समं चाप्नुयाद्दमम्। कात्यायनः।

न रोद्धव्यः क्रियावादी सन्दिग्धार्थः कथञ्चन।
आसेधयं स्तमासेध्यन्दण्ड्यो भवति धर्मतः। बृहस्पतिः।

imposed with reference to his capacity, for unnecessarily dragging the matter into court.[1]

It may, here, be observed that although the use of force subject to the reservation pointed out above, was sanctioned in order to enable the creditor to recover the debt, yet the Hindu Law did not intend that force should be used upon the debtor as a sort of punishment for his failure to repay the loan, but only with a view to obtain satisfaction of the claim. Thus, it was laid down that a debtor, when found unable to pay off the debt, should be made to work it off by performing services for the creditor suited to his capacity, provided he did not belong to a higher caste; and it was only when he was unwilling or unable even to render such services that he should be kept confined in order that he might feel the necessity of somehow paying off the debt.[2] Then, again, it was further prescribed that even in exacting services from the debtor in satisfaction of the debt, the creditor should take care not to impose a work altogether unsuitable to the social position of the debtor; you must not think that this was a mere moral recommendation, for as Katyayana declared, if a creditor without applying to the king were to make his debtor perform degrading work, then he should be punished with fine, and the debtor absolved from liability.[3]

Obtaining satisfaction by making the debtor work for the creditor: limits upon this method.

---

[1] अर्थेऽपव्ययमानन्तु कारणेन विभावितम् ।
दापयेद्धनिकस्यार्थं दण्डलेशञ्च शक्तितः । मनुः ।

[2] धनदानासहं बुद्धा स्वाधीनं कर्म्म कारयेत् ।
अशक्तो बन्धनागारे प्रवेश्यो ब्राह्मणादृते । कात्यायनः ।

अत्र कर्म्मकरणाशक्तौ बन्धनागारे प्रवेशाभिधानं सामर्थ्योत्पत्तौ कथञ्चिदृणप्राप्त्यर्थमित्यभिहितं स्मृतिचन्द्रिकायाम् ।

[3] यदि स्वादावनादिष्टमशुभं कर्म्मकारयेत् ।
प्राप्नुयात् साहसं पूर्व्वं ऋणान्मुच्येत चार्णिकः । कात्यायनः ।

There can, therefore, be no doubt that the use of force was meant as an extreme measure to be resorted to on rare occasions when the debtor dishonestly withheld payment without any just excuse, and even then it was hemmed in by a number of conditions and limitations which took away much of its apparent offensiveness.

Payment by instalment.

As regards a debtor who was really unable to pay the debt all at once by reason of poverty, it was declared that he should be allowed to pay by instalments;[1] and even when the creditor found it inconvenient and injurious to his interest to wait further by reason of the interest having reached the maximum limit allowed by the law, the debtor should be called upon to renew the bond in the event of his inability to pay it off instead of being oppressed with a demand which he was unable then to meet.

Extrajudicial method of obtaining satisfaction in other systems of law.

The power given to the creditor of realising his debt otherwise than by litigation may seem to be somewhat peculiar to our modern minds, but it had its parallel in other ancient systems of law. The fate of an insolvent debtor under the Twelve Tables is too well-known to require repetition, but those who sneer at the Hindu Law without stopping to enquire what it really contains may well be reminded of the humanity of that particular provision by which if there were several creditors they might cut off the debtor's body and divide it among them as if they were so many cannibals who could obtain satisfaction from the flesh and blood of the debtor.

Manus injectio and Pignoris capio.

Leaving that aside, two of the early Roman methods of levying execution against a judgment debtor, viz, *manus injectio* and *pignoris capio* by which the person or the property of the judgment debtor could be seized by the creditor as a pledge for the payment of the debt have been regarded as modifications

---

[1] अथ शक्तिविहीनः स्यादृणी कालविपर्य्ययात् ।
शक्त्यपेक्षमपन्दाप्यः काले काले यथोदयम् । नारदः ।

of proceedings which had originally been wholly extrajudicial but were, with the growth of the power of the courts, gradually superseded by judicial seizure, the intervention of the court serving the useful purpose of preventing unjust or unnecessary violence and introducing order and regularity into the proceedings. **Irish method of fasting upon a debtor.** Even the curious contrivance of compelling payment by sitting at the door of the debtor without taking any food had its parallel in the ancient Irish method of fasting upon a debtor described by Sir Henry Maine in his Early History of Institutions. [1] At the same time, it seems to be clear that the power which the Hindu Law accorded to the creditor of taking independent steps for enforcing the payment of the debt without the intervention of the court was so subjected to limitations and surrounded by safeguards as to afford ample protection to the debtor from unjust oppression, for apart from anything else, no creditor was, as we have seen, allowed to resort to extrajudicial methods when the debtor claimed that the controversy should be settled by a judicial trial.

Duty to pay off the debt absolute. In the contemplation of the Hindu Law, the duty of the debtor to pay off the debt was absolute, so the creditor being dead, the payment should be made to his sons or other heirs and if no such person be found who is entitled to claim the amount as the heir of the deceased, then the debtor should pay the amount to a Brahmin or throw the same into water. [3] The idea underlying this latter direction seems to be that a debt once incurred imposes a sort of burden upon the debtor that can only be discharged by repayment; so that the death of the

---

1 Lecture II, pp. 39 and 40.

2 यदा तु न सकुल्याः स्युर्न च सम्बन्धि बान्धवाः ।
तदा दद्याद्द्विजेभ्यस्तु तेष्वसत्स्वप्सु निःक्षिपेत् ॥ नारदः ।
तदभावे तु विप्रेभ्यो देयं क्षेप्यं जलेऽपि वा । प्रजापतिः ।

creditor without leaving any heir, although it may put an end to the legal obligation, does not displace the burden altogether, for apart from the existence of any individual who can legally enforce repayment, there is this imperative and absolute duty that you must not retain what is not your own.

Liability of the heirs of the debtor.

As regards the liability to pay the debt after the demise of the debtor, I have already explained in a previous lecture how the son and grandson of the debtor become fastened with the liability although they may not have inherited from the debtor assets sufficient for its discharge. The details of the rule together with its limitations having been stated there, it is unnecessary to repeat them at this place. Besides, the son and the grandson, the liability of other heirs depends upon the possession of assets and is limited to the extent of those assets. Failing these, a person who takes the widow of the deceased debtor has been declared liable to discharge the debt.[1] Considering, then, the provisions indicated above it seems that on the whole the Hindu Law is neither unduly hard upon debtors nor unnecessarily indulgent to creditors; even the restrictions on excessivé usury cannot said to be unreasonable or unsuitable to the circumstances of the country.

Method of paying off a debt : evidence of payment how it should be obtained.

As regards the method of paying off a debt, it is laid down that the mode of payment should in general correspond to the mode in which the debt was contracted. Thus when the debtor executed a document on taking the loan, a part payment of the debt should be endorsed on its back, and in the event of full payment the document should either be torn or a separate

---

[1] रिक्थग्राह ऋणं दाप्यो योषिद्ग्राहस्तथैव च।
पुत्रोऽनन्याश्रितद्रव्यः पुत्रहीनस्य रिक्थिनः। याज्ञवल्क्यः।

document of release obtained from the creditor, if, however, the document is not forthcoming, then a receipt, in a case of part-payment, and a release, in the case of full satisfaction, should be taken from the creditor; where even this is not possible, there the payment should be made in the presence of witnesses so as to obviate, as far as possible, the chances of a future dispute. Similarly a debt contracted in the presence of witnesses should be repaid in the presence of witnesses and preferably of those who were witnesses to the original transaction. These minute directions are, at all events, interesting as showing the cautious shrewdness of those who laid them down.

Order of paying off the debts: father's debt should be paid, before ones own, and grand-father's debt before the father's.

As regards the order in which debts should be paid, we find that Brihaspati says that a person should pay his father's debts, which he is liable to pay, prior to his own and his grand-father's debts even before those of his father.[1] As regards one's own debts, they should be paid in the order in which they were contracted, subject to the exception that a debt contracted from a Brahman should be paid first, and a debt payable to the king should be paid next in preference to other debts irrespective of their position in point of time.[2] It is also laid down that if a creditor can make out that a particular article was purchased with the money borrowed from him, then he has a preferential charge over that article for the payment of that loan.[3]

Debts should be paid in the order in which they were taken.

Exceptions in favour of the king and learned Brahmins.

Another exception.

Law of Suretyship.

The payment of a debt may be secured in two ways, (1) by giving a pledge, and (2) by furnishing a

---

[1] पित्र्यं पूर्व्वमृणन्देयं पश्चादात्मीयमेव च ।
तयोः पैतामहं पूर्व्वं देयमेवं ऋणं सदा । बृहस्पतिः ।

[2] गृहीतानुक्रमाद्दाप्यो धनिनामधमर्णिकः ।
दत्त्वा तु ब्राह्मणायैव नृपतेस्तदनन्तरम् ; याज्ञवल्क्यः ।

[3] यस्य द्रव्येण यत्पण्यं साधितं यो विभावयेत् ।
तत्तस्य धनिकस्यैव दातव्यं तस्य नान्यथा । कात्यायनः ।

surety. The subject of pledge has been discussed in one of my previous lectures. I now propose to give a brief account of the Hindu Law of Suretyship.

Different kinds of sureties.

A person may stand as a surety for another in several ways; hence our lawgivers mention several distinct kinds of sureties;

Three classes of sureties mentioned by Yajnavalkya. Brihaspati adds a fourth: special significance of this fourth class in explaining the growth of hypothecation.

thus Yajnavalkya speaks of three kinds of sureties; (1) sureties for appearance, (2) sureties for confidence and (3) sureties for payment.[1] Brihaspati adds a fourth class which is very similar to the third, the distinction being, that whereas a surety for payment promises that he will himself pay off the debt, if the debtor fails to make the payment, a surety belonging to this class only undertakes to produce the property of the debtor out of which the creditor may obtain satisfaction, and not to make the payment out of his own funds.[2] The character of these different kinds of sureties is summed up by Brihaspati in two lines: "One says, 'I undertake to show him,' the other says, 'he is a good man,' the third says 'I shall pay off the money', and the last says 'I shall produce his goods'.[3]" It will be at once understood that a surety of the first mentioned kind merely undertakes to ensure the appearance of the person for whom he stands as a surety, and nothing more; a surety for confidence gives a good character to a man who relying on it secures the confidence of another and thus obtains something (say a loan) which he would not have otherwise obtained; a surety for payment definitely undertakes to pay if the person for whom he stands surety fails to discharge his obligation;

---

1 दर्शने प्रत्ययी दाने प्रातिभाव्यं विधीयते । याज्ञवल्क्यः ।

2 दर्शने प्रत्यये दाने ऋणि द्रव्यार्पणेतथा ।
चतुः प्रकारः प्रतिभूः शास्त्रे दृष्टोमनीषिभिः । बृहस्पतिः ।

3 आहैको दर्शयामीति साधुरित्यपरोऽब्रवीत् ।
दाताहमेतद्द्रविणमर्पयाम्यपरोऽब्रवीत् ।

a surety for production of debtor's goods only takes upon himself to produce the goods of the debtor on the latter's default to pay off the debt.

You will remember that in one of my previous lectures I have explained how this last class of suretyship furnished an insight into the course of transition through which, in all probability, hypothecation or pledge unaccompanied by delivery of possession gradually came to be recognised; for, to my mind, a pledge, where the pledgor is allowed to retain the property pledged in his possession, on furnishing a surety, who undertakes to produce it in case the pledgor fails to discharge his liability at the proper time, furnished an intermediate stage between a pledge accompanied by delivery of possession and a mere hypothecation. As I have discussed this point at length in that lecture, it is unnecessary to dilate upon it any more at this place.

Harita mentions a fifth class corresponding to sureties for good behaviour.

To the four classes of sureties mentioned above, Hárîta adds a fifth viz., that of sureties for safety, or to be more literal, sureties who undertake to keep out of fear.[1] It will be at once seen that this exactly corresponds to that class of sureties which a man may be called upon to furnish under the Criminal Procedure Code, for instance, sureties to keep the peace, or sureties for good behaviour.

When the obligation incurred by a surety extends to his son or grandson.

It should, here, be remarked that the obligation incurred by a surety is a personal obligation, and hence the liability arising therefrom is confined to him alone, so that on his death it does not pass to his son or grandson. Consequently it has been broadly stated that neither a son nor a grandson is liable to discharge an obligation incurred by a person in his capacity as a surety for another.

[1] अभये प्रत्यये दाने उपस्थाने प्रदर्शने ।
पञ्चस्वेषु प्रकारेषु याज्ञोऽपि प्रतिभूर्भवेः । अभयस्तुपद्रव वारणमिति
वीरमित्रोदयः ।

This is, however, subject to the exception that when a person becomes surety for the payment of a debt by undertaking that in the event of the debtor not paying it off, he will himself make the payment, his position is so far assimilated to that of an ordinary debtor as to render his sons (but not his grand-sons) bound by the obligation. So Yajnavalkya declares, 'When a surety for appearance or a surety for confidence is dead, his sons are not liable to discharge the obligation, but it is otherwise in the case of a surety for payment.'[1] The position of a surety who undertakes to produce the goods of the debtor on the failure of the latter to pay off the debt is somewhat anomalous, but seeing that, as Viramitrodaya observes, there is not much difference between a surety of this class and a surety for payment it will not perhaps be unreasonable to maintain that the same rule should apply to both the cases.[2] A text of Brihaspati seems to make the point quite clear for it distinctly states that while the liability of the surety does not extend to his son when the surety was a surety for appearance or for confidence, it does so extend in the other two cases, *viz.*, when the surety undertook either to pay off the debt or to produce the goods of the debtor in the failure of the latter to discharge his obligation.[3] It should, however, be observed that even where the son of the surety becomes liable to carry out the obligation

[1] दर्शनप्रतिभूर्यत्र मृतः प्रात्ययिकोऽपि वा ।
नतत्पुत्राऋणं दद्युर्दद्युर्दानाय यः स्थितः । याज्ञवल्क्यः ।

[2] यत्तु योगीश्वरेण प्रतिभुवस्त्रैविध्यमुक्तं—'दर्शने प्रत्ययेदाने प्रातिभाव्यं विधीयते'—तत्दानार्पणयोरनतिभेदाभिप्रायेण । इति वीरमित्रोदयः ।

[3] आद्यौ तु वितथे दाप्यौतत्कालावेदितं धनं
उत्तरौ तु विसम्वादे तौ विना तत्सुतौ तथा ।

incurred by his father, the liability only extends to make good the principal and not the interest; the grandson is nowhere held liable in such a case.[1] All these rules are subject to the exception that where a surety obtains a pledge to ensure his safety, there the creditor is entitled to realise his claim including the interest from the pledge even if the surety be dead.[2]

Sureties should not be oppressed.

Turning, now, to the method of enforcing the claim against a surety, we find it laid down, that a creditor should not deal oppressively with him, but should allow him to discharge his liability slowly without hurrying him on to ruin.[3] It is unfortunate that considerations like these which did not escape our ancient lawgivers do not, often, attract the attention or draw the sympathy of our modern courts. Where there are several sureties in the same transaction, the liability arising therefrom should be distributed among them, and each held liable to the extent of his proportionate share; but when each of them has undertaken to take the entire responsibility upon himself independently of the other sureties so as to resemble the position of a single debtor it is optional with the creditor to proceed against any of them.[4]

Several sureties—their respective liabilities how determined.

प्रातिभाव्यागतं पौत्रैर्दातव्यं न तु तत क्वचित् ।
पुत्रेणापि समं देयमृणं सर्व्वमपैतृकम् । कात्यायनः ।

ऋणं पैतामहं पौत्रः प्रातिभाव्यागतं सुतः ।
समं दद्यात् तत् सुतौ तु न दाप्याविति निश्चयः । व्यासः ।

गृहीत्वा बन्धकं यत्र दर्शनेऽस्यस्थितो भवेत् ।
विना पित्राधनात्तस्मात् दाप्यः स्यात्तद्धनं सुतः । कात्यायनः ।

नात्यन्तम्पीड़नीयाः स्युः ऋणं दाप्याः शनैःशनैः । बृहस्पतिः ।

बहवः स्युर्यदि स्वांशैर्दद्युः प्रतिभुवोधनम् ।
एकच्छायाश्रितेष्वेषु धनिकस्य यथारुचि

Remedy of the surety against the debtor.

When a surety has been compelled to make any payment in discharge of his obligation, he has of course the right to recover the same from the debtor.[1] It is, however, laid down that where the surety has suffered considerable hardship in meeting the creditor's claim, there he becomes entitled to recover from the debtor double the amount that he has paid,[2] for it is but meet that he should obtain some compensation for his suffering on account of the debtor's default.

Contracts of service and letting on hire: compared to *locatio conductio* of the Roman Law.

Contracts of service and letting on hire: Commentators treat these two subjects together under the topic of non-payment of wages. The connection between the two is obvious, and it is remarkable that under the Roman Law *locatio conductio* or letting out on hire included *locatio conductio rerum*, when a person let a thing and another hired it, as well as *locatio conductio operarum*, when a person let his services and another hired them. The price or consideration for services is called वेतन or वृत्ति (wages), while the consideration for letting a thing is called भाटक or सोम ।

Wages of service: how fixed and when to be paid.

Wages depend upon contract and have to be paid before, in the middle of, or after the work as agreed upon.[3] In the absence of a contract fixing the amount of wages, the employe is entitled to remuneration which varies according to the nature of the services rendered. If the employe trangresses the direction of his employer regarding, for instance, the time or

[1] यस्यार्थे येन यद्दत्तं विधिनाभ्यर्थितेन तु ।
साक्षिभिर्भावितेनैव प्रतिभूस्तत् समाप्नुयात् । कात्यायनः ।

[2] यस्यार्थं प्रतिभूर्दद्याद्धनिकेनोपपीडितः ।
ऋणिकस्तत्प्रतिभुवे द्विगुणं प्रतिदापयेत् । नारदः ।

[3] भृत्याय वेतनं दद्यात् कर्म्मस्वामी यथाक्रमम् ।
आदौ मध्येऽवसाने तु कर्म्मणो यद्विनिश्चितम् । नारदः ।

place at which his services should be rendered and thereby causes loss to the business in which he is employed, then he shall not be entitled to get his full wages but only as much as the master thinks it fit to bestow; if, however, he brings in more profit by reason of his superior knowledge regarding the mode of his work, then the employer should give him something in addition to the fixed wages by way of rewards notwithstanding his omission to follow the exact directions with which he was supplied.[1] If several persons, being employed upon the same work fail to complete it by reason of the illness of some of them or for some other unavoidable accident of a like nature, then they should be paid severally according to the extent of work done by each, the amount to be paid being settled and apportioned according to the verdict of an arbitrator. If a person, having been engaged to do a work, falls ill before its completion, then he shall complete it after being restored to health, and no deduction shall be made from the fixed wages by reason of the delay since it arose from circumstances over which he had no control; on the other hand, if a man omits to complete a work which he has undertaken, although he is quite able to do it, and thus leaves it unfinished, then he shall not be entitled to claim even a part of the wages agreed to be paid for the work.[2] Similarly, if a person enters into a service for a definite term but gives it up before the end of the term, then he shall not get any portion of the wages unless he can show that he left the service owing to the fault of the employer, such as the use of abusive language towards the

Apportionment of wages when allowed.

Incomplete performance: how it affects the right to remuneration.

---

[1] देशं कालं च योऽतीयाल्लाभं कुर्य्याच्च योऽन्यथा ।
तत्र स्यात् स्वामिनश्छन्दोऽधिकं देयं कृतेऽधिके । याज्ञवल्क्यः ।

[2] यथोक्तमार्त्तः सुस्थोवा यस्तत् कर्म्म न कारयेत् ।
न तस्य वेतनं देयमल्पोनस्यापि कर्म्मणः । मनुः ।

employe without any fault on his part[1], if, however, it can be shown that it was owing to the employer's fault that the employe left the service, then he shall be entitled to claim remuneration *quantum meruit* in proportion to the work already done;[2] on the other hand, if the employer, on his part, dispenses with the services of the employe without any fault of his before the completion of the period of engagement, then the employe shall be entitled to get full remuneration for the entire period without any deduction, and Vishnu adds that the king may even impose a small fine on the employer for having dismissed the employe without any excuse.[3]

Refusal after engagement to work how dealt with.

It is also laid down that a man, who being engaged in a service, refuses to work without any excuse, shall not only be compelled to return the wages which he may have received in advance, but shall also be liable to be punished with a fine if he refused after having accepted wages from the employer; if, however, no wages were previously paid, then the employer alone shall be entitled to compensation for the inconvenience sustained by him on account of the improper breach of the contract of service.

Loss or destruction of any article belonging to the employer its effect—
(i) When due to negligence.
(ii) When due to an accident.
(iii) When caused deliberately out of spite.

If an employe injures or destroys any article belonging to the employer and placed under his care, out of negligence, he shall have to pay compensation for the same; but if the injury or destruction resulted from an accident, he is not answerable for the loss.[4] A text of Brihat Manu goes further, and lays down that where the employe deliberately causes the loss out of spite, there he shall have

1 कालेऽपूर्णे त्यजन् कर्म्म भृतेर्नाशमवाप्नुयात्। नारदः।

2 स्वामिदोषादपक्रामन् यावत्कृतमवाप्नुयात्। नारदः।

3 स्वामी चेद्भृतकमपूर्णे काले जह्यात् तस्य सर्व्वमेव
मूल्यं दद्यात् पणशतञ्च राज्ञे अन्यत्र भृत्यदोषात्। इति विष्णुः।

4 तद्दोषेण यद्विनश्येत् तत् स्वामिने देयमन्यत्र दैवोपघातात्। इति विष्णुः

to recoup the amount of the loss twice over by reason of his gross misconduct.[1]

Compensation for special inconvenience caused by refusal to fulfil an agreement of service.

If a servant having agreed to attend a person on a journey refuses at the last moment, and thereby causes an impediment to the journey, he shall have to pay twice the wages agreed to be paid to him as a compensation for the inconvenience caused to the employer;[2] in other cases causing less inconvenience, the amount of compensation shall be less.

Master's duty towards the servant.

If a person takes a servant with him, but abandons him in the way while he is exhausted or ill, or omits to provide him with subsistence for three days in succession, then he shall be liable to be punished by the king with the first amercement.[3]

Liability of the master for a wrong done by the servant.

If a servant does a wrong act according to the direction of the master and for his purposes, then the master shall be held responsible for the same.[4]

Letting on hire.

Principles which regulate payment by a hirer are similar in their character to those which govern the payment of wages by an employer. Thus, whoever having hired a carriage or a horse fails to take it, shall have to pay one-fourth of the fare as compensation; but once the hirer takes it away, he shall have to pay the full fare, although after having proceeded half way, he may be able to dispense with it for the rest of the journey; nay, it does not even matter whether the hirer uses the vehicle or animal, for if he takes it, he must pay

---

1 प्रमादान्नाशितं दाप्यः समं द्विर्द्रोहनाशितम्। वृहन्मनुः।

2 प्रस्थानविघ्नकृच्चैव प्रदाप्यो द्विगुणां भृतिम्। इति याज्ञवल्क्यः।

3 त्यजेत्पथि सहायं यः श्रान्तं रोगार्त्तमेव वा।
प्राप्नुयात् साहसं पूर्व्वं ग्रामेत्र्यहमपालयन्। इति कात्यायनः।

4 प्रभुणा विनियुक्तः सन् भृतको विदधाति यः।
तदर्थमशुभं कर्म्म स्वामी तत्रापराध्नुयात्। इति वृहस्पतिः।

the fare, and so long as he does not return it he shall have to pay. So also with regard to hiring of houses, shops, &c.; so long as possession is not redelivered, the hirer shall have to pay the rent.

A few remarks on the principles indicated by the rules stated above.

If we now turn round for a moment, and consider the principles that underly the rules summarised above, we find that here the law recognises an obligation arising out of mere mutual agreement even without the accompaniment of the payment or delivery of a thing as in the case of a debt; the distinction corresponds to that between real and consensual contracts of the Roman Law, and indicates a further ethical advance. The basis of the obligation rests on the reciprocal reliance caused by the agreement and the inconvenience that would arise from the failure of one of the parties to perform his part; compensation for breach of the obligation, therefore, ordinarily varies with the amount of inconvenience undergone; yet the moral aspect of the question is not also altogether lost sight of, for the law recognises the distinction between breaches of duty arising from accident, negligence and deliberate obstinacy or spite. It is also noticeable that the Hindu Law recognises that where there is an entire contract, it must be performed in its entirety; failure to perform a part in such a case disentitles the performer from claiming remuneration in proportion to the work done, unless, of course, the default arose from circumstances over which he had no control or was due to the fault of the employer himself. On the other hand, if the employer dispenses with the services of the employe before a contract of this kind is completely carried out without any fault of the latter, then the full amount of wages agreed upon for the performance of the entire work shall have to be paid. There can hardly be any doubt that a clear comprehension of the principles which led to the formulation of these distinctions indicates a great advance in juristic ideas.

Partnership.

Societas or partnership constituted a distinct class of consensual contracts under the Roman Law. The subject is discussed by the Hindu Lawyers under the head of 'सम्भूयसमुत्थान' which literally signifies an undertaking by a combination of people working together. The development of this branch of law defining the rights and obligations of partners to one another indicates a considerable amount of social, moral, and economical advance, and it is interesting to observe that the subject has attracted the attention of our law givers from a very early period.

Rights and obligations of the partners.

The share of a partner in the profits or losses of the partnership business depends either upon the amount of capital supplied by him or upon the terms of the agreement under which the partnership was started ;[1] in other words when there is a special contract defining the shares of the partners, the profits or losses arising out of the partnership transaction must be distributed accordingly, but where there is no such contract the share of each partner will be in proportion to the amount of capital supplied by him. The partners should carry out the work of partnership, according to agreement with perfect good faith towards one another, and one who has acted fraudulently and thereby cheated his co-partners should be cast out of the partnership and deprived of his share in the profits. One partner may act for all by common consent, and then his acts and deeds shall be binding upon others, as if they were the acts and deeds of all the partners. When the work of the partnership has been divided amongst the several partners

समवायेन वणिजां लाभार्थं कर्म्म कुर्व्वताम् ।
लाभालाभौ यथाद्रव्यं यथावासंविदाकृतम् । याज्ञवल्क्य।

according to their shares, one who is unable to do his part himself must have it done by an agent. If partnership goods are lost by accident, the loss will be borne by all the partners in accordance with their shares; but if the loss arises through the negligence of one of the partners, or by reason of his ignoring the prohibition of other partners or acting without their approval, it must be borne by him alone.[1] On the other hand, if a partner undergoes extra trouble to save the partnership goods from accident, he should be paid extra something for his additional work. When there is a work incidental to the partnership business which must be done by all the partners together, one who refuses to join must account for the consequent loss; for example, if, in order to recover a debt from a person who is indebted to the partnership, it is necessary that all the partners should join in making the demand or bringing a suit, but one of them refuses to join and consequently the money cannot be realised, the loss must be compensated by the partner who occasioned it by his improper conduct.

Gambling and betting.

Laying of wagers is what characterises all kinds of gambling and betting. When it accompanies some sort of play with inanimate objects such as dice and turns upon the result thereof, it is called द्यूत (gambling); when, on the other hand, it turns upon the result of some sort of contest between animate beings, as for example, on the race-course it is called समाह्वय (betting).

The practice was serverely condemned by Manu.

The practice was severely condemned by Manu who prescribed that the king should inflict corporal punishment upon those who are themselves guilty of it or induce others to join in it; gambling and betting, he said, were no better than open theft, so that the king should take special care to

[1] अनिर्दिष्टो वार्य्यमाणोऽप्रमादाद्यस्तु नाशयेत् ।
तेनैव तद्भवेद्देयं सर्व्वेषां समवायिनाम् । इति बृहस्पतिः ।

prevent them and prohibit them throughout the kingdom.[1] Gradually, however, this extreme rigour of prohibition was relaxed, and the practice surrounded by certain safeguards was legalised and even protected by the king. This divergence from the ancient rule laid down by Manu is noticed by Brihaspati who observes as follows: "Gambling was prohibited by Manu as it strikes against truth, purity and wealth; but others have sanctioned it when licensed by payment of a tax to the king; it should be presided over by a person entrusted with the duty of superintending the transaction in order to ensure the detection of fraud and sharp practice."[2] The position of the superintendent was akin to that of a licensed gambling-house-keeper. He was called upon to collect the share of the king, and was also entitled to obtain a share for himself. The gambler could recover the wager only when the gambling had taken place in an open assembly presided over by such a person, and the king had received the prescribed share, otherwise not; and if found guilty of sharp practices, he was liable to be branded and banished from the land.[3]

Gradual relaxation of the pohibition.

Conditions under which it could be practised.

Transgression of compact (सम्विदतिक्रम) is another title of litigation. The word सम्वित् does not mean a contract, but a

Transgression of compact.

---

1 प्रकाशमेतत् तास्कर्यं यद्देवन समाह्वयौ ।
तयोर्नित्यं प्रतीघाते नृपतिर्यत्नवान भवेत् ।
द्यूतं समाह्वयञ्चैव राजा राज्ये निवारयेत् । मनुः ।

2 द्यूतं निषिद्धं मनुना सत्यशौचधनापहम् ।
अभ्यनुज्ञात मन्यैस्तु राजभागसमन्वितम् ।
सभिकाधिष्ठितं कार्यं तस्कर ज्ञानहेतुतः । बृहस्पतिः ।

3 प्राप्ते नृपतिनाभागे प्रसिद्धे धूर्तमण्डले ।
जितं ससभिकेस्थाने दापयेदन्यथा न तु । इति
राज्ञा सचिह्ननिर्वास्याः कूटाक्षोपधिदेविनः । इति याज्ञवल्क्यः ।

Rules of association must e obeyed.

compact. When a body consisting of a number of individuals arrives at a certain resolution, it is the duty of everyone belonging to that particular body to abide by it, and the infringement of such a resolution furnishes a ground of action. These resolutions may be arrived at by the common consent of the members or may proceed from the king who establishes that particular body with certain specific directions. In the result, therefore, we may take it that the rules of an association must be observed by its members provided they are not opposed to the sacred law; and directions of the king establishing an institution must similarly be observed.[1] An association was usually composed of men engaged in a common undertaking or connected by a community of interest or opinion; it was directed that they should appoint from among themselves two, three or five persons to form a sort of executive committee; these persons were called advisers of the association (समूह हितवादी) or thinkers of business (कार्य्य चिन्तक). The names indicate that they were to constitute a sort of advisory board or an executive committee of the association to settle the line of action and carry it into execution, and it was laid down that their directions should be obeyed by the general members of the association.[2] It is interesting to notice the attributes which according to our lawgivers qualified a man to occupy such a position of trust; thus Brihaspati laid down that those who are spiteful, prone to lust or wrath, bashful, lazy, timid, greedy, too old, or too young should not be allowed into the executive committee which should be composed of persons who are pure, aware of the sacred law as

Constitution of an association.

Appointment of an executive committee.

निज धर्म्माविरोधेन यस्तु सामयिको भवेत् ।
सोऽपि यत्नेन संरक्ष्योधर्म्मोराजकृतश्च य: । याज्ञवल्क्य: ।

द्वौत्रय: पञ्च वा कार्य्या: समूहहितवादिन: ।
कर्त्तव्य वचनन्तेषां ग्रामश्रेणिगणादिभि: । बृहस्पति: ।

unfolded in the Vedas, expert in action, possessed of self-control, born of a good family, experienced in business, and guided by high principles.[1] Penalties were prescribed to enforce obedience to the rules of an association and the directions of its committee by the members of that association; and it was further directed that the delegates of an association approaching the king should be received by him and treated with due respect, honoured with suitable presents, and allowed to depart with their mission fulfilled.[2] All these rules and directions bear clear indications of a high stage of civilisation and they go to show that the existence of representative associations and their claim to respect and recognition even from the king were fully acknowledged by the Hindu Law; let us not, therefore, too readily fall into the delusion of thinking that institutions like these are entirely foreign to the Indian soil, but remember that foreign impact has, in many points, retarded rather than helped the natural evolution of our normal life.

Delegates of an association approaching the king should be received and treated with due honour.

What these rules indicate.

I now propose, before I close the present lecture to say a few words on the law of agency. Apart from the rules regulating the appearance by agents in a litigation with which I shall have to deal in discussing the adjective law, we find it broadly laid down by Narada that if a person employs another in an undertaking, whatever is done by the latter shall be binding on the former,[3] and

Agency.

विद्वेषिणो व्यसनिनः शालीनालसभीरवः।
लुब्धातिवृद्धबालाश्च न कार्य्याः कार्य्यचिन्तकाः।
शुचयो वेदधर्म्मज्ञा दक्षा दान्ताः कुलोद्भवाः।
सर्व्वकार्य्यप्रवीणाश्च कर्त्तव्याश्च महत्तमाः। बृहस्पतिः।

समूहकार्य्य आयातान् कृतकार्य्यान् विसर्ज्जयेत्।
सदानमानसत्कारैः पूजयित्वा महीपतिः। याज्ञवल्क्यः।

विसृष्टार्थस्तु यो यस्मिं साधिकार्थे प्रभुस्तु सः।
तद्भर्त्ता तत्कृतं कार्य्यं नान्यथा कर्त्तुमर्हति। नारदः।

Brihaspati adds that an act of the agent whether it leads to profit or loss, expenditure or income, must be accepted by the principal as binding, and he must not quarrel with it whether in or outside the country.[1] Besides this, it is pointed out by Manu that even dependent members may, when circumstances so require, enter into transactions to meet the needs of the family which it will be the duty of the head of the family not to disturb, although he may not have previously authorised them so to do;[2] in a case of this description, there arises what we may call an agency of necessity which the head of the family is called upon to ratify.

Concluding remark.

On the whole we may safely say that although the law of contract is a branch of municipal law which has received fuller development in comparatively modern times in communities thoroughly influenced by commercial activities, the Hindu Law bearing upon it is amply sufficient to meet the requirements of a simple society working out its destiny in a peaceful line of evolution.

---

[1] प्रमाणं तत्कृतं सर्वं लाभालाभव्ययोदयम्।
स्वदेशे वा विदेशे वा स्वामी तन्न विसंवदेत्। बृहस्पतिः।

[2] कुटुम्बार्थेऽध्यधीनोऽपि व्यवहारं यमाचरेत्।
स्वदेशे वा विदेशे वा तं स्वामी न विचालयेत। मनुः।

LECTURE XII

THE LAW OF TORTS AND THE LAW OF CRIMES.

Sir H. Maine's observations on the penal law of ancient communities.

Sir Henry Maine says: "The penal law of ancient communities is not the law of crimes, it is the law of wrongs, or to use the English technical word, of torts. The person injured proceeds against the wrong-doer by an ordinary civil action, and recovers compensation in the shape of money-damages if he succeeds." In illustrating this thesis, he points out that under the Roman Law offences which we are accustomed to regard exclusively as crimes were exclusively treated as torts, and not theft only, but assault and violent robbery were associated with trespass, libel and slander; all alike gave rise to an obligation or *vinculum juris,* and were all requited by a payment of money; he also shows that the old Germanic Law was similar in its character and provided money compensation even for homicide. It will perhaps be interesting to consider whether or not the ancient Hindu Law exhibited similar characteristics. It seems to me that in the Hindu Law punishment of crimes occupied a more prominent place than compensation for wrongs; and the mere payment of compensation to the individual injured, when the injury inflicted was at all serious in its character, was seldom regarded as sufficient to meet the ends of justice; of course, under certain circumstances the wrong-doer was compelled to compensate the person wronged, but the compensation was generally levied in addition to and not in substitution for the penalty which it was considered to be the duty of the king to impose.

Do they hold good in regard to the ancient Hindu Law?

In the Hindu law punishment of crimes occupied a more prominent place than compensation for wrongs; cf. the penalties.

'A king,' says Manu, 'who punishes those who do not deserve to be condemned and fails to punish those who deserve punishment becomes infamous and is ultimately doomed to hell.'[1] Neither theft, nor violence, nor any other form of serious injury to person or property could be condoned on mere payment of compensation to the party injured but it was regarded as the duty of the king to punish the culprit for his offence against the law. It may, therefore, be safely pronounced that the penal law of the Hindus was the law of crimes in the strict sense, and the law of torts occupied a comparatively subordinate and less important position in that system.

cf. the procedure.

Then, further, even apart from the nature of the penalty peculiar to the criminal law that was administered by the Hindus there was another characteristic element in the procedure to be adopted in relation to a criminal act which showed that the distinctive feature of a crime as opposed to a mere private injury was not at all lost sight of; for we find that whereas it was generally directed that neither a king nor his officers should create or foster litigation of their own accord[2] but should ordinarily refuse to take cognisance of a cause of action without a complaint from the person aggrieved, yet cases of frauds and the various other forms of crimes furnished exceptions to the general rule, for there it was directed that the king should take cognisance of them even without a complaint;[3] nay, the king was directed to employ officers to obtain information of crimes

---

1 अदण्ड्यान् दण्डयन् राजा दण्ड्यांश्चाप्यदण्डयन् ।
अयशो महदाप्नोति नरकञ्चैव गच्छति ॥

2 नोत्पादयेत् स्वयं कार्य्यं राजा नाप्यस्य पूरुषः । मनुः

3 छलानि चापराधांश्च पदानि नृपतेस्तथा ।
स्वयमेतानि गृह्णीयान्नृपस्त्वावेदकैर्विना ॥ पितामहः ।

committed within his dominion, and bring them to his notice to ensure the punishment of the culprits.[1] It is, thus, apparent from the above considerations, that although our lawgivers did not expressly say so, they condemned a crime not so much because it involved an infringement of a private right, but because it imperilled the security and the tranquillity of the people at large.

The same act may be a tort as well as a crime.

Bearing in mind the distinction which has been indicated above between a tort and a crime it will at once be seen that the same act may be a tort as well as a crime.

How far the distinction between a tort and a crime was realised by the Hindu law-givers.

When the act is looked upon from the standpoint of the individual injured and the reparation allowed to the injured party is compensation, it is treated in the light of a tort; when, on the other hand, it is looked upon as a transgression of sacred law which endangers the security of the community and is as such, visited with punishment without reference to any reparation to the individual who was specially injured, it is treated as a crime. It is no doubt true that we do not find our lawgivers to have explicitly contradistinguished the two aspects set forth above, still the difference in penalties and procedure which they have prescribed indicates that they clearly realised in what way the criminal aspect of an act differed from its aspect as a civil wrong. I shall, therefore, make no apology for trying to give you some idea about that portion of the Hindu Law which corresponded with what in England is called the Law of Torts.

TORTS.

***Injuria sine damnum*. Is it recognised by the Hindu Law?**

You are perhaps aware that under the English law of torts, there is such a thing as *injuria sine damnum*, for

[1] नृपेण विनियुक्तो यः परदोषान्ववेक्षणे ।
नृपस्य सूचयेज् ज्ञात्वा सूचकः स उदाहृतः ॥

a person may obtain compensation for an infringement of his rights although he may not have sustained any substantial damage in the shape of a definite temporal disadvantage. As Holt C. J. said in a passage of his judgment in Ashby *v.* White, which is remarkable for the force and terseness of its diction, 'a damage is not merely pecuniary, but an injury imports a damage, when a man is thereby hindered of his right. As in an action for slanderous words, though a man does not lose a penny by reason of the speaking of them, yet, he shall have an action. So if a man gives another a cuff on the ear, though it cost him nothing, no, not so much as a little *diachylon*, yet he shall have an action as it is a personal injury. So a man shall have an action against another for riding over his ground, though it do him no damage; for it is an invasion of his property and the other has no right to come there.' It seems that the Hindu Law did not take such a rigorous view of civil liability as to allow pecuniary compensation for a mere infringement of a private right when it was not accompanied by some tangible disadvantage involving a pecuniary loss, in other words, it did not recognise that a complainant could be entitled to damages although he might not have sustained any real damage. No doubt, if the act amounted to a violation of private rights and thus constituted an infringement of the sacred law, the offender would generally be liable to be punished for his transgression; but it is one thing to punish the offender for his delinquency and thereby maintain the sacredness of law and the inviolability of private rights and quite another thing to grant compensation to a person who has not sustained any actual damage requiring compensation. Hence, we find that although slander and adultery were crimes for which the offenders were liable to be punished by the king, still they were not regarded as private wrongs to be recompensed by the payment of damages to the party aggrieved. It may be quite true that many a man prizes his honour more than his purse, but our lawgivers were not imbued with that commercial spirit which could induce them to place a money value upon everything so as to make an attack on one's honour or reputation reparable by payment of pecuniary compensation. On the whole, it seems to me that under the Hindu Law no pecuniary compensation could be recorded unless the injury involved or was accompanied by actual pecuniary damage.

Injury to person.

Injury to person. It appears that for the use of personal violence, the offender not only rendered himself liable to punishment as a criminal, but the person whom he had hurt could also recover compensation for the injury sustained; the compensation seems to have been granted not only in view of the expenses which the sufferer might have incurred to recover from the effect of the violence, but also as a solatium for the pain inflicted upon him.[1] It is, however, remarkable that for an assault in the narrower sense (*i.e.*, for mere menace) no compensation seems to have been provided for although it was punishable as a crime.

No compensation for mere menace.

Injury to property: Trespass against domestic animals.

Injury to property. Whoever caused hurt to a domestic animal belonging to another became liable to compensate the owner of the animal for the consequent loss.[2] The liability arose whether the animal died or lived, although the measure of damages would not be the same in the two cases. Similarly, whoever cut or otherwise destroyed trees &c. bearing fruits or yielding some sort of produce, subjected

Cutting trees and destroying crops.

देहेन्द्रिय विनाशेतु यथादण्डं प्रकल्पयेत् ।

तथा तुष्टिकरं देयं समुत्थानञ्च पण्डितैः । कात्यायनः ।

सर्व्वपुरुषपीडा कराः समुत्थानव्ययन्दाप्याः पाल्यपशुपीडाकराश्च ।

himself to the liability of compensating the owner for his loss, the measure of compensation being the value of the usufruct lost by the owner during the time necessary for him to grow similar trees yielding similar produce.[1] In the same way, on the destruction of crops by cattle the owner of the cattle became liable to pay damages to the owner of the field.[2] If, however, the field were situated by the side of a public way, or at the outskirts of a village, and were not surrounded by enclosures, then the owner of cattle straying into it did not incur any liability; as in such a case it was the duty of the owner of the field to take the precaution of having it surrounded by fences[2], for, as Katyayana puts it, it is difficult to restrain cattle when once they have obtained the taste of crops.[3] This exception, however, did not hold good if the keeper deliberately had another's crops destroyed by his cattle or recklessly allowed them to stray into another's land for a long time without restraint, for it was intended to meet only cases of accidental destruction which the owner of the crops had not taken due care to prevent. On the whole we may take it that trespass upon another's property causing damage was regarded as a wrong for which the trespasser was held liable to pay compensation.

Conversion.

Conversion. Besides injury to property, conversion of another's property to one's own use was, also, a wrong for which the rightful owner could claim compensation from the wrongdoer. Thus, take the case of a thief who stole another's property. The property if it could be laid hold of was restored to the owner; but if it were lost and could not be recovered, the thief when apprehended was made

Restoration of stolen property.

Compensation.

---

1 यावत् सस्यंविनश्येत तावत्क्षेत्रीफलंलभेत् । याज्ञवल्क्यः ।

2 पथिग्रामविवीतान्ते क्षेत्रे दोषो न विद्यते । याज्ञवल्क्यः ।

3 दुःखेनविनिवार्य्यन्ते लब्धस्वादुरसागाः ।

to pay the price to compensate the owner apart from any penalty which might be imposed as a punishment for the crime. It is, however, remarkable that in as much as it was conceived to be the duty of the the king to protect the property of his people, if the king could not restore stolen articles to or recover their price for the owner by apprehending the thief, it was deemed to be his duty to pay the price to the owner out of his own treasury, and in his turn he could recover the same from the village officers, who by reason of their negligence, were accountable for the thief's escape.[1] The subject of conversion by a bailee has been discussed in a former lecture and need not be repeated at this place. In this way the idea of the responsibility of the king and his officers to protect the property of the people was not allowed to degenerate into mere empty words, and the security of private property was ensured.

Duty of the king to indemnify.

Fraud.

Fraud. A person cheated by fraud was entitled to damages. For instance, if a seller showed an article without defect, and then deceitfully made over a different article which was defective, the purchaser became entitled to compensation, which might even extend to double the price paid by him;[2] if, however, it was not deliberately done,

[1] देयं चौरहृतं द्रव्यं राज्ञाजानपदायतु।
अददद्धि समाप्नोति किल्विषं यस्य तस्यतत्। याज्ञवल्क्यः।२।३
यदात्वन्यतोऽपहृतं द्रव्यं दापयितुं न शक्नोति तदास्वकोषादेव राजा दद्यात्। चौरहृतमवजित्य यथास्थानं गमयेत् स्वकोषा द्वा दद्यादिति गौतमस्मरणात्। मिताक्षरा। स्तेयप्रकरणम्।

[2] निर्द्दोषं दर्शयित्वा तु सदोषं यः प्रयच्छति।
समूल्याद्द्विगुणं दाप्यो विनयं तावदेवतु। नारदः।

[3] अबुद्धि पूर्व्वक विक्रयेतु क्रयपरावर्त्तनमेव। इति
वीरमित्रोदयः। ४४१।

only the sale was to be rescinded without enforcing the payment of compensation.

Nuisance.

Nuisance. A nuisance might affect a private individual or the public in general. As an instance of the former we may cite the case of the construction of privies etc., very close to another's dwelling house so as to interfere with his comfort and convenience. In either case, the offending person was forced to remove the nuisance, and also rendered himself liable to punishment.

CRIMES.

Crimes.

Let us now turn to the law of crimes which, as I have said, occupied a more prominent place in our Hindu system. One of the main characteristics of a crime is that it makes the offender liable to be punished by the king.

Nature of the penalties prescribed.

I shall, therefore, begin with making a few observations on the nature of penalties prescribed by the Hindu Law, and some of the general principles on which they were meted out to the offenders. Punishment inflicted under the Hindu Law had various degrees and assumed various forms in order to be rendered quite flexible and keep due proportion to the enormity of the offence. I propose, therefore, at the outset to say a few words about the different kinds of punishment prescribed by the Hindu Law, and some of the principles on which they were directed to be administered.

Different kinds of punishment.

Yajnavalkya speaks of four classes of punishment, viz., censure, rebuke, pecuniary punishment, and corporal punishment, and says that these should be used either separately or jointly according to the nature of the crime.[1] Of these, mere censure was the lightest form of punishment and rebuke came after it;

धिग्दण्डस्त्वथ वाग्दण्डो धनदण्डो वधस्तथा ।
योज्या व्यस्ताः समस्ता वा ह्यपराधवशादिमे ।
याज्ञवल्क्यः । राजधर्म प्रकरणम् ।

pecuniary punishment included fine and forfeiture of property and corporal punishment included imprisonment, banishment, branding, cutting off offending limbs, and lastly death sentence. It goes without saying that the measure of punishment depended chiefly on the gravity of the offence; if the offence be not very serious, the punishment must be light, while if the offence be serious the punishment must be severe too. But besides this, our lawgivers mentioned several factors which ought, in their opinion, to be taken into consideration in order to determine the due measure of penalty to be inflicted for a crime. Thus Yajnavalkya says that the king should inflict punishment upon those who deserve the same after ascertaining and taking note of (the nature of the) offence, the time and the place (of the offence), and the strength, age, avocation and wealth (of the culprit)[1]; and the Mitakshara commenting upon this text adds, that along with these the questions whether the offence was committed with or without deliberation and whether it was the first offence or a repetition of the offence should be taken into consideration in passing the sentence.[2] In another text dealing with punishment for theft the same sage declares that the punishment should vary according to the value of the articles stolen; and the place and the time (of the offence) as well as the age and the strength (of the offender) should be taken into consideration in passing the sentence.[3] Here

Measure of punishment varies according to the gravity of the offence.

Other factors to be taken into consideration in meting out punishment.

1 ज्ञात्वापराधं देशं च कालं बलमथापि वा।
वयः कर्म्म च वित्तं च दण्डं दण्ड्येषु पातयेत्॥
याज्ञवल्क्यः। राजधर्म्मप्रकरणम्।

2 तथा बुद्धि पूर्व्वाबुद्धिपूर्व्वं सकृदावृत्त्यनुसारेण च।
इति मिताक्षरा।

3 क्षुद्रमध्यमहाद्रव्यहरणे सारतोदमः।
देशकाल वयःशक्ति सञ्चिन्त्यं दण्डकर्म्मणि।
याज्ञवल्क्यः। स्तेयप्रकरणम्।

also the Mitakshara observes that the elements for consideration thus set forth are but illustrative, since it is not possible to enumerate exhaustively the various causes determining the severity or the lightness of a sentence, they being really endless. Similarly Vasishtha lays down that punishment should be inflicted for injury and abuse having special regard to the locality, the time, the virtues, the age, the learning and the situation, and he adds that it should also be regulated according to the Sastras, and previous precedents.[1] It is not possible for me to enter into a close examination of the elements indicated above, which, in the opinion of our ancient lawgivers, should regulate the exact measure of punishment to be inflicted in each case. I may, however, be permitted to observe that the principles thus laid down presuppose a considerable advance of juristic ideas in the field of Criminal Law; in the first place, one may recollect that in many systems of Law punishments for many offences were rigidly and, if I may say so, almost inflexibly fixed and no extrinsic consideration could be laid hold of to modify them. One might suppose that the elimination of all extrinsic considerations in passing the sentences maintained the equality and uniformity of the punishment; but such is not really the case, for equality which does not take any notice of personal equations is not real equality but a mere semblance of the same, and considerations of time and place, and of the surrounding circumstances ought not to be lost sight of in awarding due punishment in each particular case. As a matter of fact it cannot be denied that our modern judges do take most of these elements into consideration in passing a sentence but

Importance of these considerations.

दण्डस्तु देशकालधर्मवयो विद्यास्थान विशेषैः हिंसाक्रोशयोः कल्प्यः ।
शास्त्राद्दृष्टान्ताच्च । वसिष्ठः ।

for want of enunciation of specific principles upon the subject, the matter does not often receive the amount of attention it deserves, and sentences passed often bear, within certain limits, the appearance of having been dictated by caprice rather than by an intelligent application of rational principles. It is, therefore, highly interesting to observe that our ancient lawgivers acutely analysed and emphasised the principal considerations which ought to be taken into account in determining the due measure of punishment to be inflicted in each particular case, while even many a modern judge does not seem to have a clear or systematised idea about them. In the second place the application of these principles afforded a practical method of modulating the sentences prescribed by law so as to make them pliable enough to meet the justice of each case without departing from the theoretical rigidity of the Sastras.

Difference of caste as a determining factor in inflicting punishment.

It must, however, be conceded that at least in one respect the admission of extrinsic considerations to influence the nature and extent of punishment seems to have been carried rather too far. It will be readily understood that I am here referring to the rules of Hindu Law making difference in caste a determining factor in inflicting punishment for an offence. Thus, it was directed that a Brahman should never be subjected to corporal chastisement, however grave the offence might be.[1] He could, however, be for very serious offences imprisoned or put in chains, and even branded and banished from the country under marks of ignominy and disgrace.[2] It cannot, there-

[1] अविशेषेण सर्वेषामेव दण्डविधिः स्मृतः ।
वधादृते ब्राह्मणस्य न वधं ब्राह्मणोऽर्हति । नारदः ।
यमोऽपि—न शारीरो ब्राह्मणस्य दण्डो भवति कस्यचित् ।

[2] गुप्तं तु बन्धने वा राजा भक्तं प्रदापयेत् । यमः
नारदोऽपि—शिरसो मुण्डनं दण्डस्तस्य निर्वासनं पुरात् ।
ललाटे चाभिशस्ताङ्कः प्रयाणं गर्दभेन च ।

fore, be said that a Brahman enjoyed absolute immunity from severe punishment in any shape, only he could not be subjected to certain forms of bodily punishment. I do not propose to endeavour to justify this distinction, but having regard to the peculiar organisation of the ancient Hindu society one may not find it difficult to understand the nature of the influences which led to its recognition. Besides this, it will also be found that apart from the special exemption of Brahmans from certain forms of bodily punishment, difference in caste also gave rise to a difference in the measure of punishment in yet another way, for ordinarily a person belonging to a higher caste was generally subjected to a lighter punishment than one belonging to a lower caste for an offence of an apparently similar description. Thus a person belonging to a lower caste abusing or assaulting a person belonging to a higher caste was subjected to a heavier punishment than a person belonging to a higher caste found guilty of a similar offence in relation to a person belonging to a lower caste.

How far this can be justified.

This may to some extent be accounted for on the ground that in cases where insult or indignity was a constituent element of the offence, the punishment was to be severe when the delinquent belonged to a lower caste in relation to the complainant, for the outrage proceeding from the former against the latter made the insult more keenly felt and consequently deserved to be put down with a heavier punishment. It should, however, be remarked that it would be a mistake to suppose that this was the universal rule and that for every offence punishment increased in severity according to the inferiority of caste of the culprit. Thus, we find, that in cases where the offence was an outcome of moral depravity, but did not involve insult to the complainant as an element to be taken into consideration in measuring the enormity of the crime, a person belonging to a higher caste who had less excuse for the same was generally imposed a heavier punishment. Thus dealing with punishment for theft, Manu said that a Sudra knowing what is right and wrong should get eight times the punishment liable to be inflicted on one ignorant of the same; a Vaishya having a similar knowledge sixteen times; a Kshatriya, similarly situated thirty-two times; and a Brahmin sixty-four times or even full hundred times, or one hundred and twenty-eight times since he knows what is right and what is wrong.[1] The Hindu Law cannot, therefore, be accused of showing unmixed or unqualified partiality towards people belonging to higher castes in the administration of criminal justice. It is also remarkable that our lawgibers distinctly declared that no one, however closely he might be related to the king, should, if found transgressing the law, be exempted from due punishment; so Yajnavalkya says, 'no one who has transgressed the law is exempt from punishment, by the king, be he a brother, a son, an object of worship (such as a preceptor), a father-in-law or a maternal uncle';[2] nay, Manu declares that where an ordinary man is punishable with a fine of one kárshápana, the king (committing the offence) should punish himself with thousand times the amount,[3] and the commentators say that he should distribute the sum among

No one exempt from punishment.

1 अष्टापाद्यन्तु शूद्रस्य स्तेये भवति किल्विषम् ।
षोड़शैव तु वैश्यस्य द्वात्रिंशत् क्षत्रियस्य च ॥
ब्राह्मणस्य चतुः षष्टिः पूर्णं वापिशतं भवेत् ।
द्विगुणा वा चतुः षष्टिस्तद्दोषगुणविद्धि सः ॥ मनुः ।८।३३७।३८

2 अपि भ्राता सुतोऽर्घ्यो वा श्वशुरो मातुलोऽपि वा ।
नादण्ड्यो नाम राज्ञोऽस्ति धर्म्माद्विचलितः स्वकात् ॥

3 कार्षापणं भवेद्दण्ड्यो यत्रान्यो प्राकृतो जनः ।
तत्र राजा भवेद्दण्ड्यः सहस्रमिति धारणा ॥

Brahmins. It would not, therefore, be quite correct to say that the Hindu Law of crimes was characterised by uniform partiality towards people belonging to higher castes and occupying loftier positions, although it cannot be denied that it gave formal recognition to the doctrine that difference in caste should, in manner indicated above, be a determining factor in fixing the due measures of punishment. I am quite aware that in working out the details the doctrine has been carried so far as to lead to directions which sometimes seem to be revolting to our modern idea of justice, equity, and good conscience; I do not propose to justify those directions, for whatever the explanation may be I do not think that they can be absolutely justified.

At the same time while condemning these inequalities sanctioned by law, one ought not to forget that so long as inequalities exist, the law cannot ignore them altogether, nor am I quite sure that it ought always to ignore them. If we look around, do we not find that even in spite of our vaunted civilisation relics of the old tendency to take a light view of offences committed by people in high position do often appear in actual practice? It may be that this tendency may sometimes carry us too far and work evident injustice, but it cannot be said that within certain limits it may not be founded on sound principles; for as I have shown above, in cases where insult to the complainant is an ingredient of the offence, the offender, when he occupies a lower station in life in relation to the complainant, really commits a graver offence than what we could impute to him if the position were reversed; moreover punishment, which is apparently the same, may affect different persons quite differently by reason of differences in their previous habits of life, and external and internal environments. With these general observations, I shall now proceed to say a few words on some of the important heads of crime under the Hindu Law.

Verbal abuse. Three classes of the offence.

वाक्पारुष्य or verbal abuse. This is one of the principal kinds of offence under the Hindu Law. It has been divided into three classes—निष्ठुर (cruel), अश्लील (indecent) and तीव्र (severe).

Truth is no defence.

It may be observed that truth is no defence in a case of verbal abuse, although falsehood may be regarded as aggravating the offence, for the gist of the offence consists in the intentional insult which the complainant suffers from the accused. Thus, Manu declares that a man who calls another one-eyed or lame or the like even with truth is liable to be fined.[1] Nothing can be finer than this solicitude on the part of our lawgivers to prevent a man from wilfully or recklessly wounding the feelings of another by improper and uncalled for abuse.

Relative position of the parties should be considered in inflicting punishment.

In inflicting punishment for verbal abuse the relative position of the parties owing to social rank and quality, should, as I have already indicated, be taken into consideration.[2]

Sureties for good behaviour, when required.

It is also laid down, that when a person threatens personal injury to another, then if the person so threatening be incapable of carrying out the threat, he should be punished with a fine; but if he be capable of inflicting the injury, then in addition to the fine, he should also be compelled to find sureties for his future good behaviour.[3]

काणं वाप्यथवा खञ्जमन्यं वापि तथाविधम् ।
तथ्यं नापि ब्रुवन् दापोदण्डं कार्षापणावरम् ॥ मनुः ।८।२७४।

दण्डप्रणयनं कार्यं वर्णजात्युत्तराधरैः ।
याज्ञवल्क्यः । वाक्पारुष्यप्रकरणम् ।

अशक्तस्तु वदन्नेवं दण्डनीयः पणान्दश ।
तथाशक्तः प्रतिभुवं दाप्यः क्षेमाय तस्य तु ।
याज्ञवल्क्यः । वाक्पारुष्यप्रकरणम् ।

Personal violence. Three different degrees of the offence.

दण्डपारुष्य or personal violence constituted another head of crime under the Hindu Law. It was laid down that usually it had three different degrees: अवगोरण (mere menace, or assault in the narrower sense of the term) निःशङ्कपातन (battery), and क्षतदर्शन (causing of wound). It may also be mentioned that use of criminal force in any form, for instance by throwing ashes, &c., on another's body, came within this offence.

Punishment varied with the relative position of the parties.

Here also punishment varied with the relative position of the parties, the use of criminal force by a person belonging to a lower caste to one belonging to a higher caste being regarded as a graver offence than in other cases.

साहस or deliberate and aggressive violence.

साहस—The word साहस is a generic term comprising various offences having the common characteristic of being attended with or accompanied by the use of force.[1] In its broader sense, therefore, it included certain offences which would also come under other descriptions of offences, but in its restricted sense it was used to denote certain specific offences such as mischief, robbery, murder, etc., characterised by deliberate and aggressive violence.

Difference between साहस and स्तेय

Understood in this way, it differentiates itself from theft and kindred offences (स्तेय) by the element of force which enters into its composition; the spring of action from which such an offence proceeds is passion or rage, whereas in cases of theft and other kinds of offences the spring of action is avarice; to put it shortly offences of the former kind are violent and aggressive in their character, while offences of the latter kind are generally secretive in their nature. Hence, the Mitakshara points out that although a साहस (or violent offence) involves either theft, or verbal abuse, or personal violence, or outrage of the modesty of a

सहसा क्रियते कर्म यत्किञ्चिद्बलदर्पितैः ।
तत्साहसमितिप्रोक्तं सहोबलमिहोच्यते । नारदः

woman as an element in its constitution yet it differentiates itself from them by the adjunct of aggressive violence which gives it a peculiar shape, and this differentiation marks out that the offence should be visited with a heavier punishment.[1] There are three different degrees of this kind of offence प्रथम (of the first degree), मध्यम (intermediate) and उत्तम (grave), and different degrees of punishment were prescribed as appropriate to them. It was also laid down that if several persons combined in striking another, they should be visited with double the ordinary punishment, and furthermore he who struck at the vital part was to receive the severest sentence. In a case of साहस in the narrower sense, as distinguished from दण्डपारुष्य and स्त्रीसंग्रहण difference in caste did not lead to any difference in sentence, but this must be understood as subject to the general rule, that a Brahmin could never be capitally punished, although in a proper case he might be chained or imprisoned, or banished from the country branded with marks of disgrace.

Three degrees of the offence.

When several people combine in striking another how they should be punished.

स्त्रीसंग्रहण—This expression signifies offences against female modesty including seduction, adultery and rape. These offences are divided into three classes with reference to the means used by the man,—for the offence may be committed by force, or fraud, or from mutual amorous desire.[2] Then, again, amorous criminal intimacy has three degrees according to the extent of the improper conduct.

Offences against female modesty.

Divided into three classes

तदिदं साहसं चौर्य्यवाक्दण्डपारुष्यस्त्रीसंग्रहणेषु व्याप्तमपि बलदर्पावष्टम्भोपाधितोभिद्यते इति दृष्टान्तविवेकार्थं पृथगभिधानम्। मिताक्षरा। साहसप्रकरणम्।

पापमूलं संग्रहणं त्रिप्रकारं निबोधत।
[2]बलोपधिकृते द्वे तु तृतीयमनुरागजम्॥

वीरमित्रोदय धृत बृहस्पति वचनम्।

It goes without saying that the offence is greater when it is committed by the use of force or fraud without the free consent of the woman, than when the woman out of free will surrenders herself. Then, again, in either case the extent of the improper conduct may differ, for the criminal intimacy may not always be equally complete. Other things being equal the gravity of the offence varies according to the relative position of the man and the woman; thus when the woman belongs to a superior caste the offence is graver than when the man and the woman are of the same caste or the woman belongs to an inferior caste. When the criminal intercourse proceeds from mutual amour the woman is also punishable, for in such a case she is not absolutely free from guilt; but in consideration perhaps of the fact that usually the first overture proceeds from the man, and the woman by reason of her weak nature ultimately succumbs to the allurement, our lawyers lay down that her punishment should be half of that of the man. Brihaspati, however, provides for an exceptional case and says that where a woman follows a man to his house and there allures him by soft touches, etc., there she shall receive higher punishment than the man,[1] the usual condition of things being here reversed. I mention these little matters only to show how shrewd our law-givers were, and how boldly they faced the realities of the world without being overcome by that sort of false sentimentalism which has influenced some of our modern systems of law to absolve a woman altogether from guilt in a case of adultery.

Extent of the improper conduct should be considered in inflicting punishment, as well as the relative position of the man and the woman.

When the woman is punishable, and how far.

स्तेय— its primary stricter sense.

स्तेय—In its primary stricter sense the word signified theft, *i.e.*, taking away the property of another without

1 स्वगृहमागत्य या नारी प्रलोभयति स्पर्शनादिना ।
कामयेत्तत्र सा दण्ड्या नरस्यार्धदमः स्मृतः ॥

his consent not by the use of force but of deceit. According to the value of the articles stolen, theft may be divided into three classes: paltry theft (क्षुद्र), theft of ordinary magnitude (मध्य) and theft of precious things (उत्तम). The word is, however, also used in a wider and more comprehensive sense to denote every offence against property which springs from avarice and is carried out by fraud and deceit. It will be understood that this involves an extension of the primary signification of the word to cover analogous offences characterised by slyness as distinguished from aggresiveness and violence. Taken in this sense, theft has been divided into two kinds: open theft (प्रकाश), and concealed theft (अप्रकाश).[1] These two expressions may remind a student of the Roman Law of the distinction drawn in that system between manifest and non-manifest theft; but though the expressions are similar, the distinction between open and concealed theft in the Hindu Law is in no way identical with the distinction between manifest and non-manifest theft of the Roman Law. The distinction drawn by the Roman Law was founded on the place or time of arrest of the offender; the manifest thief was he who was caught in the act or on the spot or at least with the thing stolen on him before he had transported it to its destination; in any other case the theft was called non-manifest, so that if the thief had once reached his destination and was afterwards taken with the thing stolen on him, he was not a manifest thief: this distinction was at one time of serious practical moment, for according to the Twelve Tables a manifest thief was condemned to death, while a non-manifest thief was only compelled to refund double the value of what he had stolen. The distinction between open theft and concealed

Divided into three classes according to the value of the stolen property.

Wider sense of the term.

It covers offences analogous to theft.

Open and concealed theft:

not to be confused with manifest and non-manifest theft of the Roman Law

[1] प्रकाशाश्चाप्रकाशाश्च तस्करा द्विविधाः स्मृताः । बृहस्पतिः

theft under the Hindu Law was based on a nice discrimination; by the expression concealed theft was meant theft in the proper sense of the word where property is dishonestly taken away from another's possession without his consent by clandestine means; open theft, on the other hand meant quite a different thing for it signified the taking away of another's property with his consent obtained by questionable means, and thus it included cheating under various pretences, taking of bribes and breach of trust. In illustration of the highly refined moral conception of the Hindu lawyers it may be mentioned that a quack who professes to be a physician without proper medical training and thus takes money from patients on false pretences, a tradesman who in selling a cheap article makes it look like a valuable one and thereby deceives women and boys, and a person who falsely wears the garb of a religious mendicant and then imposes upon the credulity of other people and does them harm; all these persons were declared to be as culpable as thieves and punishable as such. It has already been indicated that in the case of theft and other kindred offences superiority of caste was not regarded as an extenuating circumstance; it is true the punishment varied with the caste of the offender, but it varied in the reverse order, since the moral depravity which these offences indicate was less excusable in a man of a superior caste than in a low-caste offender.

Concealed theft, what it meant.

Open theft, what it included.

Here superiority of caste of the offender not an extenuating circumstance; but it rather aggravated the offence.

I have now said a few words on each of the principal divisions of crimes under the Hindu Law. It must not, however, be supposed that these exhaust the list of crimes recognised by the Hindu Law; in fact the various forms which a particular type of offence may assume are too numerous to be exhausted by enumeration, and our lawgivers are fully cognisant of it; thus speaking of the two divisions of theft and other kindred offences into open and

Enumeration of crimes not exhaustive.

concealed, Brihaspati went on to observe that these again might take a thousand different shapes according to the differences in intellect, capacity and artifice of the offenders,[1] indicating that you may classify offences into different groups according to their common characteristics, but you cannot exhaustively enumerate their different varieties. I may now add a few words on some minor offences not included in the above. We have already seen that trespass on others' goods, and encroachment on another's land were both regarded as offences in so far as they were punishable with fines. Similarly causing nuisance at a public place was regarded in the light of an offence, and punished as an offence. In short, if we are entitled to generalise from these and other instances, we may say that the intentional causing of injury in any form to the person or property of another person by the use of force or fraud was treated as an offence and regarded as punishable by the king.

A few minor offences.

Trespass.

Public nuisance.

There is yet another class of offences which deserves more than a passing notice; I mean offences against public justice. A witness, who gives false evidence, not only commits a sin, but also renders himself liable to punishment as a criminal. Similarly, a person who having knowledge about a matter in controversy refuses to give evidence is as much a sinner as a false witness and should be punished in the same way.[2] The production of fraudulent and forged document in support of one's claim was another offence belonging to this group and it appears that a person who falsely impugned a genuine document as a forgery was also deemed to be an offender of the same type. Corruption in

Offences against public justice: giving false evidence.

Refusal to give evidence.

Production of fraudulent and forged documents.

Falsely impugning a genuine document.

Corruption in a judge.

प्रज्ञासामर्थ्यमायाभिः प्रभिन्नानि सहस्रधा ।

न ददातीह यः साक्ष्यं जानन्नपि नराधमः ।
स कूटसाक्षिणां पापैस्तुल्यो दण्डेन चैव हि ॥ याज्ञवल्क्यः ।

a judge was very strongly condemned. So Yajnavalkya says that each member of a court of justice who out of partiality, or avarice, or fear acts against the law, should be made to suffer twice the punishment inflicted upon the person who loses the action.[1]

Taking bribes by a judge.

When, however, the judge works injustice by taking bribe from a litigant, the king should confiscate his property and banish him from the place.[2]

Omission to bring certain offences to the notice of the king.

It may also be mentioned that omission to bring certain offences to the notice of the king's officers was also made punishable. All these rules indicate a high stage of morality and a lofty conception regarding proper administration of justice, and we can only wonder at the extraordinary ignorance of those who maintain that the Hindu kings paid very little attention to the administration of justice within their realm.

Negligence; when it amounts to an offence.

Negligence, also, under certain circumstances amounted to an offence. Thus causing injury to men or animals by rash or negligent driving was an offence and rendered the offender punishable. In a case of rash driving it was the driver who committed the offence and was punishable as such, but in a case of negligence the employer might also be liable to punishment if he had employed an unskilful man, and the negligence was a consequence of want of skill.[3]

रागाल्लोभाद्भयाद्वापि स्मृत्यपेतादिकारिण:।
सभ्या: पृथक् पृथग्दण्ड्या: विवादाद्द्विगुणं दमम् ॥

न्यायस्थाने गृहीत्वार्थमधर्म्यं च विनिर्णयम्।
कुर्व्वन्त्यन् कोचका ये तु राजद्रव्य विनाशका:।
उत्कोचजीविनो द्रव्यहीनान् कृत्वा विवासयेत्।
व्यास:। वीरमित्रोदय:। प्रकीर्णकप्रकरणम्।

यत्रापवर्त्तते युग्यं वैगुण्यात् प्राजकस्य तु।
तत्र स्वामी भवेद्दण्ड्यो हिंसायां द्विशतं दमम्।
प्राजकश्चे द्भवेदाप्तो प्राजको दण्डमर्हति। मनु:

Abetment. Accessories to a crime.

A person, who abets the commission of an offence or helps the offender by giving him shelter and food, or does not prevent the offence while having the power to do so, is regarded as a participator in the crime and liable to punishment according to the circumstances of the case. The texts bearing upon the point have been quoted in connection with the group of offences designated by the term साहस (violent offences), but I think, the principles are applicable with necessary modifications to other offences also, and it is expressly stated by Yajnavalkya that a person who knowingly helps a thief by giving him food, shelter, fire, water, advice, materials and expenses renders himself liable to the highest amercement.

Exemption from liability. Infancy as an excuse

An infant who is incapable of differentiating right from wrong is exempted from criminal liability. There is a text which says that an infant within the eighth year is similar to a child in its mother's womb,[1] implying that he cannot be held responsible for his act. We find in the Mahabharata that the sage Anîmándavya says that an infant within the twelfth year from birth cannot incur any sin as he has no knowledge of the rules of proper conduct, and to this the sage adds two years more, and declares that he will establish the rule that no one should incur a sin for anything done by him within fourteen years of age.[2] Naturally this latter rule seems to carry the exemption a little too far, and Nilkantha in his commentary

गर्भस्थैः सदृशो ज्ञेयः आष्टमाद्वत्सरात् शिशुः ।

बालोहि द्वादशाद्वर्षाज्जन्मतो यत् करिष्यति ।

न भविष्यत्यधर्म्मोऽत्र न प्रज्ञास्यन्ति वै दिशः ।

*   *   *

मर्य्यादां स्थापयाम्यद्य लोके धर्म्मफलोदयाम् ।

आचतुर्द्दशकाद्वर्षात् न भविष्यति पातकम् ।

महाभारतम् । आदिपर्व्व । १०८

taxes his ingenuity to get out of it by laying stress on the reason of the rule and declaring that in fact the exemption from responsibility extends so long as the infant cannot discriminate between right and wrong and no definite age-limit can be prescribed to meet every case.[1]

Right of private defence.

Our lawgivers fully recognised the right of private defence and a person who in defence of his person or property, repelled the aggressor by force was exonerated from offence, and in extreme cases the right extended to causing the death of the aggressor even if he might be a Brahmin.

A few exceptions to criminal liability for theft.

While dealing with the subject of exemption from criminal liability, it may not be out of place to mention a few exceptions to criminal liability for theft. It is laid down by Manu that a traveller, who finding himself short of provisions, takes a small quantity of edibles from another's field does not deserve to be punished on that account. This is no doubt founded on the principle that a petty offence committed under pressure whereby nobody suffers much ought to be excused. We also meet with a somewhat bolder rule, undoubtedly conceived in a spirit of humanity, that it is allowable for a man who had nothing to eat for six consecutive meals, to take from another even without his consent enough to provide him with food for a day without looking for the morrow.[2]

Caution required of the king in dealing with crimes.

I have already stated that Manu declares that a king who condemns the innocent and absolves the guilty subjects himself to great disgrace and goes to hell. If

---

[1] चतुर्दशाब्दं पापमस्तीति पौराणं मतमिदम्। वस्तुतस्तु भवादितो पुण्य-पापविभागज्ञानपर्यन्तमेव पापानुत्पत्तिः।

[2] तथैव सप्तमे भक्ते भक्तानि षडनश्नता।
अश्वस्तनविधानेन हर्तव्यं हीनकर्मणः॥

Expiration for inflicting unjust sentence.

unwarily he imposes penalty unjustly, he should expiate himself by distributing among Brahmins thirty times the amount which he has so realised.

End of punishment according to the Hindu Law.

I shall now conclude the present lecture by making a few observations on the end of punishment according to the conceptions of our ancient lawgivers. I have already observed that according to Manu one of the primary objects of punishment is the protection of the people. 'Penalty,' says he, 'keeps the people under control, penalty protects them, penalty remains awake when people are asleep, so the wise have regarded punishment as a dharma or a source of righteousness.'[1]

Protection of the people.

According to this view the end of punishment is to ensure the protection of the people by creating a motive for desisting from crimes, for as Manu points out 'people are kept in check by punishment, for it is difficult to find a man who by nature sticks to the path of virtue and this world is enabled to afford sources of enjoyment through fear of punishment.'[2] Besides this, there is yet another aspect of punishment, viz., as a source of purification of the culprit himself. So Manu says, 'men who are guilty of crimes being condemned by the king become pure and go to heaven in the same way as good and virtuous men.'[3] I am disposed to think that the two ends of punishment indicated above manifest a very high ideal regarding the end of criminal justice; and

Punishment as a source of purification of the culprit.

दण्डः शास्ति प्रजाः सर्व्वा दण्डएवाभिरक्षति ।
दण्डः सुप्तेषु जागर्त्ति दण्डं धर्म्मं विदुर्बुधाः ॥ मनुः ।७।१८

सर्व्वो दण्डजितो लोको दुर्लभो हि शुचिर्नरः ।
दण्डस्य हि भयात् सर्व्वं जगद्भोगाय कल्पते ॥ मनुः ।७।२२

राजभिर्धृतदण्डास्तु कृत्वा पापानि मानवाः ।
निर्म्मलाः स्वर्गमायान्ति सन्तः सुकृतिनो यथा । मनुः ।८।३१८

it is a source of gratification to me that our lawgivers, so far as I am aware, do not give any countenance to the view that the function of a court of justice in administering criminal law is to exact the vengeance which the complainant may feel disposed to demand. Time has changed and conditions of people have changed along with it, so that punishments which at one time seemed to be just and proper may now appear to be too severe, but the ideal of punishment held out by our ancient lawgivers does not seem to require any revision though centuries have rolled by.

LECTURE XIII.

ADJECTIVE LAW.

In this lecture, I shall endeavour to place before you a short account of the adjective law according to the Hindu Sastras. In doing so, I shall try to give you some idea regarding the constitution of courts, the procedure followed in adjudicating upon litigious disputes, and the evidence by which the parties were permitted to substantiate their claim or defence.

The subject introduced.

Referring to the constitution of Courts, we find that primarily it was conceived to be the duty of the king to administer justice by hearing litigious disputes. In doing so, he was directed to take the assistance of councillors who were to act as assessors or advisers of the king. As regards their qualifications, it was declared that they should be learned in the Vedas, acquainted with the sacred law, addicted to truth, and impartial towards friend and foe;[1] and their number should be either three, five or seven, the reason for insisting upon an odd number perhaps being that in a case of difference of opinion guidance might be obtained from the opinion of the majority. When, however, the king could not himself preside over the deliberations of the Court by reason of other avocations, it was directed that he should appoint a Judge to act as his delegate along with the councillors. The Judge so appointed was called a प्राड्विवाक and it was directed that he should be possessed of self-control, belong to a respectable family, be impartial,

Constitution of Courts.

King, the supreme judge. Councillors.

Their qualification.

Delegation of the duty to administer justice to a Judge. His qualification.

[1] श्रुताध्ययनसम्पन्ना धर्म्मज्ञाः सत्यवादिनः ।
राज्ञा सभासदः कार्य्याः रिपौमित्रे च ये समाः ॥

temperate, firm, fearful for the future, virtuous, attentive and free from passion.[1] He should be selected, if possible, from among the Brahmans, or at all events from the Kshatriyas or the Vaisyas; but never should a Sudra be appointed to such a post.

Where other people present in court could give out their opinion.

It may here be mentioned that besides the Councillors selected and appointed by the king in order to assist in the deliberations of the Court, it was declared that other people versed in the law who attend the court should, if occasion arises, give their own opinion on a disputed point of law to prevent a perversion of justice; nay it was pointed out that even silence may become culpable in such a case, for Manu declares that you must not enter the assembly or must speak out what is proper, for a man becomes a sinner who, under those circumstances, either preserves silence or speaks falsely.[2]

It must not be supposed that this implies that every person who happened to be present in the court was entitled to prattle to his hearts' content on any disputed question arising in any judicial proceeding; the above remarks only applied to those who were versed in the law, and, as such, had a recognised position in the judicial assembly, although they did not hold any appointment as an adviser of the court. As regards an ordinary visitor the rule of Narada held good, *viz.*, that in a litigious dispute, one who has no appointed function should not say anything, and one who has should say what is proper without any leaning towards either party.[3]

1 दान्तं कुलीनं मध्यस्थमनुद्वेगकरं स्थिरं।
परत्रभीरुं धर्मिष्ठमुद्युक्तं क्रोधवर्जितम्। कात्यायनः।

2 सभा वा न प्रवेष्टव्या वक्तव्यं वा समञ्जसं।
अब्रुवन् विब्रुवन् वापि नरो भवति किल्बिषी॥

3 नानियुक्तेन वक्तव्यं व्यवहारेषु किञ्चन।
नियुक्तेन तु वक्तव्यमपक्षपतितं वचः। नारदः।

Distinction between the function of such men and that of a duly appointed councilor.

There was, however, this difference between the function of a duly appointed councillor and that of a learned lawyer who gave his opinion as, what we may call, *amicus curiae*; a councillor was, by reason of his post, a member of the court, and it was his duty to oppose a king if he wanted to proceed illegally, by remonstrating with him, since those councillors who follow a king, pursuing the path of injustice become participators in his act.[1] On the other hand, the duty of a lawyer who held no post ended when he gave out his opinion, and it was no part of his business to remonstrate with the king if he did not want to follow it.

Local courts of limited authority.

Besides the ordinary Court of Justice, of which the constitution has been explained above, it has been declared that families, corporations, and communities may also be charged with the decision of judicial proceedings. It must, however, be understood that these could only decide disputes which came within their special province, being disputes relating to matters which, from their very nature, fell within their special knowledge, for instance, disputes regarding trade and other local concerns. These local courts had a sort of delegated authority within their limited spheres, but their decisions were subject to appeal in the following order; a case having been decided by a family, an appeal, lay to the corporation, by a corporation to the community, and by a community to the officers appointed by the king, or in other words, to the court properly constituted to try all disputes. Narada adds that a decision arrived at by the king's court from which the king is absent is appealable to the king himself.

Gradation of courts, and right of appeal.

Having thus explained the constitution of courts, and their gradation, together with the consequent right of

Procedure.

---

1 अन्यायेनापि तं यान्तं येऽनुयान्ति सभासदः ।
तेऽपि तद्भागिनस्तस्माद्बोधनीयः स तैर्नृपः । नारदः ।

appeal, I now proceed to deal with the procedure to be followed in deciding a litigious dispute.

Complaint: No litigation without complaint.

As I have already stated no civil action could be taken cognisance of except on a complaint. It is directed that neither the king nor his officers should foster litigation by starting an action without a complainant, and, moreover,

Who were entitled to lodge a complaint.

no complaint should be taken notice of when it proceeded from a person altogether unconnected with the person aggrieved. Narada adds that a person, who comes to the court with a complaint which does not concern him, without being related to the person aggrieved as brother, father,

Exception in the case of a crime.

son, or duly appointed agent should be punished. Of course, as I have already shown, this limitation does not apply to the case of a crime, for the king may and should take notice of it even without a complaint.

Mode of lodging a complaint.

As regards the mode of lodging a complaint, it is laid down that the complainant should appear before the court in all humility, and state the facts constituting his grie-

Mode of recording a complaint.

vance, and his statement would be taken down accurately by an officer of the court called लेखक or writer. The king, or the judge, as the case may be, and the councillors may then put any questions that they think proper in order to elucidate the complaint, and when they have been ans-

If the complaint disclosed a cause of action, the defendant was to be summoned. Mode of summoning a defendant. Personal attendance when dispensed with.

wered, the whole should be taken into consideration in order to see whether the complaint discloses any proper cause of action; if it does, then the defendant should be summoned to appear through an officer of the court appointed for the purpose called साध्यपाल or by issuing a summons duly served by the court. It is, however, laid down that there are certain persons who may not be summoned to appear personally before the court, meaning thereby that they may be allowed to appear through an agent; as instances of persons who were so exempted from personal attendance we may mention persons in great distress, persons con stantly engaged in the performance of religious cremonies, persons who would suffer great loss if they were compelled to appear, persons suffering from grief, engaged in kings' business, or busily employed in some auspicious ceremony, those who are intoxicated, insane or otherwise deranged in mind as well as those who are dependent on others such as servants, young women, &c. It is unnecessary to endeavour to go through the whole catalogue of the persons exempted from personal appearance in the manner stated above, for I hope the examples already given will indicate the principles on which the exemption was based. It may, however, be interesting to add that besides those already mentioned, a bridegroom who was about to be engaged in the marriage, a soldier about to start on an expedition, and an emissary from another king were excused from personal attendance at least for the time. It should be understood that the exemption spoken of above relates to ordinary litigation, for when the charges are very grave the king may summon even those who are sick causing them to be conveyed slowly in carriages, and even an ascetic who has repaired to forest may be called in such a manner as not to arouse his anger. It should also be added that persons charged with any of the serious offences should not be allowed to appear through an agent, and then personal attendance must be insisted on.

Punishment for disobedience of summons.

A person who being duly summoned disobeys the summons without any excuse should be punished with a fine. I may now turn to a somewhat peculiar procedure recognised by the Hindu Law to ensure the attendance of a defendant.

आसेध or the imposing of legal restraint.

This was called आसेध or the imposing of legal restraint. It could be resorted to by a person about to prefer a complaint, when he found that his adversary was not paying any heed to his claim or was evading it, by way of imposing a restraint on the freedom of the defendant until the arrival of the

Four kinds of legal restraint.

summons from the court. The legal restraint which could be so imposed was fourfold; local, temporary, inhibition from going abroad, and from the pursuit of a particular work or occupation; thus the intending complainant could say to his adversary, 'I am going to complain against you at once, and the summons will come, do not leave this place until it comes, or do not engage yourself in any other work for an hour or two, or do not leave the country so as to avoid the process, or do not follow a particular occupation so long as we do not settle our dispute before the court'.

When it could not be imposed.

Almost the same persons who are exempted from personal attendance in a court are also declared to be unfit to be detained by the imposition of what I have called legal restraint. It was also laid down that any person who was so situated that it would be most inconvenient for him to have his freedom of movement interfered with, should not be subjected to any legal restraint by the intending complainant in anticipation of the complaint and the consequent issue of process from the court.

Wilful violation of legal restraint properly imposed was punished, as well as imposition of legal restraint without proper grounds.

A person who wilfully violated a legal restraint properly imposed rendered himself liable to be punished, and on the other hand, a person who imposed a legal restraint without proper grounds and under circumstances which did not justify its imposition made himself liable to penalty.

Procedure to be followed when the defendant entered appearance.

When the defendant enters appearance, the complainant is called upon to repeat his complaint in the presence of the defendant, when he does so it is again taken down and that forms the plaint in the case. On this occasion, the complainant is required to go more into details so as to make his charges quite specific, and definite as regards time, place, and so forth, and the manner in which the cause of action arose. Any serious discrepancy between the complaint as originally lodged and the plaint as recorded in the presence of the adversary may prove fatal to the cause.

A proper declaration of complaint should be significant, technically precise, comprehensive. unwavering, direct, unequivocal, conformable to the original complaint, not opposed to well-known facts, consistent, clear, susceptible of proof, concise and yet not deficient in meaning, and consistent with local and temporal conditions. A plaint should be rejected as containing a mere semblance of a true and proper complaint, if the declaration on which it is based is unnatural, or discloses no injury to the complainant, or is unmeaning, frivolous, unsusceptible of proof, or at variance with possibility. A plaint which is not altogether inadmissible but is wanting in precision or otherwise defective, may be allowed to be amended at any time before the defendant has put in his answer, but no amendment can be allowed afterwards, for otherwise there may arise what is called the fault of inability to stay (अनवस्था); since if you allow an amendment of the declaration after the answer, the defendant may ask to put in a supplementary answer, which may be followed by a fresh amendment of the declaration to be met by a fresh answer, and so on. So Narada says that 'a declaration may be amended until the answer is given in, but being stopped by the answer, the corrections must cease.'

Character of a proper declaration of complaint.

When the plaint should be rejected.

Amendment of plaint when allowed

When the plaint has been properly and correctly recorded, the defendant is to be called upon to answer to the charge laid against him. The defendant may, if necessary, obtain an adjournment for putting in his answer, but in cases of certain specified offences he should be called upon to submit his answer at once. Just as the complaint is recorded in the presence of the defendant, so the answer, in its turn, is taken down in the presence of the complaint, the utility of confronting the two parties when they unfold their cases being obvious. The answer should meet the grounds raised by the complaint

Defendant's answer.

Adjournment for answer when granted and when not.

Answer should be taken down in the presence of the complainant.

Qualities of a proper answer.

Four kinds of answers.

and he substantial, unhesitating, clear, consistent, and free from prolixity and yet not obscure. An answer may assume either of four forms ; 'a confession, a denial, a special exeeption and a plea of former judgment (*res judicata*) are the four sorts of answer,' [1] says Katyayana. There is no difficulty in understanding what a confession and a denial mean. A special exception, which is also called a plea of justification (कारणोत्तर) is thus defined by Narada, 'where the defendant admits the allegations recorded by the plaintiff as true, but urges reasons (in denial of the liability), the pl a so taken is called a special exception.' [2] Thus, virtually, it amounts to what may be called a plea of confession and avoidance, in as much as here the defendant admits at least partially, if not wholly, the allegations made by the plaintiff, but at the same time avers additional fa ts and brings forward reasons why notwithstanding the admission, the plaintiff's case should fail. A plea of *res judicata* has been thus defined by Harita, "when the defendant avers that the matter in controversy was the subject of a former litigation between him and the plaintiff when the latter was defeated, the plea is a plea of former judgment (or *res judicata*)". [3]

Nature of the answer affected the future course

You will now see how the nature of the answer affected the future course of the litigation. A judicial proceeding,

सत्यं मिथ्योत्तरञ्चैव प्रत्यवस्कन्दनं तथा ।
पूर्व्वन्यायविधिश्चैवमुत्तरं स्यात् चतुर्व्विधम् ॥
मिताक्षराधृत कात्यायन वचनम् ।

अर्थिना लिखितोयोऽर्थः प्रत्यर्थी यदि तं तथा ।
प्रपद्य कारणंब्रूयात् प्रत्यवस्कन्दनं स्मृतम् ॥
मिताक्षराधृत नारद वचनम् ।

अस्मिन्नर्थे ममानेन वादः पूर्व्वमभूत्तदा ।
जितोऽयमिति चेद्ब्रूयात् प्राङ्न्यायः स्यात्तदुत्तरम् ॥
वीरमित्रोदयधृत हारीत वचनम् ।

of litigation. Four steps in a litigation.

according to the lawgivers, ordinarily consists of four steps or stages, *viz.*, the complaint, the answer, the trial, and the deliberation followed by the decree.[1] When the answer amounts to an admission of the claim, there is no further need of any trial, and the decree follows at once ; in other cases, after the answer has been duly recorded, there arises the necessity for a trial. There the question is, who should begin ? As to this, the rule is that when the answer amounts to a denial, it is the duty of the complainant to begin and substantiate his claim by adducing evidence ; in the other two cases, the defendant must begin and substantiate his defence.[2] When the answer is of a complex character, its component parts should be separately taken into consideration, and the mode of trial in its consecutive stages should be regulated according to the nature of the pleas constituting the answer.

Trial—who should begin? This depends on the nature of the plea.

When the answer has been duly taken down, and it has been determined which of the parties is to begin, he is to be called upon to state the evidence by which he proposes to substantiate his case. Yajnavalkya says that a competent surety should be taken from each party for the satisfaction of the judgment, if it goes against him ; if a party be unable to furnish a competent surety, steps should be taken to ensure his attendance during the trial. Counter-charge against the complainant should not be taken cognisance of until the completion of the trial of

Surety for the satisfaction of the judgment.

Counter-charge not to be taken cognisance

[1] भाषा पादोत्तर पादौ क्रियापादस्तथैव च ।
प्रत्याकलित पादश्च व्यवहारश्चतुष्पदः ॥
वीरमित्रोदयधृत बृहस्पतिवचनम् ।

[2] प्राङ्न्याय कारणोक्तौ तु प्रत्यर्थी निर्दिशेत् क्रियाम् ।
मिथ्योक्तौ पूर्ववादी तु प्रतिपत्तौ न सा भवेत् ॥
मिताक्षराधृत हारीत वचनम् ।

of until the completion of the trial of the original complaint. Exceptions.

the original complaint.[1] This restriction is, of course, confined to a retort not having a tendency to refute the original complaint. Apart from this, in prosecutions for verbal abuse, personal violence, or other violent offences, recrimination is allowable so that the person complained against may without having refuted the charge, recriminate his accuser ; this, the Mitakshara explains, is allowed not for the sake of carrying on two distinct proceedings simultaneously but because the counter-charge, if made out, may serve as an extenuation leading to a mitigated punishment. It is hardly necessary to say that when the original charge has been tried out, there is nothing to prevent the person complained against from preferring a counter-charge against the complainant and demanding a trial of the same.

Production of evidence.

When the parties have duly recorded their complaint and answer, and the court has determined which party should begin, the trial commences with the party called upon to begin adducing evidence in support of his case, and after him the opposite party similarly adduces his evidence before the court.

Five persons liable to lose their cause.

The following five persons are liable to lose their cause : a person who having his case recorded in one way afterwards sets up a new case, a person who evinces his aversion to the trial by refusing to help its progress, a person who fails to appear at the time of the trial, a person who being called upon to answer keeps silent, and lastly a person who absconds with a view to avoid the process of the Court.[2]

Alteration of the case originally set up when

The Mitakshara however explains on the authority of another text of Narada that a verbal error involving an

उभयोः प्रतिभूर्ग्राह्यः समर्थः कार्य्यनिर्णये। याज्ञवल्क्यः।
अभियोगमनिस्तीर्य्य नैनं प्रत्यभियोजयेत्। याज्ञवल्क्यः।

अन्यवादी क्रियाद्वेषी नोपस्थाता निरुत्तरः।
आहूत प्रपलायी च हीनः पञ्चविधः स्मृतः। नारदः।

alteration of the case originally set up is not fatal in civil actions; should it appear in actions brought for reduction, for debt or for landed property, the plaintiff is to be amerced, but it does not annul his claim. From the specification of civil actions, it may ba inferred that in the case of a criminal prosecution such an abandonment of the case as originally laid is fatal to the charge. A litigation once started should not be compromised except with the sanction of the court.

fatal to the action, and when not.

Compromise.

Evidence is said to consist of documents, possession and witnesses; in the absence of all these, a divine test is presented. Documents are of two sorts, official and private. Possession becomes evidence by giving rise to a presumption of title. When the one adduces human evidence and the other appeals to a divine test, the king will proceed to examine the human evidence, and will not have recourse to divine test. A decision by divine test is allowable only in the absence of human evidence. This is the general rule. But in the investigation of a capital offence or assault and battery, and in all cases of violence committed long ago, both witnesses and divine test may be had recourse to. The proof of established custom among people of the same township or tribe depends on documentary evidence. There neither divine test nor witnesses are available. So also, in cases relating to pathways, roads, enclosures and watercourses, possession affords the weightiest proof.

Different kinds of evidence. Two kinds of documents.

Possession. A division by divine test when allowable.

Proof of established custom. Where possession affords the weightiest proof.

Witnesses are twofold; a witness appointed, and a witness unappointed; an appointed witness is one nominated to give testimony; an unappointed witness is one not so appointed. The minor divisions of these two classes of witnesses need not be referred to. Reliable witnesses generally possess the following qualities: "religious, generous, of respectable family, addicted to veracity, lovers

Two kinds of witnesses.

Qualities of a reliable witness.

of virtue, candid, having offspring, wealthy, conformer to traditional and written law, and in number three". An untruthful witness generally exhibits the following characteristics: he constantly shifts his position, licks the corners of his lips, his forehead sweats and his countenance continually changes colour; his mouth dries up and he falters in his speech and very often contradicts himself; he does not look up or is slow in returning answers and contorts his lips; such a person who exhibits an unnatural aspect either in body, mind, words or action is esteemed false, whether putting forward a claim on his account, or giving evidence in another's cause.

Characteristics exhibited by an untruthful witness.

Formal validity of a document.

The formal validity of a document depends on the usage of the country.

Mode of examining witnesses.

The witnesses should be made to depose having been placed near the plaintiff and defendant. Having called the witnesses, the judge shall place them on their oath and then interrogate them about the case. The proof of a negative is dependent on the establishment of an affirmative, and the establishment of an affirmative is not dependent on the proof of a negative. Hence the burden of proof lies upon him who sets up an affirmative case.

Burden of proof rests on him who sets up an affirmative case.

Ordeals.

An ordeal is not like human evidence confined to an affirmative only, but it extends indiscriminately both to affirmatives and negatives. There are several distinct forms of ordeal prescribed in the books, but I do not think it will serve any useful purpose to discuss how they were administered. It must be remembered that they were to be avoided where other kinds of evidence were forthcoming.

Deliberation and decision.

When both the parties have adduced their evidence it becomes the duty of the court to deliberate and decide which party should succeed; on such deliberation, the judgment follows embodying the decision of the court. The winning party then obtains what has been called जयपत्र or decree; this document embodies a summary of the pleadings, of the evidence adduced by the parties, of the court's deliberation thereon, and of the law applicable to the case as determined by the court.[1] It bears the signature of the judge and the mark of the royal seal.

Judgment.

Decree: what it should contain.

A decision obtained by false evidence is liable to be set aside on review. Similarly a decision obtained by fraud or force is liable to be vacated on proof that it was so obtained. So also, a litigation with women or with persons not in sound state of mind by reason of intoxication, insanity, disease, extreme distress infancy or intimidation is ineffectual and cannot produce any binding effect. A trial held during night or within closed doors or outside jurisdiction is void and so liable to be annulled.

Review.

Grounds for vacating a previous judgment.

When a judgment has been pronounced by a proper court, it becomes the duty of the king to enforce it by the exercise of his administrative powers.

Enforcement of the decree.

By protecting people in the proper enjoyment of their rights, by punishing the delinquent and by exculpating the innocent, the king pleases the whole world, and himself attains fame, victory and heavenly bliss.

पूर्व्वोत्तर क्रियापादं तत्प्रमाणं परीक्षणम् ।
निगदव्यतिवाक्यञ्च यथाशास्त्रं विनिश्चितम् ।
एतत् सर्व्वं समासेन जयपत्रेऽभिलेखयेत् । व्यासः (वी-मि)

LECTURE XIV

CONCLUDING REMARKS.

Excellence of Hindu Jurisprudence

In concluding my introductory lecture I ventured to assert that although Hindu Jurisprudence might not in all respects be as perfect as one could desire, still I hoped to be able to show that, in the main, it would not compare unfavourably with even the most developed system of ancient Jurisprudence, the Roman. After having briefly reviewed most of the principal topics of jurisprudence as dealt with by the Hindu Jurists, I feel that what I said there was not dictated by any undue partiality towards my national system, and I repeat my conviction that whatever may be the views of those self-styled critics who somehow or other start with a prejudice against everything Hindu, an honest investigator will not hesitate to endorse my assertion as founded on truth. More than four score years ago, Sir Francis Macnaghten said speaking of the Hindus: "The merit of having been the founders of their own jurisprudence cannot be denied to this people; and those who are at all conversant with the decisions of our own courts will acknowledge the analogy which exists between some of their doctrines, and some of the texts which I have cited from the Hindu Law. Where this is not to be found, a comparison may in several instances be made without disadvantage to the Hindus"; and yet when he wrote in the above strain the materials which he had in his hands were far from being complete. Since then critics have come and gone who have not hesitated to sneer at the Hindu Law without caring to descend into particulars and almost assuming that advanced judicial ideas could have no place outside certain local limits.

Comprehensiveness of the Hindu Law.

It may not, therefore, be useless to recapitulate some points of excellence which characterized the Hindu Law as developed by the sages and the commentators. In the first place, we may be permitted to observe that in point of comprehensiveness the Hindu Law in its various branches occupies a fairly high place among the systems of ancient jurisprudence. Its conception of legal liability is broad and perspicuous, and although it has generally retained the eighteen divisions of the topics of litigation as described by Manu, that has not in any way stinted its growth or prevented it from embracing within its range the various aspects of juridical relations which the complexity of human affairs may usually being about.

Loftiness of ideal.

In the second place, the administration of justice according to the Hindu system was evidently actuated by a high sense of duty, and it is impossible to deny that our lawgivers ever carried in their mind a very lofty ideal regarding the function which they had to discharge. They were not merely guided by an idea of temporary expediency, but were moved by the higher idea of 'धर्म' which in one of its phases looks upwards to revelation and in another looks forward to the permanent welfare of the entire sentient world.

Logical consistency.

In the third place, whatever else you may say, no one can complain that our lawgivers were lacking in logical consistency. The Hindu mind has ever been eminently logical; subtlety of discrimination, analytical skill, and logical accuracy in defining legal conceptions have always been its delight; and it has never enunciated a principle without perceiving what it really involves and the deductions which logically follow from it. Whoever knows anything about the manner in which legal topics have been discussed by the commentators, and the way in which, even at the present day, orthodox students of Hindu Law carry on their discussions on disputed questions, will not feel any hesitation in endorsing what I say. However high the position of a Hindu scholar may be, no opinion of his will carry any weight with an orthodox lawyer unless it stands the test of logical scrutiny applied according to the refined rules of ratiocination explained by Gautama and the logicians of his school, and the subtle principles of interpretation laid down by Jaimini and his followers. Read the work of any commentator, and you will find that at every step he has felt that ipse-dixitism will not do; he must justify his position against all possible controversy and avoid logical blunder and inconsistency.

Reasonableness, and regard for the interest of the community.

Lastly, our lawgivers have also taken care that the rules laid down by them may not be unreasonable and detrimental to the interest of the community at large. Law exists for the benefit of the people; it is a manifestation of the eternal Reason that rules this universe, and it justifies itself by being conducive to the welfare of the people who are governed by it. The king cannot override it; the judges cannot dispute its authority; and the people are bound to obey it not merely because it has the support of temporal authority, but because it draws its inspiration from the fountain of supreme wisdom. It must not be supposed that I mean to maintain that there is no rule of Hindu Law which to a modern mind may seem to be unreasonable; I have already indicated that the disparity of punishment according to difference of caste seems to us to be at least to some extent unjust and unreasonable; but I venture to affirm that mere errors in detail can furnish no reason for ignoring the guiding principle which actuated our law-givers in enunciating and expounding the law.

Practical insight of our law-givers: they were not mere dreamers.

It has been remarked that our ancestors were mere dreamers ; but we who are more asleep than awake can hardly discriminate what is a dream and what is not. It is no doubt true, and we should feel proud of it, that our forefathers meditated upon the potentialities of existence beyond the world with an earnestness unsurpassed in the history of philosophy ancient or modern ; but surely that did not make them forget the concerns of worldly life, for nothing human was alien to them ; in medicine, which has as its aim the alleviation of human suffering by curing the distempers of our physicial organism, the system introduced by them even now commands the admiration of the scientific world ; in the field of jurisprudence also their labours were equally well-directed and equally successful ; but unfortunately circumstances intervened which retarded its growth and at the present day very few among us feel any curiosity to enquire what it was like, and how far it was developed ; nay, there are people who even seem to entertain serious doubts regarding its existence. It was therefore, with a heavy sense of responsibility that I took upon myself the task of presenting a short but systematic exposition of some of the important principles of Hindu Jurisprudence in its several divisions and sub-divisions. Having regard to the novelty and the importance of the subject a more elaborate discussion would not, perhaps, have been out of place ; but travelling as I was over a long deserted ground I could not afford to run the risk of tiring out the patience of those who might be following me.

Conclusion.

Here, then, I conclude my lectures. I am aware that to a mere practising lawyer a study of the topics discussed by me in these lectures may not appear to be profitable to any considerable exent; but I venture to expect that to a student of scientific jurisprudence it will not appear to be altogether valueless. Success in the profession depends upon a combination of various conditions and influences which are not all within our control; many strive for it and a few succeed. But whether we succeed or fail in the pursuit of professional reputation, let us not forget that we have a higher duty to perform, a higher ideal to have in view, and a higher inspiration to be guided by.

Who is there among us who will not feel a thrill of pleasure and a sense of mental and moral elevation to be reminded that we also had a brilliant past, and that the wisdom of our forefathers has left its traces in the various branches of learning not excluding even those which some nations profess to be specially their own? Who is there among the students of Jurisprudence who will not feel a keen curiosity to get an insight into the conceptions and principles of a system of Jurisprudence which to say the least of it, is as old as the Roman? And, above all, who is there who will not be moved to see the manifestation of one universal reason which unfolds itself amidst the diversity of details through unexpected similarities of legal conceptions, rules and institutions? The sun arose in the east and travelled towards the west, and it is the same light which illumines the whole world; supercilious observers may think that 'east is east, and west is west, and never the twain shall meet,' but deeper insight into the institutions of the different countries discloses that it is the same universal reason which permeates the universe, and its touch makes the whole world kin.

APPENDIX A.

SOME RECENT DECISIONS ON THE INTERPRETATION OF HINDU LAW TEXTS.

1. *Gangadhar Bagla* v. *Hira Lal Bagla*, *(1916) 23 C.L.J. 372.*

A special text or statute forming an exception to a general text or statute should be construed strictly and applied only to cases falling clearly within it.

Where a Hindu widow governed by the Mitakshara School of Law, dies without issue leaving stridhan property, an adopted son of her husband taken in conjunction with another wife and a son of her husband born of the womb of a third wife inherit, as her husband's sapindas, her stridhan property, in *equal* shares.

Briddha Gautama lays down the general rule that an adopted son endowed with excellent qualities and an after born son are equal sharers. Vasishtha introduces an exceptional rule with regard to the inheritance to father's property, *viz.*, "if after he has been adopted, a legitimate son be born, then the dattaka shall obtain a fourth share."

It was held, that this exception must not be extended to property inherited from step mother.

"Consequently we should not extend its application to cases not only not comprised strictly within its letter, but undoubtedly beyond its true spirit : in this connection we may bear in mind that Hindu jurists, quite as much as English jurists (Ebbs v. Boulnois (1875) L. R. 10 Ch.

App. 479 (484) ; Co. Litt. 299a) recognise the well-known canon of interpretation that a special text or statute forming an exception to a general text or statute should be construed strictly and applied only to the cases falling clearly within it ; the Mitakshara itself recognises the principle that where an exception exists to a general rule, the exception should be confined within the strictest limits, so as not to encroach unduly upon the rule : Gangu *v.* Chandra (1907) I. L. R. 32 Bom 275 ; Anandi *v.* Hari (1909) I. L. R. 33 Bom 404 ; Dattaka Chandrika Sec. V. 27 ; Mitakshara on Prayaschitta, Ed. Moghe, p. 292 ; यावत्यबाधिते अनुपपत्ति प्रशमो न भवति तावत्बाधनीयम्''

Per Mookerjee, J. pages 387-388.

2. *Ramchandra Martand Waiker and ors.* vs. *Vinayak Venkatesh Kothekar and another*, (1914) 20C. L. J. 573 P. C.

The Hindu Law contains its own principles of exposition, and questions arising under it cannot be determined on abstract reasoning or analogies borrowed from other systems of law, but must depend for their decision on the rules and doctrines enunciated by its own law-givers and recognised expounders.

The questions were, *first,* whether the expression 'bandhu' would be confined only to those three classes of *bhinna gotra* sapindas that were mentioned in the Mitakshara, or whether any new class of heirs can be introduced under it ; and *secondly* whether the word sapinda should be understood in a wide sense to include every person related by particles of the body, or whether it should be understood in a restricted sense, so as exclude from inheritance every one related through females beyond the fifth degree, and every one related through males beyond the seventh degree.

Held, first, that the classes specified by Vijnaneswara cannot be added to ; and the case of Giridharilal Roy v. Government of Bengal, 12 M. I. A. 448, is no authority for the extension.

Held, further, that the relation of sapinda ceases for purposes both of marriage and of inheritance after five degrees in case of relationship through females.

"The limitation of five degrees clearly applies and can only apply to the *bhinna gotra* sapindas. But it is contended that this limitation is confined to prohibition in respect of marriage. As has already been observed, a part of the limitation appears to have been applied to the succession of samanagotra sapindas : their Lordships are unable to see on what principle it can be said that the other part relative to kinsmen who are equally sapindos but belong to a different gotra or sons must be restricted to matrimonial affinity.

*   *   *   *   *   *

In the absence of any authoritative text, their Lordships do not see their way merely on abstract reasoning to displace a view of the law which has received the recognition of the Courts in India and which the District Judge, an officer of great experience and learning says is accepted by " public opinion."

Per Mr. Ameer Ali. Pages 608 and 609.

3. Prasannakumar Bose v. *Sarutsasi Ghosh (1908) (I.L.R. 36 Cal. 86. Brett, Mitra and Coxe, JJ.*

On a difference of opinion between Justices Brett and Coxe, the case was referred to Mitra, J., who agreed with Brett J.

The question was whether under the Dayabhaga School of Hindu Law, the son or the married daughter is the preferential heir to the mother's *ayautuka stridhana*,

The decision depended upon the meaning of the expression *kanya* given by Jimutavahana in connection with his quotation from Manu in Ch. IV, Sec. 2, Para 16. It appears that Srikrishna and Raghunandan use the term as meaning daughter generally. But from Chap. V of the Dayabhaga it is clear that Jimutavahana used it in the sense of an unmarried daughter.

In such a conflict of opinions, that of Jimutavahana

4. *Bhupatinath Smrititirtha* v. *Ramlal Maitra (1909) I.L.R. 37 Cal. 128 F.B., Sir Lawrence Jenkins C.J., Stephen, Mookerjee, Cox and Chatterjee JJ.*

The principal question referred to the Full Bench was "Does the principale of Hindu Law, which invalidates a gift other than to a sentient being capable of accepting it, apply to a bequest to trustees for the establishment of an image and the worship of the Hindu deity after the testator's death and make such a bequest void ?"

Held on a construction of the expression 'दानेहि चेतनोद्देशविशिष्टत्यागादेव' (Dayabhaga Ch. I. Para 21) and comments thereon, read with Shoolapani's and Raghunandana's discussions as to the nature of *Sradh* and gift, &c., that the above principle of Hindu Law does not apply to such a bequest.

" The view that no valid dedication of property can be made by a will to a deity, the image of which is not in existence at the time of the death of the tastator, is based upon a double fiction, namely, first, that a Hindu deity is for all purposes a juridical person, and secondly, that a dedication to the deity has the same characteristies and is subject to the same restrictions as a gift to a human being. The first of these propositions is too broadly stated, and the second is inconsistent with the first principles of jurisprudence."

Per Mookerjee J. Page 161.

"The Hindu Law recognises dedications for the establishment of the image of a deity and for the maintenance and worship thereof. The property so dedicated to a pious purpose is placed *extra-commercium* and is entitled to special protection at the hands of the sovereign whose duty it is to intervene to prevent fraud and waste in dealing with religious endowments." Per Mookerjee J. Page 161.

APPENDIX B.

List of Sanskrit texts quoted in the book.

Page.	Foot Note. No.	TEXT	Reference.
10	1	वेदःस्मृतिः सदाचारः स्वस्य च प्रियमात्मनः । एतच्चतुर्विधं प्राहुः साक्षाद्धर्म्मस्य लक्षणं ॥	Manu II. 12
12	2	अपिवाकर्त्तृसामान्यात् प्रमाणमनुमानंस्यात् । विरोधेत्वनपेक्ष्यं स्यादसतिह्यनुमानं ॥	Purva Mimansa I. ii. 2&3.
13	1	मन्वत्रिविष्णुहारीतयाज्ञवल्क्योशनोऽङ्गिराः । यमापस्तम्बसम्बर्ताः कात्यायनवृहस्पती ॥ पराशरव्यास-शङ्खलिखिता दक्षगौतमौ शातातपो वशिष्ठश्च धर्म्मशास्त्रप्रयोजकाः ॥	Yajnavalkya I. 4 & 5
"	2	वेदार्थोपनिवन्धृत्वात् प्राधान्यंहि मनोःस्मृतं । मन्वर्थविपरीता या सा स्मृतिर्नप्रशस्यते ॥	Vrihaspati, cited by Kulluka on *Manu* I. 2.
14	1	अन्ये कृतयुगेधर्म्मास्त्रेतायां द्वापरेपरे । अन्ये कलियुगे नृणां युगरूपानुसारतः ॥	Parasara I. 21
"	2	धर्म्मशास्त्रविरोधेतु युक्तियुक्तोविधिःस्मृतः ।	Narada I. 40
15	1	स्मृत्योर्विरोधे न्यायस्तु वलवान् व्यवहारतः ।	Yajnavalkya II.21
"	2	तस्यायमाशयः-न्यायानुपष्टब्धस्मृत्यपेक्षयान्यायोपष्टब्धा-स्मृतिर्वलवतीति-न्यायानुपष्टब्ध-स्मृतेस्तात्पर्य्यान्तर-कल्पना कार्य्या ।	Viramitrodaya, Vyavahara.

16 1 श्रुतिस्तु वेदो विज्ञेयो धर्म्मशास्त्रन्तु वै स्मृतिः ।
ते सर्व्वार्थेष्वमीमांस्ये ताभ्यां धर्म्मो हि निर्बभौ ॥
योऽवमन्येत ते मूले हेतुशास्त्राश्रयाद्द्विजः ।
स साधुभिर्बहिष्कार्य्यो नास्तिको वेदनिन्दकः ॥ Manu II. 10,11.

17 1 यो मातुल विवाहादौ शिष्टाचारः समानवा ।
इतराचारवत्मात्वममात्वं स्मार्त्तवाधनात् ॥
स्मृतिमूलो हि सर्व्वत्र शिष्टाचारस्ततोऽत्र च ।
अनुमेया स्मृतिः स्मृत्या वाध्या प्रत्यक्षया तु सा ॥ Jaimini's Nyayamala, I. iii. 5.

18 1 देशजाति कुलानां च ये धर्म्माःप्राक् प्रवर्त्तिताः ।
तथैव ते पालनीयाः प्रजाः प्रक्षुभ्यतेऽन्यथा ॥
जनापरक्तिर्भवति वलं कोषश्च नश्यति ।
* * * * *
अनेन कर्म्मणा नैते प्रायश्चित्तदमार्हकाः ॥ Vrihaspati, II. 28-31.

19 1 यत्तु स्मृत्यन्तरेष्वेतत्कर्म्मकरणे प्रायश्चित्तदण्डस्मरण-
न्तदेतद्वचनानुपात्तदेशविषयमिति मदनरत्नकारः ।
वयन्तु—प्रजाप्रक्षोभादिदृष्टदोषकथनाद्राज्ञा तत्र दण्डो
न कार्य्य एव । प्रायश्चित्ताभावस्तु व्यवहार विषयः ।
परलोकशुद्ध्यर्थं प्रायश्चित्तं भवेदेवेति न स्मृत्यन्तरविरोधः ।
तत्तद्देशव्यापक-श्रुतिस्मृति-विरुद्धाचरणे व्यवहारप्रति-
बन्धिकाशक्तिस्तज्जन्यपापस्य नास्ति, नरकजनकास्त्येव ।
उपक्रम पर्य्यालोचना-देतावदर्थकतयैवचैतद्वचनोपपत्तौ
सर्व्वथा दोषाभाव-कल्पनस्यानुचितत्वात् । अतएव
आपस्तम्बेनोक्तं देश-जाति-कुलधर्म्मा—आम्नायै—रविरुद्धाः
प्रमाणमिति । येषां परम्पराप्राप्ताः पूर्व्वजैरप्यनुष्ठिताः ।
त एव तैर्न दुष्येयुराचारै र्नेतरे पुनरिति । न दुष्येयुरन्य-

वक्तार्थ्या राजदण्ड्याश्च न भवेयुरित्यर्थः । अन्यथैतयोरेव वचनयोः परस्परविरोधो दुष्परिहारः स्यादिति ब्रूमः ॥ — Viramitrodaya, Vyavahara.

21 1 वैकल्पिके आत्मतुष्टिः प्रमाणम् । — Garga cited by Kulluka on Manu, II. 6.

24 1 धर्म्मोविश्वस्य जगतः प्रतिष्ठा । — Narayan Upanishad.

25 1 धर्म्मस्य शब्दमूलत्वादशब्दमनपेक्ष्यं स्यात् । — Purva Mimansa. I. i. 3.

" 2 अन्यच्छ्रेयोऽन्यदुतैव प्रेयः । ते उभेनानार्थे पुरुषं सिनीतः ॥ तयोःश्रेयआददानस्य साधु भवति । हीयते-ऽर्थाद् य उ प्रेयो वृणीते । — Kathopanishad. I. ii.

26 1 चोदनालक्षणोऽर्थोधर्म्मः । — Purva Mimansa. II. i.

" 2 अथातः पुरुषनिःश्रेयसार्थं धर्म्मजिज्ञासा ।
ज्ञाता चानुतिष्ठन् धार्म्मिकः प्रशस्यतमो
भवति लोके प्रेत्य वा विजितं धर्म्मं । — Vasistha I.

" 3 यतोऽभ्युदयनिःश्रेयससिद्धिः स धर्म्मः । — Vaisasikha Sutras.

28 विवक्षाविशेषेण तत्समाधानात्

29 1 स्मृत्याचारव्यपेतेन मार्गेणाधर्षितः परैः ।
निवेदयति चेद् राज्ञे व्यवहार पदं हि तत् ॥ — Yajnavalkya, II. 5.

30 1 दण्डःशास्ति प्रजाःसर्व्वाः दण्ड एवाभिरक्षति ।
दण्डः सुप्तेषु जागर्त्ति दण्डं धर्म्मं विदुर्बुधाः ॥ — Manu, VII. 18.

" 2 अरक्षितारं राजानं वलिषड्भागहारिणं ।
तमाहुः सर्व्वलोकानां समग्रमलहारकं ॥ — Manu, VIII. 308.

31 1 अरक्ष्यमाणाः कुर्व्वन्ति यत्किञ्चित् किल्बिषं प्रजाः ।
तस्मात्तु नृपतेरर्द्धं यस्मात् गृह्णात्यसौ करान् ॥ — Yajnavalkya, I. 337.

33 1 तेषामाद्यं ऋणादानं निक्षेपोऽस्वामिविक्रयः ।
सम्भूय च समुत्थानं दत्तस्यानपकर्म्म च ॥
वेतनस्यैव चादानं संविदश्च व्यतिक्रमः ।
क्रयविक्रयानुशयो विवादः स्वामिपालयोः ॥
सीमाविवादधर्म्मश्च पारुष्ये दण्डवाचिके ।
स्तेयञ्च साहसञ्चैव स्त्रीसंग्रहणमेव च ॥
स्त्रीपुंधर्म्मो विभागश्च द्यूतमाह्वय एव च ।
पदान्यष्टादशैतानि व्यवहारस्थिताविह ॥ Manu, VIII. 4-7.

34 1 पदान्यष्टादशैतानि धर्म्मशास्त्रोदितानि च ।
मूलं सर्व्वविवादानां ये विदुस्ते परीक्षकाः ॥ Vrihaspati. cited in Vira. on Vyavahara-pada.

41 1 द्रव्यं गुणास्तथाकर्म्म सामान्यं सविशेषकं ।
समवायस्तथाभावः पदार्थाः सप्त कीर्त्तिताः ॥ Karikabali, I. 2.

42 यथेष्टविनियोगार्हत्वेन शास्त्रबोधितत्वमिति प्राञ्चः । Srikrishna on Daya-bhaga, I.5.

53 1 सप्त वित्तागमा धर्म्म्या दायो लाभः क्रयो जयः ।
प्रयोगः कर्म्मयोगश्च सत्प्रतिग्रह एव च ॥ Manu x.115.

55 1 परिग्रहः पूर्व्वमपरेणास्वीकृतस्यारण्यादिसाधारण-
प्रदेशसम्बन्धिनस्तृणजलकाष्ठादेः स्वीकारः । Vira. on Partition I. 13, G. Sarkar's Edn.

56 1 पृथोरपीमां पृथिवीं भार्य्यां पूर्व्वविदो विदुः ।
स्थाणुच्छेदस्य केदारमाहुः शल्यवतो मृगम् ॥ Manu, IX. 44.

57 1 येऽक्षेत्रिणो वीजवन्तः परक्षेत्रप्रवापिणः ।
ते वै शस्यस्य जातस्य न लभन्ते फलं क्वचित् ॥ Manu, IX. 49.

क्रियाभ्युपगमात्त्वेतद् वीजार्थं यत्प्रदीयते ।
तस्येह भागिनौ दृष्टौ वीजी क्षैत्रिक एव च ॥ Manu, IX. 53.

58 1 अधिगमोऽज्ञातस्वामिकस्य निध्यादेः प्राप्तिः । Vira. I. 13 G. Sarkar's Edn.

61 1 स्वजातीयस्वत्वं प्रति स्वजातीयस्वत्वं विरोधि । स्वजातीयेति करणात् पराजित नृपति-राज्यान्तर्वर्त्तितत्तत्पुरुषीयक्रमागतस्थावरादौ जयादिना जेतुर्नृपतेः करग्रहणोपयोगिस्वत्वोत्पादः । Srikrishna on Dayabhaga.

य एव नृपते धर्म्मः स्वराष्ट्रपरिपालने ।
तमेव कृत्स्नमाप्नोति परराष्ट्रं वशं नयन् ॥ Yajnavalkya, I. 342.

74 1 दानादियोग्येषु विभक्तेषु दायादेषु सत्सु तेभ्य एव स्थावरमर्पणीयमयोग्येषु निरपेक्षेषु वाऽन्येभ्यः । Apararka. Chapter on Datta-pradanika.

87 1 पण्यमूल्यं भृतिस्तुष्ट्या स्नेहात् प्रत्युपकारतः ।
स्त्रीशुल्कानुग्रहार्थन्तु दत्तं दानविदो विदुः ॥ Narada, IV. 8.

88 1 अदत्तन्तु भयक्रोधशोकवेगरुगन्वितैः ।
तथोत्कोचपरीहास-व्यत्यासच्छलयोगतः ॥
वालमूढास्वतन्त्रार्त्त-मत्तोन्मत्तापवर्जितम् ।
कर्त्ता ममायं कर्म्मेति प्रतिलाभेच्छया च यत् ॥
अपात्रे पात्रमित्युक्ते कार्य्ये वा धर्म्मसंयुते ।
यद्दत्तं स्यादविज्ञानाददत्तमिति तत्स्मृतं ॥ Narada, IV. 9,10,11

... ...

89 1 वलाद्दत्तं वलाद्भुक्तं वलाद् यदपि लेखितं ।
सर्व्वान् वलकृतानर्थानकृतान् मनुरब्रवीत् ॥ Manu, VIII. 168.

,, 2 योगाधमनविक्रीतं योगदानप्रतिग्रहं ।
यत्र वाप्युपधिं पश्येत् तत्सर्व्वं विनिवर्त्तयेत् ॥ Manu, VIII. 165.

89 3 येनागामिमनोपाधिविशेषेणाधिविक्रयदानप्रतिग्रहाः
कृतास्तदुपाधिविगमे तान् क्रयादीन् विनिवर्त्तयेत् ॥ Mit. II.12.

91 1 स्वस्थेनार्त्तेनवा दत्तं श्रावितं धर्म्मकारणात् ।
अदत्त्वा तु मृते दाप्यस्तत्सुतो नात्र संशयः ।
दत्तमित्यत्र देयमित्यपरार्कधृतः पाठः । Katyayana cited in Mit. on Yaj. II. 176.

92 1 वाचैव यत्प्रतिज्ञातं कर्म्मणा नोपपादितम् ।
ऋणन्तद्धर्म्मसंयुक्तमिहलोके परत्र च ॥ Harita cited in Vir. on Datta-pradanika.

,, 2 स्वेच्छया यः पतिश्रुत्य ब्राह्मणाय प्रतिग्रहं ।
न दद्यादृणवद्दाप्यः प्राप्नुयात् पूर्व्वसाहसम् ॥ Katyayana, cited in V. Mayukha, on Datta-pradanika.

,, 3 प्रतिश्रुत्याप्यधर्म्मसंयुक्ताय न दद्यात् । Gautama.

95 1 वणिग्वीथीपरिगतं विज्ञातं राजपुरुषैः ।
अविज्ञाताश्रयात् क्रीतं विक्रेता यत्र वाहृतः ।
स्वामिदत्तार्द्धमूल्यं तु प्रगृह्णीयात् स्वकं धनम् । Katyayana, cited in Vira. on Aswamibikraya.

96 1 हृतं प्रणष्टं यो द्रव्यं परहस्तादवाप्नुयात् ।
अनिवेद्य नृपे दण्ड्यः स तु षण्णवतिंपणान् ॥ Yajnavalkya, II. 172.

97 1 क्रेता पण्यं परीक्षेत प्राक्स्वयं गुणदोषतः ।
परीक्ष्याभिमतं क्रीतं विक्रेतुर्नभवेत्पुनः ॥ Narada, IX. 4.

98 1 क्रीत्वामूल्येन यः पण्यं दुष्कृतं मन्यतेक्रयी ।
विक्रेतुः प्रतिदेयं तत्तस्मिन्नेवाह्न्यविक्षतम् ॥ Narada, IX. 2.

द्वितीयेऽह्नि ददत्क्रेता मूल्यात् त्रिंशांशमाहरेत् ।
द्विगुणं तु तृतीयेऽह्नि परतः क्रेतुरेवतत् ॥ Narada IX. 3

,, 2 परिभुक्तन्तु यद्वासः क्लिष्टरूपं मलीमसं ।
सदोषमपितत्क्रीतं विक्रेतु र्नभवेत्पुनः ॥ Narada, IX. 7.

99 1 दत्तमूल्यस्य पण्यस्य विधिरेव प्रकीर्त्तितः । Narada, VIII. 10.
अदत्तेऽन्यत्र समयान्नविक्रेतुरतिक्रमः ।

„ 2 राजदैवोपघातेन पण्येदोषमुपागते । Yajna-valkya, II. 256.
हानिर्व्विक्रेतुरेवासौ याचितस्याप्रयच्छतः ॥

100 1 दीयमानं न ग्टह्णाति क्रीतम्पण्यञ्च यः क्रयी । Narada, VIII. 9
स एवास्य भवेद्दोषो विक्रेतुर्योऽप्रयच्छतः ॥

101 1 क्रयानन्तरं क्रेत्रा न याचितं, विक्रेत्राच न समर्पितं,
जातश्चौराद्युपद्रवस्तत्र द्वयोः समा हानिः । क्रेतृ- Smriti Chandrika
विक्रेत्रोरुभयोरपि याचनानर्पण शैथिल्येन सापराधत्वात् ।

102 1 सत्यङ्कारञ्च यो दत्त्वा यथाकालं न दृश्यते । Vyasa
पण्यम्भवेन्निसृष्टं तद्दीयमानमगृह्णतः ॥

„ „ सत्यङ्कारकृतं द्रव्यं द्विगुणं प्रतिदापयेत् । Yajna. II. 62.

अत्र पण्यद्रव्यस्योत्सर्गः सत्यङ्कारद्रव्यस्योत्सर्गोऽभिमतः । Viramitrodaya.

„ 2 सर्व्वेष्वर्थविवादेषु बलवत्युत्तरा क्रिया । Yajna, II. 23.
आधौ प्रतिग्रहे क्रीते पूर्व्वा तु बलवत्तरा ॥

103 1 पश्यतोऽब्रुवतो भूमेर्हानिर्विंशति वार्षिकी । Yajna II. 24.
परेण भुज्यमानाया धनस्य दशवार्षिकी ॥

104 1 अनागमन्तु यो भुङ्क्ते बहून्यब्दशतान्यपि । Narada, I. 87.
चौरदण्डेन तं पापं दण्डयेत् पृथिवीपतिः ॥

107 1 आर्त्तिकाले स्मर्त्तव्यास्मरणरूपया योग्यानुपलब्ध्या
भोक्तुरागमाभावनिश्चये, पूर्व्वस्वामिनस्त्यागाभावनिश्चये,

तदीय परिग्रहकृत-स्वत्वोत्पत्ति-पूर्व्वस्वामित्वध्वंसावुभावपि
कल्पयितुमशक्याविति मतद्वयमपीदमत्ययुक्तम् । Vira, on possession.

108 1 अजडश्चेदपोगण्डो विषये चास्य भुज्यते ।
भग्नन्तद् व्यवहारेण भोक्ता तद्धनमर्हति ॥ Manu, VIII. 148.

109 1 अध्यासनात् समारभ्य भुक्तिर्यस्याविघातिनी ।
त्रिंशद्वर्षाण्यविच्छिन्ना तस्य तां नविचालयेत् ॥ Vrihaspati, cited in Vir. on Bhukti.

114 1 आधिसीमोपनिक्षेपजड़बालधनैर्विना ।
तथोपनिधिराजस्त्रीश्रोत्रियाणां धनैरपि ॥ Yaj. II. 25.

115 1 सम्प्रीत्या भुज्यमानानि न नश्यन्ति कदाचन ॥ Manu, VIII. 146

116 1 आगमोऽभ्यधिको भोगाद्विना पूर्व्वक्रमागतात् । Yaj. II 27.

117 1 अन्यायेनापि यद्भुक्तं पित्रा पूर्व्वतनैस्त्रिभिः ।
न तच्छक्यमपाकर्त्तुं क्रमात्त्रिपुरुषागतम् ॥ Narada I. 91.

117 2 वर्षाणि विंशतिर्भुक्ता स्वामिनाव्याहतासती ।
भुक्तिः सा पौरुषीभूमेर्द्विगुणाच द्विपौरुषी ॥ Vyasa, cited in Vir. on Bhukti.

117 3 त्रिपौरुषी च त्रिगुणा न तत्रान्वेष्य आगमः ।
वर्षाणि पञ्चविंशन्तु पौरुषो भोग उच्यते ॥ Anonymous cited by Aparарka.

118 1 स्मार्त्तकाले क्रिया भूमेः सागमा भुक्तिरिष्यते ।
अस्मार्त्तेऽनुगमाभावात् क्रमात् त्रिपुरुषागता ॥ Narada, I. 89

Page	Line	Text	Source
26	1	दायशब्देन यद्धनं स्वामिसम्बन्धादेव निमित्तादन्यस्य स्वं भवति तदुच्यते ।	Mitakshara, on Partition
130	1	तस्मात् पैतृके पैतामहे च द्रव्ये जन्मनैव स्वत्वम् ।	Mitakshara, on Partition
136	1	स्थावरेतु स्वार्ज्जिते पित्रादिप्राप्ते च पुत्रादिपारतन्त्र्यमेव ।	Mit. I. i.27. as in Colebrooke.
137	1	सकृदुच्चरितः शब्दः सकृदर्थं गमयति इति ।	Nyaya
137	2	स्थावरादौ तु स्वार्ज्जिते पित्रादि परम्पराप्राप्ते च पुत्रादिपारतन्त्र्यं तुल्यमेव ।	Vira. I. 30. G. Sastri's Edn.
137	3	मणिमुक्ताप्रवालानां सर्व्वस्यैव पिता प्रभुः । स्थावरस्य तु सर्व्वस्य न पिता न पितामहः ॥	Yajnavalkya cited in Daya bhaga. II 22.
145	1	एकदेशोपात्तस्यैव भूहिरण्यादावुत्पन्नस्य स्वत्वस्य विनिगमनाप्रमाणाभावेन वैशेषिकव्यवहारानर्हतया अव्यवस्थितस्य गुटिकापातादिना व्यञ्जनं विभागः विशेषेण भजनं स्वत्वज्ञापनं वा विभागः । (पुरुषविशेष निरूपितांशविशेषनिष्ठत्वेन इत्यर्थः इति श्रीकृष्णः) ।	Dayabhaga. I. 8&9. as in Colebrooke.
145	2	विभागोनाम द्रव्यसमुदायविषयाणामनेकस्वाम्यानां तदेकदेशेषु द्रव्यस्य व्यवस्थापनम् ।	Mit. I. 4.
150	1	स्वं दद्यादित्यनेन चास्वभूतानामन्वाहितयाचितकाधिसाधारणनिक्षेपाणां पञ्चानामप्यदेयत्वं व्यतिरेकतो दर्शितम् ।	Mit. on Yaj. II. 175.
153	8	अदेयं यश्च गृह्णाति यश्चादेयं प्रयच्छति । तावुभौ चौरवच्छास्यौ दाप्यौ चोत्तमसाहसम् ॥	Manu cited in Vira. on Datta pradanika.

161	2	अथैतासां स्मृतीनां न्यायमूलत्वे सत्यपि तद्भोग्य पार्व्वणदातरि तस्य गङ्गायामस्थिप्रक्षेप्तुर्गयायां पिण्ड-दातुर्वा उदासीनस्याधिकारापत्तिः ।	Srikrishna on Daya XI. vi.33.
176	1	विस्रम्भहेतू द्वावत्र प्रतिभूराधिरेव च ।	Narada, I. 117
176	2	आधिर्नाम गृहीतस्य द्रव्यस्योपरि विश्वासार्थं अधमर्णेनोत्तमर्णोऽधिक्रियते, आधीयते इति आधिः ।	Mit. on Yaj. II. 57.
177	1	अधिक्रियते इत्याधिः स विज्ञेयो द्विलक्षणः । कृतकालोपनेयश्च यावद्देयोद्यतस्तथा ॥ स पुनर्द्विविधः प्रोक्तो गोप्यो भोग्यस्तथैव च ।	Narada. I. 124.
177	2	आधिर्बन्धः समाख्यातः स च प्रोक्तश्चतुर्विधः । जङ्गमः स्थावरश्चैव गोप्यो भोग्यस्तथैव च । यादृच्छिकः सावधिश्च लेख्यारूढोऽथसाक्षिवान् ॥	Vrihaspati cited in Vira. on Adhi.
181	1	आधेः स्वीकरणात् सिद्धिः ।	Yaj. II. 60
181	2	आधिस्तु द्विविधः प्रोक्तः स्थावरो जङ्गमस्तथा । सिद्धिरस्योभयस्यापि भोगो यद्यस्ति नान्यथा ।	Narada I. 139.
		गोप्याधौ भोगः स्वीकारः भोग्याधौ फलभोगः ।	Vira.
185	2	आधिर्बन्धः समाख्यातः सच प्रोक्तश्चतुर्विधः ।	Vrihaspati cited in Vira. on Adhi.
185	3	आधानं विक्रयो दानं लेख्यसाक्षिकृतं तथा । एकक्रियाविरुद्धन्तु लेख्यन्तत्रापहारकम् ॥	Katyayana cited in Vira. on Adhi.

186 2 वाल्येधिष्ठितराजपण्डितपदः शीतांशुविम्बोज्ज्वल
च्छत्रोत्सिक्तमहामहत्त्वगुपदं दत्त्वानवे यौवने ।
यस्मै यौवनशेषयोग्यमखिलक्ष्मापालनारायणः ।
श्रीमांल्लक्ष्मणसेनदेवनृपतिधर्म्माधिकारं ददौ ॥ Halayudha.

188 यावत्तावकमृणं न शोध्यते तावदेतद् गृहक्षेत्रादेदनां
विक्रयाधिकरणाद्यहं न करिष्यामीति निर्वन्धोवन्धः । Vyavahara-mayukha, on Rinadan.

189 1 परिपूर्णं गृहीत्वाधिं वन्धं वा साधुलग्नकम् ।
लेख्यारूढं साक्षिमद्वा ऋणं दद्याद्धनी सदा । Vrihaspat cited in Vira, on Rinadan

189 निक्षेपो मितहस्तस्थो वन्धो विश्वासकःस्मृतः Narada cited in Vira. on Nikshepa.

189 3 दर्शने प्रत्यये दाने प्रातिभाव्यं विधीयते । Yaj. II.53.

191 1 हिरण्ये द्विगुणीभूते पूर्णकाले कृतेऽवधौ ।
वन्धकस्य धनीस्वामी द्विसमाहं प्रतीक्षते ।
तदन्तराधनं दत्त्वा ऋणीवन्धमवाप्नुयात् ॥ Vyasa & Vrihas cited in Vira. on Adhi.

192 1 आधिःप्रणश्येद्द्विगुणे धने यदि न मोक्ष्यते ।
काले कालकृतोनश्येत् फलभोग्यो न नश्यति ॥ Yaj. II. 58,

196 1 हिरण्ये द्विगुणीभूते मृतेनष्टेऽधमर्णिके ।
द्रव्यन्तदीयं संगृह्य विक्रीणीत ससाक्षिकं ॥
रवेद्वाकृतमूल्यन्तु दद्याद्वज्जनसंसदि ।
ऋणानुरूपं परतो गृह्णीतान्यत्तुवर्जयेत् ॥ Vrihaspati cited in Vira. on Adhi.

196 2 आधाता यत्रनैवास्याद्धनी बन्धं निवेदयेत् ।
राज्ञस्ततः स विख्यातो विक्रेय इति धारणा ॥ Katyayana cited in Vira. on Adhi.
सवृद्धिकं गृहीत्वातु शेषं राज्ञे समर्पयेत् ॥

197 * नचाधेः कालसंरोधान्निसर्गोऽस्ति न विक्रयः। Manu. VIII. 143.

198 1 अत्र तु सर्व्वदेशीयशिष्टाचारविरोधः बन्धकीकृत
भूम्यादेरन्यत्राधीकरणसमाचारात् । Kulluka. on Manu VIII. 143

199 1 राजदैवोपघातेन यत्राधिर्नाशमाप्नुयात् । Vrihaspati cited in Vira. on Adhi.
तत्रान्यद्दापयेद्बन्धं धनभागाधनी भवेत् ॥

200 1 गोप्याधिभोगेनो वृद्धिः सोपकारेऽथहापिते ।
नष्टोदेयो विनष्टश्च दैवराजकृताद्दृते ॥ Yaj. II. 59.

अल्पेऽप्युपभोगे महत्यपि वृद्धिर्हातव्या समयातिक्रमात् । Mit. on same.

201 1 आधिमेकं द्वयोर्यस्तु कुर्य्यात् का प्रतिपद्भवेत् । Katyayana. cited in Vira. on Adhi.
तयोः पूर्व्वकृतं ग्राह्यं तत्कर्त्ता चोरदण्डभाक् ॥

202 1 आधौ प्रतिग्रहे क्रीते पूर्व्वातु बलवत्तरा Yaj. II. 23.

204 1 ययोर्निक्षिप्त आधिस्तौ विवदेतां यदा नरौ । Vishnu cited i Vira. o Adhi
यस्यभुक्तिर्जयस्तस्य बलात्कार कृतंविना ॥

205 1 गोप्याधौ भोगः स्वीकारो भोग्याधौ फलभोगः । Vira. on Adhi.

स्वीकरणञ्च भोग्याधौ भोगपर्य्यन्तं गोप्याधौ तु
भाण्डागारप्रवेशपर्य्यन्तं ।

209 1 ददतो यन्नवेत् पुण्यं हेमकूप्याम्वरादिकं ।
तत्स्यात् पालयतो न्यासं यथैव शरणागतं ॥
भर्त्तृद्रोहे यथानार्य्याः पुंस पुत्त्रसुहृद्दधे ।
दोषो भवेत्तथान्यासे भक्षितोपेक्षिते नृणां ॥
न्यासद्रव्यं न गृह्णीयात्तन्नाशस्त्वयशस्करः ।
गृहीतं पालयेद् यत्नात् सक्कद् याचितमर्पयेत् ॥

Vrihaspati cited in Vira. on Nikshepa.

211 1 ग्रहीतुः सह योऽर्थेन नष्ट एव स दायिनः ।
दैवराजकृते तद्दत् चेत्तज्जिह्मकारितं ॥

Narada cited in Vira. on Nikshepa

212 1 ज्ञात्वा द्रव्यवियोगन्तु दाता यत्र विनिक्षिपेत् ।
सर्व्वोपायविनाशेऽपि ग्रहीता नैव दाप्यते ॥

Katyayana cited in Vira. on Nikshepa.

219 1 भक्षितं सोदयन्दाप्यः समन्दाप्यमुपेक्षितं ।
किञ्चिन्न्यूनं प्रदाप्यः स्याद्द्रव्यमज्ञाननाशितं ॥

Katyayana cited in Mit. on Yaj. II. 66

220 1 याचनान्तरं नाशे दैवराजकृतेऽपिसः ।
ग्रहीता प्रतिदाप्यःस्यान्मूल्यमात्रंनसंशयः ।
प्रत्यर्पणविलम्वमात्रापराधे सवृद्धिकदानस्या-
न्याय्यत्वात् ।

Vyasa cited on Nikshepa in Vira.

221 1 यदि तत्कार्य्यमुद्दिश्य कालम्परिनियम्य वा ।
याचितोऽदत्तकृतो यस्मिन्नप्राप्ते न तु दाप्यते ।

Katyayana cited in Vira. on Nikshepa.

221 2 अथकार्य्यविपत्तिस्तु तस्यैव स्वामिनो भवेत् ।
अप्राप्ते वै सकालेतु दाप्यस्त्वदत्तकृतेऽपितत् ।

Katyayana cited in Vira. on Nikshepa.

222 1 स्थापितं येन विधिना येन यच्च यथाविधि । Vrihaspati cited in Vira. on Nikshepa.

तथैव तस्य तद्देयं न देयं प्रत्यनन्तरे ॥

स्थापयितेतरस्य यस्य स्थापितद्रव्यत्वमस्ति स इह प्रत्यनन्तर उच्यते ।

इति स्मृतिचन्द्रिकायां, प्रत्यनन्तरे पुत्रादाविति कल्पतरौ ॥ Vira. on Nikshepa.

,, 2 मिथोदायः कृतो येन गृहीतो मिथ एव वा ।

मिथ एव प्रदातव्यो यथादायस्तथाग्रहः ॥ Manu VIII. 195

223 1 ग्रामेच्छया गोप्रचारो भूमी राजवशेन वा । Yaj. II. 166.

224 1 धनुःशतं परीणाहो ग्रामक्षेत्रान्तरं भवेत् ।

द्वेशते खर्वटस्य स्यान्नगरस्य चतुःशतं ॥ Yaj. II. 167.

,, 2 धनुःशतं परीहारो ग्रामस्य स्यात् समन्ततः । Manu VIII 237

,, 3 ग्रामेच्छया गोप्रचारो भूमीराजवशेन वा । Yaj. II.166.

यान्त्यायान्ति जना येन पशवश्चानिवारिताः । Vrihaspati cited in Vira, on Simavivada.

तदुच्यते संसरणं न रोद्धव्यन्तु केनचित् ।

सर्व्वे जनाः सदा येन प्रयान्ति स चतुष्पथः । Katyayana cited in same.

अनिषिद्धा यथा कालं राजमार्गः स उच्यते ॥

,, ,, अवस्करस्थलश्वभ्रभ्रमस्यन्दनिकादिभिः । Narada cited in same.

चतुष्पथसुरस्थानराजमार्गान् न रोधयेत् ॥

228 1 न निषेध्योऽल्पबाधस्तु सेतुः कल्याणकारकः ।

परभूमिं हरन् कूपः स्वल्पक्षेत्रो बहूदकः ॥ Y II. 156

228 2 परक्षेत्रस्य मध्ये तु सेतुर्न प्रतिषिध्यते।
महागुणोऽल्पदोषश्चेद्वृद्धिरिष्टाक्षये सति॥ Narada, XI. 17

231 1 यादृशं फलमाप्नोति कुप्लवैः सन्तरन् जलं।
तादृशं फलमाप्नोति कुपुत्रैः सन्तरंस्तमः॥ Manu, IX. 161

236 1 औरसः क्षेत्रजश्चैव दत्तः कृत्रिमकः सुतः। Manu, IX. 159

,, 2 दत्तौरसेतरेषान्तु पुत्रत्वेन परिग्रहः।

* * * * * *

इमानि लोकगुप्त्यर्थं कलेरादौ महात्मभिः।
निवर्त्तितानि कर्म्माणि व्यवस्थापूर्ब्बकं बुधैः
समयश्चापि साधूनां प्रमाणं वेदवद्भवेत्॥ Aditya Purana cited in Udvaha-tattva.

,, 3 दत्तपदं कृत्रिमस्याप्युपलक्षणं। Dattaka Mimansa.

237 1 स्वे क्षेत्रे संस्कृतायान्तु स्वयमुत्पादयेद्धि यं।
तमौरसं विजानीयात् पुत्रं प्रथमकल्पितं॥ Manu IX. 166

238 1 माता पिता वा दद्यातां यमद्भिः पुत्रमापदि।
सदृशं प्रीतिसंयुक्तं स ज्ञेयो दत्रिमः सुतः॥ Manu, IX. 168

244 1 न स्त्री पुत्रं दद्यात् प्रतिगृह्णीयाद्वा अन्यत्रानु-
ज्ञानाद्भर्त्तुः। Vasistha. Ch. XV.

245 1 भर्त्तरि जीवति भार्य्यया स्वातन्त्र्येण तदनुमतौ न—
पुत्रीकरणीय इति भर्त्तुरनुज्ञानादन्यत्रेत्यस्यार्थः।
मृतेतु तस्मिन् यत्पारतन्त्र्यन्तदनुमतिरेवापेक्षिता।
एवं सति दृष्टार्थता भवति प्रतिषेधस्य। तस्मात्
दत्तानुज्ञे मृतेऽपि भर्त्तरि भार्य्यया दत्तकादिकरण
मविरुद्धं॥ Vira. G. Sastri Edn, II, ii.

248 1 माता पिता वा दद्यातां यमद्भिः पुत्रमापदि ।
सदृशं प्रीतिसंयुक्तं स ज्ञेयो दत्रिमः सुतः ॥ Manu, IX. 168

249 1 नत्वेकं पुत्रं दद्यात् प्रतिगृह्णीयाद्वा स हि सन्तानाय
पूर्व्वेषां । Vasishtha.

251 3 भार्य्यापुत्रश्च दासश्च शिष्यो भ्राता च सोदरः ।
प्राप्तापराधास्ताड्याः स्यूरज्ज्वा वेणुदलेन वा ॥
पृष्ठतस्तु शरीरस्य नोत्तमाङ्गे कथञ्चन ॥ Manu, VIII 299, 300.

252 1 शिष्यशिष्टिरवधेनाशक्तौ रज्जुवेणुविदलाभ्यामतनुभ्या-
मन्योन्यं घ्नन् राज्ञा शास्यः । Gautama.

शुक्रशोनितसम्भवः पुत्रः मातापितृनिमित्तकः ।
तस्यचप्रदानविक्रयत्यागेषु मातापितरौ प्रभवतः ॥ Vasistha. Ch. XV.

स्वं कुटुम्बाविरोधेन देयं दारसुतादृते । Yaj. II. 175.

253 1 निक्षेपंपुत्रदारांश्चसर्व्वस्वं चान्वये सति ।
आपत्स्वपि च कष्टासु वर्त्तमानेन देहिना ।
अदेयान्याहुराचार्य्या यच्चान्यस्मैप्रतिश्रुतं ॥ Narada IV. 4,5.

विक्रयश्चैवदानश्च न नेयाः स्युसुनिच्छवः ।
दाराः पुत्राश्च सर्व्वस्वमात्मन्येव च योजयेत् ।
आपत्काले प्रकर्त्तव्यं दानं विक्रय एव च ।
अन्यथा न प्रवर्त्तेत इति शास्त्रेषु धारणा ॥ Katayyana cited in Smriti-Chandrika.

257 1 यस्यां मनश्चक्षुषोर्निबन्धस्तस्यामृद्धिः । Apastamba

259 1 भार्य्यापुत्रश्च दासश्च त्रय एवाधनाः स्मृताः । M cited by Jimutavahana.
यत्ते समधिगच्छन्ति यस्यैते तस्यतद्धनं ॥

261 1 ऋणं पुत्रकृतं पिता न देयमितिधर्म्मतः । Katyayana cited in Vira. on Pratibhu,
देयं प्रतिश्रुतं यत्स्याद् यच्चस्यादनुमोदितं ॥

पितुरेवनियोगाद्वा कुटुम्बभरणाय वा ।
कृतं वा यदृणं कृच्छ्रे दद्यात् पुत्रस्य तत्पिता ।
„ 2 वृद्धौ च मातापितरौ साध्वीभार्य्या सुतः शिशुः । Narada cited in Vira. on Pratibhu.
अप्यकार्य्यशतं कृत्वा भर्त्तव्या मनुरब्रवीत् ॥

262 1 सौराक्षिकं वृथादानं कामक्रोध प्रतिश्रुतं ।
प्रातिभाव्यं दण्डशुल्कावशेषं पुत्रो नदापयेत् ॥ Vrihaspati

„ 2 नाप्राप्तव्यवहारेण पितर्य्युपरते क्वचित् । Katyayana cited in Viramitrodaya.
कालेतु विधिना देयं वसेयुर्नरकेऽन्यथा ।

263 1 कन्याप्येवं पालनीया शिक्षणीयातियत्नतः ।
देया वराय विदुषे धनरत्नसमन्विता ।

„ 2 पिता पितामहोभ्राता सकुल्यो जननी तथा ।
कन्याप्रदः पूर्व्वनाशे प्रकृतिस्थः परः परः ॥ Yaj. I. 63

264 1 काममामरणात् तिष्ठेत् गृहेकन्यर्त्तुमत्यपि ।
नत्वेवैनां प्रयच्छेत्तु गुणहीनाय कर्हिचित् ॥ Manu, IX. 89

„ 2 गुरोःशिष्ये पितुःपुत्रे दम्पत्योः स्वामिभृत्ययोः ।
विरोधेऽपि मिथस्तेषां व्यवहारो नसिध्यति ॥

265 2 गुरुञ्चैवाप्युपासीत स्वाध्यायार्थं समाहितः ।
आहूतश्चाप्यधीयीत लब्धं तस्मै निवेदयेत् ॥
हितं तस्याचरेन्नित्यं मनोवाक्कायकर्म्मभिः ॥ Yaj. I. 26,27.

272 1 पाणिग्रहणिका मन्त्रा नियतं दारलक्षणं ।
तेषां निष्ठातु विज्ञेया विद्वद्भिः सप्तमे पदे ॥ Manu, VIII. 227.

,, 2 महान्त्यपि समृद्धानि गोऽजाविधनधान्यतः ।
स्त्रीसम्बन्धे दशैतानि कुलानि परिवर्जयेत् ॥
हीनक्रियं निष्पुरुषं निश्छन्दो रोमशार्शसम् ।
क्षयामयाव्यपस्मारिश्वित्रिकुष्ठिकुलानि च ॥ Manu, III. 6.

1 येषां पुनर्दृष्टगुणदोषमूलकं, विधिनिषेधाभिधानं
यथा हीनक्रियमिति, नतदतिक्रमे भार्य्यात्वाभावः । Kulluka on Manu, III. 11

न सगोत्रां समान प्रवरां भार्य्यां विन्देत Vasishtha.

175 पिता रक्षति कौमारे भर्त्ता रक्षति यौवने ।
पुत्त्रस्तुस्थविरे भावे न स्त्री स्वातन्त्र्यमर्हति ॥
रक्षन्ति स्थविरे पुत्रा इत्यपि पाठः । Manu, IX.3

रक्षेत् कन्यां पिताविन्नां पतिःपुत्रास्तु वार्द्धके ।
अभावे ज्ञातयस्तेषां न स्वातन्त्र्यं क्वचित्स्त्रियाः ॥ Yaj. I. 85.

276 1 यत्र नार्य्यस्तु पूज्यन्ते रमन्ते तत्र देवताः ।
यत्रैतास्तु न पूज्यन्ते सर्व्वास्तत्राफलाः क्रियाः ॥
शोचन्ति जामयो यत्र विनश्यत्याशु तत्कुलं ।
न शोचन्ति तु यत्रैता वर्द्धते तद्धि सर्व्वदा ।

सन्तुष्टो भार्य्यया भर्त्ता भर्त्रा भार्य्या तथैवच ।
यस्मिन्नेव कुलेनित्यं कल्याणं तत्र वै ध्रुवं ॥ Manu, III. 56,57,60.

276 2 प्रजनार्थं महाभागाः पूजार्हा गृहदीप्तयः ।
स्त्रियः श्रियश्च गेहेषु न विशेषोऽस्तिकश्चनः ॥ Manu, IX. 26.

न निष्क्रयविसर्गाभ्यां भर्त्तुर्भार्य्या विमुच्यते । Manu, IX. 46.

277 1 काममन्तु क्षपयेद्देहं पुष्पमूलफलैःशुभैः ।
नतु नामापि गृह्णीयात् पत्यौ प्रेते परस्यतु ॥
आसीतामरणात्क्षान्ता नियताब्रह्मचारिणी ।
यो धर्म्म एकपत्नीनां काङ्क्षन्ती तमनुत्तमम् ॥ Manu, V. 157,158.

,, 2 न द्वितीयश्च साध्वीनां क्वचिद्भर्त्तोपदिश्यते । Manu, V. 162.

एवञ्च सति पुनर्भूत्वमपि प्रतिषिद्धं इति । Kulluka on the above.

278 1 नष्टे मृते प्रव्रजिते क्लीवे च पतिते पतौ ।
पञ्चस्वापत्सुनारीणां पतिरन्यो विधीयते ॥ Parasara, IV. 28.

न विवाहविधावुक्तं विधवावेदनं पुनः । Manu.

279 1 ऊढायाः पुनरुद्वाहं ज्येष्ठांशं गोवधं तथा ।
कलौ पञ्च न कुर्व्वीत भ्रातृजायां कमण्डलुं ॥ Adipurana.

,, 2 या पत्या वा परित्यक्ता विधवा वा स्वयेच्छया ।
उत्पादयेत् पुनर्भूत्वा स पौनर्भव उच्यते ।
सा चेदक्षतयोनिः स्याद् गतप्रत्यागतापिवा ।
पौनर्भवेन भर्त्रा सा पुनः संस्कारमर्हति ॥ Manu, IX. 175,176.

280 1 प्रतिपन्नं स्त्रिया देयं पत्या वा सह यत्कृतं ।
स्वयं कृतं वा यदृणं नान्यत् स्त्री दातुमर्हति । Yaj. II. 49

,, 1 गोपशौण्डिकशैलूष रजकव्याधयोषितां ।
ऋणं दद्यात्पतिस्तासां यस्माद्वृत्तिस्तदाश्रया ॥ Yaj. II. 48

281 1 वन्ध्याष्टमेऽधिवेद्याब्दे दशमे तु मृतप्रजाः ।
एकादशे स्त्रीजननी सद्यस्त्वप्रियवादिनी ॥ Manu, IX. 81

282 1 आधिविन्नस्त्रियै दद्यादाधिवेदनिकं समम् ।
न दत्तं स्त्रीधनं यस्यै दत्ते त्वर्द्धं प्रकीर्त्तितं ॥ Yaj. II. 148

,, 2 या रोगिणी स्यात्तु हिता सम्पन्ना चैव शीलतः ।
सानुज्ञाप्याधिवेत्तव्या नावमान्या तु कर्हिचित् ॥ Manu, IX. 82

,, 3 अधिविन्ना तु या नारी निर्गच्छेद्रुषिता गृहात् ।
सा सद्यः सन्निरोधव्या त्याज्या वा कुलसन्निधौ ॥ Manu, IX. 83

285 1 प्राप्तं शिल्पैस्तु यद्वित्तं प्रीत्याचैव यदन्यतः ।
भर्त्तुः स्वाम्यं भवेत्तत्र शेषन्तु स्त्रीधनं स्मृतम् ॥ Katyayana, cited in Dayabhaga.

287 1 न चैवगृहदासानां दानाधमनविक्रयाः ।
अस्वतन्त्रकृताःसिद्धिं प्राप्नुयुर्णानुवर्णिता ॥ Katyayana, cited in Viramitrodaya.

सौदायिके सदास्त्रीणां स्वातन्त्र्यं परिकीर्त्तितं ।
विक्रये चैव दानेच यथेष्टं स्थावरेष्वपि ॥ Katyayana, cited in Dayabhaga.

291 1 सकृत्प्रदीयते कन्या हरंस्तां चौरदण्डभाक् ।
दत्तामपि हरेत् पूर्व्वाच्छ्रेयांश्चेद्वर आव्रजेत् ॥ Yaj. I. 65.

" 2 दत्त्वा न्यायेन यः कन्यां वराय न ददाति तां ।
अदुष्टश्चेद्वरो राज्ञा स दण्ड्यस्तत्र चौरवत्॥ Narada, XII. 32.

292 1 यस्तु दोषवतीं कन्यां मनाख्यायोपपादयेत् ।
तस्य तद्वितथं कुर्य्यात् कन्यादातुर्दुरात्मनः ॥ Manu, IX. 73

" 2 प्रतिगृह्य तु यः कन्यामदुष्टामुत्सृजेन्नरः ।
सविनेयस्त्वकामोऽपि कन्यां तामेव चोद्वहेत् ॥

293 2 स्वतन्त्रस्यात्मनो दानाद्दासत्वं दारवद्भृगुः ॥ Katyayana cited in V. Mayukha on Slavery etc.

294 1 ध्वजाहृतो भक्तदासो गृहजःक्रीतदत्रिमौ ।
पैत्रिको दण्डदासश्च सप्तैते दासयोनयः ॥ Manu VIII. 415.

296 1 यश्चैषां स्वामिनं कश्चिन्मोचयेत् प्राणसंशयात् ।
दासत्वात् स विमुच्येत पुत्रभागं लभेत च ॥ Narada, V. 30.

" 2 चौरापहृतविक्रीता ये च दासीकृता वलात् ।
राज्ञा मोचयितव्यास्ते दास्यन्तेषु हि नेष्यते ॥ Narada, IV. 38.

298 1 विक्रीणमानां यो भर्त्ता दासीं विक्रेतुमिच्छति ।
अनापदिस्थः शक्तः सन प्राप्नुयाद् द्विगतं दमं ॥ Katyayana cited in Vira, on Slavery.

299 1 स्वतन्त्रोऽपि हि यत्कार्य्यं कुर्य्यादप्रकृतिं गतः ।
तदप्यकृतमेवाहुरस्वातन्त्र्यस्य हेतुतः ॥ Narada, I. 40.
कामक्रोधाभिभूतार्त्तभयव्यसनपीड़िताः ।
रागद्वेषपरीताश्च-ज्ञेयास्त्वप्रकृतिंगताः ॥ Narada, I. 41.

300 1 गर्भस्थैः सदृशो ज्ञेय आष्टमाद्वत्सराच्छिशुः ।
बाल आषोडशाद्वर्षात् पौगण्डश्चापि शब्द्यते ॥
परतो व्यवहारज्ञः स्वतन्त्रः पितरावृते । Narada, III. 35,36.

" 3. अप्राप्तव्यवहारा बालकाः पञ्चदशवर्षानधिकवयस्काः ॥ Srikrishna on Dayabhaga, III. 1. 17

301 1 तयोरपि पिता श्रेयान् बीजप्राधान्यदर्शनात् ।
अभावे बीजिनो माता तदभावे तु पूर्व्वजः । Narada cited in Vira. on Kriyapada.

" 2 बालदायादिकं रिक्थं तावद्राजानुपालयेत् ।
यावत् स स्यात्समावृत्तो यावच्चातीतशैशवः ॥ Manu, VIII. 27

305 1 जायमानो हि वै ब्राह्मणः, त्रिभिर्ऋणैः ऋणवान्
जायते । ब्रह्मचर्य्येण ऋषिभ्यो यज्ञेन देवेभ्यः प्रजया-
पितृभ्यः । एष वा अनृणो यः पुत्री, यज्वा ब्रह्मचारी च ॥ Sruti.

306 1 वृद्धिञ्च भ्रूणहत्याञ्च तुलया समतोलयन् ।
अतिष्ठद् भ्रूणहा कोट्यां वार्द्धुषिर्व्यकम्पत ह । Vasishtha.

कामं वा परिलुप्तकृत्याय पापीयसे दद्यात् ।

ब्राह्मणः क्षत्रियो वापि वृद्धिं नैव प्रयोजयेत् ।
कामन्तु खलु धर्म्मार्थं दद्यात् पापीयसेऽल्पिकां ॥ Manu, X. 117

307 1 ऋणिकेन तु या वृद्धिरधिका सम्प्रकल्पिता ।
आपत्कालकृता नित्यं दातव्या सा तु कारिता ।
अन्यथा कारिता वृद्धिर्न दातव्या कथञ्चन ॥ Vrihaspati cited in Vira, on Rinadan.

308 1 यो गृहीत्वा धनं पूर्व्वं श्वो दास्यामीति सामकम् । Vishnu cited in same.
न दद्याल्लोभतः पश्चात् तदहाद्‌वृद्धिमाप्नुयात् ॥

न वृद्धिः प्रीतिदत्तानां स्यादनाकारिता क्वचित् । Narada, I. 108
अनाकारितमप्यूर्द्ध्वं वत्सरार्द्धाद्विवर्द्धते ॥

वृद्धिं दद्युर्वत्सरातिक्रमे यथाभिहितामिति । Vishnu, cited in Vira, on Rinadan.

प्रीतिदत्तं न वर्द्धेत यावन्न प्रतियाचितं । Katyayana, cited in

311 1 कुसीदवृद्धिर्द्वैगुण्यं नात्येति सकृदाहृता । Manu, VIII. 151

312 1 तथा च याज्ञवल्क्यः—दीयमानं न गृह्णाति प्रयुक्तं यत्स्वकं धनं । मध्यस्थस्थापितं तत्स्यात् वर्द्धते न ततः परं । इति । मध्यस्थस्थापितमिति विशेषणेनाधमर्णो यदि स्वनिकटे स्थापयति तदा भवत्येववृद्धिरिति वीरमित्रोदयः । Viramitrodaya.

313 1 धर्म्मेण व्यवहारेण छलेनाचरितेन च ।
प्रयुक्तं साधयेदर्थं पञ्चमेन बलेन च ॥ Manu, VIII. 49

314 1 प्रपन्नं साधयन्नर्थं न वाच्यो नृपतेर्भवेत् ।
साध्यमानो नृपं गच्छन् दण्ड्योदाप्यश्च तद्धनं । Yaj. II. 40

„ 2 पीड़येत्तु धनी यत्र ऋणिकं न्यायवादिनं । Katyayana, cited in V. Mayukha on Rinadan.
तस्मादर्थात् स हीयेत तत्समं चाप्नुयाद्दमं ॥

न रोद्धव्यः क्रियावादी सन्दिग्धेऽर्थे कथञ्चन । Vrihaspati, cited in Vira, on Pratibhu.
आवेधयंस्त्वनासेध्यन्दण्ड्यो भवति धर्म्मतः ॥

315 1 अर्थेऽपव्ययमानन्तु करणेन विभावितं ।
दापयेद्धनिकस्यार्थं दण्डलेशञ्च शक्तितः ॥ Manu, VIII. 51

,, 2 धनदानासहं बुद्ध्वा स्वाधीनं कर्म्म कारयेत् ।
अशक्तौ बन्धनागारे प्रवेश्यो ब्राह्मणादृते ॥ Katyayana, cited in Vira, on Rinadan,

अत्र कर्म्मकरणाशक्तौ बन्धनागारे प्रवेशाभिधानं सामर्थ्योत्पत्तौ कथञ्चिदृणप्राप्त्यर्थमित्यभिहितं स्मृतिचन्द्रिकायां ॥ Smriti-Chandrika.

,, 3 यदि स्यादादावनादिष्टमशुभं कर्म्मकारयेत् ।
प्राप्नुयात् साहसं पूर्व्वमृणान्मुच्येत चर्णिकः ॥ Katyayana, cited in Vira, on Rinadan.

अथशक्तिविहीनः स्यादृणी कालविपर्य्ययात् ।
316 1 अशक्त्यपेक्ष्यमृणान्दाप्यः काले काले यथोदयं ॥ Narada, I, 161

317 2 यदातु न सकुल्याः स्युर्न च सम्बन्धिवान्धवाः
तदा दद्याद्द्विजेभ्यस्तु तेष्वसत्स्वप्सु निक्षिपेत् ॥ Narada, I, 113

वन्धभावेतु विप्रेभ्यो देयं क्षिप्यं जलेऽपिवा । Prajapati.

318 1 रिक्थग्राह ऋणं दाप्योयोषिद्ग्राहस्तथैवच ।
पुत्त्रोऽनन्याश्रितद्रव्यः पुत्त्रहीनस्य रिक्थिनः । Yaj. II. 51

319 1 पित्रं पूर्व्वमृणं देयं पश्चादात्मीयमेवच ।
तयोः पैतामहं पूर्व्वं देयमेवं ऋणं सदा ॥ Vrihaspati, cited in Vira, on Rinadan,

,, 2 गृहीतानुक्रमाद्दाप्यो धनिनामधमर्णिकः ।
दत्त्वा तु ब्राह्मणायैव नृपतेस्तदनन्तरं ॥ Yaj. II. 41

319 3 यस्य द्रव्येण यत्पण्यं साधितं यो विभावयेत् ।
तद्द्रव्यमृणिकेनैव दातव्यं तस्य नान्यथा ॥ Katyayana, cited in Vira, on same.

320 1 दर्शने प्रत्यये दाने प्रतिभाव्यं विधीयते । Yaj. II. 53

,, 2 दर्शने प्रत्यये दाने ऋणिद्रव्यार्पणे तथा ।
चतुःप्रकारः प्रतिभूः शास्त्रे दृष्टो मनीषिभिः । Vrihaspati, cited in Vira, on Pratibhu.

,, 3 आहैको दर्शयामीति साधुरित्यपरोऽब्रवीत् ।
दाताहमेतद्द्रविणमर्पयाम्यपरोऽब्रवीत् ॥ Vrihaspati, cited in same.

321 1 अभये प्रत्यये दाने उपस्थाने प्रदर्शने ।
पञ्चस्वेषु प्रकारेषु ग्राह्योहि प्रतिभूर्बुधैः । Harita cited in same.

322 1 दर्शनप्रतिभूर्यत्र मृतप्रात्ययिकोऽपि वा ।
न तत्पुत्रा ऋणं दद्युर्दद्युर्दानाय यः स्थितः ॥ Yaj. II. 54

,, 2 यत्तुयोगोश्वरेण प्रतिभुवस्त्रैविध्यमुक्तं, दर्शने प्रत्यये, दाने, प्रातिभाव्यं विधीयते । तद्दानार्पणयोरनति-भेदाभिप्रायेण । इति । Vira.

,, 3 आद्यौ तु वितथे दाप्यौ तत्कालावेदितं धनं ।
उत्तरौतु विसम्वादे तौ विना तत्सुतौ तथा ॥ Vrihaspati, cited in Vira, on Pratibhu.

323 2 प्रातिभाव्यागतं पौत्रैर्दातव्यं न तु तत्क्वचित् ।
पुत्रेणापि समं देयं ऋणं सर्व्वत्र पैत्रिकं ॥ Katyayana, cited in same.

ऋणं पैतामहं पौत्रः प्रातिभाव्यागतं सुतः !
समंदद्यात् तत्सुतौ तु न दाप्याविति निश्चयः ॥ Vyasa, cited in same.

323 2 गृहीत्वा बन्धकं यत्र दर्शनेऽस्य स्थितोभवेत् । Katyayana, cited in same.
विनापित्रा धनात्तस्माद्दाप्यः स्यात्तदृणं सुतः ॥

,, 3 नात्यन्तम्पीड़नीयाः स्युः ऋणं दाप्याः शनैः शनैः । Vrihaspati, cited in same.

,, 4 बहवः स्युर्यदि स्वांशैर्दद्युः प्रतिभुवोधनं ।
एकच्छायाश्रितेष्वेषु धनिकस्य यथारुचि ॥ Yaj. II. 55

324 1 यस्यार्थे येन यद्दत्तं विधिनाभ्यर्थिते न तु । Katyayana, cited in Vira. on same.
साक्षिभिर्भावितेनैव प्रतिभूस्तत्समाप्नुयात् ॥

,, 2 यस्यार्थं प्रतिभूर्दद्याद् धनिकेनोपपीड़ितः ।
ऋणिकस्तं प्रतिभुवे द्विगुणं प्रतिदापयेत् ॥ Narada, I. 121

,, 3 भृत्याय वेतनं दद्यात् कर्म्मस्वामी यथाक्रमं ।
आदौ मध्येऽवसाने तु कर्म्मणो यद्विनिश्चितं ॥ Narada, VI. 2

325 1 देशं कालञ्च योऽतीयाल्लाभं कुर्य्याच्च योऽन्यथा ।
तत्र स्यात् स्वामिनश्छन्दोऽधिकं देयं कृतेऽधिके ॥ Yaj. II. 195.

,, 2 यथोक्तमार्त्तः स्वस्थोवा यस्तत्कर्म्म न कारयेत् ।
न तस्य वेतनं देयं अल्पोनस्यापि कर्म्मणः ॥ Manu, VIII. 217

326 1 कालेऽपूर्णे त्यजन् कर्म्मभृतेर्नाशमवाप्नुयात् । Narada, cited in Vira. on Non payment of wages.

,, 2 स्वामिदोषादपक्रामन् यावत्कृतमवाप्नुयात् । Narada, in same.

,, 3 स्वामी चेद् भृतकमपूर्णे काले जह्यात् तस्य सर्व्व Vishnu, cited in same.
मेव मूलं दद्यात्, पणशतञ्च राजन्यन्यत्र भृत्यदोषात् ।

4 तद्दोषेण यद्विनश्येत् तत्स्वामिनि देयमन्यत्र दैवोपघातात् ॥ Vishnu, cited in same.

327 1 प्रमादान्नाशितं दाप्यः समं द्विर्द्रोहनाशितं । VribatManu cited in same.

" 2 प्रस्थानविघ्नकृच्चैव प्रदाप्यो द्विगुणां भृतिं । Yaj II. 197

" 3 त्यजेत् पथि सहायं यः श्रान्तं रोगार्त्तमिव वा ।
प्राप्नुयात् साहसं पूर्व्वं ग्रामे त्र्यहमपालयन् ॥ Katyayana, cited in same.

" 4 प्रभुणा विनियुक्तःसन् भृतको विदधाति यः ।
तदर्थमशुभं कर्म्म स्वामी तत्रापराध्नुयात् ॥ Vrihaspati, cited in same.

329 1 समवायेन वणिजां लाभार्थं कर्म्म कुर्व्वतां ।
लाभालाभौ यथाद्रव्यं यथा वा संविदाकृतौ ॥ Yaj. II. 259

380 1 अनिर्द्दिष्टो कार्य्यमाणः प्रमादाद् यस्तु नाशयेत् ।
तेनैव तद्भवेद्देयं सर्व्वेषां समवायिनां ॥ Vrihaspati, cited in Vira. on Partnership.

381 1 प्रकाशमेतत्तास्कर्य्यं यद्देवनसमाह्वयौ ।
तयोर्न्नित्यं प्रतीघाते नृपतिर्यत्नवान् भवेत् । Manu, IV. 223

द्यूतं समाह्वयञ्चैव राजा राज्ये निवारयेत् ॥ Manu, IX. 221

" 2 द्यूतं निषिद्धं मनुना सत्यशौचधनापहं ।
अभ्यनुज्ञातमन्यैस्तु राजभागसमन्वितं ।
सभिकाधिष्ठितं कार्य्यं तस्करज्ञानहेतुतः ॥ Vrihaspati cited in Vira. on Dyuta.

" 3 प्राप्ते नृपतिना भागे प्रसिद्धे धूर्त्तमण्डले ।
जितं ससभिके स्थाने दापयेदन्यथा न तु ।
राज्ञा सचिह्नं निर्व्वास्याः कूटाक्षोपधिदेविनः ॥ Yaj. II. 201,202

332 1 निजधर्म्माविरोधेन यस्तु सामयिको भवेत् ।
सोऽपि यत्नेन संरक्ष्यो धर्म्मो राजकृतश्च यः ॥ — Yaj. II, 185.

„ 2 द्वौ त्रयः पञ्च वा कार्य्याः समूहहितवादिनः ।
कर्त्तव्यं वचनं तेषां ग्रामश्रेणिगणादिभिः ॥ — Vrihaspati, cited in Vira. on Breach of Contract.

333 1 विद्वेषिणो व्यसनिनः शालीनालसभीरवः ।
लुब्धातिवृद्धबालाश्च न कार्य्याः कार्य्यचिन्तकाः ।
शुचयो वेदधर्म्मज्ञाः दक्षा दान्ताः कुलोद्भवाः ।
सर्व्वकार्य्यप्रवीणाश्च कर्त्तव्याश्च महत्तमाः ॥ — Vrihaspati, cited in same.

„ 2 समूहकार्य्य आयातान् कृतकार्य्यान् विसर्जयेत् ।
सदानमानसत्कारैः पूजयित्वा महीपतिः । — Yaj. II. 189

„ 3 विसृष्टार्थस्तु यो यस्मिंस्तस्मिन्नर्थे प्रभुस्तु सः ।
तद्भर्त्ता तत्कृतं कार्य्यं नान्यथा कर्त्तुमर्हति ॥ — Narada.

334 1 प्रमाणं तत्कृतं सर्व्वं लाभालाभं व्ययोदयं ।
स्वदेशे वा विदेशे वा स्वामी तन्न विसंवदेत् ॥ — Vrihaspati,

„ 2 कुटुम्बार्थेऽप्यधीनोऽपि व्यवहारं यमाचरेत् ।
स्वदेशे वा विदेशे वा तं स्वामी न विचालयेत् ॥ — Manu, VIII 167

336 1 अदण्ड्यान् दण्डयन् राजा दण्ड्यांश्चैवाप्यदण्डयन् ।
अयशो महदाप्नोति नरकञ्चैव गच्छति ॥ — Manu, VIII. 128

„ 2 नोत्पादयेत् स्वयं कार्य्यं राजा नाप्यस्य पूरुषः । — Manu, VIII. 43

„ 3 छलानि चापराधांश्च पदानि नृपतेस्तथा ।
स्वयमेतानिगृह्णीयान्नृपस्त्वावेदकैर्विना ॥ — Pitamaha.

337 1 नृपेणविनियुक्तो यः परदोषान्ववेक्षणे ।
नृपस्य सूचयेज्ज्ञात्वा सूचकः स उदाहृतः ॥

339 1 देहेन्द्रियविनाशे तु यथा दण्डं प्रकल्पयेत् ।
यथा तुष्टिकरं देयं समुत्थानञ्च पण्डितैः ॥ Katyayana.

,, 2 सर्व्वे पुरुषपीड़ाकराः समुत्थानव्ययन्दाप्या Vishnu.
ग्राम्यपशुपीड़ाकराश्च ।

340 1 यावत्सस्यं विनश्येत्तु तावत्क्षेत्री फलं लभेत् । Yaj. II. 161

,, 2 पथिग्रामविवीतान्ते क्षेत्रे दोषो न विद्यते ॥ Yaj. II. 162

,, 3 दुःखेन विनिवार्य्यन्ते लब्धस्वादुरसा मृगाः ॥ Katyayana.

341 1 देयं चौरहृतंद्रव्यं राज्ञा जानपदाय तु ।
अददद्धि समाप्नोति किल्विषं यस्य तस्य तत् ॥ Yaj. II. 36

यदात्वन्यतोऽपहृतं द्रव्यं दापयितुं न शक्नोति, तदा-
स्वकोषादेव राजा दद्यात् । चौरहृतं अवजित्य यथा-
स्थानं गमयेत् स्वकोषाद्वा दद्यादिति गौतमस्मरणात् । Mit. on Yaj. II. 272.

,, 2 निर्दोषं दर्शयित्वा तु सदोषं यः प्रयच्छति ।
स मूल्याद्द्विगुणं दाप्यो विनयं तावदेव तु ॥ Narada, VIII. 7

अबुद्धिपूर्व्वक-विक्रये तु क्रयपरावर्त्तनमेव । Viramitrodaya.

342 1 धिग्दण्डस्त्वथ वाग्दण्डो धनदण्डो वधस्तथा ।
योज्या व्यस्ताः समस्ता वा ह्यपराधवशादिमे । Yaj. I. 367

343 1 ज्ञात्वापराधं देशञ्च कालं बलमथापि वा ।
वयःकर्म्मच वित्तञ्च दण्डं दण्ड्येषु पातयेत् ॥ Yaj. I. 368.

„ 2 तथा बुद्धिपूर्व्वाबुद्धिपूर्व्वसकृदावृत्त्याद्यनुसारेण च । Mit. on same.

„ 3 क्षुद्रमध्यमहाद्रव्यहरणे सारतो दमः ।
देशकालवयःशक्ति संचिन्त्य दण्डकर्म्मणि ॥ Yaj. II. 275.

344 1 दण्डस्तु देशकाल-वयोविद्यास्थान-विशेषैर्हिंसा-
ञ योपयोगः कल्प्यः आगमाद्दृष्टान्ताच्च ॥

345 1 अविशेषेण सर्व्वेषामेषदण्डविधिःस्मृतः ।
वधादृते ब्राह्मणस्य न वधं ब्राह्मणोऽर्हति ॥
यमोऽपि—न शारीरो ब्राह्मणस्य दण्डो भवति कस्यचित् । Yama.
गुप्तेतु बन्धने बद्धा राजभक्तं प्रदापयेत् ।

नारदोऽपि—शिरसोमुण्डनं दण्डस्तस्य निर्व्वासनंपुरात् । Narada.
ललाटेचाभिशस्ताङ्कः प्रयाणं गर्द्दभेन च ॥

347 1 अष्टापाद्यन्तु शूद्रस्य स्तेये भवति किल्बिषं ।
षोड़शैव तु वैश्यस्य द्वात्रिंशत् क्षत्रियस्य च ॥
ब्राह्मणस्य चतुःषष्टिः पूर्णंवापि शतं भवेत् ।
द्विगुणा वा चतुःषष्टिस्तद्दोषगुणविद्धि सः ॥ Manu, VII, 337,338

2 अपि भ्राता सुतोऽर्घ्यो वा श्वशुरोमातुलोऽपि वा ।
नादण्ड्यो नाम राज्ञोऽस्ति धर्म्माद्विचलितः स्वकात् ॥ Yaj. I. 358

3 कार्षापणं भवेद्दण्ड्यो यत्रान्यः प्राकृतो जनः ।
तत्र राजा भवेद्दण्ड्यः सहस्रमिति धारणा ॥ Manu, VIII 336

349 1 काणं वाप्यथवा खञ्जमन्यं वापि तथाविधं ।
तथ्येनापि ब्रुवन् दाप्यो दण्डं कार्षापणावरं ॥ Manu, VIII' 274

,, 2 दण्डप्रणयनं कार्य्यं वर्णजात्युत्तराधरैः ॥ Yaj, II, 206

,, 3 अशक्तस्तु वदन्नेवं दण्डनीयः पणान् दश ।
तथाशक्तः प्रतिभुवं दाप्यःक्षेमाय तस्य तु ॥ Yaj. II, 209

350 1 सहसा क्रियते कर्म्म यत्किञ्चिद्वलदर्पितैः ।
तत्साहसमितिप्रोक्तं सहोवलमिहोच्यते ॥ Narada, XIV. 1

351 1 तदिदं साहसं चौर्य्यवाग्दण्डपारुष्यस्त्रीसंग्रहणेषु-
व्यासक्तमपि वलदर्पावष्टम्भोपाधितो भिद्यते इति ।
दण्डातिरेकार्थं पृथगभिधानं । Mit. on Yaj. II, 230

,, 2 पापमूलं संग्रहणं त्रिप्रकारन्निवोधत ।
वलोपधिकृते द्वे तु तृतीयमनुरागजं ॥ Vrihaspati cited in Vira. on Stri-sangraha.

352 1 गृहमागत्य या नारी प्रलोभ्य स्पर्शनादिना ।
कामयेत्तत्र सा दण्ड्या नरस्यार्द्धदमःस्मृतः ॥ Vrihaspati, cited in same.

353 1 प्रकाशाश्चाप्रकाशाश्च तस्कराद्वि विधाःस्मृताः । Vrihaspati, cited in

355 1 प्रज्ञा सामर्थ्यमायाभिः प्रभिन्नास्ते सहस्रधा । Vrihaspati, cited in same.

2 न ददाति हि यः साक्ष्यं जानन्नपि नराधमः ।
स कूटसाक्षिणां पापैस्तुल्यो दण्डेनचैव हि ॥ Yaj. II. 77.

356 1 रागाल्लोभाद्भयाद्वापि स्मृत्यपेतादिकारिणः ।
सभ्याः पृथक् पृथग्दण्ड्या विवादाद्द्विगुणं दमं ॥ Yaj. II. 4

356 2 न्यायस्थाने गृहीत्वार्थमधर्म्मेण विनिर्णयं ।
कुर्व्वन्त्युत्कोचकास्ते तु राजद्रव्यविनाशकाः ॥
उत्कोचजीविनो द्रव्यहीनान् कृत्वा विवासयेत् ॥ Vyasa, cited in Vira. Prakirna-Kanda.

„ 3 यत्र प्रवर्त्तते युग्यं वैगुण्यात् प्राजकस्य तु ।
तत्रस्वामी भवेद्दण्ड्यो हिंसायां द्विशतं दमम् ।
प्राजकश्चेद्भवेदाप्तः प्राजको दण्डमर्हति ॥ Manu, VIII, 293,294,

357 1 गर्भस्थैः सदृशो ज्ञेयः आष्टमाद्वत्सराच्छिशुः ।

„ 2 बालो हि द्वादशाद्वर्षाज्जन्मतो यत्करिष्यति ।
न भविष्यत्यधर्म्मोऽत्र न प्रज्ञास्यन्ति वै दिशः ।

मर्य्यादां स्थापयाम्यद्य लोके धर्म्मफलोदयां ।
आचतुर्द्दशकाद्वर्षाद् न भविष्यति पातकं ॥ Maha-bharata Adiparva, 108.

358 1 चतुर्द्दशादूर्द्ध्वं पापमस्तीति पौराणं मतमिदं ।
वस्तुतस्तु भक्तहेतोः पुण्यपापविभागज्ञानपर्य्यन्तमेव
पापानुत्पत्तिः । Nilakantha,

„ 2 तथैव सप्तमे भक्ते भक्तानि षडनश्नता ।
अश्वस्तन-विधानेन हर्त्तव्यं हीनकर्म्मणः ॥

359 1 दण्डःशास्ति प्रजाःसर्व्वा दण्ड एवाभिरक्षति ।
दण्डः सुप्तेषु जागर्त्ति दण्डं धर्म्मं विदुर्बुधाः ॥ Manu, VII, 18

359 2 सर्व्वो दण्डजितो लोको दुर्लभो हि शुचिर्नरः ।
दण्डस्य हि भयात्सर्व्वं जगद्भोगाय कल्पते ॥ Manu, VIII, 22

„ 3 राजभिर्धृतदण्डास्तु कृत्वा पापानि मानवाः ।
निर्म्मलाः स्वर्गमायान्ति सन्तः सुकृतिनो यथा ॥ Manu VIII, 318

361 1 श्रुताध्ययनसम्पन्ना धर्म्मज्ञाः सत्यवादिनः ।
राज्ञा सभासदः कार्य्या रिपौ मित्रे च ये समाः ॥ Yaj. II. 2.

362 1 दान्तं कुलीनं मध्यस्थमनुद्वेगकरं स्थिरं ।
परत्रभीरुं धर्म्मिष्ठमुद्युक्तं क्रोधवर्ज्जितं ॥ Katyayana, cited in Mit. on Yaj. II. 6.

„ 2 सभायां न प्रवेष्टव्यं वक्तव्यं वा समञ्जसं ।
अब्रुवन् विब्रुवन् वापि नरो भवति किल्बिषी ॥ Manu, VIII. 13.

3 नानियुक्तेन वक्तव्यं व्यवहारे कथञ्चन ।
नियुक्तेन तु वक्तव्यं अपक्षपतितं वचः ॥ Narada, ch. II, Procedure 1.

363 1 अन्यायेनापि तं दण्डं येऽनुमान्ति सभासदः ।
तेऽपि तद्भागिनस्तस्माद्बोधनीयः स तैर्नृपः ॥ Narada.

368 1 सत्यंमिथ्योत्तरञ्चैव प्रत्यवस्कन्दनं तथा ।
पूर्व्वन्यायविधिश्चैवमुत्तरं स्याच्चतुर्व्विधं ॥ Katyayana cited in Mit. on Yaj. II. 7.

„ 2 अर्थिना लिखितो योऽर्थः प्रत्यर्थी यदि तं तथा ।
प्रपद्य कारणं ब्रूयात् प्रत्यवस्कन्दनं स्मृतं ॥ Narada cited in Mit. on Yaj. II. 7.

„ 3 अस्मिन्नर्थे समानेन वादः पूर्व्वमभूत्तदा ।
जितोऽयमिति चेद्ब्रूयात् प्राङ्न्यायः स्यात्तदुत्तरं ॥ Harita cited in Vira. on Pleadings.

भाषापादोत्तरपादौ क्रियापादस्तथैवच ।
प्रत्याकलितपादश्च व्यवहारश्चतुष्पदः ॥ Vrihaspati cited in Vira.

प्राङ्न्यायकारणोक्तौ तु प्रत्यर्थी निर्द्दिशेत्क्रियां ।
मिथ्योक्तौ पूर्व्ववादी तु प्रतिपत्तौ न सा भवेत् ॥ Harita cited in Mit. on Yaj. II. 8.

उभयोः प्रतिभूर्ग्राह्यः समर्थःकार्य्यनिर्णये । Yaj. II. 10.

अभियोगमनिस्तीर्य्य नैनं प्रत्यभियोजयेत् ॥ Yaj. II. 9.

अन्यवादी क्रियाद्वेषी नोपस्थाता निरुत्तरः ।
आहूतप्रपलायी च हीनःपञ्चविधःस्मृतः ॥ Narada, on Procedure Ch. II. 33.

पूर्व्वोत्तरक्रियापादं तत्प्रमाणपरीक्षणम् ।
निगदस्मृतिवाक्यञ्च यथासंख्यं विनिश्चितं ।
एतत्सर्व्वं समासेन जयपत्रेऽभिलेखयेत् ॥ Vyasa.

INDEX

54

55

ERRATA.

N. B. For a thoroughly corrected version of the Sanskrit texts given in the Footnotes, see Appendix A.

Page	70	line	21,	*after*	point	*insert*	of
,,	,,	,,	26,	*for*	little	*read*	title
,,	72	,,	6,	,,	mudis practis	,,	nudis pactis
,,	111	,,	16,	,,	Common	,,	Canon
,,	112	,,	21,	,,	shout	,,	short
,,	113	,,	23,	,,	three	,,	thirty
,,	140	,,	3,	,,	well	,,	null
,,	146	,,	22,	,,	ownership	,,	co-ownership
,,	156	,,	31,	,,	cofirmed	,,	confirmed
,,	164	,,	5,	,,	modelled	,,	remodelled
,,	165	,,	31,	,,	Procustean	,,	Procrustean
,,	169	,,	6,	,,	beased	,,	based
,,	,,	,,	9,	,,	might	,,	right
,,	174	,,	12,	,,	interitance	,,	inheritance
,,	217	,,	29,	,,	Bernand	,,	Bernard
,,	231	,,	27,	,,	would	,,	world
,,	236	,,	6,	,,	obsoleute	,,	obsolete
,,	244	,,	25,	,,	hy	,,	by
,,	250	,,	26,	,,	inferntial	,,	inferntial
,,	255	,,	12,	*after*	in	*insert*	the
,,	258	,,	2,	*for*	father, The	*read*	father, the
,,	259	,,	7,	,,	for	,,	far
,,	272	,,	27,	,,	hemorrhords	,,	hemorrhoids
,,	284	,,	19,	,,	hemned	,,	hemmed
,,	286	,,	19,	*omit*	and		
,,	292	,,	18,	*for*	if	,,	it
,,	304	,,	8,	,,	mutumn	,,	mutuum
,,	318	,,	22,	*after*	cannot	*insert*	be